Research Methods
in Applied Settings:
An Integrated Approach
to Design and Analysis

WITHDRAWI

Research Methods in Applied Settings: An Integrated Approach to Design and Analysis

Jeffrey A. Gliner

and

George A. Morgan

Colorado State University

LAWRENCE ERLBAUM ASSOCIATES, PUBLISHERS

2000   Mahwah, New Jersey   London

Lawrence Erlbaum Associates, Inc., Publishers
10 Industrial Avenue
Mahwah, NJ 07430

Cover design by Kathryn Houghtaling Lacey

Library of Congress Cataloging-in-Publication Data

Gliner, Jeffrey A.

Research methods in applied settings: an integrated approach to
design and analysis / by Jeffrey A. Gliner and George A. Morgan.

p. cm.

Includes bibliographical references and index.
ISBN 0-8058-2992-X (cloth : alk. paper)

1. Social sciences—Research. I. Morgan, George A.
(George Arthur), 1936– . II. Title.
H62 .G523   2000
300'.7'2—dc21   99-38652
                                                                CIP

Books published by Lawrence Erlbaum Associates are printed on
acid-free paper, and their bindings are chosen for strength and dura-
bility.

Printed in the United States of America
10 9 8 7 6 5 4 3 2 1

Contents

Preface

In this book, we have provided an integrated approach to quantitative research methods and to the selection and interpretation of data analyses for graduate students in the applied behavioral sciences. The target disciplines include education, allied health, and other applied behavioral science areas as well as psychology, which is our training and background discipline.

The book offers several unusual and valuable features. The content is based on the conceptualizations of respected authors of research methods books and articles (e.g. Cook & Campbell, Kerlinger, etc.), but we have tried to make this book student friendly as well as sophisticated, partly by being consistent and clear in terminology and partly by organizing the material so that the various chapters are consistent and fit together logically. Many authors treat the different parts of their research methods books as essentially unrelated. For example, sampling is discussed as if it only applied to survey research; internal validity is discussed only in relation to experimental and quasi-experimental research; and often little attempt is made to show how the reliability and validity of a measurement (test or instrument) are related to and different from internal and external validity. Furthermore, chapters on statistics usually seem unrelated to those on design, so students can take statistics and have little idea when or why to use them. In this book, we discuss in detail both research design and interpretation of statistical analyses, and we show how the research approach and design determine the appropriate statistical analysis. However, this is not a statistics book so there are few formulas and computations.

Our approach to design and analysis is somewhat nontraditional because we have found that students have difficulty with some aspects of statistics but not others. Most can "crunch" the numbers easily and accurately with a calculator or with a computer. However, many have trouble knowing what statistics to use and how to interpret the results. They do not seem to have a "big picture" or see how the research questions and design influence data analysis. Part of the problem is inconsistent terminology. We are reminded of Bruce Thompson's frequently repeated, intentionally facetious remark at his many national workshops: "We use these different terms to confuse the graduate students." For these reasons, we have tried to present a semantically consistent and coherent big picture of what we call research approaches (experimental, comparative, and so forth) and how they lead to three basic kinds of research questions (difference, associational, and descriptive) which, in turn, lead to three kinds or groups of statistics with the same names. We realize that these and other attempts to develop and use a consistent framework are both nontraditional and somewhat of an oversimplification. However, we think the framework and consistency pay off in terms of student understanding and ability to actually use statistics to answer their research questions.

A strong feature of the book is the emphasis on helping students become good *consumers of research* by helping them to analyze and evaluate research articles. The last chapter (24) integrates many points from earlier chapters into a framework for the analysis and evaluation of research articles by using 16 questions and the six rating scales, presented in earlier chapters, to evaluate research validity, which is the validity of a whole study. Because evaluation of research studies is a major goal of our courses, we have found it helpful for students to read chapter 24 part way through the course, perhaps after chapter 5, as well as at the end. The application problems at the end of each chapter are also designed to help students become good consumers of research.

A second feature is that the text is heavily annotated with examples from our combined 60 years of teaching and research experience. It also has a large number of diagrams and tables that summarize various topics and show in a different way areas that are often confusing or prove difficult to learn well enough to apply. Visual learners may especially appreciate the figures and tables.

A third feature is that, although the book is based primarily on the quantitative research paradigm, chapter 2 deals in depth with how *the qualitative or naturalist/constructivist* paradigm differs from the quantitative or positivist paradigm. In a number of places, including chapter 2, the book points out the value of qualitative research and how it should lead quantitative researchers to be more flexible and take into account the criticisms of qualitative researchers. We also point out, of course, what we think are the weaknesses of the qualitative paradigm.

A fourth feature of the book is the division of all quantitative research questions (and we think qualitative research as well) into five categories that we call research approaches:

1. **Randomized Experimental** (has random assignment of participants to groups and an active or manipulated independent variable).
2. **Quasi-Experimental** (has an active or manipulated independent variable but without random assignment of participants to groups).
3. **Comparative** (has a few levels or categories of an attribute or nonmanipulated variable that are compared).
4. **Associational** (sometimes called correlational, has two or more variables that are related or associated for the same group of subjects).

5. **Descriptive** (research that answers descriptive questions using only descriptive statistics).

Complex studies may use more than one of these approaches; for example, "survey" studies often have descriptive as well as comparative and associational research questions. We have been able to fit all of the hundreds of studies that we and our students have evaluated into one or more of these categories based on the research questions that the investigator asked and analyzed.

This categorization of research or, more accurately, research questions, into one of five approaches has been helpful for several reasons. One concerns discussions of cause and effect. We feel that causal questions can be appropriately answered only with well-controlled randomized experiments and to a lesser extent with the quasi-experimental approach. Neither the comparative nor the associational approach is well suited to deal with cause and effect, but we realize that some complex statistics, such as cross-lag panel correlations and structural equation modeling, may provide evidence for causality from nonexperimental studies.

Another reason that our classification of research approaches is helpful is that one can follow the research process from purpose to question or hypothesis to data analysis. For example, in general, the experimental, quasi-experimental, and comparative approaches use what we call "difference inferential statistics," such as the *t* test or analysis of variance, whereas the associational approach uses "associational inferential statistics," such as correlation and multiple regression. We know that all parametric inferential statistics are relational (special cases of canonical correlation), but we think that it is helpful educationally to make this distinction, which is consistent with our framework for research approaches as well as with the information found in most basic statistics books.

A fifth feature of the book is what we call the design classification that is based on the three major types of design: between groups, within subjects, and mixed designs. These general classifications apply to the comparative approach as well as to the experimental and quasi-experimental approaches, which has been more traditional. We show that, although these three types of approach use the same general type of statistics (e.g., ANOVA), the specific statistics for between groups design are different from those for within subjects and from those in mixed designs. We also point out that the associational approach uses a different set of statistics but the data resemble those in a within subjects design.

Although our backgrounds are in psychology, we have over the last twenty or more years worked in and taught research courses in applied departments that include occupational therapy, education, human development and family studies, and consumer science and merchandising, as well as psychology. In addition, we have had in our classes students from home economics, business, music therapy, social work, and communication disorders, to mention a few of the more common areas. Thus, we feel that we have a good grasp of the types of research problems faced by master's and doctoral students in these diverse areas and have designed a book that we feel is user friendly as well as sophisticated. We think that we have a good text on research design and data analysis that will help graduate students learn about this important area that is often unnecessarily scary to students in applied fields.

We want to acknowledge the assistance of many persons whose help and advice has been critical in the development of this book. Special thanks go to our very competent and helpful word processor, Linda White. Phyllis Beard and Ruth McNeal did much of the word processing for early versions of this text. At times our many figures and tables have pushed the limits of the software. Mae Mackie, Chao-Hsien Yeh, and Mei-Huei Tsay developed many of the figures in the text. Joan Anderson, David Stephen, and Loretta Teng did the first draft of the glossary. Several teaching assistants and work–study students helped with the tasks related to the book. For example, Shelly Haddock, Nancy Leech, Maura MacPhee and Susan Tungate wrote many of the application problems. We especially want to thank the students in our classes who have used several earlier versions as their text and have provided extensive feedback, much of which we have tried to incorporate. Finally, we want to thank our wives, Gail and Hildy, for their support and help. Gail Gliner, Orlando Griego, Helena Chmura Kraemer, David MacPhee, Pat Sample, Celia Walker, and several reviewers provided helpful feedback on various chapters of the book.

—J.A.G. & G.A.M.
Fort Collins, Colorado

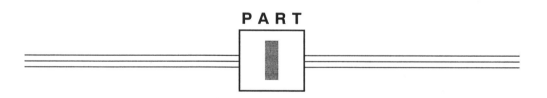

Introductory Chapters

Definitions, Purposes, and Dimensions of Research

WHAT IS RESEARCH?

Definition

What is research? Many definitions have been given, including a systematic method of gaining new information, or a way to answer questions. Smith (1981) suggests that research be broadened to **disciplined inquiry,** which

> must be conducted and reported so that its logical argument can be carefully examined; it does not depend on surface plausibility or the eloquence, status, or authority of its author; error is avoided; evidential test and verification are valued; the dispassionate search for truth is valued over ideology. Every piece of research or evaluation, whether naturalistic, experimental, survey, or historical must meet these standards to be considered disciplined. (p. 585)

Smith's (1981) definition of disciplined inquiry is worth considering in detail. An inquiry is defined by Webster (1972) as a systematic investigation of a matter of public interest. The public interest part debatable, but the systematic investigation is certainly a part of any definition of research. Regardless of the particular research paradigm to which the investigator adheres, there must be underlying guidelines for how the research is to be carried out.

In the experimental approach within the so-called **positivist,** or quantitative, framework, the investigator establishes a detailed plan prior to the study. This plan includes details such as who the participants in the investigation would be, how they would be selected, how the treatment group(s) would be assigned, what the treatment would be, how the treatment would be measured, and other details of the study.

On the other hand, if the investigator uses a qualitative framework, often called **constructivist**, or naturalistic, there are still general guidelines to follow. Although many of these guidelines come into play after the investigation begins, they are important for guiding the research.

Smith (1981) states that the research "must be conducted and reported so that its logical argument can be carefully examined" (p. 585). The term *conducted* in the definition implies that the research must be carried out. (Designing research serves no useful purpose if the research is not actually done). Also, the research must be reported, that is, written for a journal or delivered as a talk at a professional meeting. This dissemination function is important if the research is to be examined by others in detail. Smith (1981) is really saying that unless the research is conducted and reported, others cannot examine it to determine whether, given similar circumstances, they would come to the same conclusion as the investigators.

The last part of Smith's (1981) definition refers to the fact that the research must stand on its own merit. It should not matter who completes the research, how eloquent it is, or even the nature of the problem. If the research has been done systematically by following guidelines within a particular research paradigm, and it has been disseminated within a particular discipline, then that research can be tested, or verified, by others. Although there have been numerous attempts to define research, we feel that the Smith (1981) definition encompasses most.

Why do we do research? To find something out? What is it that we want to find out? Questions recently addressed within the field of education are as follows: Does class size affect student outcomes? Is cooperative learning more successful than individualized learning? Is learning mathematics a personal construction or a social construction? Should students with special needs be mainstreamed into the school system? Several questions also need to be addressed in the allied health fields: Does a particular treatment work? Are certain characteristics of therapists better than others? What makes a good therapist? Is supported employment more successful for community integration than sheltered work?

PURPOSES OF RESEARCH

There are many reasons to conduct research, not the least of which is to complete your graduate program. On a more (or less) serious note, the rationale for learning about research serves two general purposes: (a) increasing knowledge within the discipline, and (b) increasing knowledge within oneself as a professional consumer of research to understand new developments within the discipline. Increasing knowledge within the discipline is certainly a worthy and noble pursuit. For example, most research texts acknowledge something similar to the following "The selection of programs and techniques of therapeutic intervention for a particular handicapped population or handicapping condition must be based on clear empirical evidence of effectiveness" (Ottenbacher, 1986, p. 5).

Increasing Knowledge Within the Discipline

Increasing knowledge within the discipline can take many directions; three are discussed here. The first of these directions supports the *theoretical basis* of the discipline.

Theory Development.   A theory, according to Kerlinger (1986), "is a set of interrelated constructs (concepts), definitions, and propositions that present a systematic view of phenomena by specifying relations among variables, with the purpose of explaining and predicting the phenomena" (p. 9). For example, purposeful activity is a construct within the theory of occupation within the field of occupational therapy. Numerous studies have been published attempting to demonstrate that if the activity is "purposeful," the individual performing the activity will be more invested in the activity (e.g., Bakshi, Bhambhani, & Madill, 1991; Kircher, 1984; Nelson & Peterson, 1989). These studies might be conceptualized within the following research design. Two groups are formed through random assignment. One group receives a condition of exercise, for example, jumping in place. The other group also jumps in place, but does so with a jump rope and the goal of doing it well. At the end of a given time period, the two groups are measured for performance, satisfaction, or motivation to determine if the exercise-with-purpose condition was different than the exercise-without-purpose condition.

Practical Application.   A second approach to increasing knowledge within the discipline involves providing evidence for the *efficacy* of a therapeutic technique, a curriculum, or an administrative change. An example of examining therapeutic techniques can be seen in a study by Jongbloed, Stacey, and Brighton (1989). They compared the effectiveness of two approaches for treating cerebrovascular-accident patients: a functional approach and a sensorimotor integrative approach. After randomly assigning patients to one of two treatment groups, both groups were assessed for function in self-care and mobility, meal preparation, and sensorimotor integration prior to the treatment interventions and at 4 and 8 weeks after the intervention. The study is exemplary as a method to test the effectiveness of different therapeutic interventions.

Developing Research Tools.   A third approach to increasing knowledge within the discipline involves creating methods to assess behaviors. For example, Morgan, Harmon, and Maslin–Cole (1990) developed a new standardized testing procedure and set of tasks to assess mastery motivation in young children. The procedure was designed to be useful for normally developing children and also for children who are at risk for developmental problems. To compare children with different ability levels, an individualized approach to measuring mastery motivation was developed. This approach varies the difficulty of the task in accordance with the child's ability level, so that each child is given tasks that are moderately difficult for him or her. Each child's motivation is assessed with one task, from each of several graded sets of similar tasks, that is challenging (not too difficult or too easy) for that individual child. Good interobserver reliability has been obtained for the two key measures in this procedure: persistence at tasks that are challenging and pleasure after completing a part of the task. The validity of these mastery task measures has been confirmed in several ways. First, groups of children (such as those who are handicapped or at risk for developmental problems) who had been predicted to score lower on mastery motivation measures than the appropriate comparison groups did score lower. Second, there were significant relationships between persistence at tasks and several other measures that were expected to reflect aspects of the concept of mastery motivation; for example, ratings of persistence during mental tests, engrossment during free play, and mother and teacher ratings of motivation.

A. G. Fisher (1995) provides another example of instrument development with her functional assessment tool called the Assessment of Motor and Process Skills (AMPS). The AMPS allows the therapist to assess the client while the client is performing a task of his or her choice, usually in the client's home. Thus the setting for the AMPS is natural, i.e., it has ecological validity. However, what is special about the AMPS is that by using a sophisticated psychometric method called Rasch analysis (A. G. Fisher, 1993), the AMPS can be (a) used with different therapists, (b) used with different tasks, and (c) analyzed with parametric statistics because the data approximate an interval scale. Fisher has set about the task of validating the AMPS through numerous studies that examine cross-cultural differences (A. G. Fisher, Liu, Velozo, & Pan, 1992), diagnostic differences (e.g., Puderbaugh & A. G. Fisher, 1992), and age differences (Dickerson & Fisher, 1993).

Understanding Research in One's Discipline

For most students, the ability to understand research in one's discipline may be more important than making a research contribution to the profession. Dissemination of new knowledge occurs for the professional through numerous professional journals, workshops, and continuing education courses, as well as through popular literature, such as daily newspapers. Today's professional cannot simply rely on the statements of a workshop instructor or newspaper to determine what should be included or not included for future intervention in the classroom, clinic, or community. Even journal articles need to be scrutinized for weak research design, inappropriate data analyses, or incorrect interpretation of these analyses. The current professional must have the research and reasoning skills to be able to make sound decisions and to support them. In addition, research skills can help professionals in education or therapeutic sciences to be better service providers because they will know how to examine their own school, classroom, or clients, and they will note if improvement in various areas has occurred (e.g., see Ottenbacher, 1986). We present a framework for evaluating articles in several chapters and summarize it in the last chapter of the book.

RESEARCH DIMENSIONS AND DICHOTOMIES

Although we have discussed briefly the importance of learning about research, little has been said about the different forms that research may take. Several dichotomies, or dimensions, are used to describe research.

Theoretical Versus Applied

Researchers in most social science disciplines conduct research with a specific, practical application in mind, such as treatment, learning enhancement, or evaluation. Theoretical research is also done, as mentioned earlier, but most of the research projects we examine in this book are at the applied end of this dimension.

Laboratory Versus Field

A second dimension for examining research is the setting. The term *field* takes on many different meanings. Field could be a clinic, hospital, school, workplace, or home setting. Laboratory implies a structured setting that is not where the subjects or participants usually live, work, or receive therapy. In the social and health sciences, a laboratory most often refers to a room with a video camera and microphones (i.e., a somewhat unnatural setting). Research in the social sciences is usually slanted toward the field end of the dimension to be more ecologically valid, but laboratory settings provide better control over extraneous variables.

Self-Report Versus Researcher Observation

In some studies the participants report to the researcher (in writing or orally) about their attitudes, intentions, or behavior. In other studies the researcher directly observes and records the behavior of the participant. Sometimes instruments such as heart rate monitors are used by researchers to "observe" the participants' physiological functioning.

Most research in the applied social sciences and in education relies on the self-reports of the participants. However, such reports are always influenced by the fact that the participants know they are in a study; they may want to please the researcher, they may want to hide things, or they may have forgotten or not know some things. Many investigators prefer researcher-observed behavioral data, even though these data also have potential limitations. On the other hand, sensitive, well-trained interviewers may be able to establish enough rapport with participants to alleviate some of the biases inherent in self-reports.

Quantitative Versus Qualitative Research

This is the most confusing and controversial dichotomy. We believe that this topic is more appropriately thought of as three related dimensions. The first dimension deals with philosophical or paradigm differences in the approach to research. The second dimension, which is what many students mean when referring to this dichotomy, deals with the type of data and data collection method. The third dimension refers to the type of data analysis. We think that in distinguishing between qualitative and quantitative research, the first dimension (i.e., the philosophical dichotomy called positivist vs. constructivist) is the most important.

Positivist Versus Constructivist Paradigms[1].   The similarities and differences between these paradigms are discussed in detail in chapter 2. For now, note that a study could be theoretically positivistic, but the data could be subjective or qualitative. In fact, this combination is common. On the other hand, a researcher may embrace the constructivist paradigm, but some of the supporting data may be quantitative or objective. Thus, the type of data and even the data analysis is not necessarily the same as the research paradigm. However, qualitative data, methods, and analyses often accompany the constructivist paradigm, and quantitative data, methods, and analyses are usually associated with the positivist paradigm. The approach of this book lies

---

[1]Although we believe that the term *positivist* is *not* an accurate label for most quantitative social scientists, it is commonly used by qualitative or constructivist writers. It also helps us separate the philosophical or paradigm distinction from the data collection and analysis issues. Likewise, the term *constructivist* may not be the best or most common identifier for what is often called the naturalist or qualitative paradigm, but, again, it helps us make important distinctions.

within the framework of the so-called positivist paradigm, but the constructivist paradigm reminds us that human participants are complex and different from other animals and inanimate objects. Thus, we should not be overly dependent on the philosophy and methods of natural science research. Although you may find this paradigm distinction confusing now, its meaning should be clear after you read chapter 2.

Quantitative Versus Qualitative Data and Data Collection.   Quantitative data are said to be *objective*, which indicates that the behaviors are easily classified or quantified, either by the participants themselves or by the researcher. Examples of quantitative data are scores on an achievement test, time to recovery, and demographic variables such as age and gender. The data are usually gathered with an instrument (e.g., a test, physiological device, or questionnaire) that can be scored reliably with little training required.

Qualitative data are more difficult to describe. They are said to be *subjective*, which indicates that they could be hard to classify or score. Examples of qualitative date are perceptions of pain, feelings about work, and attitudes toward school. Usually these data are gathered from interviews, observations, or documents such as biographies. *Quantitative* or *positivist* researchers also gather these types of data, but they usually translate perceptions, feelings, and attitudes into numbers by using, for example, rating scales. *Qualitative* or *constructivist* researchers, on the other hand, usually do not try to quantify such perceptions. Like the authors of other quantitative or positivist research books, we believe that the approach in this book is useful for dealing with both qualitative or subjective data and quantitative or objective data.

It is important to point out that researchers within both the quantitative or positivist paradigm and the qualitative or constructivist paradigm use interview and observational methods and both are interested in objective as well as subjective data. However, constructivist researchers prefer open-ended interviews, observations, and documents such as diaries. Positivist researchers prefer structured interviews (or questionnaires), observations, and documents such as school or clinic records. We describe data collection methods in chapter 21.

Quantitative Versus Qualitative Data Analysis.   The interpretation and understanding of quantitative data analysis is a major theme of this book. It is dealt with in detail in chapters 14 to 19, which discuss many of the most common inferential statistics and show how they are related to the approaches and designs discussed in chapters 5 to 8. Qualitative data analysis involves various methods for coding, categorizing, and assigning meaning to the data, which are usually words or images. This book does not deal with qualitative data analysis techniques such as content analysis, but some researchers within the positivist paradigm do so. Constructivist researchers rarely use inferential statistics, but sometimes they use descriptive statistics (chap. 9).

Relationships Between the Four Dichotomies

Certain aspects of the four dimensions or dichotomies tend, in practice, to go together. For example, applied research tends to be done in field or natural settings, often by using self-reports of the participants. Qualitative research is almost always conducted in the field. On the other hand, theoretically oriented research tends to be done in the lab by using researcher observations.

However, there is not necessarily an association between any of these four dimensions. For example, applied research can be done in either the lab or in the field, by using either observation or self-report, and it can be either positivist (quantitative) or constructivist (qualitative). To help you visualize that these dimensions can be and often are independent, we present Fig. 1.1, which is adapted from Hendricks, Marvel, and Barrington (1990). Examples of research studies that fall into each of the eight cells in the cube would not be hard to find.

SUMMARY

Research is defined, according to Smith (1981), as "disciplined inquiry," which must be conducted and reported so that its arguments can be carefully examined. Inquiry is a systematic investigation of a matter of public interest. In the so-called logical positivist or quantitative framework, which is one of the two main research paradigms, a specific plan is developed prior to the study. In the constructivist or qualitative approach, less structure surrounds the use of specific guidelines in the research design. However, general guidelines are followed in qualitative research. All research must be conducted and reported so that it can be tested and verified by others.

There are two main purposes for research: (a) to increase knowledge within one's discipline, and (b) to increase knowledge within oneself as a professional consumer of research. Three directions are taken to increase knowledge within a discipline: expanding the theoretical basis of the discipline; testing the effec-

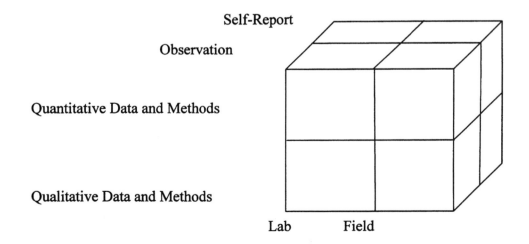

FIG. 1.1   A research cube showing the conceptual independence of these research dimensions or dichotomies. From "The Dimensions of Psychological Research," by B. Hendricks, M. K. Marvel, and B. L. Barrington, 1994, *Teaching of Psychology, 17,* 79. Copyright 1990 by Lawrence Erlbaum Associates. Adapted with permission. (Note, the vertical dimension is different from Hendricks et al.)

tiveness of practical applications, and developing research tools. Research skills are required to examine research in one's discipline.

Four important research dimensions are (a) theoretical versus applied, (b) laboratory versus field, (c) self-report versus researcher observation, and (d) quantitative versus qualitative research. The latter dichotomy has three aspects: the philosophical or theoretical framework, the type of data and how data are collected, and the type of data analysis. Although qualitative data are often collected within the constructivist paradigm, that is not always the case. Qualitative data and data analysis can be used within the positivist paradigm. The four dimensions or dichotomies are related in practice, but conceptually they are independent. It is possible to have a study that fits any combination of the four dichotomies.

STUDY AIDS

The following concepts and distinctions are discussed in this chapter and many of the concepts are defined in the glossary (Appendix A). It will help you to learn the material if you understand the meaning of each concept and can compare and contrast the paired distinctions.

Concepts

- Disciplined inquiry
- Research
- Theory

Distinctions

- Laboratory versus field research
- Positivist versus constructivist paradigm or theoretical framework
- Producing knowledge versus understanding research as a consumer
- Quantitative versus qualitative data analysis
- Quantitative versus qualitative data and data collection
- Self-report versus researcher observation
- Theoretical versus applied research

Application Problems

1. The chapter introduced several different forms that research can take: theoretical versus applied, laboratory versus field, self-report versus researcher observation, and quantitative versus qualitative. Using these dimensions or dichotomies, identify the form of research for each of the following examples. Remember that some research projects use both ends of a dimension. For instance, many projects incorporate both quantitative and qualitative data collection methods; others use both self-report and observational measures.

a. A researcher was interested to know if there were differences in the physiological arousal of men and women during arguments. She[2] recruited 30 couples, and asked them to come to the Happy Family Counseling Center. Couples were comfortably seated in an attractively decorated room. The researcher placed heart rate and blood pressure monitors on each person in the couple. They were then instructed to identify and discuss a problem area in their relationship for 20 minutes. The researcher recorded the heart rate and blood pressure for each individual to determine if there were differences between men and women and to improve therapy.

b. A therapist was interested in learning the characteristics of marriages that were based on equality. She also wanted to learn what the benefits and costs of equality were for women, men, and their relationship. She interviewed couples in their home for 2 hours, asking them open-ended questions about their previous relationships, the history of their marriage, the evolution of their egalitarian feelings and behaviors, and how they handled communication, conflict, sex and intimacy, money, children, job, and life-style issues. To analyze the data, she coded the conversation according to common themes that emerged from the interviews.

c. A model was developed to explain a family's response to a stressful event. More specifically, the model was developed to explain a family's adaptation over time given several variables, such as the nature and degree of a stressor, and the family's resources and perceptions. A researcher is interested in determining if this model applies to a particular catastrophic event—the loss of one's home to an environmental catastrophe. The researcher recruits families from a town that recently experienced an earthquake. Members of these families are mailed a questionnaire about particular variables (e.g., family resources, perceptions of the stressor event); these measures have been used in prior research of the model.

2. A researcher was interested to learn how work environment influences employees' experience of work–family conflict, or the degree to which their work responsibilities impinged on their home responsibilities and vice versa. The researcher gained permission from several company presidents to collect data from company employees.

a. Describe how the researcher might proceed if this were a field research design. What about a laboratory design?

b. How might the researcher use qualitative data collection methods to gain information? How might she use quantitative data collection methods?

c. Describe how she might use self-report measures to gather certain information? What about observational methods?

d. Would this research be applied or theoretical?

3. A researcher is interested to learn the qualities of and strategies used by dual-earner couples who are successful in balancing work and family re-

---

[2]The authors use the pronoun he and she randomly throughout the Application Problems sections.

sponsibilities. She asks each member of the couple to complete several measures of variables that she believes will be particularly relevant, such as creativity, optimism, and self-esteem. She also plans to interview each couple to learn about their strategies for balancing work and family. These interviews will begin with the question: "What is it about you or your life that you believe most leads to your success in balancing work and family?"

a. Which of the previously mentioned methods for collecting data is quantitative? Which is qualitative?

b. If the researcher uses qualitative methods of data analysis for the interview, how might they conduct this analysis?

4. A recently hired president of a university is committed to increasing the number of minority students who graduate with their bachelors' degrees. The president calls to arrange a meeting with you. In this meeting, the president explains that she wants you "to do some research on this topic." She explains that she is aware of other universities who have set and achieved this goal in prior years. She is also aware that this university has developed several programs in prior years in the effort to reach this goal. She wants you to provide her with information that will help her design specific initiatives that are most likely to produce the results she wants. What is the President asking you to do? (Or, is the President asking you to be a consumer or producer of knowledge?) What kind of skills must she believe that you have?

2

A Tale of Two Paradigms:
Quantitative and Qualitative

CONFUSION

A quantitative or a qualitative paradigm, which should I choose? There is confusion in the social and health sciences about the difference between quantitative and qualitative approaches to research. Much of the confusion about these paradigms, as indicated in chapter 1, comes from equating them with the way data are collected. Investigators often associate subjective methods of data collection, such as open-ended interviews, with the qualitative approach and objective methods of data collection with the quantitative approach. As we will see, however, the type of data collection cannot be used to distinguish adequately between the two different paradigms.

PARADIGMS

What is a paradigm? The term was coined by Thomas Kuhn (1970) but has been inconsistently defined (Komesaroff, 1986). One interpretation of a paradigm by Kuhn was that of a scientific community, or, more specifically, the beliefs that members of that scientific community share. Lincoln and Guba

(1985) refer to a paradigm as a system of ideas: "We shall call such a systematic set of beliefs, together with their accompanying methods, a paradigm" (p. 15). In our view a paradigm is a way of thinking about and conducting research. It is not strictly a methodology, but more of a philosophy that guides how the research is to be conducted. More important, a paradigm determines the types of questions that are legitimate, how they will be answered, and in what context they will be interpreted.

There are currently two major paradigms within the social and health sciences. One paradigm, often referred to as the *quantitative* paradigm, has been the dominant paradigm and is usually associated with the so-called scientific method. Qualitative theorists (e.g., Lincoln & Guba, 1985) use the term *logical positivist* to identify the dominant paradigm; however, this term is easily misunderstood and not really representative of the quantitative, dominant paradigm (Phillips, 1992). Philosophically, the logical positivists did not agree with most quantitative researchers that one can identify causal relationships, because they argued that these relationships could not be directly verified by sensory experience. On the other hand, the positivists did have respect for traditional scientific methods (Phillips, 1992). It appears that it is to the latter that Lincoln and Guba (1985) refer when they associate positivism with the dominant paradigm. Thus, even though the term positivist is not totally accurate, we, too, will use it when referring to the dominant or quantitative paradigm, in part to distinguish it from quantitative data collection and analysis, as discussed in chapter 1. The positivist case is described by Phillips (1992) as follows:

> A case can be made—that for the purposes of social science, meanings and intentions can be investigated using traditional scientific methods. That is, it can be argued that there is no epistemological difference in kind between gaining knowledge about the other objects of science and gaining knowledge about meanings and intentions. Many branches of science can provide cases where the objects of interest are not directly observable or measurable, but where their presence is inferred from what is observable. This process is hypothetical, and it is not guaranteed to be successful; but it is self-corrective by a bootstrapping process involving testing and elimination of errors. (p. 18)

Taken a step further, the implication is that science—that is, the scientific method—will allow us to discover truths about the world, both physical and social.

The other paradigm, referred to by Lincoln and Guba (1985) as the naturalistic or constructivist approach, is usually associated with a *qualitative* approach to research. Phillips (1992) points out, "Humans are not mere physical objects; and to understand or explain why a person has acted in a particular manner, the meaning (or meanings) of the action have to be uncovered—and to do this the roles of language and of social symbolisms and values have to be taken into account" (p. 5).

Lincoln and Guba (1985) stated five axioms that from their point of view as qualitative researchers, separate the two paradigms. Since that time, they have modified their position (E. G. Guba, personal communication, 1995), but it is instructive to examine these original five axioms in detail to gain a clearer picture of the differences between the two paradigms. Note that we have changed the word *naturalist,* which was originally used by Lincoln and Guba (1985), to *constructivist* because the former could be confused with "naturalism" or "naturalistic interpretation of social science," which says that the social sciences should have the same goals and methods as the natural sciences (Ary, Jacobs, & Razaviek, 1996).

Axiom 1: The Nature of Reality

Positivist Version.   There is a single tangible reality "out there" that can be fragmented into independent variables and processes, any of which can be studied independently of the others; inquiry can converge onto that reality until finally, it can be predicted and controlled.

Constructivist Version.   There are multiple constructed realities that can be studied only holistically; inquiry into these multiple realities will inevitably diverge (each inquiry raises more questions than it answers) so that prediction and control are unlikely outcomes, although some level of understanding can be achieved (Lincoln & Guba, 1985, p. 37).

Explanation and Comments.   The issue of reality that separates the positivist paradigm from the constructivist paradigm is the most important of the axioms. The nature of reality is an issue that seemingly cannot be resolved or treated on a relative scale. Either there are many realities or there is one reality, but both positions cannot exist at the same time. We think that part of the issue comes from the lack of an agreed on definition of reality. Phillips (1992) points out:

> First, there is a simple confusion here between, on the one hand, the fact that different people and different societies have different views about what is real (a fact that seems undeniable), and on the other hand the issue of whether or not we can know which of these views is the correct one (or indeed, whether there is a correct one at all). From the fact that we might not be able to reach an agreement (an epistemological matter), it does not follow that there is more than one "reality" (ontological matter). (p. 59)

Phillips (1992) follows with an example about this distinction, "And certainly, it does not follow from the fact that a tribe of headhunters socially determines its own reality, that we thereby have to accept that reality as true. What is true—if we have done our research properly—is that the members of that tribe actually do believe in their own realities" (p. 60).

The issue leads to the following question. In the social sciences, is the purpose of research to predict and control (understand the causes)? The answer to this question raises a key distinction between the two different paradigms or belief systems on how research ought to be carried out. We believe that if the purpose of research is to be able to identify causes and predict behavior, then a methodology for carrying out this research from traditional scientific methods should be undertaken. On the other hand, if the purpose of research is to describe participants' beliefs fully, then a methodology based on constructivism seems to be well adapted to this problem.

Consider the following example. A grant from the Kellogg Foundation was given to the Fort Collins community through the Family Medicine Center (Poudre Valley Prenatal Program) to help provide medical care for low-income pregnant women. From the perspective of the program evaluator, one of the general outcome variables that needed to be assessed was whether the method of health care delivery affects the health status of the mothers and infants. To determine the effect of the intervention, the program evaluator undertook a positivist approach by using a time-series design and measuring outcomes such as birth weight, Apgar scores, and so forth. On the other hand, a program evaluator also might be interested in the effect of the intervention (program), as seen through the eyes of the participants. What is it like being a participant in the Poudre Valley Prenatal Program? To answer this question, a constructivist approach appears to be the appropriate method of research. An ethnography was conducted, where the investigator interviewed participants through individual interviews and focus groups. According to the ethnographer (Gerst, 1994), there were many different viewpoints (realities), depending on the context.

Quantitative researchers have also recognized that participants have different perspectives, or points of view, and report those as variability. In addition, quantitative studies often examine factors that are related to and perhaps cause different perceptions. Just because a person states a belief, does not necessarily mean that it is "real." Sometimes people lie or hide their beliefs or are confused. It seems to us, as to Phillips (1992), that it is important to acknowledge that people have different perceptions, but it is also best to investigate why perceptions seem to be different and to be cautious about assuming that what one says is what one really believes.

Axiom 2: The Relationship of Knower to Known

Positivist Version.   The inquirer and the object of inquiry are independent; the knower and the known constitute a discrete dualism.

Constructivist Version.   The inquirer and the "object" of inquiry interact to influence one another; knower and known are inseparable (Lincoln & Guba, 1985, p. 37).

Explanation and Comments.   Axiom 2 is about how much the investigator and participants influence each other. The positivist approach to research has prided itself on the notion that the investigator is objective during the experiment. However, most investigators realize that they can be affected by the impression of the participants. A cute baby is reacted to differently than a fussy one. On the other hand, participants who know they are being investigated may change or act differently. Such psychological phenomena as the Hawthorne effect (participants are likely to change or to be more [or less] motivated simply because they know of their participation in a study; e.g., Roethlisberger & Dickson, 1939) or demand characteristics (participants' awareness of the purpose of the study) have been known for years.

In medical research, placebos are used so that the subjects will not know whether they are in the treatment or in the control group. And double blind studies are used so that the physician will not know who is getting the placebo. The issue for the positivist is to determine how much of the outcome might result from these effects. For example, Drew (1980) suggested that "if the Hawthorne effect cannot reliably be removed from the experimental group, the most effective control method would seem to be to 'Hawthorne' both groups equally" (p. 161). However, the same issue is a problem for the constructivist family of approaches. How much difference does it make if the observer is a participant as compared to a silent observer? We would argue that Axiom 2 separates the two approaches more on a relative than on an absolute basis. The positivist is usually more confident that bias can be overcome, but both paradigms need to be sensitive to this issue.

Axiom 3: The Possibility of Generalization

Positivist Version. The aim of inquiry is to develop a nomothetic body of knowledge in the form of generalizations that are truth statements free from both time and context (they will hold anywhere and at any time).

Constructivist Version. The aim of inquiry is to develop an ideographic body of knowledge in the form of "working hypotheses" that describe the individual case (everything is contextually bound) (Lincoln & Guba, 1985, p. 38).

Explanation and Comments. The issue for Axiom 3 concerns the generalization of the results from the individual study to populations, settings, treatment variables, and measurement variables (Campbell & Stanley, 1966). The theory underlying this generalization (external validity of a study) comes from proper sampling techniques. Lincoln and Guba (1985) and others are correct in their claims that few studies that take an empiricist or positivist approach have used proper sampling techniques. Unfortunately, empirical clinical studies are even more susceptible to these claims. Usually, participants are not randomly sampled from a target population. Instead, participants are usually obtained from a convenience sample (i.e., get them where you find them). The convenience sample is often found at the investigator's clinic.

There is presently less concern over the generalization issue among positivists primarily because of the relatively new methodology called meta-analysis (Glass, McGaw, & Smith, 1981). Meta-analysis allows researchers to combine the results from different studies performed in the same area of interest (by using an effect size index). Effect size in its simplest form for any study is determined by subtracting the average results of the control group from the intervention group and dividing by the pooled standard deviation of both groups. The result yields an effect size in standard deviation units. Effect sizes then can be combined with other, similar studies, resulting in a meta-analysis. When one considers that there are some meta-analyses where over 200 studies have been combined (Lipsey, 1992), the case for generalization gains considerable steam.

The constructivist often makes no claims for generalizing the results beyond what was found in the study. If one believes that the results of a study are always context specific and the investigator's biases play a large role in the data gathering and interpretation, then it follows that the results from the study cannot be generalized to other situations. This last statement is contradictory however, as one of the methods used by constructivists to establish credibility is to have a peer examine the data to determine if similar interpretations are found. Many of the qualitative studies we have reviewed have attempted to make inferences well beyond the specifics of the findings. Again, we would argue that, similar to Axiom 2, Axiom 3 separates the two approaches more on a relative than on an absolute basis. Furthermore, researchers from both approaches should be cautious about generalizing their results.

Axiom 4: The Possibility of Causal Linkages

Positivist Version.   Every action can be explained as the result of a real cause that precedes the effect temporally.

Constructivist Version.   All entities are in a state of mutual simultaneous shaping so that it is impossible to distinguish causes from effects (Lincoln & Guba, 1985, p. 38).

Explanation and Comments.   The issue for Axiom 4 becomes philosophical. For years, positivists believed that under the proper experimental conditions one could conclude that the independent variable caused the change (effect) in the dependent variable. These proper conditions always included the random assignment of participants to groups. However, few positivists were willing to make a strong statement about the causal nature of the study even if (a) they used the proper experimental methods, and (b) the dependent variable changed in the predicted direction after the manipulation of the independent variable. Instead, they frequently observed, "The data are highly suggestive that variable X caused the change in variable Y." Furthermore, statistical analyses alone do not allow for a causal statement. Instead, outcomes are viewed as probability statements; for example, "The probability that variable X could have caused the change in outcome Y is less than 5 chances in 100, assuming that the null hypothesis is true."

Constructivists rule out the concept of causality on many grounds, but perhaps the most salient is that the positivists see causality in a linear fashion, whereas others suggest that most events have multiple causes. Lincoln and Guba (1985) take a much stronger stance on the issue of causality, suggesting that it is impossible to separate cause and effect. Instead, they introduce the concept of mutual simultaneous shaping. Their idea is that

everything influences everything else, in the here and now. Many elements are implicated in any given action, and each element interacts with all of the others in ways that change them all while simultaneously resulting in something that we, as outside observers, label as outcomes or effects. But the interaction has no directionality, no need to produce that particular outcome; it simply happened as a product of the interaction-mutual shaping. (pp. 151–152)

There is no way to resolve differences between the two paradigms for Axiom 4. We are unsure whether one could place the differences on an absolute or on a relative basis. However, our views on causality are similar to the position taken by Davis (1985):

"causation" is a notorious philosophical tar pit. One of the important principles of the philosophy of science is that the working scientist depends on formulations that don't quite hold water under the scrutiny of a professional philosopher. Thus, the ideas I will spell out are the unspoken assumptions of the professional social science researcher, not the honed formulations of the professional logician. (p. 8)

Lincoln and Guba (1985) are certainly correct in pointing out that much behavior is both a cause and an effect, that there is mutual simultaneous shaping of behavior, and that causes and effects are difficult, if not impossible, to distinguish. Also, it is true that students and scholars, not to mention journalists and the public, are too loose in using words like cause, impact, and determinant. In fact, one of the key points that we want to make in this book is that such words should be used with caution and then probably only after completing a study with a tight, randomized experimental design.

Axiom 5: The Role of Values in Inquiry

Positivist Version. Inquiry is value free and can be guaranteed to be so by virtue of the objective methodology used.

Constructivist Version. Inquiry is value bound in at least five ways, as captured in the corollaries that follow:

- *Corollary 1.* Inquiries are influenced by inquirer values as expressed in the choice of a problem, evaluand, or policy option, and in the framing, bounding, and focusing of that problem, evaluand, or policy option.
- *Corollary 2.* Inquiry is influenced by the choice of the paradigm that guides the investigation into the problem.
- *Corollary 3.* Inquiry is influenced by the choice of the substantive theory used to guide the collection and analysis of data and in the interpretation of findings.
- *Corollary 4.* Inquiry is influenced by the values that inhere in the context.
- *Corollary 5.* With respect to Corollaries 1 through 4, inquiry is either value resonant (reinforcing or congruent) or value dissonant (conflicting). Problem, evaluand, or policy option; paradigm; theory; and context must exhibit congruence (value resonance) if the inquiry is to produce meaningful results (Lincoln & Guba, 1985, p. 38).

Explanation and Comments.   Axiom 5 is, in part, about introducing bias in research. It is important for all researchers to recognize that research is *not* value free. Consider the positivist who assumes that his or her research is objective. One might ask, "Who selected the independent variable(s) or the dependent variable(s)? Who selected the sampling frame? Who selected the particular treatment?" Of course, the investigator selected all aspects of the study. Therefore, the constructivists are correct in assuming that research is not value free. In addition, a part of constructivist research is to state the bias of the investigator.

On the other hand, just because the investigator may have a bias in the study does not necessarily mean that nothing can be done about bias or that the outcome will be in the direction of the investigator's choice. There are probably far more studies that fail to find significant differences between treatment and control groups than those that find significant differences. Furthermore, replication attempts by other researchers help to insure that something other than the investigator's bias is influencing the results.

Axiom 5 appears to separate the two paradigms on a relative basis. The degree of subjectivity in most constructivist studies (the investigator is the instrument to measure outcomes) seems to us usually far greater than that seen in the positivist approach. However, this difference is not all or nothing. Researchers in both paradigms should acknowledge that there will be subjectivity and bias. However, we believe that researchers should do what they can to minimize the potential effects of biases.

THE POSITIVIST APPROACH TO RESEARCH

The positivist approach is based on the so-called scientific method. Drew (1980) presents six steps to the research process that are relevant for education, health, and human services disciplines.

1. The first step involves the research question. Kerlinger (1986) refers to it as the problem-obstacle-idea stage. This initial stage involves choosing a question that has the potential to work into a researchable project. Where does the problem come from? For many, especially those in applied disciplines, the problem often comes from a clinical situation. Will a particular type of therapy lead to improvement? Will adaptive technology increase communication skills? Will a particular assessment yield the information I need? Another place from which problems may arise is the previous literature. A published study may help to formulate questions that lead to a new study.

2. The second stage suggested by Drew (1980) involves developing hypotheses. Briefly, the research problem is directed into specific questions that are testable.

3. The third step is developing a research design that allows the investigator to test the hypotheses. The major focus of the research design is to allow the investigator to control or eliminate variables that are not of direct in-

terest to the study. This allows the investigator to test or answer the research question directly.

4. The fourth stage involves data collection and analysis. Data are collected in an unbiased and objective fashion. In the traditional method, the scientist does not examine the data in detail until the study has been completed. The data, which are usually quantitative numbers, are then analyzed by using statistics.

5. The fifth step involves making inferences or interpretations from the data. However, these interpretations must be based on the original hypotheses.

6. A statement is then made as to whether the hypotheses are accepted or rejected.

Drew's (1980) example of the research process takes the form of a feedback loop. After the last step, a new research question is asked. If the hypothesis is confirmed, then a new question can be asked to gain additional information. If the hypothesis is not confirmed, the new question may be a modification of the original question.

These six steps, which are typical of those in most social science research methods books, are discussed in more detail in chapter 22 and throughout this book. It should be noted, however, that quantitative research often varies from this idealized format, which has provided a "straw man" for proponents of the qualitative or constructivist paradigm to criticize. In practice, the scientific approach is not as deductive (literature/theory ⇨ deduce hypotheses ⇨ test hypotheses) or as rigid as implied. For example, interesting findings often emerge in the data analysis stage that were not based on the original hypotheses.

THE CONSTRUCTIVIST APPROACH TO RESEARCH

The process of the constructivist approach to research also is sequential, but it is more flexible than that of the positivist. According to Lincoln and Guba (1985), "Design in the naturalistic (constructivist) sense, as we shall see, means planning for certain broad contingencies without, however, indicating exactly what will be done in relation to each" (p. 226). The constructivist approach also starts with a problem. It would be inconceivable to study a group or organization without having any thought as to why the study is being conducted. However, although the problem may be well thought out at the time of deciding on a group to study, the constructivist researcher is open to the possibility that a major change in emphasis about the problem could occur at any time during the study (emergent design). In other words, although the constructivist researcher has a general idea of what to be looking for in the study, no specific hypotheses are formed prior to the onset of the study. According to Lincoln and Guba (1985, pp. 226–249), a general sequence or plan of constructivist research would be as follows:

1. Determining a focus for the inquiry and determining the constraints of the problem.
2. Determining the fit of the paradigm to the focus.

3. Determining the fit of the inquiry paradigm to the theory.
4. Determining where and from whom the data will be collected.
5. Determining successive phases of the inquiry.
6. Determining instrumentation.
7. Planning for collecting and recording data.
8. Planning data analysis (and interpretation—our addition).
9. Planning the logistics.
10. Planning for trustworthiness.

The first three steps address the problem. However, more than just knowing that a problem needs to be researched, Steps 2 and 3 indicate that a decision must be made about whether the constructivist paradigm is the best method to approach the problem.

Step 4 addresses the particular group that will be studied, but more specifically, who in the group will provide the initial information. Steps 4, 5, and 6 are general in that the constructivist researcher is aware that once the study unfolds, different persons will need to be studied who were not specified prior to the initiation of the study. In addition, the constructivist researcher has no way of knowing what will happen after the study is initiated as far as planning further stages. Whereas the positivist researcher plans a start and end to the study, the constructivist researcher cannot know in advance how long the study will take or in what direction the study will go. However, Lincoln and Guba (1985) suggest three general phases of any constructivist inquiry: focusing on what the investigator needs to determine, determining it, and checking the findings. Step 6, instrumentation, usually implies the human instrument as observer or participant, but other types of instrumentation such as records or documents may be needed to help verify the findings of the study. Again, these instruments may not be established prior to the initiation of the study.

Steps 7 (collecting and recording data) and 8 (data analysis) appear on the surface to be similar to those followed by the positivist. However, there are differences between the two approaches. The type of data that the constructivist deals with is typically qualitative (words, photographs, etc.), or subjective. This is not to say that the constructivist cannot or does not use quantitative data, but does so less frequently than the positivist would. In addition, the type of data analysis methods for the constructivist is not based on inferential statistics. Instead, these methods are similar to descriptive statistics in determining agreement among themes, opinions, and so forth. More important, it is not just the type of data that is collected and analyzed that differs from that collected by the positivist, but when the collection and analyses take place. In the scientific method, data collection and analyses follow a particular order: the data usually are not analyzed until all of the data have been collected. Then the analysis phase takes place, which is followed by the interpretation. For the constructivist, data collection, analysis, and interpretation take place continually and simultaneously throughout the study. In a sense, a feedback system is created that operates continuously. From this system, new hypotheses may emerge, and new types of data are collected.

Step 9, planning the logistics, involves the nuts and bolts of the study, at least initially, in terms of who will carry out the inquiry, where it will be carried out, and what schedules will need to be observed. Some of the logistics include making initial contact and gaining entree, negotiating consent, building and maintaining trust, and identifying and using informants (Lincoln & Guba, 1985).

The last step, planning for trustworthiness, is analogous to the positivist's methods to evaluate research. Lincoln and Guba (1985) have made considerable efforts to develop a method of evaluation for constructivist inquiry that would carry the weight that internal and external validity carry for studies that use the positivist paradigm. Gliner (1994) suggests that some of these methods should be given higher priority than others.

TYPE OF DATA DOES NOT IMPLY A PARTICULAR PARADIGM

If one uses the nature of reality as a distinction between the positivist paradigm and the constructivist paradigm, then it can be argued that not all qualitative data will be constructivist, nor will all quantitative data fit the positivist paradigm (Gliner, 1994). Patton's (1990) examples of different program evaluation approaches help to demonstrate this point. Two of his designs were labeled as pure designs. One pure design, labeled as the pure hypothetical–deductive approach, fits the traditional positivist framework. This approach uses experimental design, quantitative data, and traditional statistical methods. The other pure design was labeled as the *pure qualitative strategy* and fits the constructivist paradigm. This approach uses constructivist inquiry, qualitative data, and content analysis.

Patton (1990) also introduced *mixed form* approaches that included characteristics from each pure-form approach. Of particular importance for distinguishing constructivist research from other research that uses qualitative data were two mixed form approaches. One mixed form approach consisted of experimental design, qualitative data collection, and statistical analysis. The other mixed form approach consisted of experimental design, qualitative data collection, and content analysis. Both of these approaches should be considered as part of the positivist paradigm because the design was experimental. Experimental designs are used to answer questions about cause and effect. Therefore, even though these two approaches used qualitative data, they should be evaluated by using traditional criteria established for positivist paradigms.

A RAPPROCHEMENT BETWEEN QUALITATIVE AND QUANTITATIVE APPROACHES?

As we have seen, philosophically, the two paradigms are different, yet the two approaches may be found together in one research article. Sometimes the two are included in the same article but are separate. Other times, the two paradigms are blended so that one paradigm sets the stage for or leads to the other paradigm (Caracelli & Greene, 1993). The field of program evaluation has numerous examples of both situations.

A classic example of using both qualitative and quantitative approaches in one study, but keeping them separate, is the work by Smith, Gabriel, Schott, and Padia (1976). These investigators evaluated an Outward Bound program. In the quantitative part of the evaluation, a unique time-series design was performed on over 300 participants in the program. The qualitative part of the evaluation used a case study approach, where one participant kept a diary of his experiences throughout the Outward Bound program.

An example where one approach leads to the other is also common in the field of program evaluation. Consider a program evaluation by Gliner and Sample (1996), which evaluated a program designed to increase community opportunities for persons with developmental disabilities. Gliner and Sample (1996) examined quantitative information collected from a quality-of-life questionnaire to select participants for further case study.

The naturalistic paradigm and the positivist paradigm represent two different philosophical approaches to research. The axioms outlined by Lincoln and Guba (1985) emphasize the differences between the two approaches. On the other hand, writers like Howe (1985) do not see the two as mutually exclusive. A few examples of the possible paradigm combinations were listed earlier. Other combinations have been described by Patton (1990), Caracelli and Greene (1993), and Creswell (1994). Lancy (1993) notes that "as the polemical debate heats up, there also is increasing evidence of rapprochement" (p. 11).

SUMMARY

A paradigm is the beliefs that members of a scientific community share. There are two major social science paradigms at present. The dominant paradigm, sometimes called positivism, is usually associated with quantitative research and methods similar to those in the natural sciences. The constructivist, or naturalist, paradigm is usually associated with qualitative research. Such researchers argue that one must take into account the roles that language and values play. Therefore, unlike a positivist, a constructivist does not put total faith in scientific methodology but leaves room for human nature.

Lincoln and Guba (1985), who are constructivist investigators, argue that there are five axioms that separate the two paradigms. The axioms deal with the following:

1. *The nature of reality.* Positivists believe in a single reality. Constructivists believe in multiple constructed realities.
2. *The relationship of knower to known.* Positivists might say the investigator is totally objective. Constructivists say the investigator cannot be totally objective; in fact, participant and researcher interact.
3. *The possibility of generalization.* Positivists might say truth statements are free from both time and context. Constructivists say that the best that can be accomplished is a working hypothesis; everything is contextually bound.
4. *The possibility of causal linkages.* Positivists believe that cause and effect can be determined at least as a probability. Constructivists believe that we are in a constant state of mutual shaping and it is impossible to distinguish cause and effect.
5. *The role of values in inquiry.* Positivists might say inquiry is value free and objective. Constructivists think that inquiry is value bound by inquiry, choice, theory, values, and conflict.

Although these dichotomies highlight differences in the paradigms, we believe that to some extent the positions attributed to the so-called positivists do not reflect the real position of most quantitative researchers. These dichotomies do reflect, however, relative differences. The positivist approach to research follows the so-called scientific method. Steps taken to create this method are to state a research question, develop a hypothesis, develop a research design, collect data, interpret the data, and accept or reject a hypothesis.

The constructivist approach to research is sequential yet flexible. The steps are to determine an area of inquiry, a belief to fit the inquiry, a fit to a theory, a collecting site, a plan for future steps, and the instrument for measurement; and to collect and record data, interpret data, plan logistics, and plan for validity.

A pure positivist approach is deductive. Within this approach you will find experimental design, quantitative data, and statistical methods. A pure constructivist approach is inductive. Within this approach you will find natural inquiry, qualitative data, and content analysis. Sometimes these two paradigms are used together in research.

STUDY AIDS

Concepts

- Deductive reasoning
- Epistemology
- Generalize
- Inductive reasoning
- Paradigm
- Reality

Distinctions

- Identifiable causes versus mutual simultaneous shaping
- Nomothetic or generalizable knowledge versus ideographic knowledge
- Positivist versus constructivist paradigm
- Positive approach (steps) versus constructivist approach to research
- Qualitative versus quantitative research
- Researcher and participants are independent versus research and participant always influence each other
- Single tangible reality versus multiple constructed realities
- Value-free versus value-laden inquiry

Application Problems

1. One of the major differences between the qualitative paradigm (constructivist inquiry) and the quantitative paradigm (logical positivism) is

the method of sampling. How do the two paradigms differ in sampling and what implications might this have for generalization?

2. What is the order of the steps in the positivist approach to research? Put the following steps in order from 1 to 6.

_____ Interpret data
_____ Develop a hypothesis
_____ Accept or reject hypothesis
_____ State research question
_____ Collect data
_____ Develop a research design

3. According to Lincoln and Guba (1985), what is the usual order of a constructivist approach for research? Put the following steps in order from 1 to 10.

_____ Determine a fit to a theory
_____ Determine the instrumentation
_____ Determine a focus of inquiry
_____ Plan for trustworthiness
_____ Determine where and from whom to collect data
_____ Determine the fit of paradigm to the focus
_____ Plan for data analyses
_____ Determine a plan for phases of the inquiry
_____ Plan to collect and record data
_____ Plan logistics

4. A researcher wants to find out if there is a relationship between gender and test anxiety.

a. Using the qualitative (constructivist) approach, describe how a researcher would create a research project to answer this question.

b. Using the quantitative (positivist) approach, describe how a researcher would create a project to answer this question.

3

Ethical Problems
and Principles

This chapter is divided into two major sections. The first provides a brief overview of the recent history of ethical problems in research with human subjects. The second is a discussion of current principles and policies.

HISTORICAL OVERVIEW

Although there have been ethical problems regarding the treatment of human subjects throughout history, it is common to begin about 60 years ago with the Nazi *research* atrocities of 1933 to 1945. Notice that, in contrast to the terminology we use in the rest of this book, we have used the phrase "human subjects" rather than "participants." The latter is a relatively recent change that emphasizes the collaborative and voluntary relationship of investigator and participant. This was definitely *not* the relationship in Nazi Germany nor, sadly, in too many examples of American research.

By Nazi research atrocities, we refer to experiments conducted by respected German doctors and professors on concentration camp inmates that led to their mutilation or death. Although it is tempting to think that these atrocities could be blamed on prison guards, soldiers, or rogue scientists, the evidence indicates otherwise (e.g., Pross, 1992). Not only were many of these doctors respected, but Germany had more advanced moral and legal regulations concerning bona fide consent and special protections for vulnerable subjects than any other country at that time (Young, 1999). As a result of the trial of these doctors, the Nuremberg code was prescribed by an international court in 1947 (see Shuster, 1997). The first principle of the code states that **voluntary consent** of human subjects is absolutely essential. Principles 2 through 8 deal with experimental design and the risks and benefits of the research. Principle 9 states the subject's right to refuse to participate or continue, and Principle 10 deals with the investigator's obligation to stop the experiments when continuing them would likely lead to harm.

Lest we think that ethical problems with human research have been confined to Nazi Germany, examples of American research can also be cited. In 1963, mentally impaired children from the Willowbrook State School in New York were given live hepatitis A virus. Their parents were not adequately informed and were even coerced into volunteering their children for the study. The Tuskegee syphilis study, which began in 1932, continued until it became public knowledge in 1972 (Heller, 1972). The study involved several hundred poor African American men in Alabama who were studied but not treated over a 40-year period, even though antibiotics were available and commonly used to treat syphilis for more than 25 years of the study. The long-term effects of this study include mistrust and suspicion in the African American community of medical research and of doctors in general (Jones, 1982).

Serious ethical problems are not, however, confined to the biomedical sciences. Milgram (1974) conducted a series of well-known experiments on obedience that sparked ethical debate both inside and outside of the behavioral sciences. His intent to perform these experiments was based on his dismay at the effects of blind obedience to Nazi commands in World War II. He decided that it was important to study the psychological mechanism that linked blind obedience to destructive behavior. He wanted to know how far ordinary adults will go in carrying out the orders of a seemingly legitimate authority. He deceived subjects into believing that they would be giving painful electric shocks to a third person, the "learner," when that person made a mistake on a particular task. The results were startling. A great many of the "teachers," who were the actual subjects in the study, obeyed without hesitation the experimenter's urging to continue to increase the presumed level of the shocks, no matter how much the learner pleaded and screamed. Milgram was especially surprised that none of the subjects refused to apply the shocks or dropped out of the study. The learner in these studies was a confederate of Milgram's and no actual shocks were transmitted by the teacher. Nevertheless, concerns about the studies and the use of deception have continued to this day. Milgram defended his work as showing that remarkable obedience was seen time and time again at several universities where the experiment was repeated. He emphasized the willingness of adults to go to almost any lengths when commanded by an authority. He did fully debrief the subjects and provided an opportunity for a friendly reconciliation with the presumably shocked learner, who was shown not to have received any actual electric shocks. Furthermore, he sent follow-up questionnaires to the former subjects and found that less than 1% regretted having participated in the study. In spite of this, it's doubtful that **institutional review boards** (IRBs) would allow this kind of study today because subjects were tricked into participating in a study that they probably would find unacceptable if they had understood it correctly.

If you think that ethical problems about research have been confined to experimental studies, Humphreys' (1970) research on the "tea room" trade indicates issues that are potentially raised by participant observations and qualitative methodology. For this study of male homosexual behavior, Humphreys received a prestigious award. He used considerable deception and violated the subjects' privacy by surreptitiously noting the license plates of men he knew had had fellatio in public restrooms. He then obtained their addresses from the Division of Motor Vehicles to interview them while pretending to be a health service worker. He suspected that the men would not grant an interview if they had known his real purpose because most of the men were married and lived with wives who would not have approved of this behavior.

In 1974 the Department of Health, Education, and Welfare published regulations on the protection of human subjects. It mandated that there be IRBs at each research institution that accepted federal funding to determine whether subjects are placed at risk, and if so, whether the benefits and importance of the knowledge to be gained so outweigh the risks that the subjects should be allowed to accept these risks. The guidelines also mandated that effective informed consent be obtained from participants in research.

PRINCIPLES AND POLICIES RELATED TO HUMAN RESEARCH PARTICIPANTS

The Belmont Report: Principles and Norms

The National Commission for the Protection of Human Subjects of Biomedical and Behavioral Research identified ethical principles and guidelines for the protection of human subjects. This report (National Commission, 1978) is often called the *Belmont Report*. The report listed three ethical principles to guide human research.

Respect for Persons.   This principle incorporates two ethical convictions. First, participants should be treated as autonomous agents, which means that the individual is capable of deliberating and making individual decisions and choices. Second, persons with diminished autonomy are entitled to protection. Such persons include children, the mentally retarded, the demented elderly, persons with various emotional or mental disorders, and prisoners.

Beneficence.   Researchers should not harm participants and good outcomes should be maximized for the participants as well as for science and humanity. This principle, like the others, is complex and requires balancing the potential benefits and the risks, as we will see following.

Justice.   Research should not be exploitative and there should be a fair distribution of risks and benefits. For example, those who bear most of the risks during research should benefit the most from it. Fair distribution is clearly not always the case and leads to ethical dilemmas that need to be considered carefully.

Sieber (1992) lists six norms of scientific behavior that follow from the *Belmont Report*:

1. The research design should be valid because only valid research yields meaningful results.
2. The researcher must be competent and capable of carrying out the procedures.
3. The risks and benefits should be identified from all perspectives. Ethical research will maximize the benefits and minimize the risks.
4. The selected subjects must be appropriate for the purposes of the study and representative of groups that will benefit from the research.
5. The researcher is responsible for what happens to the subjects and must inform them about compensation if they are harmed.
6. There must be voluntary consent.

The next section expands the topic of informed consent. That discussion and those on privacy and the assessment of risks and benefits that follow are based on Sieber's (1992) helpful book, *Planning Ethically Responsible Research: A Guide for Students and Internal Review Boards.*

Voluntary Informed Consent

Consent, like the other issues to be discussed, is considerably more complex than it might appear on the surface. Voluntary informed consent is the procedure by which participants choose whether or not they wish to participate in a study. According to the *Belmont Report* (National Commission, 1978) there are three aspects to informed consent: information, comprehension, and voluntariness. Each is described briefly and then various issues are discussed in more detail.

Information.   The information provided to participants should include the research procedure, purpose, risks, and anticipated benefits. It should provide the information that a reasonable volunteer would want to know before giving consent. How the information is given is also important. It must be in language or in a form that the participants can understand, and efforts should be made to check that it is understood, especially in cases where risks are involved. Also, it should be noted that consent is an ongoing process and that it may be withdrawn at any time during the study.

Comprehension.   The participants should have the legal capacity and the ability to understand the information and risks involved so that they can make an informed decision. Some participants (e.g., children) are not legally qualified to make decisions of consent for themselves, so others must make the decision for them. Their representative is usually the parent or guardian, but children 7 years or older also must *assent* to the procedure, indicating that they agree and want to participate.

   Comprehension also may be impaired in cases of mentally retarded or emotionally disabled persons. Again, to the extent possible, this person should be allowed to assent or not to the procedures, but a third party (e.g., the legal guardian or someone who is likely to understand the subject's situation) should be chosen to act in that person's best interest. Special care must be taken when there might be a conflict of interest between the parent or guardian and the interests of the child or other participants who do not have the legal capacity to grant consent. Both persons must voluntarily agree to the participation.

Voluntariness.   The third aspect of informed consent means that the participant has decided to participate in the study freely without threat or undue inducement. There should not be any element of force, deceit, duress, or other form of constraint or coercion. As we have seen in the Milgram studies, persons in authority can elicit unjustifiable obedience even with well-educated adults. Also, voluntariness is reduced when the research offers financial or other inducements that the potential participants would find hard to refuse, for example, large payments to poor people or promises of reduced sentences to prisoners.

   Sieber (1992) lists a number of aspects of the consent process that should be considered. Rapport should be achieved not only because participants are more likely to cooperate, but because it can strengthen the ecological validity of the study. There should be a congruence between what the researcher says and body language. It is important that the researcher not rush through this "unnecessary" aspect of the study or even give that impression. Developing the trust of the participants and understanding their personal and cultural situations is also important. This awareness is especially true for community-based research and research done in cultures that are different from the researcher's culture. The research also should be relevant to the concerns of the research population and explained in those terms.

   The issue of who should provide the consent is easy when the potential participant is an adult who is assumed to be a free agent and has the capacity to consent or not. The issue is less clear with children or other persons who may not have the capacity to give consent. The issue here is that, in situations where the participants cannot provide their own consent, we should not automatically assume that parental or guardian consent is sufficient, although in most cases it should be. Researchers should be aware that in some situations there may be a conflict of interest. For example, parents of adjudicated youth or poor parents who need the money offered by a research study might not have the interest of the child foremost.

How is consent obtained? Most IRBs require a formal signed consent form, except in certain situations specified in the federal regulations. First, a signed consent form may be omitted when subjects can easily refuse by discontinuing a phone call with an interviewer or by not returning the survey that was received in the mail. It is important, however, that the interviewer or questionnaire cover letter describes the purpose of the research and any risk involved, and states that participation is voluntary. In such cases it's generally deemed unnecessary for the subject to actually sign and return a consent form. Returning the survey or answering the questions is the subject's way of implying consent. Second, signed consent forms can be omitted when providing them would jeopardize the well-being of the participants. For example, if the research is on criminal behavior, a consent form could be subpoenaed and, therefore, could put the person in jeopardy. In research on populations vulnerable to stigmatizing effects (e.g., persons with AIDS), a signed consent form may well present more danger than protection to the participants.

The fact that a signed consent form is not required does not mean that consent is not necessary. For consent in the case of interviews and surveys, the participants still must be informed and must have the capacity to consent. In the case of criminal or stigmatized behavior, the participants should be provided with a copy of the consent statement but they do not have to sign the agreement to participate.

Another aspect of the consent process occurs in studies where there is deception or where there may be questions about the procedures after the fact. **Debriefing**, as it is called, is required when deception is involved and is a good idea even if there is no deception. Too often researchers skip a responsibility to debrief subjects by promising to make the results available later. This promise is usually not a good idea because it is often broken and is hard to follow up by the time the results are known. More realistic and important is providing the opportunity right after the study to discuss it in the context of the literature and what led to the research. This approach is often more useful to the participants than the findings of the particular study. Participants who received such informative debriefing are more likely to feel good about research and more likely to participate in future studies.

Privacy

Stemming from the ethical principle of respect for participants, a component of voluntary informed consent is that participants' privacy will be respected. To some extent much of behavioral research involves asking participants to reveal aspects of their behavior or attitudes. **Privacy** refers to a person's concern about controlling access to information about themselves (Sieber, 1992). Voluntary informed consent involves the participant agreeing to reveal certain aspects that may have been private previously. If participants feel that privacy is being invaded, answers that they provide may be distorted and, therefore, give misleading or false information. The essence of privacy is that the participant is free to choose the extent to which his or her attitudes, beliefs, and behaviors are to be shared with or withheld from others. Because behavioral scientists often collect and analyze private data, there is always the potential for a conflict between the right of privacy and the goal of the research.

Several factors influence the extent to which participants view their privacy as being invaded. One is that if the data are anonymous, that is, unidentifiable by the researcher, the participant may be more willing to share and to be reassured that their privacy is protected. It is important here to make a distinction between confidentiality and anonymity. **Anonymity** means that the person's name and other identifiers such as social security number or address are never attached to the data or even known by the researcher. In many studies the data are not anonymous, because the researcher must match more than one piece of data or the participant is seen face to face and cannot be anonymous. In all cases it is important that the data remain **confidential**. That is, there is an agreement that private information will remain private to the researcher, and the participant will not be identifiable in the reports or in conversations with other persons outside of the research team.

Federal law has little to say about privacy and social research. For example, it is not discussed as a separate topic in depth in the *Belmont Report* mentioned earlier. However, sensitive researchers will be very careful not to invade the privacy of participants in their research; IRBs are typically alert to this issue. This consideration implies that fully informed voluntary consent will be obtained ahead of time and that the researcher will assure confidentiality of the data. The participants can then decide whether or not to participate under these conditions. Presumably the participant who views the research as an invasion of privacy can simply decline to participate. However, it may be that, feeling subtle pressure to participate, the subject will distort answers. Thus, both to be sensitive to the participant's concerns about invasion of privacy and to obtain the best data, it is important to consider whether members of the planned participant group will view the research as an invasion of privacy. To learn about the privacy interests of your research population, you should ask someone who works with or is a member of the population. For example, ask teachers, parents, therapists, or experienced researchers whether they think other people in this group might think your questions are an invasion of privacy.

Researchers also need to protect the fact that an individual participated in the research at all. Confidentiality is especially important if the research is about a stigmatized group (e.g., homosexuals, depressed mothers). Thus, lists of participants need to be kept confidential and should be destroyed after the project.

Assessment of Risks and Benefits

Probably the most important concern about research ethics is that the individuals not be harmed by serving as participants in the study. The *Belmont Report* states,

"The requirement that research be justified on the basis of a favorable risk/benefit assessment bears a close relation to the principle of beneficence, just as the moral requirement that informed consent be obtained is derived primarily from the principle of respect for persons" (National Commission, 1978, p. 6).

Risk refers both to the probability of harm occurring and to the magnitude and type of harm. There are many kinds of possible harms and benefits that need to be taken into account. For example, there are psychological, physical, legal, social, and economic harms, which have corresponding potential benefits, although psychological and physical pain or injuries are the most often discussed types of risks. Others, such as potential loss of job or embarrassment, should be considered. In fact, invasion of one's privacy could be viewed as a type of harm resulting from research that is not sensitively or carefully planned.

Although it is rare to attempt to quantify the risks and benefits of a particular research study, there should be a systemic assessment of these factors. The *Belmont Report* (National Commission, 1978) states that the assessment of whether the research is justifiable should reflect at least five considerations: (a) brutal or inhumane treatment is never justified; (b) risks should be reduced to those that are necessary and consideration should be given to alternative procedures that reduce risks; (c) when research involves significant risks of serious harm, review committees should be very careful that the benefits justify those risks (for example, in medical research, an unproven treatment may promise significant benefits even though there are risks of serious side effects); (d) when vulnerable populations are involved, the appropriateness of using them should be demonstrated, including judgment about the nature and degree of risk and the level of anticipated benefits; and (e) relevant risks and benefits must be fairly explained in the informed consent procedure and form.

Sieber (1992) identifies four misconceptions about risks and benefits:

1. A ratio is not actually computed; most risks and benefits of research cannot be quantified.
2. Some risks and benefits cannot be identified accurately before the research is performed.
3. It is impossible to consider all risks and benefits ... the researchers need to focus on the most important of these, but cannot possibly anticipate everything.
4. Risks and benefits cannot be identified for each subject individually. One subject's risk may be another's benefit. (pp. 75–76)

Sieber (1992) also points out that federal regulations governing the IRBs are concerned only with harm to human subjects, not with researcher social sensitivity. However, ignoring the sensitivities of gatekeepers, community members, and society at large invites having the research prevented, interrupted, maligned, or invalidated. Furthermore, IRBs may well consider how the research may affect the community.

In addition to minimizing the risks, it is important for researchers to maximize the **benefits**. This step may be relatively easy in community-based and medical research where some clear benefit to the individual participants is envisioned. However, before the study, such benefits can only be anticipated, or there would be no need for the study.

It is less easy to achieve benefits for the participants in so-called survey research and certain kinds of laboratory experiments. Nevertheless, researchers must think about the issue of maximizing benefits in a realistic manner to avoid false promises or grandiose claims about benefits to science and society. Sieber (1992) states that it is more realistic to provide benefits to the subjects or their community, research institutions, the researcher, or the funder than it is to science and society. Benefits to participants could include an informative debriefing, workbooks or materials, a chance to share concerns or interests with the researcher, and, in some cases, the effects of the experimental treatment.

Benefits to the community could include improved relationships with a university, more understanding about the problems under study, special training, the prestige of being associated with the program and university, and materials such as books. The benefits to the researcher, institutions, and funder are more obvious, but include subtle things like future access to participants and community sites and improved "town-gown" relationships. These benefits are important but, in the view of IRBs, take a back seat to benefits to the individual and to science.

SUMMARY

This chapter provides an overview of the recent history of ethical problems in research with human subjects. In the last 60 years, there have been a number of violations ranging from the Nazi doctors' research atrocities to studies that seem in retrospect to have gone too far in terms of deception or invading privacy. The chapter also discusses principles and norms for research with human participants. The principles of respect for participants, beneficence, and justice form the basis of appropriate human research. Voluntary informed consent by participants is required, and its complexities are discussed. The ethical principles of privacy are designed to assure that the participants are free to choose how much to reveal and that what is revealed will be kept confidential. Finally, the assessment of risks and benefits is discussed and the point made that risks should be minimized. Various kinds of risks, psychological as well as physical, are discussed, as are various types of possible benefits.

STUDY AIDS

Concepts

- Assent
- Beneficence
- Debriefing
- Institutional review board (IRB)
- Justice
- Privacy

- Respect for persons
- Voluntary informed consent

Distinctions

- Anonymous versus confidential
- Risks versus benefits

Application Problems

1. Read the following scenario, then answer the questions below.

Dr. Jones, of the College of Education at Major University, is interested in the emotional well being of children raised in a traditional religious school setting. She hypothesizes that these children will be emotionally stronger than the general national norms. Because Dr. Jones serves on the Board of Directors for the school, the Principal, Sister Mary, readily agrees. Dr. Jones may meet with the 5th graders and can interview all 20 students about their family attitudes toward alcohol, tobacco, and drug use, and their resistance to violence. She also knows of a standardized instrument of emotional health. Sister Mary determines that the assessment of the children's emotional health will be useful information for the school to have in the students' records, so students will be told the interviews are part of the class. Because it is part of the class assignment, there is no need to especially inform the parents. Besides, the notices sent to parents never come back when they are sent out in lunchboxes anyway! The 20 students are about evenly split between boys and girls, three Cuban students attend, and the rest are white. Along with the standardized psychological instrument, she should be able to *snapshot* the children reasonably well, and differentiate well-being by gender, ethnicity, and family attitudes.

a. Who are the players (both apparent and not apparent) and what might be their issues?

b. Which Belmont Report principles (respect for person, beneficence, justice) pertain, and how?

c. What questions might an Institutional Review Board have about this project?

d. Should the project be approved as currently proposed?

e. How could the project be redesigned to address some of the IRB's concerns?

In the following scenarios describe what ethical issues were raised.

2. A researcher is interested in chocolate consumption and reaction time. She randomly assigns 16 students to either an experimental or control group. The students are told that as part of their final grade in the course, they must be a subject in the study. After giving eight of the students five candy bars each to eat (while she sits and watches to ensure they eat all of them) she gives all 16 students a test for reaction time. When the students have completed the test, she allows them to leave.

3. At a large university a researcher wants to find out if graduate students have better decision making skills than undergraduates. The researcher tells 30 graduates and 30 undergraduates that he will give them $50 each if they complete a difficult decision task. After the results were tabulated, the researcher posts the students' social security numbers and decision-making score on his door so the students can know how they did on the task.

Research Problems,
Variables, and Hypotheses

Theory
Summary
Study Aids
  Concepts
  Distinctions
  Application Problems

RESEARCH PROBLEMS

The research process begins with a problem. What is a **research problem**? Kerlinger (1986) describes a problem as "an interrogative sentence or statement that asks: What relation exists between two or more variables?" (p. 16). We would like to point out that almost all research studies have more than two variables. Kerlinger suggests that prior to the problem statement "the scientist will usually experience an obstacle to understanding, a vague unrest about observed and unobserved phenomena, a curiosity as to why something is as it is" (p. 11).

Two Sample Problems

Consider first the following example that happened to *J.A.G.* Some years ago, when I was working in the area of environmental physiology, I was to give a talk at the Federation of American Societies for Experimental Biology. There were many well-known scientists at my talk, and I was nervous to say the least, especially because I felt that others in the audience knew more about my topic—regional distribution of blood flow during alcohol intoxication—than I did. During the talk immediately preceding mine, a colleague sitting next to me asked how I felt. I answered that I felt fine, but I took my pulse and found my heart to be beating at a rate of about 110 beats per minute, considerably above my normal resting heart rate of 60 beats per minute but similar to my rate after moderate exercise. I wondered if this could be a healthy response. Thus I began to formulate my problem. I would phrase my problem at this stage as, *Could a high heart rate in the absence of exercise be normal?*

From here I read the literature on anxiety and heart rate, and found numerous studies that examined heart rate under conditions of speaking before audiences. The heart rate could get exceedingly high, much higher than mine had been. Also of interest was the use of pharmacological agents such as beta blockers to reduce heart rate and anxiety under these conditions. However, none of the previous studies examined the metabolic requirements (e.g., oxygen uptake and cardiac output) under these anxiety situations. On the other hand, several studies that had examined metabolic requirements on heart rate above resting were performed during the condition of exercise. These studies considered elevated heart rate following exercise to be normal because the heart must deliver an increased amount of oxygen to the tissues under higher metabolic demands. The problem now became a general question: *If we measured the metabolic demands of a situation under anxiety, would it be similar to a situation under exercise?* Now an obstacle was created that had to be removed. How could we create two situations, one under anxiety and one under exercise, that yielded similar heart rates? To remove this barrier, we decided to use a within subjects design, where each participant took part in all conditions of the study. First, we could determine the heart rate and metabolic requirements under an anxiety-provoking situation (e.g., prior to giving a talk). Next, we could have the participant exercise on a treadmill at a workload high enough to give us a heart rate identical to that experienced under anxiety and we could also measure metabolic requirements.

Now we could state our problem as, *How are heart rate and metabolic requirements related under conditions of anxiety?* Our next step would be to change the problem statement into a prediction statement, or **hypothesis**, that could be directly tested. Again, borrowing from Kerlinger (1986), "hypothesis statements contain two or more variables that are measurable or potentially measurable and that specify how the variables are related" (p.17). We will return to this example later in the chapter.

The second example is a research problem faced by *G.A.M.* and his colleagues. We had observed that infants who were born prematurely and also those who had been abused or neglected seemed to have lower motivation to master new skills and seemed to get less pleasure from trying. This clinical observation raised several issues. First, could the motivation of preverbal infants be measured? Achievement motivation in adults and older children had been assessed from stories they told in response to ambiguous pictures. Some other method would need to be developed for infants. Second, was it really the case that premature and abused or neglected infants were less motivated to master tasks? The second part of the research problem might be phrased, *Is there a relationship between prematurity and abuse or neglect and mastery motivation?* We will also return to this example to examine the selection and development of a good research problem.

Sources of Research Problems

The examples just discussed illustrate two common sources of research problems: personal experience and clinical observation. Both assume a knowledge
of the literature in the field and the ability to relate it to the experiences or observations. Often experiences at work or school can be the source of a research
problem, if you know what questions are unanswered at present and how to
translate the "vague unrest about observed or unobserved phenomena"
(Kerlinger, 1986, p. 11) into a testable research problem.

An important distinction that is sometimes confusing to students is that the
word *problem* might convey the false impression that a research problem is the
same as a personal or societal problem. Personal or societal problems, however, may lead to research problems and questions or hypotheses that can be
answered by collecting and analyzing data. For J.A.G. to worry that he would
be nervous during his presentation is not a research problem. Likewise, for
G.A.M. to be concerned about the apparent low mastery motivation of abused
or neglected children is a societal but not a research problem. The discussion at
the beginning and end of this chapter indicates how these personal and societal
problems might evolve into research problems.

One of the first steps in the research process is to read the **research literature** on and around the topic of interest so that you will be able to identify gaps
in knowledge. Appendix B discusses the research article and provides hints
about the literature review. Locke, Silverman, and Spirduso (1998) and Fink
(1998) provide useful information about reading and understanding research
and conducting **literature reviews**.

Theory is another major source of research problems. In textbook descriptions of the scientific method, the deduction of testable hypotheses from theories is presented as *the* method of choice for the behavioral sciences (e.g.,
Drew, 1980). We do not want to discount the importance or value of this source
of research problems, but we would like to make two points. Qualitative research is often said to work the other way around: observations lead to theory
inductively. Also, in applied fields, relevant theories may be hard to find. Nevertheless, we think it is important for any good research problem to be
grounded in the empirical and theoretical literature and to have a conceptual as
well as a practical base.

Characteristics of a Good Research Problem

In addition to being grounded in the empirical and theoretical literature and examining the relationships between two or more variables, a good research problem has several other characteristics. As indicated earlier, it should hold the
promise of filling a gap in the literature, or providing a test of a theory, or both.

A good research problem should also state the variables to be related clearly
and unambiguously. Often research problems start out too broadly or vaguely
stated. Appendix C provides several examples and templates for writing good
research problems. Problems should also imply several research questions.

Again, Appendix C provides examples of research questions in formats that are consistent with the framework of this book (see especially chapter 5, which also provides examples of research questions).

A good research problem should be **testable** by empirical methods; it should not be just a statement of your moral, ethical, or political position. You should be able to collect data that will answer the research questions.

Of course, the methods used must be ethical and consistent with the guidelines outlined in chapter 3. The problem also needs to be feasible, given your resources and abilities. Finally, it is desirable, especially for graduate students, to choose a problem that is of vital interest to you so that you can sustain the motivation to finish, often a difficult thing to do.

Another way of deciding on a good, appropriate research problem for a thesis or dissertation is to examine where it would lie on several dimensions.

Broad Versus Narrow.   We stated that research problems often start out too broadly. For example, *What factors cause low mastery motivation?* is too broad and probably not a feasible problem. Remember that your time and resources are limited, so practicality requires that you limit the scope of your problem. It is also important to realize that science progresses in small steps. Even large, well-funded research projects often raise more questions than they answer, and usually address only a limited piece of a broad research problem. On the other hand, you do not want the problem to be too narrow. Usually it should deal with more than a single, limited research question and two variables (see Appendix C).

Widespread Versus Limited Interest.   It might seem that you would want as many people (scholars and the public) as possible to be interested in your research. Certainly *you* should be interested and it is a good strategy to pick a problem that is of interest to your advisor. You will get more and better feedback from your advisor and committee if they have interest in and knowledge about the area. It is also desirable to choose a topic that is of widespread interest, but some topics become almost faddish and have so many studies about them that it is hard to make a contribution. If you choose a topic that is currently very popular, try to find as much recent unpublished literature as possible by attending conferences, searching the Web and ERIC (Education Resources Information Centers) documents, and writing to researchers who have recently published in the area to see if they have something new. It is a difficult task to identify gaps in the literature of a currently popular topic because a lot of work may be still in progress. This point overlaps with the next.

Well-Researched Versus Unknown Territory.   It is exciting to think that you might be the first one to explore an area. However, if that is the case, one might wonder why it is unexplored. Is the topic of limited interest? Are there practical, ethical, or financial reasons? Is the topic too specialized or narrow? Of course, there are interesting and important topics that are relatively unexplored and are not faced with these objections, but they are not easy to identify.

Quantitative researchers tend to emphasize finding gaps in the literature, so they tend to study relatively well-researched areas. Qualitative researchers, on the other hand, de-emphasize finding literature ahead of time and tend to explore less well-researched topics, seeing where their observations lead them.

VARIABLES

A variable has one defining quality. It must be able to vary or have different values. For example, gender is a variable because it has two values, female or male. If we are studying differences between men and women, gender is a variable. On the other hand, if we are studying only women, gender is not a variable; it is a constant. *Age* is a variable that has a large number of values. Type of treatment or intervention (or type of curriculum) is a variable if there is more than one treatment or there is a treatment and a control group. Number of days to recover from an ailment, a common measure of the effect of a treatment, is also a variable. Similarly, amount of mathematics knowledge is a variable because it can vary from none to a lot.

Definition of a Variable

Thus, we can define the term **variable** as a characteristic of the participants or a situation in a given study that has different values in that study. In quantitative research, variables are defined operationally and are commonly divided into independent variables (active or attribute), dependent variables, and extraneous variables. Each of these topics are dealt with in the following sections.

Operational Definitions of Variables

An **operational definition** describes or defines a variable in terms of the operations used to produce it or techniques used to measure it. When quantitative researchers describe the variables in their study, they specify what they mean by telling how they measured the variable. Demographic variables like age, gender, or ethnic group are usually measured simply by asking the participant to choose the appropriate category from among those listed. Each type of treatment (or curriculum) is usually described or defined much more extensively so that the reader knows what the researcher meant by, for example, a cognitively enriching curriculum or sheltered work. Likewise, abstract concepts such as mathematics knowledge, self-concept, or mathematics anxiety need to be defined operationally by describing in detail how they will be measured or implemented in a particular study. To do this, the investigator may provide sample questions or append the instrument, or provide a reference where more information can be found.

Independent Variables

Active Independent Variables.   This first type of independent variable is often called a manipulated variable. A frequent goal of research is to investigate the effect of a particular intervention on a particular outcome. A study might examine the effect of a new kind of splint to increase functional movement in people who have had a spinal cord injury. The independent variable is the type of splint. A second study might examine the effect of a new teaching method, such as cooperative learning, on student performance. The independent variable in this case is the type of teaching method. In these two examples, the variable of interest is something that is given to the participants. Therefore, an **active independent variable** is a variable, such as a workshop, new curriculum, or other intervention, one level of which is given or presented to one group of participants but not to another, usually within a specified period of time *during the study*.

In traditional experimental research, independent variables are those that the investigator can manipulate; they presumably cause a change in a resulting behavior, attitude, or physiological measure of interest. An independent variable is considered to be manipulated when the investigator has given one value to one group (experimental condition), and another value to another group (control condition).

However, there are many circumstances, especially in applied research, when we have an active independent variable, but this variable is not directly manipulated by the investigator. Consider the situation where the investigator is interested in a new type of treatment. To conduct the study, it turns out that rehabilitation center *A* will be using that treatment. Rehabilitation center *B* will be using the traditional treatment. The investigator will compare the two centers to determine if one treatment works better than the other. Notice that the independent variable is active but has *not* been manipulated *by the investigator.*

Thus, active independent variables are *given* to the participants in the study but are not necessarily manipulated by the experimenter. They may be given by a clinic, school, or someone other than the investigator. From the participants' point of view, the situation was manipulated.

Attribute Independent Variables. Unlike some authors of research methods books, we do not restrict the term independent variable to those variables that are manipulated or active. We define an independent variable more broadly to include any predictors, antecedents, or presumed causes or influences under investigation in the study. Attributes of the participants, as well as active independent variables, would fit within this definition. For the social sciences, education, and disciplines dealing with special-needs populations, nonactive independent variables are especially important. Type of disability or level of disability is often the major focus of a study. Disability certainly qualifies as a variable because it can take on different values even though they are not "given" in the study. For example, cerebral palsy is different from Down syndrome, which is different from spina bifida; yet all are disabilities. Also, there are different levels of the same disability, which may take on values defined by functional level or anatomical level. Spinal cord injury is a good example of the latter. However, we cannot give levels of spinal cord injury. Specifically, we cannot assign or make one group of people into the category of quadriplegia and another group of people into the category of paraplegia. People already have defining characteristics, or *attributes,* that place them into one of these two categories.

The different disabilities are already present when we perform our study. Thus, we are also interested in studying a class of variables that cannot be given during the study, even by other persons, schools, or clinics.

A variable that cannot be given, yet is a major focus of the study is called an **attribute independent variable** (Kerlinger, 1986). In other words, the values of the independent variable are an attribute of the person. For example, gender, age, ethnic group, or disability are attributes of a person. Another common label for an attribute independent variable is a measured variable. However, we dislike this label because one could easily confuse an attribute independent variable with the dependent variable, which is also measured.

Other methodologists, especially experimental psychologists, have referred to attribute independent variables as nuisance variables (Kirk, 1982) because, from a strict experimentalist standpoint, the researcher would make an attempt to get rid of, or control, these variables. Sometimes demographic variables such as gender or ethnic group are called moderator or mediating variables because they serve these functions. However, in education and the health sciences, we often have a substantive interest in attribute variables.

Type of Independent Variable and Inferences About Causes. When we analyze data from a study, the statistical analysis does not differentiate between whether the independent variable is an active independent variable or an attribute independent variable. However, even though we give the label independent variable to both active and attribute variables, there is a crucial difference in interpretation. A significant change or difference following manipulation of the active independent variable may reasonably lead the investigator to infer that the independent variable caused the change in the dependent variable. However, a significant change or difference between or among values of an attribute independent variable should *not* lead one to the interpretation that the attribute independent variable caused the dependent variable to change. This important distinction is amplified in the next chapter when we compare the experimental (active) and individual differences (attribute) approaches to research.

Levels of the Independent Variable. Earlier, in defining a variable, we said that it must take on different values. When describing the different values of an independent variable, the word **level** is commonly used; it does not necessarily imply that the values are ordered.[1] Suppose that an investigator is conducting a study to investigate the effect of a treatment. One group of patients is assigned to the treatment group. A second group of patients does not receive the treatment. The study could be conceptualized as having one independent variable, treatment type, with two levels, treatment and no treatment. The independent variable in this example would be classified as an active independent variable. Suppose instead that the investigator was interested primarily in comparing

---

[1]The terms categories, values, groups, and samples are sometimes used interchangeably with the term levels, especially in statistics books. Likewise, the term factor is often used instead of the term independent variable.

two different treatments but decided to include a third no-treatment group as a control group in the study. Now the study could be conceptualized as having one independent variable, treatment type, with three levels, the two treatment conditions and the control condition. Again, the independent variable in this example is an active independent variable. This variable could be diagramed as follows:

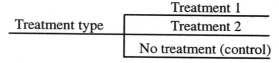

Now, let's think about gender, which is an attribute independent variable with two levels, male and female. It could be diagramed as follows:

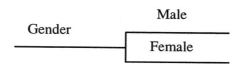

The design of a study with one independent variable is often called a *single factor* design and the appropriate statistics are called single factor or basic statistics (see chap. 14–15).

More Than One Independent Variable.   We could expand our study of three levels of treatment by adding gender as a second independent variable. When more than one independent variable is included in a study, the investigator is often interested not only in the effect of each independent variable by itself, but in the interaction between the two independent variables. We discuss variables, levels, and interactions in more detail in later chapters because most published studies and theses have more than one independent variable. Studies with two independent variables are called *two-factor*, or *factorial, designs.*

Dependent Variables

The dependent variable is the outcome or criterion. It is assumed to measure or assess the effect of the independent variable. Dependent variables are scores from a test, ratings on questionnaires, readings from instruments (electrocardiogram, galvanic skin response, etc.), or measures of physical performance. When we discuss measurement, we are usually referring to the dependent variable. Specifically, scale of measurement, standardization, reliability, and validity are all terms that are important for choosing and describing the dependent variable (see chap. 9 and 20). Just as it is common for a thesis or published study to have more than one independent variable, it is common to have several dependent variables or measures, for example, performance and satisfaction. Dependent variables also have at least two levels, but it is common for them to have many ordered levels (i.e., from low to high).

Extraneous Variables

Extraneous variables are not of interest in a particular study, but they could influence the dependent variable. Environmental factors (e.g., temperature or distractions), time of day, other attributes of the participants, and characteristics of the investigator, teacher, or therapist are some possible extraneous variables that need to be controlled by methods such as holding them constant, randomization, statistics, or matching. We discuss these variables in more detail in several later chapters.

Ordered Versus Unordered or Nominal Levels of Variables

Another important feature of any variable is that the levels may be unordered categories or they may be ordered and, perhaps even continuous; that is, variables may have an infinite number of ordered categories on a continuum. Remember, earlier it was stated that a variable must vary; that is, it must be able to take on different values. Most of our examples of independent variables (e.g., gender, treatment type) had levels or categories that were not ordered. The categories in such variables are essentially labels or names and the variables are said to be *nominal* (from "name") *variables*. For example, the independent variable gender has two, nonordered levels, female and male. Nominal variables, according to Kerlinger (1986), "have simple requirements: all the members of a subset are considered the same and all are assigned the same name and the same numeral" (p. 36). For example, all females are considered the same and assigned to the category of female. All males are the same and assigned to the category of male, but the categories are not ordered such that females are more or less than males.

On the other hand, ordered variables have a set of values that vary from low to high within a certain range (e.g., a 1–7 rating of satisfaction), such that a larger value of the variable indicates more of it than a smaller value of the variable, and there is an assumption that there are or could be an infinite set of values within the range (Kerlinger, 1986). Weight and time to recovery are continuous variables, but many ordered variables have only a few levels or categories, such as high, medium, and low. We expand on this introduction to measurement in chapter 9.

Other Considerations About Variables

For the most part, the studies we discuss have independent variables that have a few levels and dependent variables that have many ordered levels. However, in the associational approach discussed in chapter 5, both independent and dependent variables usually have many ordered levels. Also, there are some studies in which the independent variables have many levels and the dependent variable has two or a few levels, and there are even studies where both variables have only a few levels. We discuss these different combinations of independent and dependent variables and how they are analyzed later in the book.

Some variables (e.g., knowledge of mathematics or self-concept) could be either the independent variable or the dependent variable (or even an extraneous variable), depending on the study. These variables are usually a changeable characteristic of the participant (like an attitude or personality characteristic); if one of these is used as the independent variable, it is an attribute independent variable.

Individual participants do *not* have to vary on a characteristic or variable—it is the group that must have more than one value (e.g., some men and some women). In some studies, participants may change over time or as a result of an intervention. In these studies, there are repeated measures of the same variable (e.g., a pretest and a posttest on math knowledge).

Groups or Sets of Variables

In analyzing complex research articles (see chap. 24), students often have difficulty distinguishing between **variables and the levels of variables**. The reason that this sorting is difficult is that in complex studies researchers have many variables that they often group into what might be called sets of similar variables. For example, age, gender, education, and marital status variables could be grouped together and referred to collectively in an article as demographics. Similarly, verbal, quantitative, and analytical scores on Graduate Record Exams (GRE) could be called GRE scores. The confusion arises if one mistakenly assumes that the sets or groups of variables (demographics and GRE scores) are the variables, and the actual variables (age, gender, GRE verbal, etc.) are the levels.

How can one avoid this confusion? Thoughtful reading is the key, but some tips may help. Remember that a variable has to have at least two levels, but a level or category is a single value.[2] Thus, if something can vary from low to high (e.g., age or GRE verbal) or has two or more nominal values (e.g., gender), it has to be a variable, not a level.

HYPOTHESES AND RESEARCH QUESTIONS

Now that we have discussed variables in detail, let's return to hypotheses. Broadly speaking, a hypothesis is a predictive statement about the relationship between two or more variables. In later chapters, we expand on this definition. In chapter 11, we discuss null (no difference) hypotheses that are tested when we use inferential statistics. However, for now we can use the general definition. In chapter 5 we describe two basic kinds of research questions (difference and associational), which are like hypotheses in question format. However, it is important to point out that *any* research hypothesis or question can be phrased as a relationship between variables. Also note that most studies have several hypotheses or research questions. We examine this scenario in the next chapter and throughout the book.

---

[2]In some cases a level may be a range of values (e.g., ages 21–30 years), but in these cases the values in a given range are treated as if they were all the same (e.g., young adult or given a single group code such as 3).

The Anxiety and Heart Rate Problem Revisited

Earlier, we stated one research problem as, *How are heart rate and metabolic requirements related under conditions of anxiety?* Perhaps a clearer way to state the problem is, *Do metabolic requirements differ between the conditions of anxiety and exercise when heart rate is held constant*? By examining our problem statement closely, we can determine that a number of variables may be involved. Heart rate, metabolic requirements, exercise, and anxiety all might be variables. But remember, a variable must be able to vary. Let's reexamine our study. Under one condition, called anxiety, heart rate and metabolic requirements are measured. Under a second condition, which is exercise, heart rate and metabolic requirements are also measured. Therefore, one variable might be labeled *type of condition* with two levels, anxiety and exercise. Type of condition is an active or manipulated independent variable, and anxiety and exercise are levels or categories of that variable, not variables themselves, because in this study they do not vary. A second *set* of variables is metabolic requirements, which is operationally defined by cardiac output and oxygen uptake. These are the two dependent variables. Do we have another variable? What about heart rate? Remember that, in our study, we are attempting to create two different situations, anxiety and exercise, with identical heart rates. However, the two conditions yield identical heart rates; therefore, heart rate cannot be a variable because it will not vary in the two situations of this study. That is, heart rate is controlled rather than allowed to vary in this study.

Broadly speaking, our research problem asks whether there will be a relationship between the situation and metabolic requirements. More specifically, we hypothesized that the exercise condition would produce significantly higher cardiac output and oxygen uptake than the anxiety condition when heart rate was equal. Were the hypotheses tested? Yes, Gliner, Bedi, and Horvath (1979) tested the hypothesis for the metabolic requirement of cardiac output. Gliner, Bunnell, and Horvath (1982), replicated the study for cardiac output and also measured oxygen uptake. In both studies, the hypothesis was supported.

The Mastery Motivation Problem Revisited

Earlier we stated the second research problem as, *Is there a relationship between prematurity and abuse or neglect and mastery motivation?* Actually, this general problem led to two separate studies. One study compared premature infants to full-term infants matched on gestational age, and the other compared three groups of infants: abused, neglected, and low risk (control group).

In the first study, the independent variable was gestational status, with two levels, preterm and full term. This is an attribute independent variable. In the second study, the independent variable might be called risk status, or type, with three levels: abused, neglected, and low risk. Again, this is an attribute variable because it was not and could not ethically be manipulated or given to the children. If an intervention were given to some infants but not others, that variable—intervention type—would be an active independent variable.

What are the outcome or dependent variables in this study? Two aspects of mastery motivation were measured, task persistence and mastery pleasure, each of which is a variable. They are not two levels of one variable because each varies from low to high and infants had scores on both.

What about age? It was not a variable because all infants were 12 months gestational age. Likewise, infants are not a variable. All of the participants were infants, so, as we see in chapter 10, they are the *population* studied.

THEORY

Where does theory come into play for our problems, variables, and hypotheses? First we should define theory. Kerlinger (1986) suggests that a theory explains natural phenomena, which is a goal of science, and he defines it as, "A theory is a set of interrelated constructs (concepts), definitions, and propositions that present a systematic view of phenomena by specifying relations among variables, with the purpose of explaining and predicting the phenomena" (p. 9). Krathwohl (1993) suggests that a theoretical orientation should be presented at the beginning of an article as the basis for understanding the rest of the article. He does not believe that a theory must be a part of the article; instead, explanation, rationale, or point of view could be substituted to satisfy, to some extent, the same purpose as theory. However, none of these concepts are as strong as a theory. A number of books deal extensively with the role of theory in research, but we have chosen to emphasize research design and how it influences data analysis and the interpretation of results.

The issue in contemporary social and health science research is not so much whether theory is important and how it should fit into an article, but how important should theory be in designing research? We agree that theory is important and that the value of a study depends, in part, on whether the results support a theory or not. However, theory-driven research is not necessarily well designed and analyzed, which is the focus of this book.

SUMMARY

A research problem is a statement that asks whether there is a relationship between two, or likely more, variables. It results when a researcher has experienced an obstacle to understanding.

A variable is a characteristic of the participants or situation of a given study that has different values or levels. There are a number of points to remember about variables:

   1. There are three main types of variables:

   a) Independent variables, which are the *presumed* causes, influences, or antecedents in the study. We differentiated two types of independent variable:

   1) Active, which is a variable that is given to the participants, usually for some specified time period. It may be, but is not always, manipulated and controlled by the investigator.

2) Attribute, which is an observed or measured characteristic of the participants or environment that either was not or cannot be manipulated by the investigator.

   b) Dependent variables, which are the presumed outcomes or criteria.

   c) Extraneous variables are not of interest in this study but they could influence the dependent variable.

2. If everyone in a study is the same on a given characteristic, that characteristic is constant—not a variable—in the study. For example, in a study of 9-year-old boys' learning of mathematics in one of two curricula, the participants' age and gender (9-year-old boys) are not variables.

3. The difference between the variable and the levels, or categories, of a variable is important. The variable itself has or is given a name that encompasses all of the levels or categories (e.g., treatment type, gender, or ethnicity). The levels are the names of the specific categories or groups or values (e.g., experimental versus control, male versus female, Asian versus African versus European). In this context, level does not necessarily imply order, and one level is not necessarily higher or lower than another.

4. Variables can have either nominal (unordered) levels or categories or have ordered levels.

5. Some variables (e.g., knowledge of mathematics or self-concept) could be either the independent variable or the dependent variable (or even an extraneous variable), depending on the study. These variables are usually a changeable characteristic of the participant (like an attitude or personality characteristic); if one of these variables is used as the independent variable, it is an attribute independent variable.

6. Individual participants do not have to vary on a characteristic or variable—it is the group that must have more than one value (e.g., some men and some women). In some studies there are repeated measures of the same variable (e.g., a pretest and a posttest on math knowledge) and individuals may change over time in a longitudinal study.

The research problem is usually stated more broadly than the research hypotheses or questions. Most studies have several hypotheses or questions that indicate predicted or possible relationships between variables. In chapter 5 we describe six specific types of research questions and five types of research approaches that form the basis for an understanding of research design and data analysis.

STUDY AIDS

Concepts

- Hypothesis
- Literature review

- Operational definition
- Research literature
- Research problem
- Research question
- Testable
- Theory
- Variable

Distinctions

- Active versus attribute independent variable
- Independent versus dependent versus extraneous variable
- Levels of one variable versus a set or group of variables
- Ordered versus unordered or nominal variables
- Research problem versus personal or societal problem
- The variable (itself) versus levels or categories of the variable

Application Problems

Provide the following information for each hypothesis.

1. Name the independent/antecedent/predictor variable.
2. Is the independent variable active or an attribute?
3. How many levels of this variable are there?
4. Are the levels ordered or nominal?
5. Name the dependent/outcome variable?
6. Is the population of interest named? What is it? (see p. 55)
7. Give an operational definition of each variable. If active, how might the independent variable be manipulated? If an attribute, how will the attribute be measured? How will the dependent variable be measured?
   a. Family conflict is associated with absenteeism rates in clerical workers.
   b. A workshop on visual imagery improves memory in college students.
   c. The number of faculty members at a committee meeting is related to the length of the meeting.
   d. The amount of child abuse is related to the age of parents when they married.
   e. A voters' political party is related to their attitude toward gun control.
   f. Whether a pregnant woman's diet was high, medium, or low in folic acid affects the birth weight of her child.
   g. Students given an exercise program have reduced levels of stress.
   h. The gender of the instructor is related to students' evaluation of the instructor.
   i. Participation in an anxiety reduction workshop is related to test performance.

Research Approaches
and Designs

5

Overview of Research Approaches and Questions

Study Aids
    Concepts
    Distinctions
    Application Problems

OVERVIEW

The general purpose of all research studies, except those that we call (purely) descriptive, is to look for relationships between variables (see Fig. 5.1). We divide approaches to research into three general types: *experimental, individual differences* (or nonexperimental), and *descriptive*. The first type of approach has an active independent variable, the second has an attribute independent variable, and the descriptive approach does not have an independent variable. We use the label descriptive approach more narrowly than some writers to indicate studies that do not use inferential statistics to test hypotheses.

Next, we divide both the experimental and the individual differences approaches into two specific approaches: randomized (or true) experimental versus quasi-experimental and comparative versus associational. These four specific approaches all seek to find relationships among variables; they differ in terms of purposes and in what kinds of hypotheses or research questions they answer. Figure 5.1 indicates the specific purpose for each of the five specific approaches. Notice that the randomized experimental approach is the best suited to determine causes. None of the other approaches can provide solid evidence about whether the independent variable caused a change in the dependent variable, but the quasi-experimental approach provides some evidence for causality if the approach is strong. For a discussion of the strength of quasi-experiments see chapter 7.

In the section that follows we discuss the utility of these five approaches in producing conclusions about cause and effect. We also examine the similari-

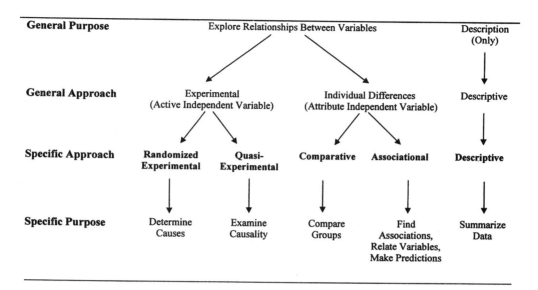

FIG. 5.1 Schematic diagram of five basic approaches to research and their purposes.

ties and differences between each of the five approaches and demonstrate that most studies are actually more complex because they combine two or more of the approaches. Table 5.1 shows the five specific research approaches and the criteria that distinguishes them.

RESEARCH APPROACHES WITH AN ACTIVE INDEPENDENT VARIABLE

The Randomized Experimental Research Approach

For a research approach to be called randomized (or true) experimental, two criteria must be met. The first criterion is that the researcher must randomly assign participants to groups or conditions. (We have used the word *condition* in addition to *group* because under certain circumstances a group can undergo both the control and the intervention conditions.) As you can see from Table 5.1, this criterion is what differentiates randomized experiments from quasi-experiments, but it is the most difficult to achieve. Much applied research involves groups that are already intact or in existence such as classrooms or rehabilitation settings, and it is not possible to change those assignments. Thus, such research is not considered to be randomized experimental.

The second criterion that must be satisfied for the research approach to be considered randomized experimental is that the independent variable must be active as defined in the last chapter. In addition the researcher usually is able to control the independent variable. In other words, the researcher can decide exactly what the treatment will be and when and to whom it will be given. For example, she or he will be able to randomly assign one level of the independent variable to the intervention condition and the other level of the independent variable to the control condition. These aspects of randomized experiments are also shown in Table 5.1.

Random Assignment.   Why is random assignment so important? The concept of randomness implies that there is no bias. When the investigator randomly assigns participants to groups, it means that each participant has an equal chance to be in either the intervention group or the control group. Random does not mean haphazard or any old way, as it sometimes does in popular language. One could use a computer-generated random number table or a method like the one described in the next paragraph to randomly assign participants to groups.

For example, suppose there are 20 participants in a study. The study calls for 10 persons to be in each of two groups. The investigator can take 20 pieces of paper, and on half of the pieces print a zero and on the other half print a one.

TABLE 5.1
A Comparison of the Five Basic Quantitative Research Approaches

Criteria	Randomized Experimental	Quasi- Experimental	Comparative	Associational	Descriptive
Random assignment of participants to groups by investigator	Yes	No	No	No (only one group)	No groups
Independent variable is active	Yes	Yes	No (attribute)	No (attribute)	No independent variable
Independent variable is controlled by the investigator*	Usually	Sometimes	No	No	No
Independent variable has only a few levels or categories	Usually	Usually	Usually	Sometimes	No independent variable
Relationships between variables or comparison of groups	Yes (comparison)	Yes (comparison)	Yes (comparison)	Yes (relationship)	No

*Although this is a desired quality of randomized experimental and quasi-experimental designs, it is not sufficient for distinguishing between the randomized experimental and quasi-experimental approaches.

Then, the investigator places all 20 pieces of paper in a bowl, and shakes the bowl to mix up the pieces of paper. Now, when each participant comes in for the study, the investigator reaches into the bowl and pulls out a piece of paper. If the paper has a zero on it, the participant is assigned to the control group. If the paper has a one on it, the participant is assigned to the intervention group. (It is important in this situation that the investigator does not put the piece of paper back into the bowl after each participant's assignment is made.) This procedure continues until all 20 participants have been assigned to either the intervention or the control group.

Therefore, prior to the intervention, the assumption is made that the participants in the two groups are equivalent *in all other respects*, including demographic characteristics and the dependent variable, if that is to be measured before the intervention. In the practical situation, two small groups of 10 persons each, as in the above example, may not be equal because the concept of randomness only makes things equal in the long run, with relatively large numbers of participants in each group (e.g., 30). However, after random assignment, even if the two groups are not exactly equal, the differences between them are considered to be unbiased and can be adjusted statistically.

Random Assignment Versus Random Selection or Sampling.   It is very important to understand these two concepts and to know the difference between them. The concept *random,* or unbiased, is, of course, common to both concepts and to several other phrases, such as random order and random assignment of treatments to groups, which we discuss in this and later chapters. Random sampling or random selection of participants from the population, if done in a study, comes before *random assignment* to groups in the procedure. As we see in chapter 10, random selection has to do with who the participants in the study will be, and how they are selected. In the ideal situation, described in depth in chapter 10, the sample is selected to be representative of all the possible participants who fit the selection criteria. For example, in the DiPasquale–Lehnerz (1994) study described in the following section, the theoretical population of interest might have been all the persons in the world who had spinal cord injuries. For practical reasons, the researcher chose to study persons with such injuries from one rehabilitation center rather than randomly selecting a sample of such persons from around the world or the United States. As we show in chapter 10, this type of convenience sample is common and often necessary. Nonrandom sampling affects the generality *(external validity)* of the study, but it is not relevant as far as the approach is concerned. Thus, random selection or sampling is not shown in Table 5.1. A randomized experiment may or may not use random selection or sampling. Although a study with a weak sampling procedure can still be a randomized experiment, its overall quality will be reduced, as discussed in chapter 24. It is also true that inferential statistics assume that the sample studied is a random sample of the population of interest. If it is not, the statistical results may be misleading. Nevertheless, a randomized experiment does not necessarily involve random sampling.

Random assignment of the participants to the intervention versus control groups is relevant for *internal validity* and for inferring causation. Random assignment has to do with how participants got into their particular groups. Was the assignment done randomly, as illustrated by the 20 pieces of paper example? Or was there a degree of bias?

An Example.   Consider a study by DiPasquale–Lehnerz (1994), who was interested in using orthoses (hand splints) to increase hand function with persons who had cervical-6 level spinal cord injuries. Using participants at the rehabilitation center where she worked (note, there was not random sampling), DiPasquale–Lehnerz randomly assigned participants to one of two groups. One group (intervention) received the hand splints. A second group (control) did not receive the hand splints. DiPasquale–Lehnerz measured hand function at 4 weeks, 8 weeks, and 12 weeks into the study by using the Jebson hand function test and other strength measures.

Is the DiPasquale–Lehnerz study a randomized experiment? The study satisfied the second criterion because the independent variable was active (manipulated). She also decided what the treatment would be and which group should get the treatment, so she had control over the independent variable. The first criterion was also met because she was able to randomly assign participants to groups. Thus, the study was a randomized experiment.

Inferring Causation.   Porter's (1997) three criteria for cause are necessary for postulating that an independent variable caused a change in a dependent variable. The three criteria are that the independent variable must precede the dependent variable, the independent variable must be related to the dependent variable, and there must be no third variable that could explain why the independent variable is related to the dependent variable.

Did the independent variable precede the dependent variable in the DiPasquale–Lehnerz study? The procedures of the study were, first, the random assignment of participants to groups, and the assigning of the independent variable (treatment) to one of the groups. Next, the treatment was given and, finally, the researcher measured the change in the groups. Thus, the independent variable preceded the dependent variable in the study. Were extraneous variables ruled out? DiPasquale–Lehnerz randomly assigned participants to groups, and then randomly assigned treatments to groups. The groups were presumed to be equal prior to the introduction of the intervention and were treated identically during the study except for whether or not they had a splint. Therefore, if there was a change in the dependent variable in the group that received the intervention, and no change in the group that did not receive the intervention, it would be difficult to postulate a third variable being responsible for any change in the dependent variable. Was there a relation between the independent variable and the dependent variable? Unfortunately, there were no statistically significant differences between groups. Therefore, even though DiPasquale–Lehnerz satisfied the conditions of a randomized experiment, in this particular study the independent variable failed to cause a change in the dependent variable.

Summary of the Randomized Experimental Approach.   The DiPasquale–Lehnerz study used one of several specific experimental designs—the pretest–

posttest control group design—which will be described in chapter 7.[1] What this specific experimental design has in common with, and what distinguishes it from, the other four research approaches that are described in this chapter is shown in Table 5.1. Note that random assignment of the participants by the investigator to levels, or groups, or conditions is what distinguishes the randomized experimental approach from the quasi-experimental approach. In the randomized experimental approach there are also several characteristics in common with quasi-experiments: an active independent variable (e.g., treatment type) that has only a few categories or levels (e.g., treatment and control). The table also shows that, in experiments, usually the investigator has some control over the independent variable, and the groups are compared (e.g., the treatment is compared to the control).

The Quasi-Experimental Research Approach

We divide the quasi-experimental approach into three categories, which we describe in more detail in chapters 7 and 8. These categories are *pretest–posttest designs, time-series designs,* and *single subject designs.*

The *pretest–posttest quasi-experimental* research approach is similar to the randomized experimental approach, but fails to satisfy the condition of random assignment of participants to groups. In these designs, for example, participants are already in intact groups, such as two different classrooms, prior to the study. Both groups are measured (pretest) prior to the introduction of the independent variable. One group receives the independent variable and the other group does not get the independent variable. At the end of the study, both groups are measured again (posttest).

Note in Table 5.1 that quasi-experimental designs have an active independent variable with a few categories and also involve a comparison between, for example, an intervention and a control condition. However, there is a word of caution about the active independent variable. In the randomized experimental approach, the researcher usually has control over the independent variable in that one level can be randomly assigned to the experimental condition, and one level can be randomly assigned to the control condition. The strength of the quasi-experimental design is based, in part, on how much control the investigator actually has in manipulating the independent variable and deciding which group will receive which treatment. In chapter 7 we illustrate how different levels of control of the independent variable affect the strength of the quasi-experimental design. The strength of the design influences how confident we can be about whether the independent variable was the cause of any change in the dependent variable.

Time-series designs include single group time series designs and multiple group time series designs. Time-series designs are different from pretest–

---

[1]It should be noted that if there is a pretest and posttest, as in this study, the design is no longer a basic single factor design. We discuss other types of design in later chapters. For now, ignore the pretest and think of the randomized and quasi-experimental designs as comparing two groups on a posttest that measures the dependent variable.

posttest designs seen in the randomized and quasi-experimental approach. In pretest–posttest designs there are only two measurement periods. In time-series designs there are numerous measurement periods prior to and after the introduction of the intervention. Whereas single group time series designs include only one group, the intervention group, multiple group time series designs add a control group along with the multiple measurements.

Single subject designs also include multiple measurement periods similar to time series designs. However, single subject designs include few participants, rarely more than four. Each participant becomes a separate study. In one type of single subject design, the intervention is given and withdrawn repeatedly for each of the participants. The single subject design is especially appealing to those working in clinical or applied settings because of the difficulty of obtaining large samples of participants. Because of the unique nature of single subject designs, we discuss them in a separate chapter.

RESEARCH APPROACHES WITH ATTRIBUTE INDEPENDENT VARIABLES

Table 5.1 also shows that the associational and comparative approaches are similar in several ways; for example, they are used to study attribute independent variables, the investigator does not use random assignment, and the investigator does not have control over the independent variables. For these reasons, associational and comparative approaches are often referred to as nonexperimental approaches. Because of their focus on studying patterns of individual differences in attributes of participants, we have grouped them together under a general approach with that name. In fact, most survey-type research includes both comparative and associational research questions, so it is common for one study to use both approaches. Neither approach provides good evidence that the independent variable is the cause of differences in the dependent variable.

The Comparative Research Approach

The comparative approach differs from the randomized experimental and quasi-experimental approaches because the investigator cannot randomly assign participants to groups and because there is not an active independent variable. Table 5.1 shows that, like randomized experiments and quasi-experiments, comparative designs usually have a few categories of the independent variable and make comparisons between groups. Studies that use the comparative approach examine the *presumed* effect of an attribute independent variable. Some authors call this approach *causal comparative*, but we think that term is unwise because this approach is not well suited to establishing causes.

An example of the comparative approach comes from a study by Murphy and Gliner (1988), who compared two groups of children on a series of motor performance tests. The investigators were attempting to determine whether the differences between the two groups resulted from perceptual or motor processing problems. One group of children who had motor problems was compared to a second group of children who did not have motor problems. Notice that the independent variable in this study was an attribute independent variable with two levels: with motor problems and without motor problems. Thus, it is not possible for the investigator to randomly assign participants to groups, or to provide the independent variable; the independent variable was not active. However, the independent variable had only a few categories and a statistical comparison between the two groups was done.

Note that comparative studies do not meet Porter's (1997) criteria for attributing causality, because it is impossible to control perfectly for other variables that are extraneous to this study. For example, children with motor problems might differ from the control children in many ways (e.g., education, ethnic group, economic status) in addition to motor problems. A good comparative study would try to control for some of these factors by matching or by using another technique, but we could never be certain that the groups were equivalent in all respects, as we could be if random assignment to groups were possible. Thus, we should not state in our conclusions that this disability *caused* any differences in motor performance that were found. We *can* say that there were significant differences, if they were indicated by our statistics.

You might ask, "Why do a comparative study if we cannot make conclusions about what caused what?" In part the answer is that if you are interested in attribute independent variables, you have no other choice than an individual difference (comparative or associational) approach. Attributes, in general, cannot be given or manipulated in a study. Some attributes, such as self-confidence or anxiety, do vary from time to time, or situation to situation, so they could be active, or manipulated, variables. However, in recent years it is usually considered unethical to do so. Thus, with some exceptions, we must use the comparative approach if we want to study an attribute of participants.

Adding Levels to the Independent Variable

In the randomized experimental, quasi-experimental, and comparative approaches, it is often desirable to have more than two groups (i.e., more than two levels of the independent variable). An example from the comparative approach would be a study that compared three groups—first, third, and fifth grade students—on an aspect of cognitive development. Again, this study does not meet the requirements for a randomized experimental or quasi-experimental study, because the independent variable is an attribute of the students and was not manipulated. Note that the independent variable (grade in school) in this case has three ordered levels.[2]

It is also possible to compare a relatively large number of groups or levels (e.g., 5 or 10) if one has enough participants so that the group sizes are adequate (e.g., 20 or more in each). However, this is atypical, and if there are five

---

[2]This type of study is called cross-sectional (versus longitudinal) because different children are assessed at each age.

or more *ordered* levels of the independent variable, we would recommend that you use the associational approach and statistics that we discuss later in this chapter.

There are two reasons for adding levels to a single independent variable: (a) to control for "no treatment" effects in an experimental study, and (b) to help determine the complete relationship between the independent and dependent variables.

Controlling for No Treatment Effects.   The addition of a third (or more) level to a single independent variable in experimental studies, where two different treatments or interventions are compared, may improve the research considerably. For example, a study by Jongbloed, Stacey, and Brighton (1989) compared two types of treatment in stroke rehabilitation. The independent variable, treatment, had two levels, sensori-integrative treatment and functional treatment, and thus two experimental groups. Although the authors randomly assigned participants to groups to produce good internal validity, the results were hard to interpret because of the failure to include a control group that did not receive treatment. In other words, the study could only compare which of the treatments worked better, but there was no way to evaluate whether either treatment was better than no treatment at all. Had the authors added a third level or group, which did not receive any treatment, the study would have been improved. Similarly, if you started with a new treatment and a control or no treatment group, you would obtain additional information if you added a group with an alternative or traditional treatment.

Determining the Complete Relationship.   The second reason for adding a level to a single independent variable is to determine more precisely a relationship between the independent and dependent variables. An example involves the relationship between task difficulty and mastery motivation (Redding, Morgan, & Harmon, 1988). Mastery motivation, the dependent measure, was defined as persistence at the task. Task difficulty, the independent variable, was determined with another group of children. If the study had used only very easy and very difficult tasks, the investigators would have found no difference in persistence, as shown in the following graph:

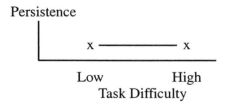

It would appear that task difficulty did not affect persistence, or that there was no relationship between task difficulty and persistence. Now consider the relationship when another level (medium difficulty) is added to the independent variable. The relationship is described in the following graph:

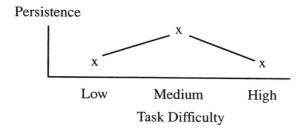

Notice that adding the third level indicates that there is an inverted U relationship between difficulty and persistence. Persistence increases as difficulty increases, up to a point, but then is lower as difficulty gets high. Had the medium difficulty condition not been included, the actual relationship between task difficulty and persistence would have been missed.

Although it is often considered desirable to add a third or more level to a single independent variable, it does not change the general design classification. A study that has two treatments is *a single factor* (one independent variable) design with two levels. If we add a third (or more) level, it would still be a single factor design; there are just more levels or groups to compare.

Summary of the Approaches That Compare Groups

In each of the three previous approaches (randomized experimental, quasi-experimental, and comparative) an attempt was made to compare two or more levels or groups of the independent variable in terms of their scores on the dependent variable. Regardless of whether the independent variable was active or attribute, it had a few categories, usually less than five. In other words, the levels of the independent variable fit into a few nonoverlapping categories or levels. For example, in the DiPasquale–Lehnerz (1994) experimental study, the participants either received a hand splint or did not receive a hand splint (two levels). Likewise, in the comparative study by Murphy and Gliner (1988), the participants either had a motor problem or did not. As we have seen, studies that compare groups can have more than two categories (e.g., two treatments and a control), and the categories can be ordered (e.g., high, medium, and low on an attribute) or not (e.g., three nominal categories like Protestants, Catholics, and Jews).

The Associational Research Approach

Now we would like to consider an approach to research where the independent variable is usually continuous or has several ordered categories, typically five or more. Suppose that the investigator is interested in the relationship between giftedness and self-concept in children. Assume that the dependent variable is self-concept as measured by the Perceived Competence Scale for Children (Harter, 1985). The independent variable is giftedness. If giftedness had been divided into high, average, and low groups (a few ordered categories), the research approach would be the comparative approach discussed previously. On the other hand, in the typical associational approach, the independent variable giftedness is *continuous* or has at least five ordered levels. In other words, all participants would be in a single group measured on two continuous variables: giftedness and self-concept. A correlation coefficient could be performed to determine the strength of the relationship between the two variables (see chap. 16). Nevertheless, even a very strong relationship between these variables does not justify the conclusion that high giftedness causes high self-concept. Some authors label this approach correlational because the typical statistic is a correlation coefficient. However, that is not the only statistic used and we think it is better to have a more generally applicable label, namely, associational.

We discuss the complex (more than one independent variable) associational approach and statistics used with it in detail in chapter 19. We want to mention here that multiple regression is a common associational statistic that is used when the question is whether a combination of several independent variables predicts the dependent variables better than any one predictor alone. For example, multiple regression is used by schools and companies to determine the best combination of entrance or application factors, such as test scores, grades, and recommendations, to predict success in college or on the job.

It is arbitrary whether a study is considered to be comparative or associational. For example, a continuous variable such as age can always be divided into fewer levels such as young and old. However, we make this distinction for two reasons. First, we think it is usually unwise to divide a variable with many ordered levels into a few because information is lost. For example, if the cut point for "old age" was 65 years old, persons who are 66 and 96 years old would be lumped together, as would persons who are 21 and 64 years old, and persons who are 64 and 65 years old would be in different age groups. Second, different types of statistics are usually, but not always, used with the two approaches. We think this distinction and the similar one made in the section on research questions will help you decide on an appropriate statistic, which we have found is one of the hardest parts of the research process.

SUMMARY DIAGRAMS FOR THE FIRST FOUR APPROACHES

Figure 5.2 is a schematic diagram illustrating the four approaches discussed so far: randomized experimental, quasi-experimental, comparative, and associational. These diagrams present the information from Table 5.1 in a different way. They also serve as a preview of Table 7.2, which illustrates several different specific experimental designs.

THE DESCRIPTIVE RESEARCH APPROACH

This approach is different from the other four in that only one variable is considered at a time so that no comparisons or relationships are made. Table 5.1 shows that this lack of comparisons or relationships is what distinguishes this approach from the other four. Of course, the descriptive approach does not meet any of the other criteria, such as random assignment of participants to groups.

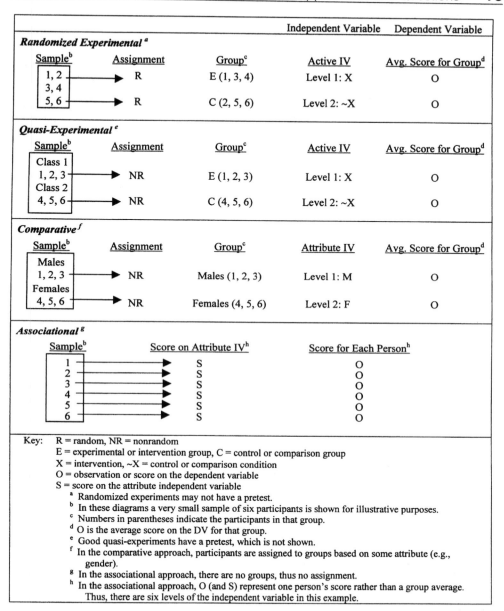

			Independent Variable	Dependent Variable
Randomized Experimental [a]				
Sample[b]	Assignment	Group[c]	Active IV	Avg. Score for Group[d]
1, 2 3, 4	R	E (1, 3, 4)	Level 1: X	O
5, 6	R	C (2, 5, 6)	Level 2: ~X	O
Quasi-Experimental [e]				
Sample[b]	Assignment	Group[c]	Active IV	Avg. Score for Group[d]
Class 1 1, 2, 3	NR	E (1, 2, 3)	Level 1: X	O
Class 2 4, 5, 6	NR	C (4, 5, 6)	Level 2: ~X	O
Comparative [f]				
Sample[b]	Assignment	Group[c]	Attribute IV	Avg. Score for Group[d]
Males 1, 2, 3	NR	Males (1, 2, 3)	Level 1: M	O
Females 4, 5, 6	NR	Females (4, 5, 6)	Level 2: F	O
Associational [g]				
Sample[b]		Score on Attribute IV[h]		Score for Each Person[h]
1		S		O
2		S		O
3		S		O
4		S		O
5		S		O
6		S		O

Key: R = random, NR = nonrandom
E = experimental or intervention group, C = control or comparison group
X = intervention, ~X = control or comparison condition
O = observation or score on the dependent variable
S = score on the attribute independent variable
[a] Randomized experiments may not have a pretest.
[b] In these diagrams a very small sample of six participants is shown for illustrative purposes.
[c] Numbers in parentheses indicate the participants in that group.
[d] O is the average score on the DV for that group.
[e] Good quasi-experiments have a pretest, which is not shown.
[f] In the comparative approach, participants are assigned to groups based on some attribute (e.g., gender).
[g] In the associational approach, there are no groups, thus no assignment.
[h] In the associational approach, O (and S) represent one person's score rather than a group average. Thus, there are six levels of the independent variable in this example.

FIG. 5.2   Schematic diagrams of four research approaches.

Most research studies include some descriptive questions (at least to describe the sample), but most do not stop there. In fact, it is rare these days for published quantitative research to be purely descriptive; we almost always examine several variables and their relationships. However, political polls and consumer surveys are sometimes only interested in describing how voters as a whole react to an issue or what products consumers in general will buy. Exploratory studies of a new topic may just describe what people say or feel about that topic. Furthermore, qualitative or constructivist research may be primarily descriptive.

Most research books use a considerably broader definition for descriptive research. For example, some experimental design books use the term *descriptive research* to include all research that is not randomized experimental or quasi-experimental. Others do not have a clear definition and use the word descriptive almost as a synonym for exploratory or sometimes correlational research. We think it is clearer and less confusing to restrict the term descriptive research to questions and studies that use only descriptive statistics, such as averages, percentages, histograms, and frequency distributions, that are not tested for statistical significance with inferential statistics.

COMBINATIONS OF RESEARCH APPROACHES

It is important to note that most studies are more complex than implied by the earlier examples. In fact, almost all studies have more than one hypothesis or research question and may use more than one of the previously discussed approaches. It is common to find a study with one active independent variable (e.g., type of treatment) and one or more attribute independent variables (e.g., gender). This type of study combines the randomized experimental approach (if the participants were randomly assigned to groups) and the comparative approach. When such a study considers both independent variables together, it no longer has a basic or single factor design. We discuss studies with two (or more) factors in later chapters. Most survey studies include both the associational and comparative approaches. Most studies also have some descriptive questions, so it is common for published studies to use three approaches or even more.

RESEARCH QUESTIONS OR HYPOTHESES AND STATISTICS

Three Types of Basic Hypotheses or Research Questions

In chapter 4, we introduced the concept of hypothesis, which was defined as a predictive statement about the relationship between variables. Research questions are similar to hypotheses but in question format. Now we want to expand on that general definition by splitting research questions into three types: *basic difference questions, basic associational questions,* and *basic descriptive questions*. For difference and associational questions, basic means that there is one independent and one dependent variable. For descriptive questions, basic means that there is one variable.

Remember that both difference and associational questions have as a general purpose the exploration of relationships between variables (see Fig. 5.3). This similarity agrees with the statement by statisticians that all parametric inferential statistics are relational, and it is consistent with the notion that the distinction between the comparative and associational approaches is somewhat

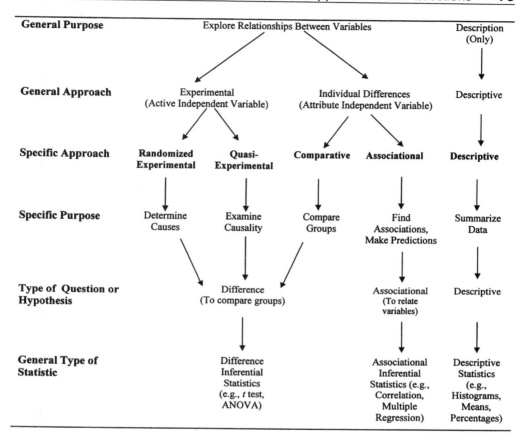

FIG. 5.3.   Schemaic diagram showing how the general type of statistic and hypothesis or question used in a study correspond to the purposes and the approach.

arbitrary.[3] However, we believe that the distinction is educationally useful. Note that difference and associational questions differ in specific purpose and the kinds of statistics they use to answer the question.

For the different type of questions, we compare groups or levels of the independent variable in terms of their scores on the dependent variable. This type of question typically is used with the randomized experimental, quasi-experi- mental, and comparative approaches. For an associational question, we associate or relate the independent and dependent variables. Descriptive questions are not answered with inferential statistics; they merely describe or summarize data.

_____

[3]We use the term associational for this type of research question, approach, and statistic rather than the terms relational or correlational to distinguish these terms from the general purpose of difference and associational questions or hypotheses. Also, we wanted to distinguish between correlation, as a specific statistical technique, and the broader types of approach, question, and groups of statistics.

The format and an example of each of these types of question or hypotheses is given in Table 5.2. Difference hypotheses are used when the research approach is randomized experimental, quasi-experimental, or comparative. As you might guess, associational hypotheses are used with the associational approach. We think it is advisable to use the research question format when one does not have a clear directional prediction and for the descriptive approach. More details and examples for stating research problems and questions are provided in Appendix C.

Difference Versus Associational Inferential Statistics

We think it is educationally useful, although not commonly explicit in statistics books, to divide inferential statistics into two types corresponding to difference and associational hypotheses or questions. Difference inferential statistics are usually (but not always) used for the randomized experimental, quasi-experimental, and comparative approaches, which test for differences between groups (e.g., using analysis of variance, also called ANOVA). Associational inferential statistics test for associations or relationships between variables and use a type of correlation or multiple regression analysis.[4] We use this contrast between difference and associational inferential statistics in chapter 13 to describe how to select an appropriate statistic.

Six Types of Research Questions: Basic and Complex

Remember that many studies are more complex than implied by the earlier examples. In fact, most studies have more than one hypothesis or research question and may use more than one of the research approaches. It is common to find a study with one active independent variable (e.g., treatment) and one or more attribute independent variables (e.g., gender). This type of study combines the randomized experimental approach (if the participants were randomly assigned to groups) and the comparative approach, and has two difference hypotheses. We see in chapter 17 that there are actually three hypotheses. This *set* of three questions can be considered a complex difference question because the study has two independent variables. They could both be active or both attribute; it would still be a study with a complex difference question. Likewise, complex associational questions are used in studies with more than one independent variable considered together.

Table 5.3 expands our overview of research questions to include both basic and complex questions of each of the three types: *descriptive, difference, and associational.* We use the terms basic and complex because the more common names, univariate and multivariate, are not used consistently in the literature.

---

[4]We also realize that all parametric inferential statistics are relational, so this dichotomy of using one type of data analysis procedure to test for differences (when there are a few levels of the independent variable) and another type of data analysis procedure to test for associations (when there is a continuous independent variable) is somewhat artificial. Both continuous and categorical independent variables can be used in a general linear model (regression) approach to data analysis. However, the practical implications are that most researchers adhere to the above dichotomy in data analysis.

TABLE 5.2

Examples of Three Kinds of Research Questions/Hypotheses

1. Basic Difference (Group Comparison) Hypotheses or Questions
- Use for randomized experimental, quasi-experimental, and comparative approaches
- For this type of hypothesis, the levels or categories of the independent variable (e.g., anxiety) are used to split the participants into groups (e.g., high and low), which are then compared to see if they differ in respect to the average scores on the dependent variable (e.g., grade point average [GPA]).
- An example. Persons with low and high anxiety will differ on average scores. In other words, the average GPA of the high anxiety persons will be significantly different from the average GPA for low anxiety persons.

2. Basic Associational (Relational) Hypotheses or Questions
- Use for the associational approach
- For this type of hypothesis or question, the scores on the independent variable (e.g., anxiety) are associated with or related to the dependent variable (e.g., GPA).
- An example. There will be a negative association (correlation) between anxiety scores and GPA. In other words, those persons who are high on anxiety will tend to have low GPAs, those with low anxiety will tend to have high GPAs, and those in the middle on the one variable will tend to be in the middle on the other variable.

3. Basic Descriptive Questions
- Use for descriptive approach
- For this type of question, scores on a single variable are described in terms of their central tendency, variability, or percentages in each category/level.
- An example. The average GPA was 2.73.

The table also includes references to tables in other chapters and examples of the types of statistics that we include under each of the six types of questions. Appendix C provides examples of research questions for each of the six types.

Note that complex descriptive statistics (e.g., a cross-tabulation table) could be tested for significance with inferential statistics; if they were so tested they would no longer be considered descriptive. We think that most qualitative or constructivist researchers ask complex descriptive questions because they consider more than one variable or concept at a time, but they seldom use inferential or hypothesis testing statistics. Furthermore, complex descriptive statistics are used to check reliability and to reduce the number of variables (e.g., with factor analysis).

TABLE 5.3

Summary of Types of Research Questions

Type of Research Question (Number of Variables)	Statistics (Example)
1) Basic descriptive questions: one variable.	Table 9.2, chap. 9 (mean, standard deviation, frequency distribution)
2) Complex descriptive questions: two or more variables, but no use of inferential statistics.	Chap. 9, 19, 20 (box plots, cross-tabulation tables, factor analysis, measures of reliability)
3) Basic or single factor difference questions: one independent and one dependent variable. Independent variable usually has a few levels (ordered or not).	Table 13.1, chap. 14, 15 (*t* test, one-way ANOVA)
4) Complex or multifactor difference question: three or more variables. Usually two or a few independent variables and one or more dependent variables considered one at a time.	Table 13.3, chap. 17, 18 (factorial ANOVA)
5) Basic associational questions: one independent variable and one dependent variable. Usually at least five ordered levels for both variables. Often they are continuous.	Table 13.2, chap. 16 (correlation tested for significance)
6) Complex or multivariate associational questions: two or more independent variables and one dependent variable. Usually five or more ordered levels for all variables but some or all can be dichotomous variables.	Table 13.4, chap. 19 (multiple regression)

Note.   Many studies have more than one dependent variable. It is common to treat each one separately (i.e., to do several *t* tests, ANOVAs, correlations, or multiple regressions). However, complex statistics (e.g., MANOVA and canonical correlation) are used to treat several dependent variables together in one analysis.

SUMMARY

Figure 5.3 and Table 5.1 provide most of the key points made in this chapter. Note that the top row of Fig. 5.3 lists two general purposes of quantitative research: discovery of relationships and description. Remember that chapter 4 began with a definition of a research problem as a question about the relationship between two or more variables. This is the broad sense in which all the approaches, except the descriptive, seek to establish relationships between variables.

For more specific purposes, you can see from Fig. 5.3 that the randomized experimental approach is the only one whose purpose is to determine or identify causes; however, quasi-experiments help us examine possible causes. The comparative, the quasi-experimental, and the randomized experimental approaches enable us to compare groups. Thus, all three of the approaches on the left side of Fig. 5.3 use difference hypotheses (as discussed earlier) and inferential statistics that test for differences between groups (e.g., *t* tests and analysis of variance). Note that there is no distinction between the statistics used in experiments to determine causes and those used in comparative studies that only tell us that there is a difference between groups.

Note also in Fig. 5.3 that the specific purpose of the associational approach includes finding associations, relating variables, and also making predictions from the independent or predictor variables to scores on the dependent or criterion variable(s). Although somewhat of an oversimplification, the associational approach uses a different type of hypothesis (associational) and different inferential statistics (correlation and multiple regression) than do the comparative, quasi-experimental, and randomized experimental approaches.

Table 5.4 provides some of the information in Table 5.1 in a different way. It brings together the discussion of ordered versus nominal variables from chapter 4 and the discussion of the five approaches in chapter 5.

TABLE 5.4
Most Common Types of Variable for the Independent and Dependent Variables Within Each of the Five Research Approaches

Research Approach	Independent Variable	Dependent Variable
Randomized experimental	Nominal	Many ordered
Quasi-experimental	or a few	levels
Comparative	ordered levels	(approximately
Associational	Many ordered levels	continuous)
Descriptive	NA	

STUDY AIDS

Concepts

- Basic or single factor approaches, designs, and questions
- Cause or inferring causation
- Complex designs and questions
- Research hypothesis
- Research question
- Variable controlled or manipulated by the experimenter

Distinctions

- Active versus attribute independent variable
- Difference versus associational versus descriptive research questions and statistics
- Experimental versus individual difference research approaches
- Pretest–posttest versus time-series versus single subject quasi-experimental designs
- Random assignment of participants to groups versus random selection of participants to be included in a study
- Randomized experimental versus quasi-experimental versus comparative versus associational versus descriptive approach to research
- Relationships among variables versus description of a variable

Application Problems

1. Listed below are some differences between the five approaches to research. Match the description that best fits the type of approach. Explain.

   1. Experimental
   2. Quasi-experimental

   3. Comparative
   4. Associational

   5. Descriptive

   A. Compares groups
   B. Asks questions that describe the data
   C. Examines causality
   D. Associates the many levels of one variable with the many levels of another
   E. Randomized assignment, tries to determine causality

Choose which research approach best describes the following scenarios. Describe why.

2. A researcher wants to know if drinking caffeine helps students get better grades on a math exam. He randomly assigns students to two groups – one that he gives caffeine to drink and one he does not. He gives each participant a mathematics examination.
3. A study is done to investigate type of classroom seats and test performance. The subjects are from two English classes at a local high school. One class is assigned to meet in a room with pillows on the floor for seats. The other class is to meet in a traditional classroom.
4. A grade school teacher is interested in whether more males or females use their left hand as their dominant hand. She asks her class of 28 students to write down whether they are right or left-handed.
5. A study is done to analyze whether a high level of stress (measured on a 0–100 scale) is related to a high level of loneliness (measured on a 0–100 scale).
6. You are interested in comparing the effects of two different types of therapy, music therapy and occupational therapy, on pain perception in people with chronic arthritis. You have two different rehabilitation settings at your disposal. Describe how a randomized experimental design would differ from a quasi-experimental design.

CHAPTER

Internal Validity

RESEARCH VALIDITY

One of the main objectives of this book is to help you learn to evaluate the merit of a research study. Validity is the term most often used to judge the quality or merit of a particular study. We use the term research validity when discussing the merit of a whole study to distinguish the term from *validity* of the *measurement* of a variable. It is necessary to learn about research validity for two reasons. The first is that it helps develop criteria by which to design and judge one's own research. Second, and perhaps more important, it makes you a better consumer of research. Persons embarking on careers in applied areas need to be able to judge the merit of research. For example, if one is to pick and choose among alternative treatment or intervention modalities, one needs to be able to evaluate the research literature.

From the work of Cook and Campbell (1979), we have divided research validity into four components:

1. measurement reliability and statistics
2. internal validity
3. measurement validity and generalizability of the constructs, and
4. external validity.

Our present discussion focuses on internal validity because of its direct relation to the design of research. The discussion of the other three components of research validity are found in chapter 23 (measurement reliability and statistics; measurement validity and generalizability of the constructs) and chapter 10 (external validity). In chapter 24, we present a summary of the framework for analyzing and evaluating research that is based on earlier chapters and these four dimensions of research validity.

INFERRING CAUSE

A major goal of scientific research is to be able to identify a causal relationship between two variables. For those in applied disciplines, the need to demonstrate that a given intervention or treatment causes a change in behavior or performance is extremely important. However, there is considerable disagreement among scholars as to what is necessary to prove that a causal relationship exists. Those professing the constructivist paradigm do not believe that a causal relationship can be determined (Lincoln & Guba, 1985). However, most scientists would at least subscribe to some probabilistic statement about the causal relationship between two variables.

How is cause inferred? In chapter 5 we introduced three criteria that must occur to infer a causal relationship (Porter, 1997). We repeat these three criteria: (a) the independent variable must precede the dependent variable in time, (b) a relationship must be established between the independent variable and the dependent variable (in the social sciences this relationship is usually determined statistically), and (c) there must be no plausible third (extraneous) variable that also could account for a relation between the independent and dependent variables.

Four of the five specific research approaches (randomized experimental, quasi-experimental, comparative, and associational) discussed in the last chapter attempt in different ways to satisfy Porter's three prerequisites. All four can, but do not always, meet the first two criteria. The randomized experimental and, to a lesser extent, the quasi-experimental approaches are usually successful in meeting Porter's third condition. The comparative and associational approaches are not well suited to establishing causes, but some things can be done to control for extraneous variables. In this chapter and the next we show that the degree to which a design meets Porter's three conditions for inferring cause is highly related to its strength and internal validity.

Although the comparative and associational approaches are limited in what can be said about causation, they can lead to strong conclusions about the differences between groups and about associations between variables. Furthermore, they are the only available approaches, if the focus of your research is on attribute independent variables. The descriptive approach, as we define it, does not attempt to identify causal relationships or, in fact, any relationships. It focuses on describing variables.

Now, we will discuss internal validity, which is, in part, dependent on which of the approaches is used, and on the strengths and weaknesses of the designs within each of the four approaches. Remember that conclusions about causes can be made with more certainty from randomized experimental than from the quasi-experimental or comparative approaches, even though these three approaches use similar group comparison or difference statistics for data analysis.

INTERNAL VALIDITY

Cook and Campbell (1979) defined internal validity as "the approximate validity with which we can infer that a relationship is causal" (p. 37). Internal validity depends on the strength or soundness of the design and influences whether one can conclude that the independent variable or intervention caused the dependent variable to change.

Cook and Campbell (1979) proposed a list of "threats" to internal validity, several of which are especially likely to be present in the poor and weak quasi-experimental designs described in chapter 7. Randomized experimental designs have fewer threats to internal validity and, thus, are more likely to allow valid conclusions about causation.

We have grouped Cook and Campbell's threats to internal validity into two main types: *equivalence of groups on participant characteristics* (e.g., equivalence of the intervention and control groups) and *control of (extraneous) experience or environmental variables*. Random assignment of participants to the groups, which is a characteristic of randomized experiments but not of quasi-experiments, is the best way to assure equivalence of the groups. Control of extraneous experiences and the environment depends on the specific study, but is generally better for randomized experiments and for studies done in controlled environments like laboratories. Although internal validity is often discussed only with respect to randomized and quasi-experiments, we believe the concept also applies to the comparative and associational approaches. Thus, our discussion is intended to apply to all types of research.

Equivalence of Groups on Participant Characteristics

Campbell and Stanley (1966) described a number of specific threats to internal validity, several of which (e.g., selection, statistical regression, experimental mortality, and various interactions) are participant factors that could lead to a lack of equivalence of the participants in the two (or more) groups and thus influence the dependent variable. We have found the labels of Campbell and Stanley's threats confusing and their categories more complex than necessary for a basic understanding of internal validity. Another problem with the emphasis on threats to internal validity is that a threat often only instructs you about what might result if the groups are not equivalent. In other words, they tell you what is wrong. They do not get at what we feel is one of the most important points about internal validity: how do we correct the problem?

In research that compares differences among groups, a key question is whether the groups that are compared are *equivalent in all respects* prior to the introduction of the independent variable or variables. In randomized experimental research, by definition, equivalence is achieved through random assignment of participants to groups, if there are at least 30 in each group. However, in quasi-experimental, comparative, or associational research, random assignment of participants to groups has not or cannot be done. Other methods, such as random assignment of treatments to similar intact groups, analysis of covariance, matching, or checking for pretest equality of groups after the fact, are attempts to make the groups equal or at least to see how different they are.

The random assignment of treatments to similar intact groups, an aspect of a strong quasi-experimental design, is often useful for reducing initial participant differences when random assignment of participants to groups cannot take place. The effect of this method is enhanced if there is no reason to believe that the groups are unequal, as would be true if participants assigned themselves to the groups, for example, if they chose a particular class or teacher in a school. Consider a study by Tuckman (1992), who was interested in determining how planning changed student motivation. Student motivation was defined as the amount of effort put forth by college students on a voluntary, course-related task. All of Tuckman's participants were enrolled in one of four sections of a course in educational psychology. Tuckman randomly assigned two of the sections to receive the intervention, while the other two sections did not receive the intervention. However, the students were not randomly assigned to the individual sections. If there were no reasons to believe that the students in the four classes were different and if these turned out to be significant differences between the intervention and nonintervention conditions, then a convincing argument could be made that it was the intervention and not the characteristics of the participants that made the difference in the study. One way to check if the four classes were different before the intervention would be to compare relevant pretest scores.

A common method of attempting to achieve participant or group equivalence, when random assignment of participants to conditions cannot be undertaken, is analysis of covariance (ANCOVA), which is discussed in chapter 18. It is often used in a design that compares two groups and the participants in each group receive a pretest and a posttest. Because participants are not randomly assigned to groups, the design is called a nonequivalent control group design (chap. 7). However, in quasi-experiments, rather than use the pretest as the covariate (which is common when participants have been randomly assigned to groups), it is best to use a separate measure, which is related to the dependent variable, as the covariate. For example, Griffin (1992) used academic aptitude as the covariate in a study that measured change in concept acquisition. Iverson, Iverson, and Lukin (1993) used grade point average as a covariate to control for selection bias across gender in a study investigating instructional strategy. A problem with ANCOVA is that certain statistical assumptions must be met (see chapter 18).

Equivalence of Groups in Comparative Studies.   ANCOVA can also be used in studies with an attribute independent variable. In this case a separate measure, such as IQ or education, is used as the covariate to control for group differences in such important variables.

Matching of participants on characteristics other than the independent variable is another method of approaching participant or group equivalence. This technique is especially popular in the comparative approach, where a *diagnostic group* is compared to a *normal* group. For example, Beatty and Gange (1977) compared 26 persons with multiple sclerosis to an equal number of persons without the diagnosis to assess motor and intellectual functioning. Before the study, they matched the participants on age, gender, and education. If participants are not different with the exception of the diagnosis, then the authors could conclude that differences between the two groups might be attributed to the disease. Often in comparative studies, investigators check after the study to see how well matched the groups were for demographic measures collected during the study. If the groups are similar, a degree of internal validity is shown.

Even if one or more of the methods listed earlier is undertaken to achieve group equivalence in place of random assignment of participants to groups, actual equivalence can never be assumed. That is why the specific quasi-experimental designs described in chapter 7 are labeled nonequivalent groups designs.

Additional problems involved in making groups equivalent include characteristics that seem equal initially, but lead to different developmental trajectories over time and, thus, group differences that are not a result of the independent variable. Differences between groups in maturation rates, genetic predisposition, or factors leading to participant attrition are examples. Regression to the mean of extreme groups is another example of where differences in characteristics of participants that may not be initially obvious appear over time because the initial score was not the true score. Although this problem is unlikely to happen if there has been random assignment of participants to groups, the issue arises often in quasi-experimental designs, where change over time is one of the independent variables. These problems are discussed in greater detail in the next section about Cook and Campbell's (1979) threats to internal validity.

Equivalence in Associational Studies. If the research approach is associational, that is, there is only one group. (Note that our associational approach has often been referred to as the correlational approach, but we prefer associational so that the term is not confused with a correlation coefficient). In the associational case, equivalence of participant characteristics comes down to the question of whether those who score high on the independent variable of interest are similar to those who score low for other attributes that may be correlated with the dependent variable. For example, if the independent variable was education and the dependent variable was income, we should be cautious about interpreting a high correlation as indicating that more education causes a higher income. Are the highly educated participants equal to the poorly educated for other possible causal factors such as IQ, parent's education, and family social status? If it is likely that the high scorers are not equivalent to the low scorers for variables such as age, gender, or ethnicity, statistically controlling for the variables on which the high and low participants are unequal is one method of achieving some degree of this aspect of internal validity within the associational research approach.

Cook and Campbell's Threats Related to Participant Characteristics

Although we have found some of Cook and Campbell's (1979) names for the various threats to be confusing and difficult to remember, we use them here because they are commonly seen in the literature and research methods books.

Statistical Regression. Sometimes the purpose of a study is to benefit a particular group who may be above or below the average. An example may be children in a Head Start program. What often happens when performing this type of research is that the scores from this group on the posttest improve relative to their scores on the pretest regardless of the intervention. Because these scores were low to start with, they may have moved or "regressed" toward the mean or average of all scores. Conceptually, what is happening in the internal validity threat of regression to the mean is that there is measurement error in the dependent variable (reliability is less than perfect). Because the dependent variable (pretest) is used in the screening, only those children who score low on the pretest may be selected to be in the study. However, since there is measurement error, a proportion of students selected into the "catch-up" group should not actually be in that group. Hence, when tested a second time (posttest), their "true score" is more apt to be reflected, which will naturally represent an increase from the pretest. Therefore, the investigator does not know if the posttest score is a reflection of the intervention or of the statistical problem of regression to the mean.

Experimental Mortality. Although the name sounds bad, the type of mortality referred to in this situation involves participants leaving the study, called attrition. Problems are created if the percentage lost is large, or if there is differential loss between or among groups, or both. For any of these mortality problems, the result could lead to a biased posttest score if the rationale for leaving the study is related to the independent variable in the study. This is especially the case if either the intervention or the control condition prompts participants to drop out. For example, if the intervention is found by participants to be onerous or not effective, they may quit the study. Likewise, if participants are in the control condition and feel cheated, they may withdraw.

Selection.   We think this threat should be called *participant assignment* because the problem arises in how participants are assigned to a particular group, treatment, or intervention, not in how they were selected from the population. Problems are created when participants are not randomly assigned to the treatment groups even if a pretest suggests that the groups are equal. Although the groups should be called nonequivalent, the extent of this problem depends on how the participants entered into the groups and whether that process was biased.

Interactions With Participant Assignment.   How participants were assigned to groups presents problems. In addition, if there are biases in assignment, they may interact differentially between or among the groups, with other factors such as maturation, environmental events, or instrumentation. These assignment interactions make it difficult to conclude that posttest differences among groups are due to the effect of the intervention.

Control of Extraneous Experience or Environment Variables

We have grouped several other threats to internal validity under a category that deals with the effects of extraneous (variables other than the independent variables) experiences or environmental conditions during the study. Thus, we have called this internal validity dimension control of extraneous experience and environment variables. Cook and Campbell (1979) addressed this problem when discussing threats to internal validity that random assignment does not eliminate (p. 56). Many of these threats occur because participants gain information about the purpose of the study while the study is taking place. The first aspect of this category has to do with whether extraneous variables or events *affect one group more* than the other. For example, if students learn that they are in a control group, they may give up and not try as hard, exaggerating differences between the intervention and control groups. Or, the opposite may occur and students in the control group overcompensate, eliminating differences between the two groups. In the associational approach, the issue is whether the experiences of the participants who are high on the independent variable are different from those who are low on the independent variable.

A second issue is whether something other than the independent variable is affecting the dependent variable for *all groups.* This problem is, of course, more likely to be serious when the treatment continues over an extended time period and in longitudinal research. Historical events and maturation could affect both groups equally, obscuring any group differences. The results could be misinterpreted if, for example, one concluded that significant pretest to posttest gains (or losses) in two intervention groups resulted from the treatments rather than from uncontrolled common (e.g., Hawthorne-type) experience or maturation. This is not uncommon in studies that investigate a clinical intervention. As a result of the problems of withholding treatment to patients, often two different treatments are compared without a control group that did not receive any treatment. If both groups improve, but do not differ from each other, then a conclusion that both treatments worked equally well may not be correct. Instead, maturation or a common experience could have affected both groups equally. Of course, in longitudinal studies, maturation *is* the variable of interest. This issue is complex. In randomized experimental designs in a laboratory, these experiential and environmental variables are usually well controlled, but in quasi-experimental designs, and especially in the comparative and associational approaches, such experiences may be inadequately controlled.

A good study should have moderate to high internal validity on both dimensions of internal validity (equivalence of groups on participant characteristics and control of extraneous experience or environment variables) or, if not, the author should be, at the very least, cautious *not* to say that the independent variables influenced, impacted, or caused the dependent variables to change. For the evaluation of internal validity, refer to the rating scales in Fig. 6.1. Each scale should be used to rate the study as a whole.

Cook and Campbell's Threats Related to Experiences or Environment

Maturation.   The internal validity threat called maturation takes place when participants in the study change as a function of time, not necessarily from physical maturation. Time, in the case of randomized experimental and quasi-experimental research, is from the pretest measurement period to the posttest measurement period. Some of these changes are physical which could result from growing older. But other changes are less obvious. For example, patients may get better over time without any treatment. The maturation threat makes it difficult to determine whether it was the intervention or something else that made the difference in the dependent variable.

History or Environmental Events.   This threat to internal validity takes place when an event, which may be related to the independent variable but is not of specific interest to the investigator, occurs at some time between the pretest and the posttest. Consider a situation in which you are interested in the effect of a particular type of teaching method. During the period that your intervention is taking place, the students in your class are exposed to a reading from another class on the merits of your teaching method. The environmental events threat does not allow for a conclusion that would say that it was your teaching method, and only your teaching method that made the difference in the study.

Repeated Testing.   The repeated testing threat to internal validity most often occurs when the investigator uses a pretest and a posttest in the study, and the two are identical or similar. The problem results from a possible carryover

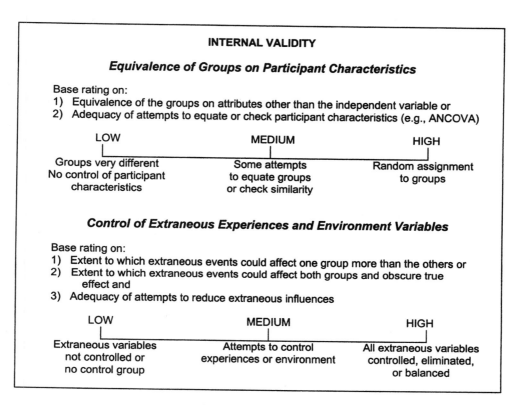

FIG. 6.1.   Evaluating the internal validity of the findings of a study.

from the pretest that might alert the participants about the study and how they might behave. Or, if the study involves learning, the pretest may have information that is included in the posttest, which would make it difficult to eliminate from the true posttest scores. Several studies have not found repeated testing to be a major problem.

Instrumentation.   When using the same pretest and posttest in a research design, it is possible that the scoring of the test may change, especially if the interval between the pretest and the posttest is relatively long. An example of this type of change could be a calibration drift in an instrument that measures reaction time. Even slight changes will prevent the investigator from concluding whether the change resulted from the intervention or to the change in calibration. Cook and Campbell called this type of threat to internal validity *instrumentation.* A common problem involving the instrumentation threat is when the pretest and posttest measurement tool involves raters. People often change their criteria over time. Even worse, one or more of the raters may leave the study and have to be replaced with different raters. Repeatedly establishing high interrater reliability is one method of circumventing this problem.

SUMMARY

In this chapter, we introduced the importance of research validity to the research process. Internal validity, one of the four components of research validity, was defined and divided into dimensions, equivalence of groups on participant characteristics, and control of extraneous or environmental variables. Threats to internal validity were described under each dimension of internal validity. Controlling these threats to internal validity through specific research designs is the topic of our next chapter.

STUDY AIDS

Concepts

- Control of extraneous experience or environment variables
- Equivalence of groups on participant characteristics
- Experimental mortality
- History or environmental events
- Instrumentation
- Interactions with participant assignment
- Internal validity
- Maturation
- Repeated testing
- Research validity
- Statistical regression
- Selection
- Threats to internal validity

Distinctions

- Equivalence of groups on participant characteristics versus control of extraneous experience or environment variables
- Internal validity versus external validity
- Maturation versus history or environmental events
- Repeated testing versus instrumentation
- Research validity versus measurement validity

Application Problems

1. Match each research example with the main threat to internal validity that it contains.
   a. maturation

b. history-environmental events
c. repeated testing
d. instrumentation
e. selection-assignment
f. experimental mortality
g. statistical regression

_____ A control group takes a pretest about social studies knowledge. Some of them are intrigued and decide to read up on the topic before the posttest.

_____ The research assistants become bored and don't do their observations as carefully near the end of the study.

_____ An experiment is conducted to assess a new history teaching method. School districts that volunteer serve as the experimental group and those that don't volunteer serve as the control group.

_____ A researcher is interested in the long term effects of an election on the political attitudes of voters. Prior to the election, the views of 100 voters are assessed. Afterwards the researcher is able to re-assess the attitudes of 74 voters.

_____ This is defined as any event other than the manipulation of the independent variable that occurs between the pretest and the posttest.

_____ At the start of the school year, the math achievement of a group of children is assessed. They are then all exposed to a new math program, and re-examined at the end of the school year.

_____ A psychiatrist selects a group of patients with the most extreme symptoms. After 1 month of therapy, the patients have markedly improved.

For the following four studies:
a. What research approach was used?
b. State the research question in the format illustrated in Table 5.2.
c. What general type of statistic would probably be used?
d. Evaluate the equivalence of the groups on participant characteristics and evaluate the control of extraneous experiences.

2. Researchers were interested in effects of different types of television programming on the aggressive behavior of pre-school aged children. Children from a pre-school were randomly assigned to spend 30 minutes viewing one of two different types of television programming. One group watched violent animated cartoons such as Power Rangers, and in an adjacent room, the other group watched programming that modeled pro-social behavior such as Barney. During the hour after the viewing, aggressive acts initiated by individual children from both view groups were counted by observers. They compared the two groups on number of aggressive behaviors.

3. In this study, the researchers were interested in comparing the way in which three types of reinforcement affected the conditioning of children to use the word "they" when making up sentences. Subjects were brought to the lab and then randomly assigned to three groups: (a) Children in the material reinforcement condition received an M & M candy immediately after using the word "they" at the beginning of a sentence; (b) Children assigned to the

praise condition were reinforced by the experimenter saying "good"; and (c) Children in the symbolic reinforcement condition were simply given a plus mark.

4. A professor wants to know whether student anxiety (on an anxiety inventory with scores from 1–10) influences test performance scores on the midterm exam.

5. The organizers of a required week-long graduate course were interested in which of two teaching-training approaches was most effective. Two sections of the course (on trauma assessment and intervention) were taught. One teacher utilized a traditional structured didactic approach. The other teacher used new approach-curriculum, utilizing a high proportion of experiential components. One section met in the afternoon and the other section in the morning. Students could sign up for either session. However, the instructors were unknown to the students and the students had no prior awareness of the differing approaches-curriculums. The sections were of equal size and the students were demographically similar. Students were pre-tested to assess their prior knowledge, and at the end of the course students were tested on the content of the course.

Specific Research Designs for Randomized Experimental and Quasi-Experimental Approaches

Concepts
Distinctions
Application Problems

RESEARCH DESIGN

In chapter 4 we introduced two different types of independent variables, active and attribute. We also described how an independent variable has different values, which we called levels. In addition, we described the dependent variable as the outcome measure or criterion of the study. How participants become assigned to the levels of the independent variable, in part, determines the type of quantitative research approach, which was the topic of chapter 5. In chapter 6 we introduced the concept of internal validity, and how it should be used to judge the merits of a study. It is worth going back to chapter 5 and reviewing Fig. 5.1 to examine the relationship between type of independent variable and type of quantitative research approach. The randomized experimental and quasi-experimental approaches have an active independent variable, whereas the comparative and associational approaches have an attribute independent variable.

In this chapter we introduce the concept of research design. We discuss *specific* research designs that fit into the randomized experimental and quasi-experimental research approaches. A specific research design helps us visualize the independent variables of the study, the levels within these independent variables, and when measurement (dependent variable) will take place. When the operations from these specific research designs are examined, they help the researcher determine the internal validity of the study. We introduce specific research designs here, so that we can examine these designs with respect to internal validity, and point out some of the threats to internal validity that we discussed in chapter 6.

Both randomized experimental and quasi-experimental approaches have an active independent variable, with at least one level being some type of intervention or manipulation given to participants in the intervention group. Usually there is also a comparison or control condition (or treatment), which is given as another level of the independent variable. There can be more than two levels or groups. Unfortunately, in some poor quasi-experimental designs, there is only one level, so no comparisons can be made. Before discussing specific designs, we want to introduce some terminology to help conceptualize each design.

DESIGN TERMINOLOGY

- R = random assignment to the group
- NR = nonrandom assignment to the group
- O = observation of the dependent variable
- X = intervention (one level of the independent variable)
- ~X = no intervention (or the usual intervention)
- E: = experimental or intervention group[1]
- C: = control or comparison group[2]
- M = matching

POOR QUASI-EXPERIMENTAL DESIGN

One-Group Posttest-Only Design

An example of this design, often referred to as the one-shot design, would be an evaluation of a new curriculum in a school system. The investigator introduces the curriculum (X), and then decides that it might be useful to determine if it is working. At the end of the semester, the investigator uses some form of measurement (O) to determine the students' response to the new curriculum. The design is shown as follows:

NR   E: X   O

This diagram and those that follow indicate a time sequence. First, there is nonrandom assignment of participants to the intervention group, then the treatment, and, finally, a posttest takes place. The problem with the design is it does not satisfy even the minimum condition for a research problem, which is investigation of a relationship or comparison. Note that the intervention is not a variable because there is only one level. Does the one group posttest-only design have any value? If nothing else, it provides pilot data (a common term to indicate exploratory data) for a future study. The investigator could compare the

[1]To simplify the examples in this chapter, we have mainly described designs with only one intervention group and one control group. However, it is common to have more than two groups. We have discussed some such examples and the reasons for them in chapter 5.

[2]In quasi-experiments, it is better to use the term comparison group rather than control group because, especially with poor and weak quasi-experiments, there is little that is "controlled." For similar reasons, quasi-experiments are labeled nonequivalent group designs.

results to data from an earlier group or from the same group at an earlier time. However, if this were done, the design would no longer be a one-group posttest-only design.

One-Group Pretest–Posttest Design

The one group pretest–posttest design can be shown as follows:

NR   E: O_1 X O_2

Pretest   Intervention   Posttest

The operations for this design are that an observation in the form of a pretest is given first, then the intervention is given, and finally, a second observation in the form of a posttest is recorded. An example of this type of design is demonstrated in a study by Moisan (1990). Moisan was interested in the effects of an adaptive ski program on the self-perceptions and performance of children with physical disabilities. Unfortunately, early in the study, the children from the control group withdrew, leaving her with only the intervention group relatively intact (this high dropout rate may have occurred because the intervention group got to participate in a ski program, whereas the control group did not receive this intervention or anything comparable). Therefore, the only comparison left for Moisan was from the pretest to the posttest.

The problem with the one-group pretest–posttest design is that the comparison is not with a second group (a control group). Instead, the comparison in the one group pretest–posttest design is between the pretest and the posttest within the same group. Because there is no comparison group, the design is susceptible to most of the threats to internal validity.

Environmental events are a possible threat to internal validity in this design, because the lack of a control group prevents the investigator from knowing, for example, whether other activities in school at the same time as the intervention might be producing the facilitation. Maturation is a possible threat to internal validity because the students are getting older and may be better coordinated and stronger at the same time as the intervention. Carryover effects are a possible problem in this design because taking the pretest could influence the posttest.

In the Moisan (1990) study, equivalence of the groups was definitely a problem because students volunteered (were self-assigned rather than randomly assigned) to be in the intervention group. Even if the intervention group had initially been similar to the control group, the high dropout rate (called experimental mortality by Cook & Campbell, 1979) would likely have meant that the groups who took the posttest had different characteristics.

If one cannot find an acceptable comparison group for the one-group pretest–posttest design, increasing the number of dependent variables one can add control toward interpreting the results. For example, among the measures that Moisan (1990) used in her study was the Self-Perception Profile for Children (Harter, 1985). This measurement tool has several domains. Some of these domains are scholastic competence, social acceptance, athletic competence, and behavioral conduct. Not all of these measures would be expected to improve as a result of the intervention. Therefore, Moisan could have predicted which measures should change from the intervention. If only those measures changed that Moisan predicted would change, then more confidence could be placed in the intervention as being responsible for changes in those measures. Cook and Campbell (1979) refer to this modification as the nonequivalent dependent variables design.

Posttest-Only Design with Nonequivalent Groups

This design can be shown as follows:

$$NR \qquad E: \qquad X \quad O$$
$$NR \qquad C: \qquad \sim X \quad O$$

There is no random assignment to groups and no pretest, so it is impossible to determine the equality of the groups prior to the treatment. Hence, the design is weak. Cosby (1989) provides an example of this type of design. An investigator is interested in a relaxation training program to reduce cigarette smoking. The participants in the intervention group are given a relaxation training program. The participants in the comparison group do not receive relaxation training. At the end of the study, both groups are measured on a smoking frequency measure. As Cosby (1989) points out:

> It is likely in this case that participants in the first group chose to participate in the program, and the subjects in the second group are simply smokers who did not sign up for the training. The problem of selection differences arises because smokers who choose to participate may be different from those who do not. (pp. 70–71)

Thus, this design is likely to be weak on equivalence of the groups on participant characteristics.

BETTER QUASI-EXPERIMENTAL DESIGNS

Pretest–Posttest Nonequivalent Comparison Group Designs

The pretest–posttest designs within the quasi-experimental approach are usually referred to as nonequivalent comparison group designs. The design appears as follows:

$$NR \qquad E: \quad O_1 \quad X \quad O_2$$
$$NR \qquad C: \quad O_1 \quad \sim X \quad O_2$$

Notice that there is *no random assignment* of the participants to the two (or more) groups in this design. The sequential operations of the nonequivalent comparison group design are as follows. First, measurements are taken on two different groups prior to an intervention. Then, one group receives the intervention, and the other group does not receive the intervention. At the end of the intervention period, both groups are measured again to determine if there are differences between the two groups. The design is considered to be nonequivalent because even if the two groups have the same mean score after the pretest, there may be characteristics that have not been measured that may interact with the treatment to cause differences between the two groups that are not caused strictly by the intervention. We have classified the nonequivalent comparison group design into three different strengths of quasi-experimental design that look alike when diagrammed, but vary in how participants are assigned to groups or conditions and how much control the investigator has over the independent variable.

Weak Quasi-Experimental Designs.   This design occurs when trying to evaluate situations where attendance is voluntary. It has some of the problems mentioned earlier. The researcher does not randomly assign participants to groups. In fact, *participants assign themselves* to the groups. A second problem is that the researcher does not have control over the independent variable because the participants presumably choose a particular group to receive a particular intervention or treatment. A design of this type is especially common when trying to evaluate educational or therapeutic workshops. People who want to attend the workshop volunteer to be in that condition or group. A comparison group is composed of people who do not wish to be in the workshop, or a sample of people who may not have cared one way or another. Regardless, since at least one group has volunteered, the researcher cannot randomly assign one group to one condition, and the other group to the other condition. Therefore, any eventual difference between the group that received the intervention and the group that did not receive the intervention must be tempered by this potential bias.

Moderate Strength Quasi-Experimental Designs.   This design also involves less control by the investigator over the independent variable, and, as in all quasi-experiments, the participants are not randomly assigned to groups. The moderate strength quasi-experimental design fits between the weak quasi-experimental design and the strong quasi-experimental design from equivalence of groups prior to the intervention. In this design, participants do not select themselves into intact groups, but are in these groups as a result of other factors, which are not related to the intervention. Examples of these factors include students scheduling classes around availability, or people choosing hospitals for convenience. The critical difference between this version of the design and strong quasi-experiments is that the investigator is not able to randomly assign the *treatment* to certain groups. Instead, the investigator takes advantage of a situation where it is known that one setting (e.g., school or hospital) will receive the intervention and another setting will not receive the intervention. An example demonstrates this design.

Gilfoyle and Gliner (1985) were interested in attitude changes toward handicapped children by nonhandicapped children. An educational puppet show (All of the Kids on the Block) was used as the active independent variable in this study. Three groups (schools) were used. Two intervention groups viewed the puppet show but the other group (control) did not. For the intervention groups, a pretest was given prior to the intervention, and a posttest was given following the intervention. The comparison group also received a pretest and posttest during the same time intervals as the intervention groups. The dependent variable from the pretest and posttest was a scale used to measure attitudes of personal feelings or perceptions of disability.

Did the Gilfoyle and Gliner (1985) study meet the criteria for a randomized experiment? There was an active independent variable (the puppet show), but did the investigator randomly assign participants to groups? No, the groups (schools) were intact prior to the investigation. Did the investigator have control over the independent variable? No, the investigator could not randomly assign the treatment to two groups and no treatment to a third group. Instead, the groups were selected because the researcher knew that two schools were going to view the puppet show and another school was not going to view the puppet show. Therefore, this design is not as strong as the next design because the investigator could not randomly assign the intervention. The relative strength of this design rests on two questions. First, why did two schools get the intervention and the other school not get the intervention? Second, are students in the schools that received the intervention different from students in the school that did not receive the intervention? If there is no reason to suspect bias relative to the dependent variable for either question, then the design is almost as strong as the type discussed next. On the other hand, if there is a reason to believe that there is bias in the groups that received the treatment and differences between the students in the intervention and control schools, such as familiarity with handicapped children or ethnic composition, then the design is considerably weaker.

Strong Quasi-Experimental Designs.   This design might be used in an environment such as an elementary school that has two fifth-grade classrooms, and with an active independent variable such as a new curriculum. In this environment, the children already have been assigned to one of the two classrooms or groups for a particular semester; thus the investigator cannot randomly assign participants to groups. However, in the strong quasi-experimental approach, the investigator has control over the independent variable by randomly assigning the new curriculum (treatment) condition to one (intact) classroom and the old curriculum condition to the other. The strength of this quasi-experimental design is that it is similar to a random experimental design except that participants have not been randomly assigned to groups or conditions. In some intact situations, such as classrooms within a school, the assignment of students to different classrooms may be almost random (i.e., there was no intentional bias introduced in the assignment); in those cases, the strong quasi-experimental design is almost equivalent to a randomized experimental design on internal validity.

In chapter 6, we mentioned a study by Tuckman (1992). We recall the study as an example of the strong quasi-experimental design. Tuckman was interested in determining how planning changed student motivation. Student motivation (the dependent variable) was defined as the amount of effort put forth by college students on a voluntary, course-related task. For our purposes, the important point was the assignment of participants to groups. Tuckman had four different groups. All of Tuckman's participants were enrolled in one of four sections of a course in educational psychology. Tuckman randomly assigned one level of the independent variable, "using the planning form," to two sections. The other two sections did not use the planning form. Is the Tuckman (1991) study a randomized experiment?

There was an active independent variable. Tuckman had control over the independent variable; he randomly assigned the planning condition (treatment) to two groups and the other two groups did not get the planning condition. However, Tuckman was not able to randomly assign participants to groups, so this was not a randomized experiment. Not satisfying this condition may or may not be a major problem, depending on how students assigned themselves into each class section. If their choices were similar to chance, then the Tuckman study could be considered almost as strong as a randomized experiment. On the other hand, if there was some systematic reason for students choosing one section over another section (such as preference for teacher or time of day), then there was a bias in the methodology, and all conclusions must take this bias into consideration.

Table 7.1 summarizes the two issues that determine the strength of a pretest–posttest quasi-experimental design: control over the independent variable (indicated by random assignment of treatments to intact groups) and equivalence of participant characteristics. Remember that there is no random assignment to the groups in any quasi-experimental design, so the groups are never totally equivalent.

Time-Series Designs

A second general category of quasi-experimental designs is called time-series designs. Similar to the quasi-experimental designs mentioned earlier, there is no random assignment of participants to groups. The two most common types of time-series designs are *single group time-series designs* and *multiple group time-series designs* (see Cook & Campbell, 1979; Huck, Cormier, & Bounds, 1974). Also, subcategories within each type of time-series design are *temporary* versus *continuous treatment*.

TABLE 7.1
Issues That Determine the Strength of Quasi-experimental Designs

Strength of Design	Random Assignment of Treatments to Intact Groups	Participant Characteristics Likely to be Similar
Strong	Yes	Yes, assuming no bias in how participants were assigned to groups
Moderate	No	Maybe
Weak	No	No, because participants self-assigned to groups

Single Group Time-Series Designs.   The logic behind these designs, or any time-series design, involves convincing others that a baseline (i.e., several pretests) is stable prior to an intervention so that one can conclude that the change in the dependent variable results from the intervention and not other environmental events. For example, consider the one group pretest–posttest design that we discussed under the heading of poor quasi-experimental designs.

The one group pretest–posttest design can be viewed as follows:

NR   E: O_1 X O_2

                Pretest   Intervention   Posttest

The problem with this design is that if there is a change from the pretest to the posttest score, it is not known whether the change resulted from the intervention or from another event that could be happening at the same time that had not been controlled. Now, suppose we add an earlier observation period (pretest 1, taken 6 months prior to the study) to this design as follows:

NR   E: O_1 O_2 X O_3

            Pretest 1   Pretest 2   Intervention   Posttest

Suppose also that there was no change observed between Pretest 1 and Pretest 2 prior to the intervention. But after the intervention, a change was observed in the posttest. This design would be more convincing if even more observations took place prior to the introduction of the independent variable, and still no change had occurred. It is common in time-series designs to have multiple measures before and after the intervention, but there must be multiple pretests to establish a baseline.

The single group time-series design with temporary treatment is as follows:

NR   E: $O_1 O_2 O_3 O_4 XO_5 O_6 O_7 O_8$

An example of this single group time-series design could involve a company that was interested in the effects of a workshop on being a team player. Observations would take place prior to the workshop on some relevant measure, such as cooperative interactions. The workshop is given after four baseline measures on cooperative interactions. The workshop is a temporary intervention, and observations are recorded immediately after the intervention and three later times. One would expect that if the workshop was successful, there would be an immediate increase after the intervention relative to the preceding baseline periods, and the effects might or might not be long lasting.

The single group time-series design with continuous treatment is a variant of the design with temporary treatment. This design is as follows:

NR   E: $O_1 O_2 O_3 O_4 \sim XO_5 \ XO_6 \ XO_7 \ XO_8$

An example of this type of design might be a school implementing a new curriculum. Observations of the old curriculum might take place with standardized reading scores from previous semesters. These same measurements could be examined during the new curriculum intervention. The new curriculum is not a temporary intervention like a workshop, but takes place continuously until replaced. This design is especially popular when there are student records with many repeated measures that can be used for observations and when it is not possible or practical to implement a control group.

Multiple Group Time-Series Designs.   These time-series designs are similar to those for the single group, but are stronger by adding a comparison group that receives the same number of measurement periods, but does not receive the intervention.

The multiple group time-series design with temporary treatment is seen as follows:

$$\text{NR} \quad \text{E:} \quad O_1 \, O_2 \, O_3 \, O_4 \quad XO_5 \, O_6 \, O_7 \, O_8$$

$$\text{NR} \quad \text{C:} \quad O_1 \, O_2 \, O_3 \, O_4 \, \sim XO_5 \, O_6 \, O_7 \, O_8$$

We can provide an example of this type of design by extending our workshop example from the single group time-series design. Suppose that the company that is trying to promote cooperation through the team player workshop establishes a comparison group by examining cooperative interactions among those workers that did not attend the workshop. Or, a more common occurrence would be to examine workers at a similar company (perhaps another branch) that did not receive the workshop.

The multiple group time-series design with continuous treatment is the final time-series design that we discuss. This design can be seen as follows:

$$\text{NR} \quad \text{E:} \quad O_1 \, O_2 \, O_3 \, O_4 \quad XO_5 \, XO_6 \, XO_7 \, XO_8$$

$$\text{NR} \quad \text{C:} \quad O_1 \, O_2 \, O_3 \, O_4 \sim XO_5 \sim XO_6 \sim X \, O_7 \sim XO_8$$

If we return to our school curriculum example, the single group time-series design with continuous treatments could be extended to the multiple group time-series design with multiple treatments by adding a comparison group, perhaps from another district. This comparison group would just receive the traditional curriculum.

Conclusions.   Time-series designs (especially single group time-series designs) have become important designs in educational settings, where it is often not practical to introduce a control group. The key advantage of such a time-series design, in contrast to the one group pretest–posttest poor quasi-experimental design, is the repeated observations or records, which provide a degree of assurance that changes are not caused by other environmental events or maturation. Another type of quasi-experimental design, single subject designs, is discussed in detail in the next chapter.

RANDOMIZED EXPERIMENTAL DESIGNS

Posttest-Only Control (or Comparison) Group Design

The posttest-only control group design can be shown as follows:

$$
\begin{array}{llll}
\text{R} & \text{E:} & \text{X} & \text{O} \\
\text{R} & \text{C:} & \sim \text{X} & \text{O}
\end{array}
$$

The sequential operations of the posttest-only control group design are to assign participants randomly to either an intervention or control group (it should be remembered that more than two groups may be used with any of these designs). Then, the intervention group receives the intended intervention and the control group receives either a different intervention or no intervention. If two different interventions are used, this design could be called a posttest-only comparison group design. At the end of the intervention period, both groups are measured by using a form of instrumentation related to the study (dependent variable).

An example of the posttest-only control group design is a study in which the investigator is interested in a particular intervention. Laconte, Shaw, and Dunn (1993) investigated the effects of participation in a developmentally appropriate affective education program. Students who were at risk for dropping out were randomly assigned to an intervention group or a control group. The intervention group received a 15-week group treatment that involved a rational–emotive curriculum. At the end of the 15-week session, both groups were tested on a self-concept scale.

The key point for the posttest-only control group design is the random assignment of participants to groups. One can assume that if participants are assigned randomly to either one or the other group, the two groups are equivalent prior to the intervention. Therefore, if there are differences on the dependent measure following the intervention, it can be assumed that the differences result from the intervention and not from differences in participant characteristics. Remember that equivalence of participant characteristics is a key dimension of internal validity. Does random assignment of participants to groups always make the groups equivalent? With large numbers (say 30 or more in a group) of participants or a homogeneous sample of participants, the investigator can be confident that random assignment will yield equivalent groups. However, with smaller numbers in the sample, or very heterogeneous participants, less confidence can be placed in random assignment providing equivalent groups. In the latter cases, a different experimental design, the pretest–posttest control group design, is suggested.

Pretest–Posttest Control Group Design

The pretest–posttest control group design can be shown as follows:

R	E:	O_1	X	O_2
R	C:	O_1	~X	O_2

The sequential operations of the pretest–posttest control (or comparison) group design are as follows. First, participants are randomly assigned to groups. Then, each group is measured on the dependent variable (pretest). The intervention group then receives the intervention, and the control group receives the traditional treatment. Because the control group participants may drop out of the study or not try hard to do well on the posttest, it is rare and not desirable for the control group to receive no treatment at all. After the intervention period, both groups are measured again on the dependent variable (posttest).

The pretest–posttest control group design is the most common randomized experimental design. Any time a treatment is compared to a control group across two time periods, usually pretest and posttest, this is the design that is used. It is randomized experimental because the participants are randomly assigned to groups prior to the initial measurement (pretest) period. The reason for using this design as compared to the posttest-only control group design is to check for equivalent groups before the intervention. On the other hand, the disadvantage is that if a pretest is used, it could bias the participants about what to expect of the study, and it could influence them in some way; that is, there could be carryover effects. The investigator must weigh the advantages of giving a pretest, that is, gaining information about the equivalency of groups, with the disadvantage of possibly biasing the posttest. Often the decision is made by the sample size. If each group is composed of at least 30 participants after random assignment, the researcher may choose to use the posttest-only control group design, because with that number of participants it is expected that the concept of randomness should work and both groups would be expected to be equivalent. On the other hand, if each group has only 10 participants, and the groups are heterogeneous, then the pretest–posttest control group design is probably best because it is possible that random assignment did not make the groups equivalent and further statistical adjustment (analysis of covariance) may be necessary.

Solomon Four-Group Design

One method of dealing with the possible effect of the pretest in the randomized experimental approach is to include intervention and control groups that receive the pretest, and intervention and control groups that do not receive the pretest. This randomized experimental design, called the Solomon four-group design, appears as follows:

R	E_1:	O_1	X	O_2
R	E_2:		X	O_2
R	C_1:	O_1	~X	O_2
R	C_2:		~X	O_2

The sequential operations of the Solomon four-group design are as follows. First, participants are randomly assigned to one of the four different groups. Then, two of the groups (E_1 and C_1) are measured on the dependent variable (pretest). The other two groups (E_2 and C_2) do not receive a pretest. Then, two groups (E_1 and E_2) receive the intervention. One group that receives the intervention was pretested (E_1) and one group that receives the intervention was not pretested (E_2). In addition, two groups do not receive the intervention: one that was pretested (C_1) and one that was not pretested (C_2). Therefore, the Solomon four-group design allows the investigator to test the effects of a pretest in addition to testing the effects of the intervention. However, to determine the effects of the pretest on the posttest, the investigator must double the number of participants—hardly worth the cost and effort in most situations.

Randomized Experimental Design With Matching

The last specific experimental design, which is commonly used, is one where participants are matched on some characteristic prior to the introduction of any of the conditions of the study. The characteristic that is used for the match must be related to the dependent variable; otherwise, matching is a waste of time and results in a loss of power. The sequential operations of the experimental design with matching are as follows. First, the investigator measures all of the participants on some characteristic (variable) that appears to be related to the dependent variable, such as intelligence. Next, if the independent variable has two levels, the investigator divides all of the participants into pairs of participants from their scores on the intelligence test. (If there were three levels or groups, the participants would be divided in triads.) The idea is to have pairs that are as close as possible on the variable of intelligence. For example, if there were 6 participants with IQ scores of 122, 110, 99, 102, 113, and 120, then the three pairs might be 122 with 120, 113 with 110, and 102 with 99. After all pairs are formed, the investigator randomly assigns one member of the pair to the intervention group and the other member of the pair to the control group. The key to the randomized experimental design with matching is to make it as if the 2 participants are identical (at least as far as the characteristics of interest). Therefore, it is as though 1 participant is receiving both conditions of the study, even though there are actually 2 different participants in each pair.

SUMMARY

Table 7.2 provides a summary diagram of the various specific designs discussed in this chapter. Remember that random assignment of participants to groups is what differentiates randomized experiments from quasi-experiments. We have discussed the strengths and weaknesses of each design, pointing out threats to internal validity where appropriate. Remember that the randomized experimental designs have the strongest internal validity and provide the best information about whether the independent variable caused changes in the dependent variable.

TABLE 7.2
Summary of Specific Designs for Experiments and Quasi-Experiments

Type of Design	Assign.	Grp.	Pre.	I.V.	Post.
Poor quasi-experimental designs					
One-group posttest-only design	NR	E:		X	O
One-group pretest–posttest design	NR	E:	O	X	O
Posttest-only design with	NR	E:		X	O
Nonequivalent groups	NR	C:		~X	O
Quasi-experimental designs					
Pretest–posttest nonequivalent	NR	E:	O	X	O
comparison group designs	NR	C:	O	~X	O
Single group time-series design					
With temporary treatment	NR	E:	OOO	X	OOO
With continuous treatment	NR	E:	OOO	XOXO	XOXO
Multiple group time-series designs	NR	E:	OOO	X	OOO
With temporary treatment	NR	C:	OOO	~X	OOO
With continuous treatment	NR	E:	OOO	XOXO	XOXO
	NR	C:	OOO	O O	O O
Randomized experimental designs					
Posttest-only control group designs	R	E:		X	O
	R	C:		~X	O
Pretest–posttest control group design	R	E:	O	X	O
	R	C:	O	~X	O
Solomon four-group design	R	E_1:	O	X	O
	R	E_2:		X	O
	R	C_1:	O	~X	O
	R	C_2:		~X	O
Randomized experimental design with	M R	E:		X	O
matching	M R	C:		~X	O

Note. Assign. = assignment of subjects to groups (NR = nonrandom, R = random, M R = matched then randomly assigned); Grp. = group or condition (E = experimental, C = control or comparison); Pre = pretest (O = an observation or measurement; a blank means there was no pretest for that group); I.V. = active independent variable (X = intervention, ~X = control or comparison treatment); Post = posttest (O = a posttest observation or measure).

STUDY AIDS

Concepts

- Multiple group time-series designs
- One-group posttest-only design
- One-group pretest–posttest design
- Pretest–posttest control group design
- Pretest–posttest nonequivalent comparison group designs
- Posttest-only control group design
- Posttest-only design with nonequivalent groups
- Randomized experimental design with matching
- Single group time-series designs
- Solomon four-group design

Distinctions

- Control group versus comparison group
- Poor quasi-experimental versus better quasi-experimental versus randomized experimental designs
- Random assignment of participants to groups versus random assignment of treatments to groups
- Random assignment versus nonrandom assignment of participants to groups
- Weak quasi-experiments versus moderate strength quasi-experiments versus strong quasi-experiments

Application Problems

For the following three scenarios:
   a. Identify the independent variable(s). For each, state whether it is active or attribute.
   b. Identify the dependent variable(s).
   c. Identify the specific design name (e.g. posttest only control group design). If the approach is quasi-experimental, evaluate its strength.
   1. You are a researcher in science education who is interested in the role of diagrams in instruction. You wish to investigate whether using diagrams in place of text will facilitate comprehension of the principles and concepts taught. To do so, you have developed a 12th grade physics unit that incorporates the liberal use of diagrams. You plan to compare student's knowledge of physics before and after the instructional unit. You will teach one of your classes using the diagram unit and the other using the text only unit.
   2. The purpose of this study was to determine whether type of class could alter attitudes toward persons with disabilities. Two classes at a large university were studied. One class, Survey of Human Disease, placed emphasis on specific diseases and handicapping conditions. The emphasis was on how these condi-

tions differed from each other. The other class, Handicapped Individual in Society, placed emphasis on abilities and did not address how handicapping conditions were different for this study. Twenty different volunteers from each class served as subjects for this study. At the end of the first semester, all subjects were tested on the Attitude Toward Disabled Persons Scale (ATDP).

3. A researcher wants to study the effects of social worker support on homeless peoples' job attainment. There are two similar mission sites. A social worker spends a month at one of the sites, but not the other. The people at the sites did not differ in average age, gender, and education. At the end of a year, she collects the following data on the two groups from labor department records for the previous two years: monthly totals of the number of days of employment.

4. Explain the rationale for a randomized experimental design with matching.

5. Health educators administering a large wellness program are interested in whether structured classes or support groups seem to have the greater influence on healthy attitudes toward food. Individuals voluntarily sign up for either the classes or the support groups. Their plan is to randomly select 30 participants from the classes and 30 from support groups and (with their permission) administer an eating attitudes instrument as a pretest and as a posttest to assess change in attitudes over time. One of the health educators expressed the concern that taking the eating attitudes test prior to the course would have an affect on posttest scores because participants will already be familiar with items on the instrument and may attempt to provide the socially desirable response. Practice effects would be an issue. What could they do to address this?

6. Describe how a researcher could explore the impact of a new curriculum on attendance:

    a. Utilizing a single group time-series design.

    b. Diagram the design and give the specific design name.

    c. Why is a time-series design stronger than a similar design that is not a time-series design?

7. Subjects are matched in pairs on key attribute variables of test scores and age, and then the children in each matched pair are randomly assigned to one of two groups, one receiving the intervention and one receiving no intervention.

    a. What specific type of experimental design is this? Explain.

Single Subject Designs

In this chapter, we describe a subcategory of quasi-experimental time-series designs that can be used with very few participants. These single subject designs have many of the characteristics that govern traditional group time-series designs, such as the numerous repeated measures on each participant and the initiation and withdrawal of treatment. However, using very few participants increases the flexibility of the design and leads to completely different methods of data analysis. Therefore, we have chosen to devote a separate chapter to these types of designs. The topic of single subject designs is complex, and contains too much material to be covered completely in a single chapter. For those interested in a complete treatment of the topic, we suggest the text by Kazdin (1982). For a clinical perspective on single subject design, Ottenbacher (1986) is an excellent work. For the analysis of single subject designs, we suggest Kratochwill and Levin (1992).

Single subject designs became prominent in the field of psychology in the 1960s, resulting in two journals, *The Journal of the Experimental Analysis of Behavior* and the *Journal of Applied Behavior Analysis*. The conceptualization of single subject designs is explained as follows. In a traditional group design, 10 participants might be assigned to receive the treatment, and 10 participants would not receive the treatment. At the end of a particular time period, the two groups are compared to determine if the treatment was successful. If the group that receives the treatment performs significantly better than the group that does not receive the treatment, then a judgment is made that the treatment was successful. Note that only one treatment was given 1 time to 10 participants and no treatment was given to the other 10 participants. Participants were measured prior to the intervention and after the intervention. Now consider a situation where 1 participant (or sometimes as many as 3 or 4 participants) receives the same treatment 10 times and, in addition, the treatment is withheld over 10 different times to the same participant. Each participant would be measured 20 times. If each time the treatment was given, an increase in the desired behavior occurred, and each time the treatment was withdrawn, the desired behavior failed to occur, one could conclude that the treatment was successful in increasing the desired behavior.

We can describe single subject designs as time-series designs where an intervention (active independent variable) is given to very few participants, four or fewer. In most situations, the independent variable is initiated and withheld numerous times throughout the study. In some situations (e.g., multiple baseline single subject designs), the removal of the independent variable is not necessary to be included as a single subject design. Single subject designs are quasi-experimental designs because they must include an active independent variable. In addition, there is no random assignment of participants to treatments. This should not be confused with case study types of designs. Case study designs fall under qualitative research methods, where descriptions of participants in natural settings are the rule. Case studies are often used to describe an unusual case, or to provide more descriptive evidence to support a quantitative study such as a program evaluation.

In this chapter we introduce the two major types of single subject designs, *ABAB* or reversal designs, and *multiple baseline designs*, and we provide examples for both. Next, we discuss the methods of observation and lengths of time of measurement periods in single subject designs. Then we discuss the analyses of these types of designs. Finally, we discuss the internal and external validity of single subject designs.

REVERSAL DESIGNS

Reversal designs, often referred to as *ABAB* designs, are the original single subject designs and are still the most common type of single subject design. In these designs, the first *A* stands for the baseline period, where the participant is usually observed for a number of time periods. The key here is that the participant is observed until the baseline is relatively flat. This is a large departure from traditional group designs, where the amount of time allotted to the experimental and control treatments is decided prior to the study. In single subject designs, the investigator plots the data for each measurement period on graph paper to determine if the behavior during baseline (or treatment) is increasing, decreasing, or leveling off. The first *B* period refers to the first intervention period. After the baseline has leveled off, the investigator initiates the treatment or active independent variable. Again, the investigator plots the data from each session to determine the effect of the treatment. If one were to stop here (hence an *AB* design), it would be easy to see the threats to internal validity, especially control of extraneous variables, that could arise. Because there has been only one baseline and one treatment phase, it is difficult to know whether it is the treatment or another variable that is making the difference. Therefore, once the treatment data appear to level off (a relatively flat line), the investigator withdraws the treatment, and initiates a second *A* phase. The investigator observes this phase for several periods (three at the minimum) until the behavior levels off. Then the investigator initiates the second *B* or treatment phase. This completes the minimum reversal design, with two *A* or baseline phases and two *B* or treatment phases. It should be noted that having two *A* and two *B* phases does not eliminate all threats to internal validity, and that the more *A* and *B* phases inserted, the more convincing is the design of the study, similar to any time-series design.

What should happen in a typical *ABAB* single subject study? Figure 8.1 demonstrates a single subject *ABAB* design. One would expect that during the initial baseline period (A_1) there may be some fluctuation of responses, but after the first few periods, the participant's responses (dependent variable) should habituate or level off. During the initial treatment period (B_1), behavior should increase (or decrease if the treatment is designed to reduce an undesirable behavior; such as aggression). One would expect this behavior to increase up to a point, and then to level off. Next, during the withdrawal of the treatment (A_2 period), the expectation is that performance will decrease (although perhaps not as low as the A_1 period) and then begin to stabilize. When the stabilization has occurred, the reintroduction of the treatment (B_2 period) takes place, and performance should increase above that of all of the preceding phases.

Although the preceding paragraph outlines the ideal results of an *ABAB* single subject design, things rarely happen exactly as planned. Perhaps the most common problem involves stabilization of performance for each phase of the study. First, it often takes time to reach a stable baseline. How long should the investigator wait until the baseline stabilizes? Usually, the baseline should stabilize within five or six periods. If the performance is still irregular (i.e., high one day and low the next), then the investigator should look for external influences to explain why the participant is performing so irregularly. Sometimes, it just takes a little while to habituate to the setting. Other problems that may interfere with stabilization may involve reactivity to the measure of performance. If the measure of performance requires that an observer be present, this may cause reactivity by the participant.

Stabilization of the initial baseline is a common problem in *ABAB* designs, but it is not the only problem. A second problem is related to treatment withdrawal. Many single subject designs institute a treatment that has a permanent effect. If this is the case, then in the second baseline (A_2) phase, one would expect that there might be little or no drop in performance. If there is no drop in performance, then one would expect an increase in performance in the second intervention (B_2) phase to a level substantially higher than that of the first intervention (B_1) phase.

The *ABAB* single subject reversal design does not necessarily mean that there should only be two baseline phases and two intervention phases. Most *ABAB* designs use at least three *A* and three *B* phases, and many use more. Actually, using only two *A* and two *B* phases is the minimum that could pass for a single subject study. More *A* and *B* phases make the study more convincing, and hence increase internal validity. In addition, the investigator is not limited

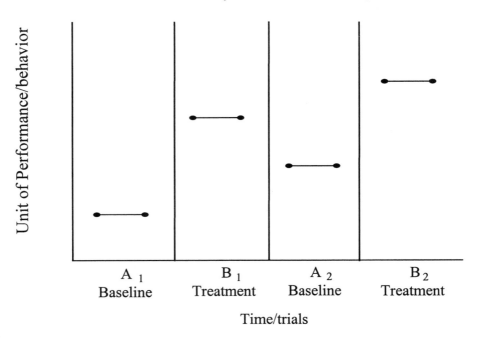

FIG. 8.1. A graphic representation of the hypothetical data of an *ABAB* single-subject experimental design.

to just the phases of *A* and *B*. Consider a situation where after the initial *A* phase, the investigator initiates a treatment in the *B* phase. However, the treatment fails to increase performance above that observed during the baseline period. If this were a traditional between groups type of design, the investigator would be stuck with a study that failed to reject the null hypothesis. Instead, in a single subject design, the investigator could modify the treatment and introduce it (*C*) after the *B* phase. Thus the design might be something like *ABCAC*. The point to remember is that a strength of single subject designs is that they are flexible, and just as you are not predetermined by the number of sessions contributing to any particular phase, you are also not predetermined to use just an *A* and *B* phase.

An example of a reversal design with only two baseline periods and two intervention periods can be seen in a study by Dunlap, Foster–Johnson, Clarke, Kern, and Childs (1995). They attempted to produce functional outcomes on 3 participants who had severe disabilities. They examined two dependent variables at the same time, on-task behavior and problem behavior. Their baseline periods consisted of standard outcomes, whereas the intervention periods consisted of functional outcomes. Figure 8.2 (adapted from Dunlap et al., 1995) shows the data for 1 of the 3 participants. Notice that during the baseline period, the on-task behavior is dropping, and then leveling off, whereas the problem behavior is level for the most part. During the first intervention phase, the on-task behavior increases immediately, and then levels off, while the problem behavior remains uniformly low. In the second baseline period, the on-task behavior has decreased to that seen in the initial baseline period, and the problem behavior has increased above that seen in the initial baseline period. During the second intervention, which only had one session, the on-task behavior increased, and the problem behavior decreased below the average of the previous period. We return to Fig. 8.2 when we discuss the evaluation of single subject designs.

MULTIPLE BASELINE DESIGNS

Multiple baseline single subject designs were introduced more recently than reversal designs. The major reasons for the introduction of multiple baseline designs is that (a) in clinical situations the removal of treatment was often considered unethical, especially if the treatment appeared successful; and (b) many of these studies were being performed when the patient, in one form or another, was responsible for the payment of the treatment. In multiple baseline studies, in the initial stages of the study, as many as three baselines may be recorded simultaneously. These baselines may represent responses of three different *participants*, responses of three different *behaviors* of the same participant, or the responses of the same participant in three different *settings*. The key to multiple baseline single subject studies is that the investigator intervenes at a randomly selected time, and observes the effect on only one of the baselines while the other two baselines should be unchanged. This type of design eliminates the internal validity threat of history because one would expect that if some external event was altering behavior, it would affect all participants, settings, or behaviors, not just one.

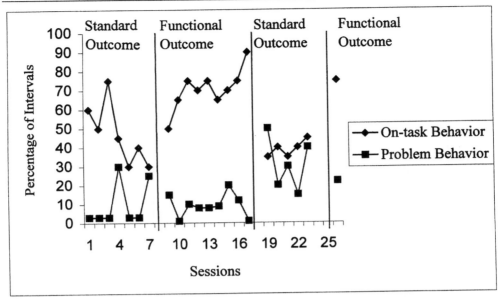

FIG. 8.2.   Results showing the effects of the standard versus functional outcome assignments on on-task and problem behavior. From "Modifying Activities to Produce Functional Outcomes: Effects of the Problem Behaviors of Students with Disabilities," by G. Dunlap, L. Foster-Johnson, S. Clark, L. Kern, and K. E. Childs, 1995, *The Journal of the Association of Persons with Severe Handicaps* (JASH),Vol. 20, No. 4, p. 253. Copyright 1995 by The Association for Severe Handicaps (TASH). Adapted with permission.

Multiple Baseline Across Subjects Designs

The most common multiple baseline design is multiple baseline across subjects. Its popularity is partially as a result of the ease of completing this type of study, especially in a clinical setting. The procedure for carrying out this type of design is as follows. Initially, the investigator selects 3 (or perhaps 4) different participants for the study. All 3 participants are observed concurrently in a baseline phase, and their responses for each baseline period are plotted on a graph (see Fig. 8.3). Next, the investigator gives the intervention to 1 of the participants, while continuing to obtain a baseline on the other 2 participants at the same time. After a given number of periods, the intervention is started with the second participant, continued with the first participant, and a baseline is continued for the third participant. Again, after a number of baseline periods, the intervention is started with the third participant, and continued with the first 2 participants.

An example of a multiple baseline across subjects design can be seen in a study by Bambara and Agar (1992), who examined the frequency of self-directed leisure activities in 3 adults with moderate developmental disabilities. The intervention was self-scheduling. The main point to notice is the staggered baseline across the 3 participants, which is similar to that shown in Fig. 8.3. The first participant, P1, had a baseline of several weeks and then received the intervention. Meanwhile, P2 and P3 continued to be in the baseline condition. After several more weeks, P2 started the intervention, while P3 continued the baseline condition. Finally, P3 received the intervention.

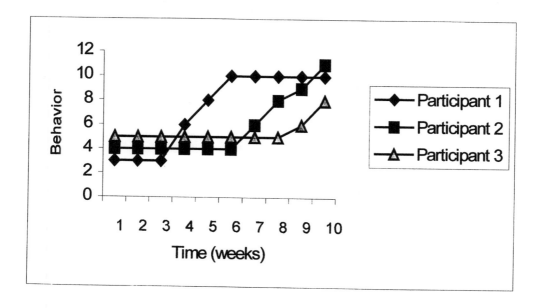

FIG. 8.3.   Results of a multiple baseline arcoss subjects design.

Multiple Baseline Across Behaviors Design

This second type of multiple baseline design is less popular than the multiple baseline across subjects design, especially in clinical settings. The procedure for this type of design is that three different behaviors of the same participant are targeted for change by the investigator. Instead of recording baseline data for 3 different participants, as in multiple baseline across subjects designs, baselines for three different behaviors are recorded concurrently. Then, an intervention is started with one of the behaviors, while baselines continue to be recorded on the other two behaviors.

Next, the second behavior is targeted with an intervention, while the first behavior continues with the intervention. Last, the third behavior is targeted with an intervention, while the other two behaviors continue to receive the intervention. For this type of design to be successful, one must assume that the treatments affect each targeted behavior independently. In other words, when one behavior is being treated, it is important that the other behaviors are not affected. On the other hand, if treating one behavior affects the second behavior, then the design will not be successful because all behaviors will change at the same time. For example, in the field of occupational therapy, where most treatments are assumed to be holistic, it is difficult to find behaviors that would be increased or eliminated by treatments that are independent of each other. On the other hand, the prominent use of operant conditioning techniques in the field of special education makes this type of design ideal because specific behaviors can be targeted without affecting other behaviors.

Multiple Baseline Across Settings Design

This type of multiple baseline design is similar to multiple baseline across behaviors single subject design. Usually a single participant is used in the study. However, in multiple baseline across settings studies, a single behavior is usually targeted, but in at least three different settings. The procedure for this type of design is that baseline responses are collected on 1 participant in three different settings. For example, one setting might be the therapist's office or clinic. A second setting might be at the participant's home. The third setting might be at the participant's school. After a number of baseline periods, intervention could begin at the clinic. During this time, baseline responses at school and at home would still be recorded. Next, after a few periods, intervention might start at home. Meanwhile, no intervention would be attempted at school. Last, the intervention at school would be tried. The multiple baseline across settings single subject design suffers from some of the same problems as the multiple baseline across behaviors design. For the design to be successful, one would expect changes in response in each setting to be independent of each other. However, realistically, a therapist would hope that treatment would generalize across settings, just as it might be expected to generalize across behaviors. If this is the expectation, then multiple baseline across behaviors design and across settings design are probably not good designs to use.

Flexibility, Random Assignment, and Multiple Baseline Designs

One of the strengths of reversal designs is flexibility. If one treatment is not working, why not modify the treatment? More important, a carefully performed reversal single subject design pays close attention to stable baselines. The investigator has the flexibility to wait within a particular phase of the design until the response is stable. On the other hand, the stronger the multiple baseline design, the less flexibility. The key to a strong multiple baseline design is randomly deciding ahead of time which of the 3 participants, behaviors, or baselines will get the intervention first and when the treatment will begin for each participant, behavior, or baseline. Random assignment of treatment to a particular participant, behavior, or setting means that the intervention must go ahead, even if the baseline is not stable, while baselines of other participants, behaviors, or settings might be quite stable. The random assignment lends credibility to the design, but it reduces flexibility considerably. A further problem with random assignment might be that a particular order of interventions with behaviors or settings might be considered advisable. For example, if one is planning a multiple behavior across settings design at clinic, home, and school, it is doubtful that home or school would be planned as a target setting before the clinic. However, random assignment precludes this from happening.

MEASUREMENT PERIODS AND INSTRUMENTS

The number of measurement periods may change between one phase and another in a reversal design. One should wait until each phase is stable before instigating or withdrawing treatment. This adds to the flexibility of the design. On the other hand, each measurement period (session) must be the same length of time. You cannot record responses on a participant for ½ hr one day and 1 hr on the next day. This invalidates the design, because the number of responses per period or session would have no meaning for comparison.

A second measurement issue to consider when performing single subject designs is that the type of instrument selected could seriously compromise the study. Each session must yield a score or a number of responses. If there are a limited number of responses per session, then your instrument may not be sensitive enough for the study. There are two popular types of measures (dependent variables) used in single subject designs: paper–pencil tests and behavioral observation.

Paper–Pencil Tests

These types of instruments, which often are standardized, help insure the internal validity of the study (instrument reliability and statistical validity). However, if you decide to use a standardized instrument such as a paper-and-pencil test, then you must determine both the length of the instrument, and how often you could use it without the participant getting bored, or becoming unreliable in responding. Typically, paper-and-pencil tests are used only once a week and usually in conjunction with some other measure such as observation.

Behavioral Observation

Observation of the participant's behavior is probably the most common form of measure in single subject designs. Certain rules should be followed when using observation.

1. It is best to have the observer be someone different from the teacher, parent, or therapist.
2. It is best to have the observer be as discrete as possible (i.e., a passive observer who is another student, students in the classroom, or an observer watching through a one-way mirror).
3. The critical responses to be judged should be well defined *prior* to the study.
4. More than one judge should be used to record the responses.
5. Interrater reliability should be carried out among judges prior to the study.

EVALUATION OF THE RESULTS OF SINGLE SUBJECT DESIGNS

The early studies using single subject designs, especially those done with rats or pigeons, typically had very stable baselines and intervention periods. In addition, the number of baseline and intervention periods far exceeded those that are used in studies with humans, especially clinical studies. For both of these reasons, the early single subject studies did not use statistical analysis to convince the appropriate audience that interventions were successful. Instead, the investigators believed that the graphic displays were convincing. However, single subject studies with humans, especially reversal designs, usually have fewer baseline and intervention periods than animal studies. In addition, the baseline periods are often shorter and less stable. Perhaps an even greater problem for visual analysis of single subject designs is *serial dependency* (Parsonson & Baer, 1992). Since single subject designs are repeated measures or within subjects designs, a problem arises that each data point is usually not independent from the previous or following data point. In other words, if one knows the value of a particular data point, the value of the next data point could be predicted. It appears that serial dependency may cause inconsistency in agreement on the effect of the intervention in single subject designs. Considering all of these problems, there has been an increasing emphasis given to using some form of statistical analysis in addition to visual analysis.

Visual Analysis of Single Subject Designs

When exploring a single subject graph visually, the key is to look for patterns in the data, especially as the phases change from baseline to intervention, and back to baseline. A reexamination of Fig. 8.2 shows definite changes in on-task behavior as each phase of the study changes. On the other hand, the changes in problem behavior are not as convincing, especially when changing from the first baseline to first intervention phase. Kazdin (1982) discussed the use of certain criteria for visual inspection of single subject designs. One criterion introduced by Kazdin is referred to as *level*. Level is the change from the last measurement in a phase to the first measurement in the next phase. For example, in Fig. 8.2, an increase in level can be seen for the on-task behavior between the first baseline and first intervention periods, and the second baseline and second intervention periods. A decrease in level can be seen between the first intervention period and the second baseline period for the on-task behavior. Sometimes, just examining change in level can be misleading. For example, in Fig. 8.2, notice that the level decreases for problem behavior between the second baseline phase and the second intervention phase. However, careful examination of the problem behavior during the second baseline phase shows a variable pattern of increase and then decrease. From this pattern, one might expect a decrease on the next measurement period, regardless of an intervention. Because the criterion of level does not always reflect the pattern of a particular phase, one could use *mean level*, as a second, more stable criterion (Kazdin, 1982). Mean level refers to the average of the points in one phase compared to the average of the points in the next phase.

A third criterion for visual analysis suggested by Kazdin (1982) was that of *trend*. A trend indicates a definite direction of the points within a phase. The trend could be positive (going up), negative (going down), or flat (going in neither direction). In Fig. 8.2, the trend in on-task behavior during the first baseline phase is negative, but shifts to positive during the first intervention phase. On the other hand, the trend is fairly flat during the first intervention phase for problem behavior.

Ottenbacher (1986) used two more criteria for visual analysis of single subject designs. One criterion for visual analysis recommended by Ottenbacher is that of *variability*. If one looks within any particular phase, a line could be fit through the points in the phase. The amount of distance the point falls from that line is a good measure of the variability within the phase. For example, in Fig. 8.2, the second baseline phase shows a large amount of variability for the problem behavior, yet very little variability for the on-task behavior.

The second criterion for visual analysis suggested by Ottenbacher (1986) was *slope*. The slope refers to the angle of increase or decrease of the measurement points. Slope has become important as an indicator for visual analysis of single subject designs because often, as one shifts from baseline to intervention, the trend may remain the same, but the angle increases during the intervention. This can happen if the baseline period fails to stabilize.

To help evaluate single subject designs, some researchers suggest, in addition to the preceding criteria, that *trend lines* be drawn for each phase of the study. These trend lines could be "split-middle" lines (White, 1974) or least squares regression lines. The split-middle procedure uses medians and produces a trend line through a baseline such that half of the data points are above the line and half are below the line. Conceptually, if this line is extended through the intervention period, then one could judge the effect of the intervention relative to the baseline. If approximately half of the baseline points are above the line and half are below the line during the intervention period, then one could conclude that no effect has taken place. On the other hand, if almost all of the data points are above the line during the intervention, then one would conclude that an effect has taken place. For the split middle or least squares approaches to have meaning, a considerable number of data points must be used. Parsonson and Baer (1992) commented, however, that when judges used trend lines, they tended to ignore some of the other important criteria that were listed earlier.

Statistical Analysis of Single Subject Designs

Although visual analysis has been one of the strengths of single-subject designs, sometimes the data from these designs are not convincing. Therefore, investigators who use these designs have resorted to statistical tests to determine if interventions have made a difference. Kazdin (1982) discussed the use of traditional statistical tests, such as a *t* test to compare the difference between a baseline and intervention period, or a single factor analysis of variance to compare all phases of an *ABAB* design. However, he also cautioned that these tests should not be used if serial dependency existed. Kazdin (1982) suggested the use of time-series analysis when serial dependency problems existed. However, the requirement of at least 20 data points per phase brings these types of analyses for human single subject designs into question because we seldom can afford that many data points (see McCleary & Welsh, 1992 for a more detailed description of time-series analyses in single subject designs).

Nonparametric tests such as the Mann–Whitney U test, the Fisher exact test, and the sign test have also been suggested (Edgington, 1992).

There is an increasing interest in using randomization tests in single subject designs. Levin, Marascuilo, and Hubert (1978) demonstrate the simplicity of this type of procedure. They provide, as an example, the analysis of an *ABAB* design. As we stated earlier, in the traditional reversal design with only two baseline phases and two intervention phases, the results that would be expected are as follows. The lowest level of response would be expected in the first baseline phase. The next lowest level of response would be expected in the second baseline phase. The first intervention phase should have a higher level of response than either of the two baseline phases. The highest level of response should be the second intervention phase. This could be depicted as $A_1 < A_2 < B_1 < B_2$ If one were to hypothesize this outcome, and the results did, in fact, occur in this order, then the probability of this occurrence is 1 in 24 or about .05. The idea is that there are four factorial possible outcomes of two A phases and two B phases, i.e., $4 \times 3 \times 2 \times 1$ possibilities, which equal 24. In addition to the predicted outcome, there are 23 others such as $A_1 > A_2 > A_3 > A_4$. Although this is an oversimplification, randomization tests have become popular in single-subject designs (see Edgington, 1992 for a more in-depth analysis).

CONSIDERATIONS OF INTERNAL AND EXTERNAL VALIDITY OF SINGLE-SUBJECT DESIGNS

Levin et al. (1978) discussed the internal validity and external validity problems in single subject designs. The internal validity problems relate to problems in random assignment. With only 1 participant, there cannot be random assignment of participants to treatments (although the multiple baseline across participants does allow for random assignment to different lengths of the baseline). More important, the order of the treatment phases also cannot be randomly assigned. A third problem is the possible carryover effects from one phase to another. On the other hand, the *ABAB* design reduces the threats of confounding variables (outside influences other than the independent variable). The problems in external validity for single subject designs are even more obvious. The random selection of 1 participant, or even a small number of participants, is unusual because the participants are usually selected because of a particular behavioral or physical problem. However, as stated by Levin et al. (1978), "since the ABAB design has found favor with applied behavioral researchers, for now we will have to accept it as a given and do the best with it we can, despite its limitations" (pp. 171–172).

Although flexibility in trying out different treatments has some advantages, it also has drawbacks. What eventually works for one client or participant may not work for another. Of course, some of the unsuccessful treatments may work for another person. Thus, if we tried many treatments, we should be careful in concluding that the successful treatment will work for all clients or participants.

SUMMARY

We described single subject designs as a subcategory of quasi-experimental time-series designs that can be used with very few participants. Using very few participants increases the flexibility of the design and leads to completely different methods of data analysis. These single subject designs use numerous repeated measures on each participant and the initiation and withdrawal of treatment.

We introduced the two major types of single subject designs, *ABAB* or reversal designs, and multiple baseline designs, and provided examples for both. The *ABAB* design is more flexible than multiple baseline designs, but often takes longer to carry out and is dependent on stable baselines. Multiple baseline designs are easier to carry out, but to insure strong internal validity, random assignment to a particular intervention time period must be instituted. This reduces flexibility in multiple baseline designs.

The methods of measurement for single subject designs are usually observation and paper-and-pencil tests. We discussed their strengths and weaknesses. Two types of evaluation of single subject designs are visual analysis and statistical analysis. One must be cautious when interpreting the results from a single subject design study, especially with respect to external validity.

STUDY AIDS

Concepts

- Behavioral observations
- Level
- Multiple baseline across behaviors design
- Multiple baseline across settings design
- Multiple baseline across subjects design
- Multiple baseline designs
- Paper–pencil tests
- Reversal designs
- Slope
- Trend
- Variability

Distinctions

- Level versus mean level
- Level versus trend versus slope
- Multiple baseline across subjects design versus multiple baseline across behaviors design versus multiple baseline across settings design
- Reversal designs versus multiple baseline designs
- Single subject designs versus traditional group designs

Application Problems

1. An ABAB reversal design is considered to be more flexible than multiple baseline designs. Why?

2. What are the advantages of selecting a multiple baseline across subjects design as compared to a reversal design?

3. An investigator performs a multiple baseline across subjects design. He has three participants in the study, labeled A, B, and C. All three participants will receive the same treatment. After observing the participants for 5 days, the researcher decides to start the treatment with participant B since her baseline was the most stable. After 3 more days, treatment is instigated with participant C since his baseline is more stable than participant A. After 6 more days, treatment is started with participant A. What are the advantages and disadvantages of this method of deciding the order of treatment?

4. You are conducting a study to determine the effects of a specific treatment using a single subject design. You decide to use a reversal design (ABAB). After five sessions, a stable baseline was established (phase A). You introduce your treatment during phase B, and after eight sessions there has been no increase on your measure. You decide to modify your treatment and introduce the new treatment as phase C. After five sessions you notice an increase easily visualized on your graph. What should be your next steps (phases) to establish internal validity?

5. The following single-subject study is an ABA design. Cathy was having a difficult time succeeding at her mail sorting job. Her job coach decided to try a new cuing system with Cathy, which involved verbal redirects when Cathy's attention would get off of her work. For the baseline period, the job coach counted how many letters Cathy could sort in 15 minutes. After eight measurement periods, Cathy had a stable baseline. Her job coach then instituted the verbal redirects, and measured Cathy for eight more measurement periods. After this, the job coach stopped the redirects and measured Cathy for the last eight measurement periods. The measures for each section are listed below:

A	B	A
50	65	60
60	70	65
35	70	65
45	75	70
50	80	70
45	80	65
50	85	60
50	90	65

a. Graph the measurements.
b. Describe how level, trend, and slope relates to the graph.
c. Form a conclusion about the study.

6. The following single-subject study is an ABAB design. Brad is a young man with mental retardation. An occupational therapist (OT) has been as-

signed to assist Brad in learning his job. He is at risk for losing his job because he is forgetting to do certain tasks on a regular basis. The OT decides to try a self-monitoring checklist with Brad to see if that will help him keep track of his duties. For 2 work weeks the OT monitors Brad's work, counting how many assigned tasks Brad completes without cuing. At the end of 2 weeks, she decides to start Brad with a checklist, and count his task completion. After 8 work days, Brad seems to be fairly stable in his work routine. The OT then removes the checklist and monitors Brad for 10 more work days, and counts his task completion. After this period, the OT reinstates the checklist. The measures for each section are listed below:

A	B	A	B
11	17	14	19
12	18	13	20
13	16	14	22
11	18	15	21
12	17	13	23
9	18	13	22
10	18	14	21
11	17	13	22
12		12	23
9		13	23

a. Graph the measurements.
b. Describe how level, trend, and slope relate to the graph.
c. Form a conclusion about the study.

Understanding the Selection and Use of Statisics

CHAPTER

Measurement
and Descriptive Statistics

Study Aids
    Concepts
    Distinctions
    Application Problems

MEASUREMENT

According to S. S. Stevens (1951), "In its broadest sense measurement is the assignment of numerals to objects or events according to rules" (p. 1). As we have seen in chapter 4, the process of research begins with a problem that is made up of a question about the relationship between two or more variables. Measurement is introduced when these variables are operationally defined by certain rules that determine how the participants' responses are translated into numerals. These definitions can include unordered categories in which the numerals do not indicate a greater or lesser degree of the characteristic or the variable. Stevens went on to describe four scales of measurement that he labeled: nominal, ordinal, interval, and ratio. These types of measurements vary from the unordered (nominal) to the highest level (ratio). However, because none of the statistics that are commonly used in social sciences or education require the use of ratio scales, we will not discuss them extensively. Furthermore, this categorization is not the most useful one for determining which statistics are appropriate, so we present an alternative categorization proposed by Helena Chumura Kraemer (personal communication, March 16, 1999).

Before presenting Kraemer's *levels of measurement*, it is important to at least summarize what S. S. Stevens (1951) meant by normal, ordinal, interval, and ratio scales because these terms are seen in the literature. However, first we would like to anticipate some common confusions. Recall, the brief discussion in chapter 4 on ordered versus unordered variables and categorical versus continuous variables. These terms and those for the scale (nominal, ordinal, interval) are sometimes used inconsistently. Figure 9.1 should be helpful in clarifying these somewhat overlapping and confusing terms.

Stevens' Scales of Measurement

Nominal Scales or Variables. These are the most basic or primitive forms of scales in which the numerals assigned to each category stand for the *name* of the category, but have no implied order or value. For example, in a study males may be assigned the numeral 1 and females may be coded as 2. This does not imply that females are higher than males or that two males equal a female or any of the other typical mathematical uses of the numerals. The same reasoning applies to many other true categories such as ethnic groups, type of disability, or section number in a class schedule. In each of these cases the categories are distinct and nonoverlapping, but not ordered; thus each category in the variable ethnic group is different from the other, but there is no necessary order to the categories. Thus, the categories could be numbered 1 for Asian American, 2 for Latin American, 3 for African American, and 4 for European American or the reverse, or any combination of assigning a number to each category. What this implies is that you must *not* treat the numbers that are used for identifying the categories in a nominal scale as if they were numbers that could be used in a formula, added together, subtracted from one another, or used to compute an average. Average ethnic group makes no sense. However, if one asks a computer to do average ethnic group, it will do so and give you meaningless information. The important thing about nominal scales is to have

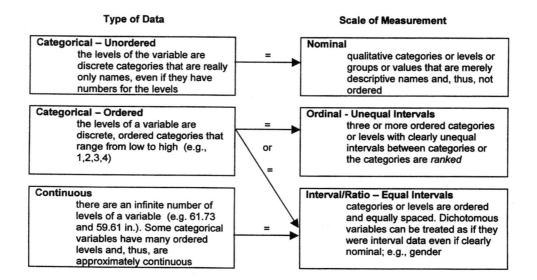

FIG. 9.1. Definitions and correspondence of several measurement terms.

clearly defined, nonoverlapping or mutually exclusive categories that can be coded reliably by observers or by self-report.

It should be pointed out that qualitative or constructivist researchers rely heavily, if not exclusively, on nominal scales and on the process of developing appropriate codes or categories for behaviors, words, and so forth. Qualitative coding may seem different because often it is much more detailed and sophisticated, and because it is unusual to assign numerals to the various categories. Although using qualitative or nominal scales does dramatically reduce the types of statistics that can be used with your data, it does not altogether eliminate the use of statistics to summarize your data and make inferences. Therefore, even when the data are nominal or qualitative categories, one's research may benefit from the use of appropriate statistics. We return shortly to a discussion about the types of statistics, both descriptive and inferential, that are appropriate for nominal data.

Ordinal Scales or Variables (Unequal Interval Scales). In ordinal scales there are not only mutually exclusive categories as in nominal scales, but the categories are ordered from low to high in much the same way that one would *rank* the order in which horses finished a race (i.e., first, second, third, ... last). Thus, in an ordinal scale one knows which participant is highest or most preferred on a dimension, but the intervals between the various ranks are not equal. For example, the second-place horse may finish far behind the winner but only a fraction of a second in front of the third-place finisher. Thus, in this case there are unequal intervals between first, second, and third place with a very small interval between second and third and a much larger one between first and second.

Interval and Ratio Scales or Variables. Interval scales not only have mutually exclusive categories that are ordered from low to high, but the categories are equally spaced; that is, they have equal intervals between them. Most physical measurements (length, weight, money, etc.) have equal intervals between the categories and, in fact, are called ratio scales because they have, in addition, a true zero, which means in the above examples, no length, no weight, or no money. Few psychological scales have this property of a true zero and thus even if they are very well constructed equal interval scales, it is not possible to say that one has no intelligence or no extroversion or no attitude of a certain type. The differences between interval and ratio scales are not important for us, because we can do all of the types of statistics that we have available with interval data. As long as the scale has equal intervals, it is not necessary to have a true zero.

Distinguishing Between Ordinal and Interval Scales. It is usually fairly easy to tell whether categories are ordered or not, so students and researchers can distinguish between nominal and ordinal data. That is good because this distinction makes a lot of difference for which statistics are appropriate, as we shall see. However, it is considerably harder to distinguish between ordinal and interval data. While almost all physical measurements provide either ratio or interval data, the situation is less clear for psychological measurements. When we come to the measurement of psychological characteristics such as attitudes, often we cannot be certain about whether the intervals between the ordered categories are equal, as required for an interval-level scale. Suppose we have a 5-point scale on which we are to rate our attitude about a certain statement from strongly agree as 5 to strongly disagree as 1. The issue is whether the intervals between a rating of 1 and 2, or 2 and 3, or 3 and 4, or 4 and 5 are all equal or not. One could argue, and we often do, that because the numbers are equally spaced on the page and because they are equally spaced in terms of their numerical values, the participants will view them as equal intervals, and thus they will have psychologically equal intervals. However, especially if the in-between points are identified (e.g., strongly agree, agree, neutral, disagree, and strongly disagree), it could be argued that the difference between strongly agree and agree is not the same as between agree and neutral; this contention would be hard to disprove.

Some questionnaire or survey items have responses that are clearly not equal intervals. For example, let's take the case where the participants are asked to identify their age as one of five categories: less than 21, 21 to 30, 31 to 40, 41 to 50, and 51 and above. It should be clear that the first and last categories are much larger for number of years covered than the three middle categories. Thus, the age intervals would not be equal. Another example of an ordered scale that is clearly not interval, would be one that asked how frequently participants do something. The answers go something like this: every day, once a week, once a month, once a year, and once every 5 years. You can see that the categories become wider and wider, and therefore are not equal intervals. There is clearly much more difference between 1 year and 5 years than there is between 1 day and 1 week.

Kraemer's Levels of Measurement

Helena Chumura Kraemer, professor of biostatistics at the Stanford University Medical School, proposed the following four levels of measurement, which are similar to Stevens', but more useful for deciding on an appropriate statistic.

Dichotomous Variables.   A dichotomous variable, one with two levels or categories (e.g., Yes or No, Pass or Fail) is sometimes assumed to be nominal. We contend that, although some such dichotomous variables are clearly nominal (e.g., gender) and others are clearly ordered (e.g., math grades—high and low), all dichotomous variables form a special case (see Table 9.1). Statistics such as the mean or variance would be meaningless for a three-or-more category nominal variable (e.g., ethnic group or marital status, as described earlier). However, such statistics do have meaning when there are only two categories. For example, if the average gender was 1.55 (with males = 1 and females = 2), then 55% of the participants were females. Furthermore, as we show in chapter 19 for multiple regression, dichotomous variables, called "dummy" variables, can be used as independent variables along with other variables that are interval scale. Thus, it is not necessary to decide whether a dichotomous variable is nominal, and it can be treated in some cases as similar to an interval-scale variable.

Nominal Variables.   These variables have three or more unordered categories. This level is the same as Stevens' nominal scale of measurement, so we will not repeat that information.

Ordinal Variables.   These variables have three or more ordered categories. The values of the variable do not have equal spaces between them, or the responses are not normally distributed, or both. Again, this level is similar to Stevens' ordinal scale of measurement, so we will not repeat that information.

Normally Distributed Variables.   These variables not only have mutually exclusive categories that are ordered from low to high, but also the responses or scores are at least approximately normally distributed in the population sampled. Normally distributed is an assumption of many parametric inferential statistics (see chap. 13), and is also important for the appropriate use of a number of the most common descriptive statistics discussed in this chapter (e.g., mean and standard deviation).

Table 9.1 shows this information in tabular form.

Confusion About Terms

Unfortunately, the literature is full of confusing terms to describe the measurement aspects of variables. *Categorical* and *discrete* are sometimes used interchangeably with *nominal*, but we think that nominal is better because it is possible to have ordered, discrete categories. *Continuous, dimensional,* and *quantitative* are terms that you will see in the literature for variables that vary from low to high, and are assumed to be normally distributed.

Most of the preceding information is summarized in the top part of Table 9.2. This should provide a good review of the concept of levels of measurement of a variable. The bottom section of Table 9.2 provides additional information and examples about the appropriate use of various kinds of descriptive statistics for dichotomous, nominal, ordinal, or normal data. We should point out here that it is always important to know the level of measurement of the dependent variable in a study. Also, when the independent variable is an attribute, we should make a judgment about the level measurement. Usually with an ac-

TABLE 9.1

Descriptions of Kraemer's Levels of Measurement

Level	Description
Dichotomous	= 2 categories either unordered or ordered
Nominal	= 3 or more unordered or nominal categories
Ordinal	= 3 or more ordered categories, but clearly unequal intervals between categories or ranks
Normal	= 3 or more ordered categories. Scores on this type of variable are at least approximately a normal (bell-shaped) distribution

tive independent variable, the assumption is that the categories of the independent variable are nominal categories, but in certain cases (drug dosages, for example), even an active independent variable could be measured on an interval level scale such as no drug, 10 mg, 20 mg, and 30 mg.

An example that illustrates three levels of measurement and may be helpful is one of an afternoon at the horse races. The numbers worn by the jockeys represent a nominal scale because the numbers identify the names of the jockeys, but the numbers do not tell us anything else about the jockeys, except perhaps their pole position for a certain race. The betting is based on an ordinal scale: whether the selected horse comes in first, second, or third (i.e., win, place, or show). It does not matter if the horse wins by a nose or by 10 lengths, a win is a win. Thus, these ranks form an ordinal scale that does not necessarily have

TABLE 9.2

Selection of Appropriate Descriptive Statistics for One Dependent Variable

| | *Level or Scale of Measurement of Variable* | | |
	Nominal	*Ordinal*	*Normal*
Characteristics of the variable	- Qualitative data - Not ordered - True categories: only names, labels	- Quantitative data - Ordered data - Rank order only	- Quantitative data - Ordered data - Normally distributed
Examples	- Gender, school, curriculum type, hair color	- 1st, 2nd, 3rd place, ranked preferences	- Height, good test scores, good rating scales
Frequency distribution	Redhead- 33% Blond- 44% Brunette - 22%	Best - 37% Better - 37% Good - 25%	5 - 9% 4 - 18% 3 - 27% 2 - 27% 1 - 22%
Frequency polygon	No[a]	OK[b]	Yes[c]
Bar graph or chart	Yes	Yes	OK
Box and whiskers plot	No	Yes	Yes
Central Tendency			
Mean	No	No	Yes
Median	No	Yes	OK
Mode	Yes	OK	OK
Variability			
Standard deviation	No	No	Yes
Interquartile range	No	Yes	OK
How many categories	Yes	OK	OK

[a] No means not appropriate at this level of measurement.
[b] OK means not the best choice at this level of measurement.
[c] Yes means a good choice with this level of measurement.

equal intervals. However, the money you receive, if you picked a winner, is normally distributed.

THE NORMAL CURVE

Figure 9.2 is an example of a normal curve. Many of the dependent variables used in the behavioral sciences that are scaled at the interval or ratio level fit a normal curve. Examples of such variables that fit a normal curve are height, weight, and many psychological variables. Notice that for each of these examples, most people would fall toward the middle of the curve, with fewer people at the extremes. If the average height of men in the United States were 5ft 10in., then this measure would be in the middle of the curve. The heights of men who are taller than 5ft 10in. would be to the right of the middle on the curve, and those of men who are shorter than 5ft 10in. would be to the left of the middle on the curve.

The normal curve can be thought of as derived from a frequency distribution. It is theoretically formed from counting an "infinite" number of occurrences of a variable. Usually when the normal curve is depicted, only the X axis (abscissa) is shown. To determine how a frequency distribution is obtained, you could take a fair coin, and flip it 10 times, and record the number of heads on this first set or trial. Then flip it another 10 times and record the number of heads. If you had nothing better to do, you could do 100 trials. (We hope you have something better to do with your time.) After performing this task, you could plot the number of times, out of each trial of 10 that the coin turned up heads. What would you expect? Of course, the largest number of trials probably would show 5 heads out of 10. There would be very few, if any trials, where

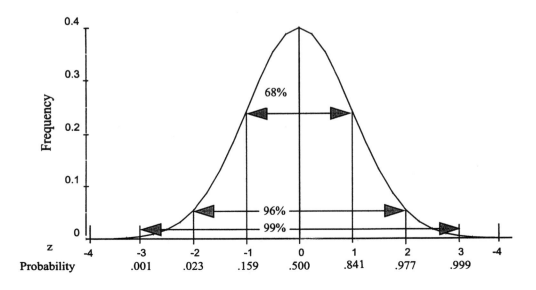

FIG. 9.2.   Frequency distribution and probability distribution for the Normal curve.

0, 1, 9, or 10 heads occur. It could happen, but the probability is low, which brings us to a probability distribution. If we performed this experiment 100 times, or 1,000 times, or 1,000,000 times, the frequency distribution "fills in" and looks more and more like a normal curve.

The normal curve is also a probability distribution. Visualize that the area under the normal curve is equal to 1.0. Therefore, portions of this curve could be expressed as fractions of 1.0. For example, if we assume that 5ft 10in. is the average height of men in the United States, then the probability of a man being 5ft 10in. or taller is .5. The probability of a man being over 6ft 5in. or less than 5ft 5in. is considerably smaller. It is important to be able to conceptualize the normal curve as a probability distribution because statistical convention sets acceptable probability levels for rejecting the null hypothesis at .05 or .01. As we shall see, when events or outcomes happen infrequently, that is, only 5 times in 100 or 1 time in 100 (way out in the left or right tail of the curve), we wonder if they belong to that distribution or perhaps to a different distribution. We return to this point numerous times later in the book.

Properties of the Normal Curve

The normal curve has five properties that are always present.

1. The normal curve is unimodal. It has one "hump," and this hump is in the middle of the distribution. The most frequent value is in the middle.
2. The mean, median, and mode are equal.
3. The curve is symmetric. If you folded the normal curve in half, the right side would fit perfectly with the left side; that is, it is not *skewed*.
4. The range is infinite. This means that the extremes approach but never touch the X axis.
5. The curve is neither too peaked nor too flat and its tails are neither too short nor too long; it has no *kurtosis*. Its proportions are like those in Fig. 9.2.

Areas Under the Normal Curve

All normal curves, regardless of whether they are narrow or spread out, can be divided into areas or units in terms of the standard deviation. Approximately 34% of the area under the normal curve is between the mean and one standard deviation above or below the mean. If we include both the area to the right and to the left of the mean, 68% of the area under the normal curve is within one standard deviation from the mean. Another 13.5% of the area under the normal curve is accounted for by adding a second standard deviation to the first standard deviation. In other words, two standard deviations to the right of the mean accounts for an area of approximately 47.5%, and two standard deviations to the left and right of the mean make up an area of approximately 95% of the normal curve. If we were to subtract 95% from 100%, the remaining 5% relates to that ever-present probability or *p* value of .05 needed for statistical significance. Values not falling within two standard deviations of the mean are seen as relatively rare events.

The Standard Normal Curve

All normal curves can be converted into standard normal curves by setting the mean equal to zero and the standard deviation equal to one. Because all normal curves have the same proportion of the curve within one standard deviation, two standard deviations, or more of the mean, this conversion allows comparisons among normal curves with different means and standard deviations. Figure 9.2, of the normal distribution, has the standard normal distribution units underneath. These units are referred to as z scores. If you examine the normal curve table in any statistics book, you can find the areas under the curve for one standard deviation ($z = 1$), two standard deviations ($z = 2$), and so forth. Any normal distribution can be converted into a standard normal distribution.

DESCRIPTIVE STATISTICS

The Importance of Levels of Measurement for Descriptive Statistics

The bottom of Table 9.2 also illustrates whether and how a number of familiar descriptive statistics would be used if the data (i.e., dependent variable) were nominal, ordinal, or normally distributed. Frequency distributions would look similar in all three cases; the only difference is that with nominal data the order in which the categories are listed is arbitrary. Thus, we have listed redhead, blond, and then brunette. If there are three redheads, four blonds, and two brunettes, then 33%, 44%, and 22% are in each category. However, redheads could be put after brunettes or between blonds and brunettes because the categories are not ordered. In ordinal data you can see that the order would be invariant. For normally distributed data, the frequency distribution would look similar to the normal curve in Fig. 9.2.

Frequency distributions indicate how many participants are in each category, whether those be ordered or unordered categories. If one wants to make a diagram of a frequency distribution there are several choices: three of them are frequency polygons, a bar chart, and box and whisker plots. As shown in Table 9.2 and in Fig. 9.3, a frequency polygon or histogram, which connects the points between the categories, is best used with normal data. Frequency polygons should not be used with nominal data, because there is no necessary ordering of the points. Thus it is better to make a bar graph or chart of the frequency distribution of variables like gender, ethnic group, school curriculum, or other nominal variables because the points that happen to be adjacent in your frequency distribution are not by necessity adjacent (see Fig. 9.4).

For ordinal and normal data, the box and whisker plot is useful (see Fig. 9.5); it should not be used with nominal data, because with nominal data there is no necessary ordering of the response categories. The box and whisker plot is a graphical representation of the distribution of scores and is helpful, as indicated in the following section, in distinguishing between ordinal and normally distributed data (see Tukey, 1977).

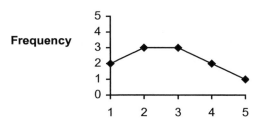

FIG. 9.3.   Sample frequency polygons for normal-level data.

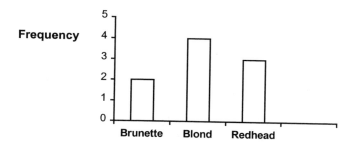

FIG. 9.4.   Sample frequency distribution bar chart for the nominal scale of hair color.

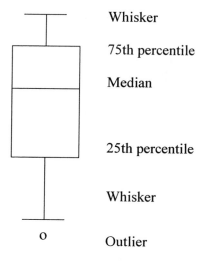

FIG. 9.5.   A box and whisker plot for ordinal and normal data.

Measures of Central Tendency

Three main measures of the center of a distribution are available: mean, median, and mode. As you can see from Table 9.2, any of them can be used with normal data, whereas with ordinal data, the mean is usually not appropriate. The *mean* or arithmetic average takes into account all of the available information in computing the central tendency of a frequency distribution; thus, it is usually the statistic of choice, assuming that one has normal data. The *median* or middle score is an appropriate measure of central tendency for ordinal level data. The median may be a better measure of central tendency than the mean under certain circumstances, namely, when the frequency distribution is skewed markedly to one side. For example, the median income of 100 midlevel workers and a millionaire is substantially lower and reflects the central tendency of the group better than the average income, which would be inflated in this example, and for the country as a whole by a few people who make very large amounts of money. For normally distributed data, the median is in the center of the box and whisker plot. Notice that in Fig. 9.5 the median is not in the center of the box. Finally, the *mode*, or most common category, can be used with any kind of data but generally provides you with the least precise information about central tendency. One would use the mode as the measure of central tendency if there is only one mode, it is clearly identified, and you want a quick noncalculated measure.

We demonstrate the calculation of the mean here, because of its common use in both descriptive and inferential statistics. The formula for the population mean called μ is the same as the formula for the sample mean called ($\overline{X}$). To calculate the mean or average of a set of numbers, we add or sum (Σ) the numbers (X), and then divide by the number of entries (N). We use capital X to refer to individual scores (often referred to as raw scores).

The formula for the sample mean (*) is as follows:

$$\overline{X} = \frac{\Sigma X}{N}, \tag{1}$$

*Where: X = individual or raw scores in the sample, and
N = the number of scores in the sample.

Calculation of the Mean.   Suppose that 10 people took a test that we will call Form B. We want to know the mean of the 10 scores. The scores are shown in Table 9.3.

We calculate the mean by using Equation 1:

$$\overline{X} = \frac{\Sigma X}{N}$$

$$\overline{X} = \frac{700}{10}$$

$$\overline{X} = 70.$$

TABLE 9.3
Scores for Ten Participants on Form B

Participant	Form B
1	75
2	62
3	93
4	66
5	77
6	63
7	54
8	43
9	82
10	85

Measures of Variability

Variability tells us about the spread or dispersion of the scores. In the extreme, if all of the scores in a distribution are the same, there is no variability. If they are all different and widely spaced apart, the variability will be high. You can see from Table 9.2 that the standard deviation, the most common measure of variability, is only appropriate when one has normally distributed data.

For ordinal data, the *interquartile range*, seen in the box plot (Fig. 9.5) by the distance between the top and bottom of the box, is the best measure of variability. Note that the whiskers indicate the expected range and scores outside that range are shown as outliers. The presence of *outliers* is a warning of non-normality or errors with the data. With nominal data one would need to ask how many different categories there are and what are the percentages in each.

Calculation of the Standard Deviation.   Because it is common in both descriptive and inferential statistics, we show how to calculate the standard deviation.

The formula for the sample standard deviation (s) is as follows:

$$s = \sqrt{\frac{\Sigma x^2}{N-1}}. \qquad (2)$$

In this formula we are going to sum the squares of numbers, but notice that the numbers that we square and add are not raw scores (large Xs), but deviation scores (the mean subtracted from each raw score), because the standard deviation is a measure of how scores vary about the mean. We will do an example calculation of the standard deviation by using the same sample of scores that we used for the mean in the previous section.

We start by creating Table 9.4 from the scores on Form B. The procedure is as follows as seen in Table 9.4. We subtract the mean, 70, from each of the raw scores.

TABLE 9.4

Calculation of the Standard Deviation

Participant	X (Form B Score)	$\bar{X}$	x	x^2
1	75	70	5	25
2	62	70	−8	64
3	93	70	23	529
4	66	70	−4	16
5	77	70	7	49
6	63	70	−7	49
7	54	70	−16	256
8	43	70	− 27	729
9	82	70	12	144
10	85	70	15	225
Total				2,166

These deviation scores can be seen under the column x. If we added these scores, the total would be zero. (The sum of the deviations around the mean always equals zero. This property of the mean becomes important when we consider degrees of freedom of the t test in chapter 14.) Next we square each of the deviation scores in column x, which gives us the scores in column x^2. Then we add the scores in column x^2, which yields the number 2,166. We divide this number by the number of participants minus one and take the square root to arrive at the standard deviation.

We complete the calculation of the standard deviation as follows:

$$s = \sqrt{\frac{\Sigma x^2}{N-1}}$$

$$s = \sqrt{\frac{2166}{9}}$$

$$s = \sqrt{240.67}$$

$$s - 15.51.$$

The calculation of the standard deviation is conceptually easy to follow. One problem is that the sample mean is not usually an even number, making subtraction tedious and possibly leading to calculation errors. The raw score formula looks worse, but is easier to accomplish because we are dealing with the original numbers or scores.

The raw score formula for the sample standard deviation is as follows:

$$s = \sqrt{\frac{\Sigma X^2 - \frac{(\Sigma X)^2}{N}}{N-1}}. \tag{3}$$

CONCLUSIONS ABOUT MEASUREMENT AND THE USE OF STATISTICS

First, researchers should try to measure each construct on the highest level consistent with reliability and validity. The accuracy of estimation and the power of tests depends strongly on how sensitive the measurement is to individual differences among participants and on access to the more powerful parametric methods. Thus, given the choice, one would hope to obtain sounder results by using normal level data than by using ordinal level data, and ordinal measurement rather than nominal measurement. However, sacrificing reliability or validity to have a higher level of measurement means that you will have greater accuracy or power to get the wrong answers!

Second, researchers also should use the most powerful methods consistent with the nature of their data. Thus, as we discuss in chapters 13 and 14, independent samples t tests, which are based on the means and standard deviation, are valid for normal data with equal variances in the two groups being compared. Typically, they are the most powerful tests available to compare two groups. However, if the data are ordered but grossly non-normal, or normal but with grossly unequal variances, the two-sample t test may not give the right answers. Then the Mann–Whitney (M–W) nonparametric test would be preferred. The sacrifice in power is relatively minor. However, the M–W test requires ordinal data. So, if the data were nominal or dichotomous, one would use instead the chi-square contingency test. Then there would be a major sacrifice in power. Thus, a researcher who chooses to dichotomize normal data and use the chi-square (often done) is being very wasteful. A researcher who uses the t test for nominal data (seldom done) would produce misleading results.

SUMMARY

The chapter provides an overview of levels of measurement and how they influence the appropriate use of statistics. We divide variables into four levels: dichotomous, nominal, ordinal, and normally distributed. Dichotomous variables have only two levels; nominal have three or more unordered levels. Ordinal variables have three or more ordered levels, but, like ranks, the intervals between levels are not equal. Finally, normal variables have at least approximately a normal (bell-shaped) frequency distribution. Properties of the normal curve are discussed because many statistics assume that responses are normally distributed, and many behavioral variables are distributed at least approximately normally. Three ways of plotting frequency distributions (frequency polygons, box and whisker plots, and bar charts) are described and illustrated. Similarly, the three measures of central tendency (mean, median, and mode) are described, as are three measures of variability (standard deviation, interquartile range, and number of categories).

STUDY AIDS

Concepts

- Box and whisker plot
- Interquartile range
- Normal distribution or curve
- Outlier
- Skewness
- Standard deviation
- Standard normal curve

Distinctions

- Dichotomous versus nominal versus ordinal versus normal levels of measurement
- Mean versus median versus mode
- Nominal versus ordinal versus interval scales of measurement
- Ordered versus unordered categories or levels of a variable

Application Problems

1. Name and describe Stevens' four levels of measurement; provide examples.
2. How are Kraemer's levels of measurement similar and different from Stevens'?
3. Why is it important to know or determine the level of measurement for your data?
4. Which measures of central tendency are appropriate to use with data at each level or scale of measurement?
5. For the examples below, state the level or scale of measurement:
   a. Urban, suburban, rural
   b. Young, middle-aged, old
   c. 15,16,17,18, 19, 20, 21 … years
   d. Strongly agree, agree, neutral, disagree, strongly disagree
6. Both dichotomous variables and nominal variables are categorical. Why is it informative to calculate the mean with a dichotomous variable, but not with a nominal variable?
7. How does the normal curve differ from the standard normal curve?
8. The following scores were recorded from students in a statistics class. Determine the mean, median, mode, and standard deviation.
   89, 93, 81, 93, 73, 93, 85, 89, 75, 85, 90, 70
9. A student in a large undergraduate class (approximately 500) scores one standard deviation above the mean on her first midterm. Her score is higher than what percentage of the class?
10. Another student in this same class scores two standard deviations below the mean. What percentage of students have higher scores?

10

Sampling and External Validity

WHAT IS SAMPLING?

Sampling is the process of selecting *part* of a larger group of participants with the intent of generalizing from the smaller group, called the sample, to the population, the larger group. If we are to make valid inferences about the population, we must select the sample so that it is representative of the total population.

Political pollsters and market researchers have developed and refined the process of sampling so that they are usually able to estimate accurately the voting or purchasing intentions of the population of the United States from samples as small as a few hundred participants. We are all familiar with public opinion and voting surveys that are usually done by telephone interviewers, who may use random digit dialing techniques to select the persons whom they choose to call. If the questions are clear and the participants answer them truthfully and accurately, a random sample of approximately 1,000 participants is enough to predict, within plus or minus 3%, what the whole population of the United States would say or feel about a certain issue.

You may also be familiar with the Nielsen television ratings that are based on information gathered about the TV viewing of a few thousand presumably representative households. These ratings are then extrapolated to indicate the presumed percentage of the total TV-viewing population of the United States that would have watched a certain show, and this determines advertising rates. A similar Nielsen system, called Scantrack, has been developed to assess the specific shopping behaviors of a small sample of American consumers. Consumers scan the bar codes on the items that they purchase so that Nielsen can report to manufacturers information not only about the number and types of items purchased, but, perhaps more importantly, profiles of the people who are buying.

With a few notable exceptions, these modern survey techniques have proven to be useful and accurate in predicting or reporting information about the attitudes and behaviors of the American public. Historically, however, there have been examples of major miscalculations that can be traced in part to inadequate sampling techniques. One of the often-cited examples is that of the grossly erroneous prediction, by a *Literary Digest* poll, of a sample of several million respondents, that Franklin Roosevelt would lose the 1936 presidential election, when, in fact, he won by a landslide. One of the problems with this poll was that the sample was selected from automobile registrations, telephone directories, and other related sources. This led to oversampling of affluent and higher educated individuals who were not representative of the voting public, especially during the middle of the Great Depression. In addition, only about 20% of the selected sample actually returned their questionnaires. Thus, one needs to obtain a representative sample to describe a population for marketing or election purposes.

Advantages of Sampling

Selecting less than the total population is an advantage for researchers for several reasons. First, it is less expensive to interview, observe, or send surveys to a smaller group of people than to a very large one. Second, it clearly takes less time to study a sample of participants than it would to study a whole population. Third, better quality control can be obtained if one has a reasonable amount of time to devote to the assessment of each participant rather than trying to spread oneself too thin over a larger group.

Key Concepts

It is necessary to define a few key concepts related to sampling to understand sampling as it occurs in the research reported in the social science and education literature. Figure 10.1 should help you visualize these key concepts and the relationships among them.

Participants, Cases, or Elements.   These are the people or objects or events that are of interest in a particular study. In the social sciences the participants are usually individual people (children or adults), but they also could be

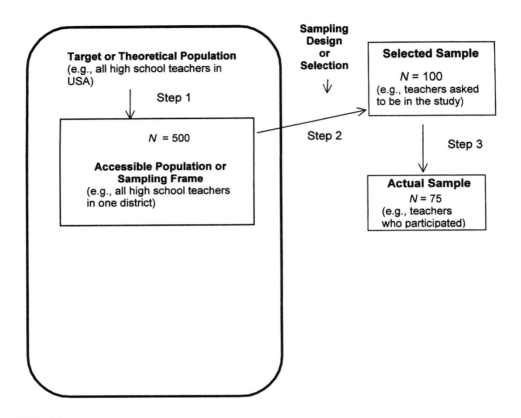

FIG. 10.1.   Schematic diagram of the sampling process.

groups of people such as married couples, siblings, families, teams, schools, and so on. They could be animals such as white rats, or events such as television programs or car accidents.

Theoretical or Target Population.   This includes all of the participants of theoretical interest to the researcher and to which he or she would like to generalize. Examples of theoretical populations are all third-grade children in the United States, all Hispanic males in the Southwest, and all women over 80 years in the world. It is rarely possible to study or even sample these target or theoretical populations for both economic and practical reasons. We usually do not have access to such broad groups, especially if we are attempting to observe or measure them in a face-to-face situation. Unfortunately, the theoretical population is usually not specified in published research articles. One has to infer it from the context and any generalizations made in the results and discussion.

Accessible Population.   This is sometimes called the survey population and frequently called the *sampling frame.* As the name implies, the accessible population is the group of participants to which the researcher has access, perhaps through a telephone or membership directory. The accessible population might also be an organization or group such as a class to which the researcher has entry. Examples of accessible populations might be the third graders in a particular school or school district, Hispanic men who belong to certain fraternal organizations in selected cities in the Southwest, or couples who are on a mailing list developed by an international marketing firm.

Selected Sample.   This is the smaller group of participants who are selected from the larger accessible population by the researcher and asked to participate in the study. In some cases, the accessible population may be so small, or defined so narrowly, or both, that it is not necessary to sample the participants. Rather, every participant in the accessible population is asked to participate in the study. Unless this accessible population is representative of the theoretical population, this selected sample is called a convenience sample, even though no actual sampling was done at this step.

The selection can be performed in several different ways as described following under Types of Sampling. The point is that the selected sample is composed of the participants that the researcher has selected, but not all of this sample necessarily participates in the study.

There are many reasons that participants in the selected sample do not end up in the actual data for the study. Some decline participation, perhaps, by not returning the researcher's questionnaire or by telling the telephone interviewer that they do not wish to participate. Others have moved or are not able to be reached on the telephone. Still others may drop out later in the process, either by returning a partially completed questionnaire or by providing answers that are judged to be suspect or, perhaps, by dropping out in the middle of the study.

Actual sample.   These are the participants who complete the study and whose data are actually used in the data analysis and in the report of the study's results. The ratio of the size of the actual sample to the selected sample is known as the *response rate*. A low response rate may lower the quality of the sample, or even make the study invalid, if the persons who responded are different in important ways from those who did not respond. Thus, in evaluating research it is important to know the response rate and to know whether the responders were similar to nonresponders.

Sampling Design.   This is the process by which the selected sample is chosen. Several of the most often used sampling designs are described later under Types of Sampling, Probability Sampling, and Nonprobability Sampling.

Strata.   These are variables (e.g., race, geographical region, age, or gender) that could be used to divide the population into segments. The researcher is usually knowledgeable about these dimensions and assumes that they are important in obtaining a representative sample. The strata are used, as described following, in obtaining a stratified random sample. They are also used in specifying the quotas in a quota sample.

Clusters.   Sometimes called sampling units, clusters are collections or groups of potential participants that do not overlap. The participants in a given cluster are usually geographically grouped together. Clusters include towns, schools, and hospitals; they are important for cluster probability sampling, which is described later in the chapter.

Representative Sample.   By representative, we mean a sample that represents the population, that is, is a small replica of the population. It has, on all of the key variables, the same proportions as in the whole population. Each participant represents a known fraction of the theoretical population so that the characterization of the population can be re-created from the sample. A representative sample is most likely obtained by using the techniques described below as probability sampling.

Steps in Selecting a Sample and Generalizing Results

There are many ways to select a sample from a population. The goal is to have an actual sample that is *representative* of the target or theoretical population. Obtaining a representative sample is not easy, because things can go wrong at several stages of the research process. Figure 10.1 shows the concepts that we have described and also the three steps (shown with arrows) from the theoretical population to the actual sample.

The first step is from the theoretical population to the accessible population. It may be that the accessible population or sampling frame is not representative of the theoretical population. This is a common problem because researchers often do not have access to the geographical, socioeconomic, or other range of participants to which they would like to make inferences or generalizations. Often, especially if we need to measure participants in a face-to-face contact, we are limited to a specific location and to groups that are available to us such as persons in a certain school, hospital, or organization.

The second step in the sampling process is called the *sampling design* or selection of participants. This step, between the accessible population and the selected sample, is the step that is usually described in the methods section of articles and is the step over which the researcher has the most control. We expand on this step in the next section, Types of Sampling.

The third step takes place between the selected sample and the actual sample. The problem here is that participants may not respond to the invitation to participate, or may drop out of the study, or both, so that the actual sample may be considerably smaller than the selected sample; that is, there is a low response rate. The actual sample may be unrepresentative of the selected sample. This is often a problem with mailed surveys, especially if the survey is sent to busy people such as small business owners. In these cases, less than 25% of the questionnaire recipients may return them. Thus, even if the selected sample was representative of the theoretical population, the actual sample may be unrepresentative.

TYPES OF SAMPLING

There are two major types of sampling designs or procedures that are used in obtaining the selected sample: probability and nonprobability sampling techniques. *Probability sampling* involves the selection of participants in a way that is nonbiased. In a probability sample, every participant or element of the population has a known, nonzero probability of being chosen to be a member of the sample (Stuart, 1984). In *nonprobability sampling*, there is no way of estimating the probability that each participant has of being included in the sample. Therefore, bias is usually introduced. Nonprobability samples are used when probability samples, which rely on random or systematic selection of participants, are not feasible. The advantages of nonprobability samples are economy and convenience. In fact, most published studies in the social sciences and education use nonprobability sampling, or the entire accessible population, if it is small. These samples may be useful in examining the relationship between variables or the differences between groups, but they are clearly not the best way to describe or make generalizations about the whole population.

Probability Sampling

When probability sampling is used, inferential statistics enable researchers to estimate the extent to which results from the sample are likely to differ from what we would have found by studying the entire population. Four types of probability sampling are described briefly.

  1. Simple Random Sampling.   The best known and most basic of the probability sampling techniques is the simple random sample, which can be defined as a sample in which all participants or elements have an equal and independent chance of being included in the sample. If we put 100 pieces of paper (numbered from 1 to 100) in a hat, shake the hat, and draw out 10 without replacing them, this process would approximate a simple random sample. In such a sample, each participant has an equal and independent chance of being selected or picked as 1 of the 10 persons to be asked to participate in the study. This type of probability sample will produce a representative sample if the number of participants selected is relatively large. However, if the number selected is small, like the 10 numbers drawn from the hat, the sample might not be a small replica of the total population.

  In an actual research study we would draw or select our random sample by using a random number table or computer-generated random numbers rather than by selecting numbers out of a hat. Assuming that there are 900 participants in the accessible population, all of the possible participants in the accessible population or sampling frame would be listed and numbered from 1 to 900 . Then, if we decided to select a sample of 90, we would start by unsystematically picking a starting point in the random number table and proceeding in a systematic and planned manner down the rows or across the columns to select the first 90 nonrepeated numbers listed in the random number table. Table 10.1 is an example of a small part of a random number table. (Complete tables can be found in most statistics books.) To select numbers from 001 to 900, one would need three digits, so one could use, for example, the three right-hand columns in the set of random numbers. Let's say we started by nonsystematically picking the number 11508, which is about halfway down the left-hand set of 5-digit numbers. The three right-hand digits are 508, so the first participant to be selected would be number 508, the second participant would be number 449, and the third 515. However, we would skip number 986 because that number is outside the range of 1 to 900 in the sampling frame. We would continue down the list by skipping numbers larger than 900 and any that had already been picked until we had selected 90 of the original 900 potential participants for this simple random sample.

Although the simple random sample is the prototype of a probability sampling method, it is used relatively infrequently, in part because it may be time consuming to number the entire list, if it is long. Also, many times there is no list of the population of interest. A more frequent equivalent of the simple random sample is systematic sampling with a random start, which will be discussed next. To use either simple random or systematic sampling, the population has to be finite and there has to be a list or directory of persons in the population.

2. Systematic Random Sampling.   To obtain this type of sample, we start by using the random number table to select a number between 1 and 10 because, as in the previous example, we have decided on a one-tenth sample of the population. If we randomly selected, for example, the fourth person on the list as the first participant, then we would systematically select every tenth participant, starting from the fourth. Thus, the sample would include the person on the list who was 4th, 14th, 24th, 34th, and so on, and would include 90 participants. Some research books warn against systematic samples if a list is ordered, especially in a reoccurring pattern, which would have a differential effect on the resulting sample, depending on where one started. For example, suppose we had a list of 90 youth soccer teams, each of which had 10 players, and their goalie was always the fourth person listed for each team. If we used the selection process from our example, starting randomly with number four, we would select only goalies for this 90-person sample (or no goalies if the random start had begun at a different number). Thus, we should examine the list with the interval (e.g., 10) to be used in mind. However, Fowler (1993) states that this is rarely a problem and in al-

TABLE 10.1

Small Section of a Random Number Table

55515	81899	04153	79401
46375	81953	etc.	etc.
15792	35101		
37824	etc.		
11508			
37449			
46515			
30986			
63798			

most all cases a systematic sample with a random start will produce the equivalent of a simple random sample.

3. *Stratified Random Sampling.*   If important characteristics of the accessible population or sampling frame, such as gender or race, are known ahead of time (i.e., are noted on the sampling frame), then we can reduce the sampling variation and increase the likelihood that the sample will be representative of the population by stratifying the sample on the basis of these key variables. In our previous example, suppose that we wanted to be sure that a representative number of goalies was chosen as part of the sample. We would use a stratified random sampling technique. The list or sampling frame would be rearranged so that all the goalies were listed together, and then one tenth of them would be selected randomly with either a simple random sampling technique or a systematic sampling technique with a random start. The same techniques could be used for selecting a sample from each of the other positions. Stratifying ensures that the sample contains exactly the proportion of goalies (one tenth) as in the overall population.

When participants are geographically spread across the country or a state, it is common to stratify from geography so that appropriate proportions of the selected sample come from the different regions of the country or state. It is also common to stratify on the rural, suburban, and urban characteristics of the sample if these are identifiable in the sampling frame.

We would now like to describe two more complex types of sampling. One is a variant of the stratified sampling procedure just described, and the second is a multistage sampling procedure designed to make sampling geographically diverse participants more practical.

3a. *Stratified Sampling With Differential Probabilities of Selection.*   Sometimes stratified sampling will lead to one or more sizable groups of participants and one or more very small groups of participants. For example, if we wanted to compare various ethnic groups, the number of Hispanics, African Americans, and especially Asian Americans and Native Americans would be small in a moderate-sized sample that was representative of the total population of the country. If we wanted to compare different ethnic groups, it is desirable to have the groups equal or at least of a substantial size (maybe 30 or more). Therefore, one might want to oversample the minority group members to have enough in each group to make reasonable comparisons with the Caucasian or White sample.

In our example of the soccer teams, the goalies would be similar to minority ethnic group members in that, if we did a one-tenth sample of the 90 goalies, we would end up with a sample of only 9 goalies, which is too small for reasonable comparisons with the group of nongoalies. We might, for example, want to sample half of the 90 goalies to get a large enough sample to compare.

We should take caution because, if we draw conclusions later about a total population from the sample, adjustment for the fact that the group had been oversampled would need to be undertaken. That is, if we were interested in the height of soccer players, we could not just take the average of the heights of the oversampled goalies and of the nongoalies. We would have to weight the goalies less so that the overall average height would not be distorted by the fact that there were five times as many goalies in our sample as would be representative of the population.

4. Cluster (Random) Sampling.   Cluster sampling is a two-stage sampling procedure that is especially useful when the population is spread out geographically, or there is no single overall list of individuals in the accessible population, or both. The basic strategy is to first select specific clusters or groups of participants by using a probability sampling method such as simple random sampling. The second stage is to randomly select all, or a proportion of, participants from the clusters.

Take, for example, the situation where we are interested in sampling one tenth of the students from a large number of schools. The task of going to each of, say, 100 schools and selecting 1 out of every 10 students would be difficult in terms of time and expense. A less expensive alternative would be to select randomly 1 out of five schools (i.e., 20), and then randomly select half of the students in those schools as the one-tenth sample. There are, of course, various combinations of the proportions that one might be selected on the first step and on the second step. For example, a common strategy is to randomly select just enough geographically compact clusters (e.g., schools or communities) so that one will have the needed number of participants if one selected all of the students in the selected clusters and did not select any students from the other schools (i.e., select 10 schools and then all students from those 10 schools). Some precision in sampling is sacrificed because the sample of schools, even if randomly selected, could be unrepresentative of the larger population of schools, but often cost considerations outweigh this minor loss in precision.

Concluding Comments on Probability Sampling.   Figure 10.2 provides diagrams of the five probability sampling methods that we just described. Notice that all of them involve randomization at some point in the process of selecting participants. However, they differ in whether the accessible population is stratified in some way (indicated by horizontal lines) and in what proportion a stratum or cluster is selected. The numbers in the boxes represent a single potential participant and his or her subject number. These diagrams do not include all of the possible combinations of the four main sampling strategies, but give a good idea of the methods used by researchers who attempt to obtain a representative sample and a high population external validity. With a probability sample, descriptive statistics from the sample also describe the population. However, with stratified samplings with different proportions, one would need to weight the results appropriately to describe the population.

Nonprobability Sampling

Nonprobability samples are those in which the probability of being selected is unknown, often because there is no sampling frame or list of the members of the accessible population. Time and cost constraints also lead researchers and pollsters to use nonprobability samples. Although nonprobability samples

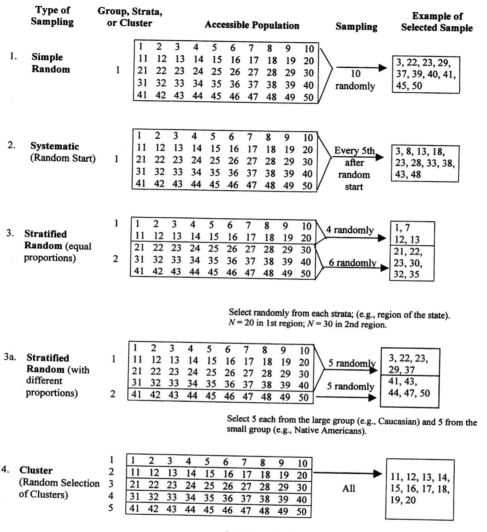

FIG. 10.2. Schematic diagrams of five probability sampling methods for a sample of 10 from an accessible population of 50.

may appear to be similar to probability samples in the demographics of the selected participants, the results can be distorted, and the assumptions of probability theory and sampling error do not apply. The first type of nonprobability sampling, quota sampling, is often used by public opinion pollsters, political pollsters, and market researchers because the resulting samples look representative of the population and the cost of obtaining the data is considerably less than would be required to obtain a probability sample.

Quota Sampling.   In quota sampling, the investigator sets certain parameters for the interviewers he or she has hired to follow, but some degree of latitude or discretion is allowed in the selection of the actual participants. For example, the interviewer may be directed to certain city blocks or telephone exchanges that may have been chosen randomly or in some other way to be representative, and then is asked to find and interview a certain number of participants from each block or telephone exchange. It is possible that there may even be further restrictions such as obtaining a certain proportion of men and women, younger and older participants, and so forth, but the actual participants are selected by the interviewer because they are home and willing to participate when asked. This technique saves money in part because participants who are not available are not called back. In house-to-house surveying, the interviewer may be tempted to skip certain households, that is, those that are located on upper floors, that are in dilapidated condition, or have a barking dog.

Purposive Sampling.   This procedure is used to select a sample from the participants, or groups of participants such as voting districts, that are judged to be appropriate or especially informative for the purpose of the research. The participants are handpicked from the accessible population so that they presumably will be representative or typical of the population. This technique is sometimes used by political pollsters who have information about previous elections that indicates which voting districts are typical in forecasting how larger entities, such as the state, will vote. The interviewer then polls people in that district to make extrapolations and generalizations about the larger unit.

This type of sampling is especially confusing to students and new researchers because it does not seem to be clearly defined. Researchers are often tempted to say that their sample is purposive because they selected the types of participants in which they were interested. Qualitative researchers also may claim that their sample was purposively selected as may focus group organizers. Sometimes this may be the case, but other times it appears to be a way of avoiding acknowledging that their sample is really a convenience or accidental sample (to be discussed following). We think that a purposive sample is much like a quota sample in that one must make an attempt to select a sample that is representative of the population of interest.

Take the soccer sample as an example; if we wanted to know how players evaluated the fairness of the league or the quality of the refereeing, we might purposively select players who were on teams that were about average in terms of wins, losses, and goals. Or we might select some players who did well in terms of competition, some who did about average, and some who did poorly. As another example, perhaps one would ask teachers to select children they felt were representative of the class. However, unless more detailed instructions are given, it might well turn out that the teachers would select children that they felt would make them or the school look good rather than representative children.

We would not consider it purposive sampling if teachers were asked to identify children with, for example, dyslexia, or if a social service agency was asked to identify family caregivers of Alzheimer patients who were in their files. This technique is similar to what Fowler (1993) calls *screening* in the case of telephone interviewers who exclude households that do not have participants of the desired types (e.g., women consumers over 60 years old). The sampling would only be purposive if, *given the list of dyslexic children* or *family caregivers of Alzheimer patients*, we attempted to pick typical or representative cases from those lists.

As an aside, if the selection of participants to be contacted is done by using probability techniques such as random digit dialing, and we screen out participants who do not fit the selection criteria, we would still end up with a probability sample. However, if we select cases from the accessible population purposefully, not randomly or systematically, the resulting sample will be a nonprobability sample. Like quota sampling, purposive sampling is an attempt to make the sample representative of the population, but it will probably not achieve the goal of complete representativeness.

A purposive sample is different from a convenience sample in that at least an attempt has been made to select participants so that they are representative of that accessible population, not just those who are convenient and available.

Convenience Sampling.   Unfortunately, this is probably the most common sampling method used in student projects, including theses and dissertations. It is also often used by researchers in experimental laboratory studies and by those who do qualitative research, as well as by any researcher with limited resources available for sampling. As the name implies, the participants are selected on the basis of convenience rather than chosen in a serious attempt to select participants who are representative of the theoretical population. Examples of convenience or accidental sampling are the use of students in ones' class, the use of passers by at a certain location (e.g., the student center or a mall), members of certain clubs, church groups, students in a school, or employees of a company that happen to be willing to cooperate. After the data are collected, researchers often examine the demographic characteristics of their convenience sample and conclude that the participants are similar to those in the larger population. This does not mean that the sample is, in fact, representative, but it does indicate an attempt by the researcher, at least after the fact, to check on representativeness. Convenience samples result whenever the accessible population is not representative of the theoretical population (Step 1 in Fig. 10.1), even if all of the members of the class, club, or clinic were assessed. The sample is also one of convenience if the participants are selected (Step 2) in a haphazard way from the population (e.g., volunteers are used).

Snowball Sampling.   Snowball sampling is a modification of convenience or accidental sampling that is used when the participants of interest are from a population that is rare or at least whose members are unknown to you. These might be persons with unusual attributes, beliefs, or behavior patterns who do not belong to known groups with identifiable lists of members, for example, drug addicts. A few participants who meet the characteristics are found and then asked for references or names of other people they may know who fit into the same category. Then these other people are asked for additional references, and so forth, thus the name *snowball sampling*. This is clearly a convenience or accidental sample. Sampling similar to this is common in the qualitative paradigm.

Why Are Nonprobability Samples Used So Frequently?

In addition to the cost and time efficiency advantages that were mentioned earlier, there are other reasons for using nonprobability samples. First, it may not be possible to do a probability sample of the participants. This is true for student researchers and others on limited budgets who cannot afford the costs of postage or of purchasing a comprehensive mailing list, or the cost of travel to interview geographically diverse participants.

Some researchers, perhaps especially those who use controlled laboratory and experimental designs, are not primarily interested in making inferences about the population from the descriptive data, as is the case in survey research. These researchers are more interested in whether the experimental treatment has an effect on the dependent variable, and they assume that if the treatment is powerful, the effect will show up in many kinds of participants. In fact, the use of nonhuman animals in medical and behavioral research assumes that we can generalize some results, even from other species, to humans.

In other types of research, the investigator is primarily interested in the relationship between variables and may assume that the relationship will hold up in a wide variety of human participants. Thus, some say, perhaps inappropriately, that it is not necessary to have a representative sample of the population to make generalizable statements about the *relationship* between two or more variables. Implicitly, many researchers imply that external population validity, which is directly related to the representativeness of the sample, is less important than internal validity.

Aspects of a Study that Lead to an Unrepresentative Sample

The following summary describes some of the things that lead to a sample that is unrepresentative of the target population.

1. First, an accessible population that is not representative of the theoretical population, but is picked for its *convenience*, may be selected. With this kind of accessible population, for example schools in a certain city in an unrepresentative part of the country, the sample would not be representative of the theoretical population even if it was chosen randomly from this accessible population.

2. The obvious way to obtain an unrepresentative sample is to use a nonprobability sampling design or method.

3. If there is a poor response rate, the representativeness of the sample is likely to be compromised. The response rate is the number of people interviewed or responding divided by the total number of people sampled. This denominator includes all the people who were selected but did not respond for a variety of reasons: refusals, language problems, illness, or lack of availability. It does not include those who were *screened* out because they

did not fit the selection characteristics, did not have a working telephone, or whose questionnaire was returned because it was not deliverable. The effect of nonresponses on the results of the survey depends on both the percentage of people who are not responding and the extent to which those who did not respond are biased in some way, that is, different from the rest of the sample who did respond.

4. High experimental mortality for certain groups and not others can produce a nonrepresentative sample. For example, if an experiment turned out to be unpleasant or irritating to males but not to females, there might be a much larger percentage of males who drop out during the study, thus leading to a biased sample, even if everything up to that point had been based on probability sampling.

5. Certain assumptions, such as "minority youth are more likely to engage in deviant behavior," can lead to sampling biases. In this case, minority youths may be oversampled (see MacPhee, Kreutzer, & Fritz, 1994).

How Many Participants?

One of the most often asked questions is, "How many participants do I need for this study?" The answer can be complex, but we will try to give some general guidelines here. One part of the answer depends on the people you ask and the discipline in which they work. National opinion surveys almost always have a thousand or more participants, while sociological and epidemiological studies usually have at least several hundred participants. On the other hand, psychological experiments and clinical trials in medicine with 10 to 20 participants *per group* are common, and in some clinical and educational areas, single-subject designs are often used. To an extent these dramatic differences in sample sizes depend on differences in types of designs, measures, and statistical analyses, but they are also based in good part on custom (Kraemer & Thiemann, 1987).

Some authors suggest that the sample be as large as is feasible for the investigators and their budget. Other things being equal, it is true that a larger sample will more likely detect a significant difference or relationship and lead to the rejection of the null hypothesis. However, two points should be made.

First, *representativeness is a more important consideration than sample size*. If the sample is not representative of the population, it can be huge and still give misleading results. For example, remember that there were two and a half million respondents to the 1936 *Literary Digest* poll that predicted the defeat of President Roosevelt.

Second, very large samples will detect differences or relationships that may have little practical or societal importance. If we are trying to *describe* a population with a statistic such as the mean or percentage, we want to be as accurate as possible, and a large sample, if appropriately drawn, will reduce the sampling error. However, in most social science and educational research, we are not interested in describing the population. Rather, we want to identify the key factors that may influence the dependent variable or help us to predict it. We have relatively less interest in finding factors that account for very small percentages of the variance. Thus, in some ways a large sample can be detrimental to identifying important results. For example, with 1,000 participants, a large proportion of correlations probably will be statistically significantly different from zero, but many of them may account for only 1% or 2% of the variance and, thus, not be of much practical importance.

Thus, the size of the sample should be large enough so one does not fail to detect significant findings because the sample was too small, but a large sample will not necessarily help one distinguish between the merely statistically significant and the societally important findings. This important point raises the issue of statistical power that we discuss in depth in chapter 23.

For now we will only mention a rule of thumb that some authors suggest: one should include a minimum of 30 participants per major group in a sample. Thus for associational (one group) designs, one might have as few as 30 participants, but for comparative, quasi-experimental, and experimental designs one should have approximately 30 in each group that is being compared. The latter part of the recommendation seems excessive to us. With a strong treatment or low within-group variability, groups as small as 10 can be compared.

In chapter 23 we address the topic of *power* and how to calculate it, which is the technically correct way to plan ahead of time how many participants are needed to detect a result of a certain effect size. The Kraemer and Thiemann (1987) book provides a relatively easy way to find the needed sample size.

EXTERNAL VALIDITY

In this chapter, we again discuss aspects of *research validity*, the validity or quality of a whole study. In chapter 6, we discussed *internal validity*, the validity related to the design of the study. Research validity also depends on sampling. Now we discuss *external validity*, an aspect of research validity that depends in part on the quality of the sample.

External validity was defined by Campbell and Stanley (1966) as follows: "External validity asks the question of generalizability: To what populations, settings, treatment variables, and measurement variables can this effect be generalized?" (p. 5). Some researchers have a tendency to judge external validity as contingent on internal validity (discussed in chap. 6). For example, they might suggest that because the study had poor internal validity, then external validity also must be poor. However, we think that external validity, like internal validity, should be judged separately, before the fact, and not be judged on the basis of internal validity.

Evaluating External Validity

Questions dealing with the external validity of a study are based on the principle that a good study should be rated high on external validity, or, if not, the author should at least be cautious about generalizing the findings to other measures, populations, and settings. Figure 10.3 provides scales to rate each of our two main aspects of external validity.

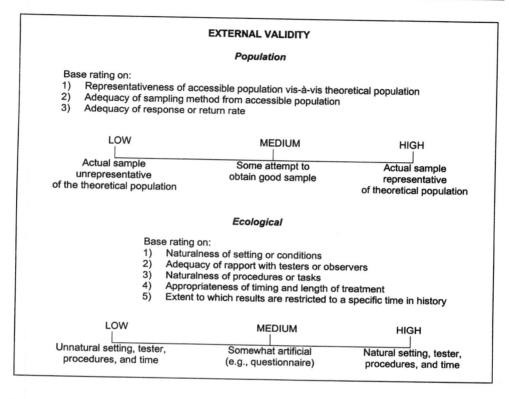

FIG. 10.3.   Evaluating the external validity of the findings of a study.

Population External Validity

This first aspect of external validity is a selection problem that involves how participants were selected to be in the study. Were participants randomly selected from a particular population, or were they a convenience sample? As discussed earlier in this chapter, most quantitative studies in the social sciences have not used random selection of participants, and thus, are not high on population external validity. However, the issue of population external validity is even more complex than an evaluation of the sampling design, that is, how the sample was selected from the accessible population. The evaluative rating of population validity should be based on all three issues in Figure 10.3.

The real question is *whether the actual final sample of participants is representative of the theoretical or target population.* To evaluate this, it is helpful to identify (a) the *apparent theoretical population,* (b) the *accessible population,* (c) the *sampling design,* (d) the *selected sample,* and (e) the *actual sample* of participants who completed the study. It is possible that the researcher could use a random or other probability sampling design, but has an actual sample that is not representative of the theoretical population either because of a low response rate or because of the accessible population is not representative of the theoretical population. The latter problem is almost universal, in part as a result of funding and travel limitations. Except in national survey research, we almost always start with an accessible population from the local school district, community, clinic, animal colony, and so on.

Ecological External Validity

The other aspect of external validity is called ecological validity. It has to do with whether the conditions, settings, times, testers, procedures, or combinations of these factors are representative of real life, and, thus, whether the results can be generalized to real-life outcomes. Obviously, field research is more likely to be high on ecological external validity than are laboratory procedures, especially if they are highly artificial. We would rate most of the self-report measures, especially questionnaires, to be artificial because they are not direct measures of the participants' actual behavior in a typical environment.

An example of a problem with ecological validity is the traditional stranger approach (e.g., see Morgan & Ricciuti, 1969; Spitz, 1965). Although methods varied, it was typical in the 1960s to test 6–12-month-old infants in a somewhat unnatural setting (lab playroom) with a male stranger who approached and picked up the baby in a short series of predetermined steps. In the name of experimental control, no attempt was made to have the researcher or stranger's behavior be contingent on the baby's behavior. This procedure, and even the existence of fear of strangers, was criticized by Rheingold and Eckerman (1973) who showed that a slower, more "natural" approach by a female stranger produced almost no crying or attempts to get away. Of course, the determinants of infant fear are complex, but it was clear that early studies were not high on ecological validity. They had traded ecological validity for better control of the environmental and independent variable aspects of internal validity.

As another example of a problem in ecological validity, if an educator is interested in the effect of a particular teaching style on student participation, the classroom should be similar to that of a normal classroom. Similarly, if the investigator asked students to come at night for the study, but these students normally attended class during the day, then there is a problem in ecological external validity. The investigator must ask if a representative method was used for selecting the setting and time, or if a convenience method was used. For high ecological validity, an intervention should be conducted by a culturally appropriate intervenor (teacher, therapist, or tester) for an appropriate length of time.

Finally, there is the question of whether the study is specific or bound to a certain time period, or whether the results will be applicable over a number of years. Attitudes about certain topics (e.g., school vouchers) may change over a short period of time so that results may not be generalizable even a few years after the study. An evaluative rating of the ecological validity of a study should be based on all five issues raised in this section and in Figure 10.3.

SAMPLING AND THE INTERNAL AND EXTERNAL VALIDITY OF A STUDY

We have discussed the internal and external validity of a study and noted that external validity is influenced by the representativeness of the sample. Much of this chapter has been about how to obtain a representative sample and what problems may arise in the process of sampling. It is important to note again, as indicated in Fig. 10.4, that the internal validity of a study is not directly affected by the sampling design or the type of sampling. Thus, a study, as is the case with many randomized experiments, may have a small convenience sample, and still have high internal validity because random assignment of participants to groups eliminates many threats to internal validity. Figure 10.4 is a schematic diagram that extends and simplifies Fig. 10.1 to show how the two

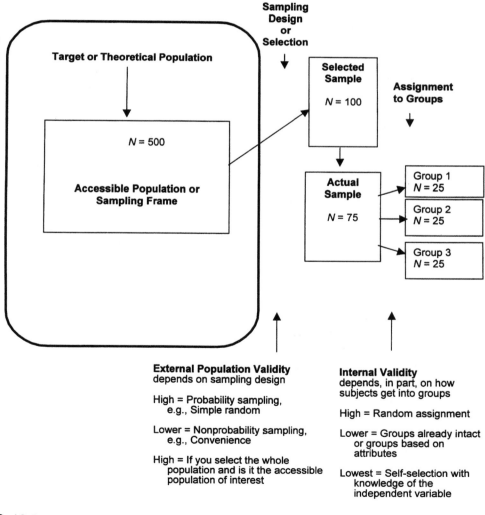

FIG. 10.4.   Random sampling versus random assignment to groups and their relationships to external and internal validity.

uses of the word random have different meanings and different effects on internal and external validity. *Random selection,* or sampling of who is asked to participate in the study, is important for high external validity. On the other hand, *random assignment,* or placement of participants into groups, is important for high internal validity. This distinction, which is often confused or misunderstood, is important for evaluating the quality of a research study and its internal and external validity.

SUMMARY

Sampling is the process of selecting part of a larger group (the accessible population) with the intent of generalizing from the smaller group (the sample) to the population. We identify two kinds of populations, theoretical or target versus accessible, and we discuss difficulties in obtaining an accessible population that is representative of the theoretical population of interest. Sampling (the sampling design) is the method used to select potential participants (the selected sample) from the accessible population. Several good sampling designs (probability sampling) are discussed; these designs include simple random, systematic with a random start, stratified, and cluster sampling. Several common but less desirable sampling methods (quota, purposive, and convenience) are also described. Finally, we discuss external validity and how to evaluate its two major components, population external validity and ecological external validity. Random selection of participants is useful to produce high population external validity, whereas random assignment of participants to groups is important for high internal validity.

STUDY AIDS

Concepts

- Cluster
- External validity
- Representative sample
- Sampling
- Sampling design
- Strata

Distinctions

- Population versus sample
- Population versus ecological external validity
- Probability versus nonprobability sampling
- Quota versus purposive versus convenience sampling
- Random sampling versus random assignment of participants to groups
- Selected sample versus actual sample

- Simple random versus systematic random versus stratified random versus cluster (random) sampling
- Stratified sampling with equal versus differential proportions
- Theoretical or target population versus accessible population

Application Problems

1. A researcher distributed questionnaires (surveys) to all employees of a municipal agency to obtain feedback regarding their jobs at this particular agency. Of 720 questionnaires distributed, 605 completed, usable surveys were returned. In this project what was: (a) the target population? (b) the accessible population? (c) the selected sample? (d) the response rate? Was any sampling done? Evaluate the external population validity overall.

2. The Fort Choice municipal agency was interested in employee feedback. A decision was made to survey a representative sample of employees. The units comprising the agency ranged from very small, 14 to 18 employees, to fairly large units of more than 100 employees. The researchers wanted to be certain that all units were represented in proportion to their size in the survey. What kind of sampling approach might they use?

3. The county office on aging is interested in the perceived needs of older adults in their service area. A telephone survey is planned. A systematic random sample of 25% of the older adults with birth dates prior to 1938 is generated from voter registration lists. Describe how this would be done and then discuss the strengths and weaknesses of the external validity of this approach.

4. A researcher is interested in studying men's and women's reactions to a violent crime show on national TV.
   a. Describe an appropriate probability sampling technique she might use.
   b. What are some problems that might affect external validity?

5. A researcher has a limited research budget, so he decides to look only at the high schools within a midwestern community of 50,000 people. There are three high schools. He makes a list of all the students for each grade level (8th–12th). He randomly samples 10 students from each grade level at each school (150 students total). Name and critique the sampling used in this study.

6. A researcher decides to do a laboratory experimental study of sleep deprivation on math performance. He randomly assigns students from his convenience sample to two groups. One group is kept awake all night and given a math test in the morning. The other group is allowed to sleep as long as they want before they take their math test in the morning. Critique this study on the basis of ecological validity.

7. Dr. G is evaluating a large national grant. The purpose of the grant is to evaluate how well revised science education courses are taught at the community college and university level. There are 10 community colleges and 10 universities involved with the grant, each with one science education course with 40 students in a class.
   Describe how you would carry out a 10% sampling procedure for:
   a. Simple random sample
   b. Stratified random sample

c. Cluster (random) sample

Label the type of sampling technique in the following example, and state whether it is a probability or nonprobability sampling technique.

8. A university professor was interested in whether her new and improved curriculum was turning out the best possible teachers. When the students completed their student teacher experience, the professor looked over the students' cumulative GPA and their student teacher evaluations. Of the 75 students who completed the program, the professor took the 10 students who had done well, 10 from the middle, and the 10 students who had done poorly, and interviewed them.

CHAPTER

11

Introduction to Inferential Statistics and Problems With Null Hypothesis Significance Testing

The goal of this chapter is to introduce inferential statistics and then to discuss some problems with the traditional use of inferential statistics to test null hypotheses. Key concepts to be covered in this chapter are hypothesis testing, exploratory data analysis, type I and type II errors, confidence intervals, and effect sizes.

HYPOTHESIS TESTING

As discussed in the last chapter, rarely are we able to work with an entire population of individuals. Instead, we usually try our treatment or intervention on a sample of individuals from the population. If our treatment is successful, we can infer that the results apply to the population of interest. Inferential statistics involves making inferences from *sample statistics*, such as the sample mean ($\bar{X}$) and the sample standard deviation (s) to *population parameters* such as the population mean (μ) and the population standard deviation (σ). When we refer to sample statistics, we use Roman letters (our alphabet); when we refer to population parameters, we use Greek letters.

A Difference Hypothesis Example

Suppose we are interested in the relationship between exercise and cardiovascular health in women. A hypothesis is formed that women who exercise regularly will have better cardiovascular health than those who do not exercise regularly. (As described in chap. 5, this is a difference hypothesis.) Inferential statistics provides us with a way to test this hypothesis, that is, to make a decision about the relationship between exercise and cardiovascular health. (We are never 100% certain that this decision is correct.) To test our hypothesis, we need to reformulate it into two statements or hypotheses, the *null hypothesis* and the *alternative hypothesis*. However, before we actually specify the null and alternative hypotheses for our study, we need to *operationalize* our variables. The independent variable, exercise, will be defined as either use of a stationary bicycle 45 min per day, 5 days per week, for 6 weeks at a work load of 50% of maximum capacity, or no exercise. The dependent variable, heart rate, is an indicator of cardiovascular health and will be measured in beats per minute. If our hypothesis is correct, we would expect that persons who exercise will have a lower heart rate than those who do not exercise, because low heart rate is considered to be an index of cardiovascular fitness.

The Null Hypothesis (H_0) and Alternative Hypotheses (H_1).   These hypotheses can be shown as follows:

$$H_0: \mu_I = \mu_C,$$

$$H_1: \mu_I < \mu_C,$$

where μ_I = intervention population mean, and

μ_C = control population mean.

The *null hypothesis* states that the mean heart rate of the population of those who receive the intervention is equal to the mean heart rate of the population of those who do not receive the intervention. If the null hypothesis is true, the intervention of exercise has not been successful in changing heart rate. The *alternative hypothesis* states that the mean heart rate of the population of those who receive the intervention will be less than the mean heart rate of the population of those who do not receive the intervention. If the null hypothesis is false, or rejected, the intervention of exercise has been successful in altering resting heart rate. In most cases, the goal of the research is to reject the null hypothesis in favor of the alternative hypothesis.

Notice that we did not set up our null and alternative hypotheses by using sample means, which would appear as follows:

$$H_0: \bar{X}_I = \bar{X}_c ,$$

$$H_1: \bar{X}_I < \bar{X}_c$$

where ($\bar{X}_I$ = intervention group sample mean, and

$\bar{X}_c$ = control group sample mean.)

The use of sample means is not correct. Why not? (Remember that we are discussing *inferential* statistics.) This method of writing the hypotheses states that we are comparing one *sample* to another *sample*. But our goal is to generalize to a *population*. Therefore, we state our null and alternative hypotheses in terms of the population means.

Three Ways to State the Alternative Hypothesis.   Specifying our alternative hypothesis in the exercise example as the intervention population mean being lower than the control group population mean is just one method of expressing the alternative hypothesis. Actually there are three choices. One choice is to specify the alternative hypothesis as nondirectional. This is expressed as follows:

$$H_1: \mu_I \neq \mu_c \quad .$$

This equation indicates that you predict the intervention will be significantly different from the control, but you are not sure of the direction of this difference. A nondirectional alternative hypothesis is often used when comparing two different treatment methods. The other two choices for alternative hypotheses are directional positive:

$$H_1: \mu_I > \mu_c \quad ,$$

and directional negative:

$$H_1: \mu_I < \mu_c \quad .$$

Directional alternative hypotheses are used most often when comparing a treatment to a control condition. Although it may appear that these choices are arbitrary, two things are important to keep in mind. First, the type of alternative hypothesis selected should be informed by the literature review. When there is previous research to support your intervention, then a directional hypothesis should be used. Sometimes there is not strong support for your intervention. This could be due to conflicting reports from previous studies or from little research done with your intervention. In these cases a nondirectional alternative hypothesis should be used. A second important point to remember about selecting the alternative hypothesis is that there are statistical consequences attached to the type of hypothesis you select. These consequences often lead to the conclusion of "no free lunch." We discuss this second issue later in the chapter.

Now that we have the proper terminology for our null and alternative hypotheses, we need to consider our population of interest for the exercise study. If we are interested in generalizing to all women, that would be our *theoretical population*. Perhaps a subset of all women, such as all women graduate students in the United States is our theoretical population. However, we may have access only to women graduate students who are currently attending a certain university. Therefore, women graduate students at that university are our *accessible population*.

The Inferential Process. Figure 11.1, adapted from Shavelson (1981, p. 335) for our study, provides insight into the inferential process. At the far left of the figure is a box that represents the population. The heart rates of women graduate students at the university is our dependent variable. For our purposes, we will assume that heart rate is distributed normally. What do we mean by distributed normally? (We examined the normal curve in some depth in chapter 9.) We mean that most of the women graduate students have resting heart rates near the average, about 70 beats per min (bpm). As we move toward the extremes or "tails" of the distribution, say 85 bpm or 55 bpm, there are few women who have these heart rates. What is important for inferential statistics is that values that occur infrequently (i.e., at the extremes of the distribution), are often regarded as belonging to, perhaps, a different population distribution with a different population mean.

Note that we rarely know the actual characteristics of the population distribution. Under many conditions we can assume it to be normal. However, there

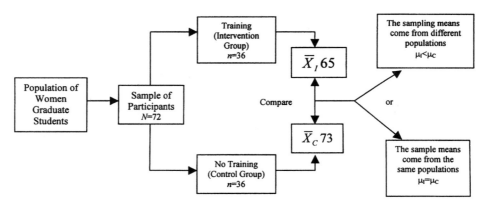

(a) Selection of sample from population

(b) Assignment of participants to groups

(c) Experiment conducted

(d) Outcome of experiment

(e) Decision based on result of inferential statistic

FIG. 11.1 Schematic diagram of the process of making an inference about the difference between two groups. From *Statistical Reasoning for the Behavioral Sciences* (p. 335), by R. J. Shavelson, Copyright © 1981, Boston: Allyn and Bacon. Adapted by permission.

may be times when we cannot assume this distribution to be normal; then we will use nonparametric, or distribution-free statistical tests.

From our accessible population (women graduate students) we sample or select, perhaps randomly, 72 women. (Note that this is step (a) in Fig. 11.1.) This step is best done by selecting names from a total list of women students in such a way that all students have an equal chance of being selected for our study. Frequently the sample is one of convenience, not randomly selected.

In the next step (b), we assign participants to groups. Assuming approval from the Human Research Committee and that all 72 participants have given voluntary consent to be in either group at the researcher's discretion, we randomly assign 36 women to be in the exercise (intervention) group and 36 women to be in the nonexercise (control) group.[1] Again, random assignment implies that each student had an equal chance to be in either group. If the participants cannot be randomly assigned to either group, the study is a quasi-experiment rather than a randomized experiment. Remember the difference between *random selection*, which is important for *external validity*, and *random assignment*, which is important for *internal validity*.

Moving to the right in Fig. 11.1, we see that the next step (c) is to conduct the study. Now, the intervention group (one level of the independent variable) will exercise on a stationary bicycle for 45 min a day, 5 days a week, for 6 weeks (training). The control group (the other level of the independent variable) will refrain from exercise for the next 6 weeks (no training). You may ask, What if some members of the control group were habitual exercisers prior to the study? It is hard to say what effect this would have on our study, but it illustrates a type of problem (extraneous variable) that you might encounter.

After 6 weeks, we ask the participants to come into our laboratory, and we measure their heart rate, step (d). We find the mean heart rate of the intervention group to be 65 bpm and the mean heart rate of the control group to be 73 bpm. We know the two means are different. The mean of the intervention group is lower, supporting our hypothesis that exercise increases cardiovascular health. From these results, can we form a conclusion to reject the null hypothesis (that there is no difference between the exercise and no exercise conditions) in support of the alternative hypothesis (that the exercise condition will reduce heart rate)? Before we make this decision, a second study is helpful.

Suppose that we repeated the same study with new participants, but used the same number of participants and the same method of selection and random assignment. However, in this new study, neither group exercises for 6 weeks. Now, at the end of the 6-week period, we measure the mean heart rate of both groups. Will the means be identical? Probably not, because there are individual differences among the members of each sample. We are not measuring the whole population, only a sample of the population, so we would expect the means to be different, as a result of random fluctuation. That is, even without introducing a treatment, and even if the two samples were equivalent, we

---

[1]It is important to point out that the two different samples of 36 participants in each group could be considered as samples from two *different* but *identically distributed* populations rather than from a single population.

would expect the two means to be different by chance alone. Therefore, we need to use inferential statistics to help make the proper decision.

Now back to our original study. After performing the proper statistical test, we can form one of two conclusions. We can conclude that the intervention group mean really is less than the control group mean. In other words, we can conclude that the intervention group mean now represents the mean of a population of trained women, and the control group mean represents the mean of a population of untrained women. This conclusion defines a *statistically significant difference* and is demonstrated in the upper portion of the right-hand section of Fig. 11.1.

A second conclusion could be that there is no difference between the two means (lower portion of the right-hand section of the figure). In other words, the difference between means was simply from random fluctuation. This latter conclusion would imply that the two groups still come from the same underlying population, and that this amount of exercise does not make a difference in cardiovascular health as defined for our study.

Which conclusion do we make? How much of a difference between the two means is needed before concluding that there is a significant difference? Inferential statistics provides us with an outcome (a statistic) that informs us of the decision to make. Which conclusion do we make? How much of a difference is needed between the two? Even after performing inferential statistical procedures on our data, we are still making a decision with a degree of uncertainty.

In our example of women and exercise, we stated that there were two possible decisions that we could make from our sample data. Either we would reject the null hypothesis and conclude that the two groups come from two different populations (top of Fig. 11.1, step (e)), or we would not reject the null hypothesis and conclude that the samples come from the same population (bottom of Fig. 11.1, step (e)). The decision to reject or not reject the null hypothesis is determined for us by subjecting our sample data to a particular statistical test. An outcome that is highly *unlikely* under the null hypothesis (i.e., one that results in a low probability value) leads us to reject the null hypothesis. An outcome that is not unlikely will result in a failure to reject the null hypothesis.

Type I and Type II Errors

Although inferential statistics informs us of the decision to make (i.e., reject or do not reject the null hypothesis), there is still a possibility that the decision we make may be incorrect. This is because our decision is based on the probability of a given outcome. The statistic is associated with a particular probability. For example, a t value calculated on our sample data may result in a probability of .04. This states that the probability of our outcome (a difference this large between the two sample groups) would occur only 4 times in 100, if the null hypothesis is true. While a result of this magnitude would lead us to a decision to reject the null hypothesis in favor of an alternative hypothesis, there is a possibility that we are in error. In other words, the null hypothesis may be true. What is the probability of making an error about the null hypothesis in this situation? The answer is 4 out of 100 or .04. Therefore, while inferential statistics informs us to either reject or not reject the null hypothesis from our sample data, each decision can either be correct *or* it can be in error.

Any time we conduct a study from the sample data, four outcomes are possible. Two of the outcomes are correct decisions and two of the outcomes are errors.

Correct Decisions:

1. Do not reject the null hypothesis when it is true (i.e., there is no difference).
2. Reject the null hypothesis when it is false (i.e., there is a difference).

Errors:

1. Reject the null hypothesis when, in fact, it is true (type I error).
2. Do not reject the null hypothesis when it is false (type II error).

We are never sure if the decision we have made is correct (what is actually true in the population), because we are basing our decision on sample data.

Figure 11.2 (adapted from Loftus & Loftus, 1982, p. 225) helps us to conceptualize the four possible outcomes that we have just discussed. The curve on the right represents the population distribution if the null hypothesis is true, and the curve on the left represents the population distribution under the alternative hypothesis if the null hypothesis is false. The line drawn perpendicular to the X axis in this illustration represents the .05 decision point, or significance level. We establish this level *prior* to the study. It is customary to decide that any difference between our two sample means that is large enough to yield a statistical outcome that could occur less than 5 times in 100 ($\alpha = .05$) if the null hypothesis is true should result in a rejection of the null hypothesis.

First, we will describe the curve on the right, or the population distribution if the null hypothesis is true. Most of this curve (95%) is to the right of the .05 decision point or statistical significance level line. Only a small portion of this curve is to the left of the statistical significance line. We call the portion to the left of the statistical significance line alpha (α). This also refers to the probability of making a type I error. Therefore, in this example, because the area of the curve to the left of the significance level line is 5%, the probability of a type I error (a) is .05. The remaining portion of the curve (the part of the curve to the right of the significance line) is the probability of making a correct decision. This is $1 - \alpha$. It is $1 - \alpha$, because α is .05. Because we are dealing with the population distribution associated with the null hypothesis, the correct decision would be to not reject the null hypothesis, assuming it is true. In our present example, the probability of making a correct decision to not reject the null hypothesis is .95 ($1 - \alpha = 1 - .05 = .95$).

The curve on the left in Fig. 11.2 is referred to as the population distribution related to the alternative hypothesis. The area of this curve to the right of the statistical significance line is called beta (β). It is relatively small, but not usually as small as alpha. Beta depicts an area of the curve (the alternative hypothesis

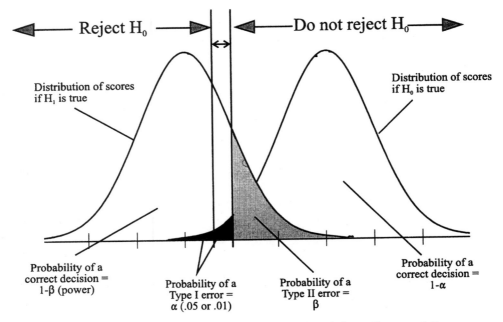

FIG. 11.2.   Type I and Type II errors related to the null and alternative population distributions. Adapted from *Essence of Statistics* (p. 225), by G. R. Loftus and E. F. Loftus, 1982, Monterey, CA: Brooks/Cole. Adapted by permission.

curve) associated with another other type of error. The area β provides the probability of making the error of not rejecting the null hypothesis when it is false, or should be rejected. This type of error is called a type II error. The area of the alternative hypothesis curve that falls to the left of the significance line is the probability of making a correct decision. This correct decision, because it deals with the alternative hypothesis curve, is rejecting the null hypothesis when it is false, that is, when it should be rejected. The probability of making this correct decision is 1 − β. Our goal in research usually is to reject the null hypothesis in favor of an alternative hypothesis, so the area or probability 1 − β is very important. We would like to increase this area as much as possible. Because of its importance, 1 − β is called power. We discuss power in more detail in chapter 23. Table 11.1 summarizes our discussion of type I and type II errors.

TABLE 11.1

Type I and Type II Errors

	True in the population	
Decision Based on Data From Sample	Null is True	Null is False
Reject null	Type I error (α)	Correct decision ($1 - \beta$) Power
Do not reject null	Correct decision ($1 - \alpha$)	Type II error (β)

Statistical Decision Making

We return now to directional and nondirectional alternative hypotheses. Remember that earlier in the chapter we stated that there are statistical consequences associated with the type of alternative hypothesis selected. If we hypothesize a directional negative alternative hypothesis, it would be conceptualized similar to Fig. 11.2. The distribution of scores under the alternative hypothesis is to the left of the distribution of scores under the null hypothesis. If, as in Fig. 11.2, we establish our significance level, α, at .05, then a statistical outcome that is to the left of this .05 value would result in a rejection of the null hypothesis. A similar conceptualization would result for an alternative hypothesis that is directional positive. Here, a statistical outcome that is to the right of the .05 value would result in a rejection of the null hypothesis.

Now, suppose instead that our alternative hypothesis is nondirectional, as seen in Fig. 11.3. We would have two distributions of scores under the alternative hypothesis. One distribution would be to the right of the distribution of scores under the null hypothesis, and the other distribution would be to the left of the distribution of scores under the null hypothesis. If we keep our significance level at .05, then it would mean that to reject the null hypothesis in either direction, the statistical outcome would have to exceed the .025 level rather than the .05 level. Therefore, it is more difficult to reject the null hypothesis using a nondirectional hypothesis. However, you are less likely to make a critical mistake. In other words, if you select a directional alternative hypothesis, and the result was a significant difference in the opposite direction, you can only conclude a failure to reject the null hypothesis, or no significant difference. It should be noted that because we are using both ends or tails of the distribution

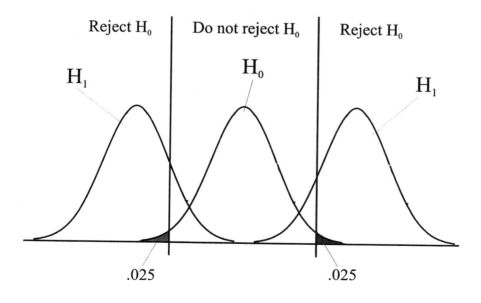

FIG. 11.3.   Alternative nondirectional hypotheses.

under the null hypothesis when stating a nondirectional hypothesis, a test of this hypothesis is referred to as a *two-tailed* test.

A last word on the philosophy of hypothesis testing is that when the null hypothesis is not rejected, it is *never actually accepted.* The correct conclusion to form is that the null hypothesis was not rejected. While one may question the difference between the terms *accept* and *not reject,* the problem with the former is that there could be many reasons why our study did not result in a rejection of the null hypothesis. Perhaps another, more powerful study, might result in a rejection of the null hypothesis. Loftus and Loftus (1982, p. 242) provide an interesting and humorous discussion of the logical implications of finding something, as opposed to the logical implications of not finding something.

Interpreting Inferential Statistics

The rationale for null hypothesis significance testing was provided earlier in this chapter, when we used as an example a basic difference question comparing two groups. Here we present an overview of how to interpret *any* of the inferential statistics described in this book. Selection and interpretation of each of the specific statistics in the tables is presented in the following chapters. For each statistic (i.e., t, F, χ^2, r, etc.), the calculations produce a number or *calculated value* from the specific data in your study. To interpret that calculated value, it is compared to *critical values* found in a statistical table or in the computer's memory, taking into account the degrees of freedom, which is usually based on the number of participants. See the left side of Fig. 11.4 for *approximate* critical values when the study has about 50 participants or is a 2×2 chi-square.

The middle column of Fig. 11.4 shows how to interpret any inferential test once you know the probability level (p) from the computer or whether the calculated value is greater than the critical value. In general, if the calculated value of the statistics (t, F, etc.) is relatively large, the probability, or p, is small, (e.g., .05, .01, .001). If the probability is *less than* the preset alpha level (usually .05), we can say that the results are *statistically significant* or that they are significant at the .05 level or that $p < .05$. We can also reject the null hypothesis of no difference or no relationship. We do not usually say so, but we could think about the level of confidence $(1 - p)$ in the results as shown on the right side of Fig. 11.4.

Note that computer printouts such as those from SPSS (Statistical Package for the Social Sciences) make interpretation of the various statistics easy by printing the actual significance or probability level (p) so you do not have to look up a critical value in a table. This translates all of the common inferential statistics into a common metric, the significance level (Sig. in SPSS). This level is also the probability of a type I error or the probability of rejecting the null hypothesis when it is actually true. Thus, regardless of what specific statistic you use, if p is small (usually less than .05), the finding is statistically significant and you reject the null hypothesis.

When you interpret inferential statistics, it is not enough to decide whether to reject the null hypothesis. If you find that the statistic is statistically significant, you need to answer two more questions.

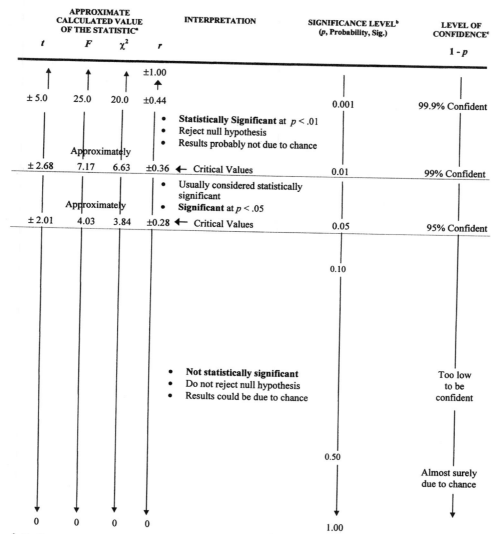

APPROXIMATE CALCULATED VALUE OF THE STATISTIC[a]				INTERPRETATION	SIGNIFICANCE LEVEL[b] (p, Probability, Sig.)	LEVEL OF CONFIDENCE[c]
t	F	χ^2	r			$1 - p$
			±1.00			
± 5.0	25.0	20.0	±0.44		0.001	99.9% Confident
				• **Statistically Significant** at $p < .01$ • Reject null hypothesis • Results probably not due to chance		
	Approximately					
± 2.68	7.17	6.63	±0.36 ← Critical Values		0.01	99% Confident
				• Usually considered statistically significant • **Significant** at $p < .05$		
	Approximately					
± 2.01	4.03	3.84	±0.28 ← Critical Values		0.05	95% Confident
					0.10	
				• **Not statistically significant** • Do not reject null hypothesis • Results could be due to chance		Too low to be confident
					0.50	Almost surely due to chance
0	0	0	0		1.00	

[a] For these examples, $df = 50$ for t test; $df = 1, 50$ for F (ANOVA); $df = 1$ for χ^2; $df = 50$ for r (Pearson Correlation). **With other df, the critical values will be higher or lower!**
[b] This is the probability that the results are due to chance, i.e., probability of a type I error.
[c] This is the probability or level of confidence that the results are not due to chance.
Note. When the output indicates that the probability or significance = 0.000, you should state that $p < 0.001$ in your paper because there is always a small probability of a type I error.

FIG. 11.4.   Interpreting inferential statistics.

First, *what is the direction of the effect?* Difference inferential statistics compare groups so it is necessary to state which group performed better. We discuss how to do this in chapters 14, 15, 17 and 18. For associational inferential statistics (e.g., correlation), the sign is very important, so you must indicate whether the association or relationship is positive or negative. We discuss how to interpret correlations in chapter 16.

Second, *what is the size of the effect?* In the next section we discuss problems with null hypothesis significance testing and recommend that you include confidence intervals or effect size measures or both in the description of your results. The general method of computing effect sizes converts the difference between the groups into a common metric, standard deviations, as discussed in chapter 9.

PROBLEMS WITH NULL HYPOTHESIS SIGNIFICANCE TESTING

There has been an increase in resistance to null hypothesis significance testing (NHST) in the social sciences during recent years. Although researchers have periodically objected to the use of NHST throughout the past three decades (e.g., Bakan, 1966; Rozeboom, 1960), the intensity of objection has increased recently, especially within the disciplines of psychology (Cohen, 1990, 1994; Schmitt, 1996a) and education (Robinson & Levin, 1997; Thompson, 1996). These objections focus around numerous criticisms. We address two major problems here because of their relevance for data analysis. Both problems involve misinterpretation of statistical significance. In addition, we describe two types of solutions to these problems, calculation of confidence intervals and effect sizes.

Adding Confidence Intervals Helps

The first problem with NHST involves the interpretation of a statistically significant difference in the form of an all-or-none decision. There is a tendency to accept something as significant or not significant, rather than acknowledge that statistical significance implies a probability of uncertainty. In addition, when we dichotomize statistical significance in this way, we become removed from the actual data of our study. One alternative approach to NHST is to create *confidence intervals.* When we conduct a study to determine which of two interventions or treatments works better, our result is usually expressed as a difference between the means of the two intervention groups, or between an intervention and a control group. It is important to remember that this difference between means is a difference between two *sample* means. This difference between the two sample means is called a point estimate. We would like to believe that this mean difference or point estimate is a good estimation of the actual mean difference between the two population means (population parameter). However, because this is only a difference between two sample means, we are not sure how close this estimation is to the actual *population* difference between means. To determine how close our difference between two sample means is from our population difference between means, we need to create a confidence interval. This confidence interval is a range of the dependent variable that should contain the true population difference between means. We are never totally sure that our confidence interval includes the population parameter, so we must estimate the confidence interval with, for example, a 95% confidence interval. This interval means that 95% of the differences between sample means that we compute would contain the true population parameter.

Confidence intervals provide more practical information than does NHST. For example, suppose one knew that an increase in reading scores of 15 points obtained on a particular instrument would lead to a functional increase in reading performance. Two different methods of instruction are compared. One method results in a statistically significant gain compared to the other method. According to NHST, we would reject the null hypothesis of no difference between methods and conclude that our new method is better. If we apply confidence intervals to this same study, not only can we determine a 95% interval that contains our population parameter, but we can see if the lower bound of that interval is greater than 15 points on our reading test. If the lower bound is greater than 15 points, we conclude that using this method of instruction would increase functional reading levels.

Cortina and Dunlap (1997) have argued that to create a confidence interval you need the same information that would be used for NHST (e.g., in a *t* test, the difference between sample means, the estimated standard error of the difference between means, and the critical value for the .05 alpha level for the particular degrees of freedom). Therefore, we will demonstrate how to create confidence intervals for the *t* test for independent samples described in chapter 14.

Including Effect Size Is Necessary

A second major problem with NHST also concerns the interpretation of statistical significance. This second misinterpretation of statistical significance occurs when one assumes that a statistically significant outcome gives information about the size of the outcome. A statistically significant outcome only describes a relationship that is unlikely to occur, assuming the null hypothesis is true, but it does not tell the extent of that relationship. Therefore, it is important to state, in addition to information on statistical significance, the size of the effect. An *effect size* is defined as the strength of the relationship between the independent variable and the dependent variable. For example, if one is comparing an intervention group to a control group, the effect size (*d*) could be computed by subtracting the mean of the control group from the mean of the intervention group and dividing by the pooled standard deviation of both groups as follows:

$$d = \frac{\overline{X}_I - \overline{X}_C}{s_{pooled}} \quad .$$

Another method of expressing effect sizes is as a correlation coefficient, *r*, (Rosenthal, 1994). Chapter 16 provides a discussion of correlation and how to interpret it. Using this method, effect sizes are always less than 1.0, varying between −1.0 and +1.0.

Unfortunately, there are many different effect size measures and little agreement about which to use. Although *d* is the most commonly discussed effect size measure, it is not usually available from the popular computer packages such as SPSS. The correlation coefficient, r, or similar measures of the strength of association, are more commonly available in statistical outputs.

   Although the *Publication Manual of the American Psychological Association* (APA, 1994) recommends that researchers report effect sizes, few researchers did so before 1999 when The APA Task Force on Statistical Inference stated that effect sizes should always be reported for your primary results (Wilkinson & The Task Force, 1999). Because in the past few published articles have presented effect sizes, we do not discuss them much in chapters 14–19. In the future, it is likely that most articles will discuss the size of the effect as well as whether or not the result was statistically significant and the direction of the effect.

Interpreting Effect Sizes   Assuming that you have computed either d or r, how should it be interpreted? Cohen (1988) provides a rule of thumb for interpreting the practical importance of both d and r as follows:

small effect	$d = .2$	$r = .1$
medium effect	$d = .5$	$r = .3$
large effect	$d = .8$	$r = .5$

Cohen provides research examples of small, medium and large effects to support the suggested d and r values. Most researchers would not consider a correlation (r) of .5 to be very strong. However, Cohen argues that a d of .8 (and an r of .5, which he shows are mathematically equivalent) are "grossly perceptible and therefore large differences, as (for example) the mean difference in height between 13- and 18-year-old girls" (p. 27).

   We discuss effect sizes again in chapter 23. In that chapter we show how effect sizes can be combined in a meta-analysis to accumulate knowledge.

SUMMARY

A conceptual view of inferential statistics was provided, along with an example. Inferential statistics involves making inferences from *sample statistics*, such as the sample mean and the sample standard deviation, to *population parameters* such as the population mean and the population standard deviation. Hypothesis testing, a primary principle of statistics, was introduced. We defined the null hypotheses and demonstrated three different ways to set up the alternative hypothesis, nondirectional, directional positive, and directional negative. A significant outcome was shown in our example, along with type I and type II errors. A type I error was defined as rejecting a true null hypothesis. A type II error was defined as failure to reject a false null hypothesis.

   Hypothesis testing has been under criticism for several years, more now than ever. Reasons for this criticism included incorrect interpretation of statistical significance. Alternatives and additions to significance testing were discussed, including confidence intervals and effect sizes. Because a statistically significant finding may be small and of little practical importance, it is desirable to know the size of the effect. Unfortunately, for a variety of reasons, researchers historically have not reported effect sizes. Because a statistically significant finding may be small and of little practical importance, it is desirable to know the size of the effect. Unfortunately, for a variety of reasons, researchers historically have not reported effect sizes.

STUDY AIDS

Concepts

- Alternative hypothesis
- Confidence intervals
- Directional hypothesis
- Effect size
- Nondirectional hypothesis
- Null hypothesis
- Population parameters
- Sample statistics
- Statistically significant difference
- Type I error
- Type II error

Distinctions

- Directional hypothesis versus nondirectional hypothesis
- Null hypothesis versus alternative hypothesis
- Sample statistics versus population parameters
- Type I versus Type II errors
- Tests of significance versus confidence intervals

Application Problems

For problems 1 to 4. Provide nondirectional and directional alternative hypotheses.

1. There is no difference between reform teaching methods and traditional teaching methods in students' mathematics achievement data.
2. There is no difference between supported employment and sheltered work in successful community participation.
3. There is no difference between exercise and no exercise in cardiovascular health.
4. There is no difference between students who perform well and students who do not perform well on teacher evaluations.

For problems 5 to 8, describe in words, the Type 1 Error, the Type 2 Error, and the two correct decisions.

5. A study is performed to determine if reform teaching methods are better than traditional teaching methods.

6. A study is performed to determine if people in supported employment participate more in the community than people in sheltered workshops.

7. A study is performed to determine if those who exercise have lower resting heart rates than those who do not exercise.

8. A study is performed to determine if students with high grades give better teacher evaluations than students with low grades.

9. A common practice in research is to establish the probability of a Type 1 Error at 0.05 and a Type 2 Error at 0.20. Why do you think researchers are more willing to accept a Type 2 Error?

10. A researcher performs a study comparing two different groups. There are 26 participants in each group. She analyzes the data using a t test. Her t value is 2.53. Should she reject the null hypothesis? Why?

11. A researcher performs a study comparing three different groups. There are 17 participants in each group. He analyzes the data using a single factor ANOVA. His F value is 3.23. Should he reject the null hypothesis? Why?

12. What are two general problems with null hypothesis significance testing? How can these problems be alleviated?

13. A researcher decides to display his results as a confidence interval. He cannot decide between a 95% confidence interval or a 99% confidence interval. Which of the two intervals do you think will be larger and why?

14. What are the two different methods of computing effect sizes?

General Design Classifications

Study Aids
    Concepts
    Distinctions
    Application Problems

INTRODUCTION

In chapter 7 we discussed specific research designs, such as the posttest-only randomized experimental design and the nonequivalent pretest–posttest control group design. These specific research designs help us visualize the operations of a study, especially for internal validity. In the present chapter, we consider general design classifications. General design classification is especially important for determining the proper statistical approach to be used in data analysis. Within the randomized experimental, quasi-experimental, and also comparative approaches, all designs must fit into one of three categories or labels that we call general design classification.

GENERAL DESIGN CLASSIFICATIONS

Between Groups Designs

Between groups designs are defined as designs where each participant in the research is in *one and only one* condition or group. For example, in a study investigating the effects of teaching style on student satisfaction, there may be three groups (or conditions or levels) of the independent variable, teaching style. These conditions could be traditional, reform, and a combination of the two. In a between groups design, each participant receives only one of the three conditions or levels. If the investigator wished to have 20 participants in each group, then 60 participants would be needed to complete the research.

Within Subjects or Repeated Measures Designs

Within subjects designs, the second type of general design classification, are conceptually the opposite of between groups designs. In these designs, each participant in the research *receives or experiences all of the conditions* or levels of the independent variable to complete the study. In the investigation of the effects of the independent variable (teaching style) on the dependent variable (student satisfaction), there still would be three conditions or levels to the independent variable. These conditions again are traditional teaching style, reform teaching style, and a combination of the two. In a within subjects design, each participant would experience and be measured for student satisfaction on all three conditions or levels of the independent variable. If the researcher wished to have 20 participants for each condition, only 20 participants would be needed to carry out the research, because each participant undergoes all three conditions of the independent variable in the research. Because each participant is assessed more than once, that is, for each condition, these designs are also referred to as *repeated measures* designs.

Within subjects designs have appeal because of the reduced number of required participants and the reduced error variance that results when each participant is his or her own control. However, often these designs may be less appropriate than between groups designs because of the possibility of *carryover effects*. If the purpose of the study is to investigate conditions that may result in a long-term or permanent change, such as learning, it is not possible for a participant to be in one condition, and then "unlearn" that condition to return to the previous state to start the next condition. Within subjects designs may be appropriate if the effects of order of presentation are negligible when participants are asked, for example, to evaluate several topics. Order effects can be controlled by presenting the conditions to participants in different orders (e.g., in random orders or counterbalanced so that, for example, half receive condition *A* first and half receive condition *B* first). When there is a pretest and a posttest, we have repeated measures and a within subject design for one of the independent variables.

Mixed Designs

The previous two classifications have only one independent variable. A mixed design has at least *one between groups independent variable* and at least *one within subjects independent variable*; thus, it has a minimum of two independent variables.[1] A between groups independent variable is any independent vari-

---

[1] There are some introductory research design texts (e.g., Cosby, 1989) that describe a mixed design as a design that has at least one active independent variable and one attribute independent variable. The problem with this characterization of a mixed design is that it could be confused with the mixed design as defined in this book, and then it would be incorrectly analyzed statistically because both independent variables are between groups variables, which require a different type of ANOVA than a mixed (between and within) design. To avoid confusion, a between groups design with one active independent variable and one attribute independent variable could be referred to as a *generalized randomized blocks design* (Kirk, 1982). However, the proper data analysis does not distinguish between active or attribute independent variables, only that they are between groups independent variables.

able that sets up between groups conditions. A within subjects independent variable is any independent variable that sets up within-subjects conditions. Let us return to our example of investigating the effect of the independent variable, teaching style, on the dependent variable, student satisfaction. If teaching style is a within subjects independent variable, as in the second example earlier, we would additionally need a second independent variable that is a between groups independent variable to complete the criteria for a mixed design. The second independent variable for this example could be the type of student in the class. Student type is a between groups independent variable, with two levels, traditional and nontraditional. Therefore, this example satisfies the criteria for a mixed design: two independent variables: one a within subjects variable (teaching style) and the other a between groups variable (student type).

MORE DESIGN CONSIDERATIONS

Number of Independent Variables

A mixed design must have a minimum of two independent variables, one a between groups independent variable and the other a within subjects independent variable. Between groups designs and within subjects designs also may have more than one independent variable (usually no more than three), although the minimum requirement for each of these designs is only one independent variable. If the researcher decides to use more than one independent variable in either a between groups design or a within subjects design, these additional independent variables also must be between groups independent variables (in a between groups design) and within subjects independent variables (in a within subjects design). Otherwise, the design would be called a mixed design.

Type of Independent Variable

Previously all independent variables were described as *active* (i.e., the independent variable is manipulated or given to one group but not to a second group) or *attribute* (the investigator is interested in a quality that is a characteristic of one group of people that is not characteristic of a second group of people). In a between groups design, the independent variable may be either an active or an attribute variable. Thus, between groups designs can use the randomized experimental, quasi-experimental, or comparative approach. For example, the workshops, new curricula, and interventions described in chapters 4 and 5 were active, and the designs were between groups. The examples of gender, giftedness, and type of disability were attribute independent variables used in between groups designs.

On the other hand, in a within subjects design, the independent variable is usually active. Thus, the approach is usually randomized experimental (if the order of the conditions is randomized) or quasi-experimental. This becomes clear if we consider an example of students with learning disabilities, an attribute independent variable. Suppose that we are interested in the reading speed of students who are learning disabled and those who are not learning disabled.

A student cannot be both learning disabled and not learning disabled at the same time. Likewise, a person cannot be both female and male. However, in some cases, there can be a within subjects design and an attribute independent variable.

Three Cases of Within Subjects Designs With an Attribute Independent Variable.   These cases use the comparative approach. One case involves a situation where participants are assessed on several parts of a particular instrument, such as the Assessment of Motor and Process Skills (A. G. Fisher, 1993). This instrument provides separate scores for motor and process skills. If the investigator is interested in comparing the motor scores to the process scores, the design becomes a within subjects design with two levels. The independent variable is type of skill, an attribute with two levels. A similar example of a within subjects design with an attribute variable (comparative approach) is in a questionnaire study where the participants are asked to rate several aspects of their personality, motivation, or attitudes, and then these aspects are compared. For example, eight aspects of workers' perceptions of the importance of "margin in life" were compared by Hanpachern, Morgan, and Griego (1998). However, if the independent variable is a stimulus, such as a product or a design, the independent variable would be considered active because the specific designs or products used are "given" by the experimenter and the features can be manipulated. Then the approach would be experimental.

A second case in which the independent variable in within subjects designs is not active involves *matching* participants. Matching refers to a situation in which participants are combined into pairs (or triads) to make each member of the pair as much alike as possible on some measure relevant to the dependent variable. For example, a researcher is interested in quality-of-life issues for persons with developmental disabilities. Specifically, he is interested in determining if people who work in supported employment have a higher quality of life than do people who work in sheltered employment. However, previous research has indicated that there is a relationship between intelligence and quality of life (the dependent variable for the study). Therefore, prior to the study, the researcher determines the intelligence level for all of the participants ($N = 20$). Then he matches (forms pairs of participants) their intelligence level. The participants with the two highest intelligence levels would form the first pair. Participants with the third- and fourth-highest intelligence levels would form the next pair. The matching process would continue until all 20 participants had formed 10 pairs of participants. Now the researcher can form two equal groups by starting with the first pair of participants and randomly assigning one member of a pair to the supported employment group and the other member of the pair to the sheltered work group. This continues until all 10 pairs of participants have been randomly assigned to one of the two groups.

The important consideration for research designs that use matching is that they change into the category of *within subjects designs.*[2] Although partici-

---

[2]Designs that involve matching subjects into pairs (or triads) and then randomly assigning one member of each pair to a particular group are called *randomized blocks designs*. However, statistically these designs are analyzed like within subjects designs.

pants are in one, and only one group, as demonstrated in the quality-of-life study, the design is not a between groups design, because the groups are not independent. The investigator matched the participants before assigning them to groups. To understand matching conceptually, remember the definition of a within subjects design—each participant undergoes all conditions of the study. In the matching design, we are trying to make each pair of participants as though they were the same participant by matching on a criterion relevant to the dependent variable. For the first pair of participants, one participant undergoes the supported employment condition and the other participant undergoes the sheltered work condition. However, from a statistical standpoint, it is as though the same participant underwent both supported employment and sheltered work conditions. (The lack of statistical independence would be obvious if the pairs of participants were twins; see the next section.)

Although we do not usually recommend matching of participants as a common research strategy, there are certain circumstances where the investigator may wish to match pairs of participants. These situations usually take place when the sample size is relatively small and heterogeneous for the dependent variable.

As implied earlier, there is a third within subjects design case in which the independent variable is not active. This occurs when the members of the groups to be compared are related in an important way. The design is said to be *a related samples* or *paired samples design*. Obviously, identical twins should be treated statistically as if they were the same person, so one would use a within subjects analysis for them. Perhaps less obviously, the same would be true for couples, parent and child, and teacher and student. These examples would be treated statistically as within subjects designs.

Change Over Time (or Trials) as an Independent Variable.   In within subjects designs there can be a third type (neither, active, or attribute) of independent variable, change over time or trials. This third type of independent variable is extremely important in randomized experimental and quasi-experimental designs because pretest and posttest are two levels of this type of independent variable. *Longitudinal studies*, in which the same participants are assessed at several time periods or ages, are another important case where change over time is the independent variable.

Consider the following study that uses a pretest–posttest control group design (chap. 7). Participants are randomly assigned (R) to one of two groups, an intervention group (E), which receives a new curriculum, and a control group (C), which receives the old curriculum. Participants are measured prior to the intervention (O_1) and after the intervention (O_2), perhaps at the end of the semester. The design can be viewed as follows:

$$R \qquad E: \qquad O_1 \qquad X \qquad O_2$$
$$R \qquad C: \qquad O_1 \qquad {\sim} X \qquad O_2$$

It is a mixed design because there are two independent variables, one a between groups independent variable, and the other a within subjects independent variable. The independent variable, type of curriculum, is a between groups independent variable because each participant experiences only one of the two curriculums. The other independent variable in this study, change over time, is a within subjects independent variable because participants within each group were measured more than once in the study. This independent variable is referred to as change over time because the second measurement period took place at a later time than the first measurement period. Change over time is considered a third type rather than an active independent variable because you cannot actively manipulate change over time; the posttest always comes after the pretest.

DIAGRAMING DESIGNS

Between groups, within subjects, and mixed designs can be diagramed to help visualize what is happening in the research. In addition, the method of diagraming that we recommend (Winer, 1962) depicts how the data are entered into the computer for future statistical analyses.

Between Groups Designs

These designs always have the data for a single subject or group placed *horizontally* into a row on the page. Suppose that we have a between groups design with two independent variables, teaching style and gender. Each independent variable has two levels (teaching style, traditional or reform; and gender, male or female). Notice that we have simplified the diagram by including the names of the levels but not the variable name, as we did in chapter 4. Therefore, the design would be as follows, assuming 40 participants were assigned to the four groups:

```
                  ┌─── Female   (Grp 1, n = 10)        O
     Traditional ─┤
                  └─── Male     (Grp 2, n = 10)        O

                  ┌─── Female   (Grp 3, n = 10)        O
     Reform       ─┤
                  └─── Male     (Grp 4, n = 10)        O
```

The four groups are formed by the conditions [Traditional - Female], [Traditional - Male], [Reform - Female], and [Reform - Male]. In this example, each participant in each group is observed or measured once (O) on the dependent variable, perhaps some measure of achievement.

You might ask why we do not usually display the diagram in blocks form, as follows:

		Gender	
		Female	*Male*
Teaching Style	Traditional	Grp 1 (N = 10)	Grp 2 (N = 10)
	Reform	Grp 3 (N = 10)	Grp 4 (N = 10)

One reason we do not use the block diagram method is that this method works well only as long as there are no more than two independent variables. When there are more than two independent variables, the third independent variable would be visualized on a third dimension. More importantly, the block diagram does not represent the way the data would be entered into the computer for proper analysis. The following diagram partially illustrates the way that these data would be prepared for entering into the computer. (Only the first and last subject in each group of 10 are shown.) Notice the similarity to the first diagram.

Group	Participant No.	Teaching Style	Gender	Achievement
1	1	1	1	53
1	10	1	1	75
2	11	1	2	67
2	20	1	2	77
3	21	2	1	82
3	30	2	1	75
4	31	2	2	86
4	40	2	2	92

Let's add a third between groups independent variable, age, with two levels, young and old. Because 8 groups are needed to complete the design, we would need 80 participants for the study. This between groups design with three independent variables can be diagramed as follows:

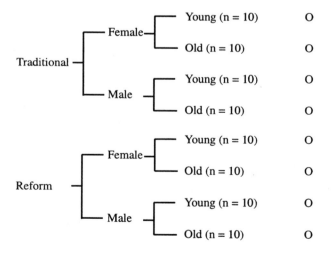

Within Subjects Designs

In contrast to between groups designs, within subjects designs are always diagramed by using columns, and the data are entered for analysis that way. Suppose we have a study that uses a within subjects design. There are two independent variables, both within subjects independent variables. The first independent variable is change over time, with two levels, pretest and posttest.

The second independent variable is our teaching style independent variable, with two levels, authoritative and participatory. However, because both independent variables are within subjects independent variables, each participant must undergo all conditions of the experiment.

Note that the dependent variable (O) scores are what go in each column. The design is diagramed as follows:

	Pretest Reform (condition 1)	Posttest Reform (condition 2)	Pretest Traditional (condition 3)	Posttest Traditional (condition 4)
($n = 10$)	O	O	O	O

In this design, only 10 participants are needed to complete the study. However, each participant must undergo all four conditions.[3]

Mixed Designs

This type of design is diagramed by combining the between groups design and the within subjects design. A common example of a mixed design would be a research study to evaluate the effects of a new curriculum. The between groups independent variable would be the curriculum, with two levels, new curriculum and old curriculum. The within subjects independent variable would be time, with two levels, before the evaluation and after the evaluation. Because the diagram is relatively simple, we have included the variable name as well as the levels.

	Type of curriculum	Pretest	Posttest
(Grp 1, n = 10)	1	O	O
(Grp 2, n = 10)	2	O	O

Notice that each participant is in only one group, but all participants in each group are measured before the intervention and after the intervention.

Describing the Various Types of Design

Within the methods section of a research paper, often there is a subsection designated Design or Design/Analysis. The purpose of this section is to identify the independent variable(s), dependent variable(s), and design in randomized experimental, quasi-experimental, and comparative studies. Most journals will not allow space to diagram the design, so the appropriate procedure is to describe the design. Designs are usually described in terms of (a) the general type of design (between groups, within subjects, or mixed); (b) the number of independent variables; and (c) the number of levels within each independent variable.

---

[3]In some cases the posttest for the first level (reform) serves as the pretest for the second level (traditional) of one independent variable, necessitating only three observations.

Single Factor Designs

If the design has one independent variable only (either a between groups design or a within subjects design), then it should be described as a *single factor design*. (Factor is another name for independent variable.) For example, a between groups design with one independent variable and four levels would be described as a single factor design with four levels. If the same design was a within subjects design with four levels, then it would be described as a single factor repeated measures design with four levels. Note that "between groups" is not stated directly in the first example, but is implied because there is no mention in that example of repeated measures.

Between Groups Factorial Designs

When there is more than one independent variable, then the levels of *each* independent variable become important in the description of the design. For example, suppose a design has three between groups independent variables, and the first independent variable has two levels, the second independent variable has three levels, and the third independent variable has two levels. The design is written as a $2 \times 3 \times 2$ factorial design (factorial means two or more independent variables). Again, between groups is not explicitly mentioned, but is implied because there is no mention of repeated measures, as in a within subjects design description. Because the design is a between groups design, the number of groups needed to complete the study is $2 \times 3 \times 2$, or 12 groups.

Within Subjects Factorial Designs

On the other hand, if the design is a within subjects design with two independent variables, each with two levels, then it is described as a 2×2 within subjects design or, more commonly, a 2×2 factorial design with repeated measures on both factors.

Mixed Designs

Such a design might have two between groups independent variables with three and four levels, respectively, and have one within subjects independent variable with two levels. It would be described as a $3 \times 4 \times 2$ factorial design with repeated measures on the third factor.

Remember, when describing a design, that each independent variable is given one number, the number of levels for that variable. Thus a design description with three numbers (e.g., $2 \times 4 \times 3$) has *three* independent variables or factors, which have 2, 4, and 3 levels, respectively. A single factor design is specifically classified or described in words, not with numerals and multiplication signs. Note that the dependent variable is not part of the design description, so is not considered in this section. Table 12.1 provides examples for

TABLE 12.1

Examples of Design Classifications

Single Factor	One Independent Variable
Between	Single factor design with ___ levels
Within	Single factor repeated measures design with ___ levels
Mixed	NA

Two Factor	Two Independent Variables
Between	___ × ___Factorial design
Within	___ × ___Design with repeated measures on both factors
Mixed	___ × ___(Mixed) Design with repeated measures on the last factor

Three Factor	Three Independent Variables
Between	___ × ___ × ___Factorial design
Within	___ × ___ × ___Design with repeated measures on all factors
Mixed	___ × ___ × ___Design with repeated measures on last (or last two) factors

Note. The dependent variable is not part of the design classification and, thus, is not mentioned. The number of levels for an independent variable is inserted in each blank.

describing the between, within, and mixed designs for studies with one, two, and three independent variables.

CLASSIFICATION OF SPECIFIC EXPERIMENTAL DESIGNS

Although specific experimental designs (see chap. 7) are important for assessing internal validity, they do not help to determine selection of the proper statistical analysis. However, any specific research design can be expressed as a general design. We provide three examples of how specific research designs fit into general design classifications. These examples are the Solomon four-group design, the pretest–posttest nonequivalent control group design, and a within subjects randomized experimental design.

Solomon Four-Group Design

Of particular interest for this design is how it fits into our general design classification of between groups, within subjects, or mixed designs. A first guess is that it is a mixed design because at least two of the groups receive a pretest and a posttest. However, closer examination of this design indicates that the investigator is really not interested in the pretest scores, only in the effects that taking a pretest has on the posttest. Therefore, the design is actually a between groups design with two independent variables. More specifically, the design is a 2 × 2 factorial design. The two independent variables are pretest (yes or no) and intervention (yes or no), each with two levels. The design can be viewed schematically as follows:

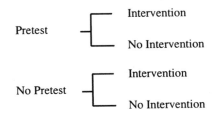

Pretest–Posttest Non-Equivalent Control Group Design

This specific research design fits the general design classification of a mixed design. There are two independent variables. One independent variable is type of intervention, a between groups independent variable with two levels, treatment and no treatment. The second independent variable is change over time, a within subjects independent variable with two levels, pretest and posttest. The design can be seen as follows:

	Pretest	*I.V.*	*Posttest*
Treatment	O	X	O
No Treatment	O	~X	O

Notice that the pretest–posttest control group design, a design that fits the randomized experimental approach, has the same general design classification, mixed, as the pretest–posttest nonequivalent comparison group design, a quasi-experimental approach.

Within Subjects Randomized Experimental Design

The third example is one that we did not explicitly describe in chapter 7 because we had not yet discussed within subjects designs. In the simplest case, this design has two levels and can be shown as follows:

		Condition 1	*Test*	*Condition 2*	*Test*
R	Group 1	X	O	~X	O
R	Group 2	~X	O	X	O

The participants are randomly assigned to either Group 1, which receives the experimental condition first and then the control condition, or Group 2, which receives the control condition and then the experimental. Of course, this design can have problems if there are carryover effects from the experimental condition. The approach is considered randomized experimental if the *order* in which participants receive the conditions is randomized. If not, the approach is quasi-experimental. This type of design is frequently used in studies where participants are asked to evaluate stimuli (e.g., foods) and in evaluating diets, exercise, and similar events assumed not to have long carryover effects.

Table 12.2 describes how each specific research design fits the general design classification (last column). This classification (between groups, within subjects, or mixed) determines, in good part, the appropriate type of difference

TABLE 12.2
Classification of Specific Designs for Experiments and Quasi-Experiments

Poor Quasi-Experimental Designs	Assign.	Grp.	Pre.	I.V.	Post.	Class.
One Group Posttest Only Design	NR	E:		X	O	None
One Group Pretest–Posttest Design	NR	E:	O	X	O	Within
Posttest-Only Design with	NR	E:		X	O	Between
Nonequivalent Groups	NR	C:		~X	O	
Quasi-Experimental Designs						
Pretest–Posttest Nonequivalent	NR	E:	O	X	O	Mixed
Comparison Group Designs	NR	C:	O	~X	O	
Single Group Time-Series Designs with Temporary Treatment	NR	E:	OOO	X	OOO	Within
with Continuous Treatment	NR	E:	OOO	XOXO	XOXO	Within
Multiple Group Time-Series Designs with Temporary Treatment	NR	E:	OOO	X	OOO	Mixed
	NR	C:	OOO	~X	OOO	
with Continuous Treatment	NR	E:	OOO	XOXO	XOXO	Mixed
	NR	C:	OOO	O O	O O	
Randomized Experimental Designs						
Posttest-Only Control Group Design	R	E:		X	O	Between
	R	C:		~X	O	
Pretest–Posttest Control Group Design	R	E:	O	X	O	Mixed
	R	C:	O	~X	O	
Solomon Four-Group Design	R	E1:	O	X	O	Between
	R	E2:		X	O	2-factor
	R	C1:	O	~X	O	
	R	C2:		~X	O	
Randomized Experimental Design with Matching	M R	E:		X	O	Within
	M R	C:		~X	O	

Abbreviations are: Assign. = assignment of subjects to groups (NR = non random, R = random, M R = matched then randomly assigned). Grp. = group or condition (E: = experimental, C: = control or comparison). Pre = pretest (O = an observation or measurement; a blank means there was no pretest for that group). I.V. = active independent variable (X = intervention, ~X = control or other treatment). Post = posttest (O = a posttest observation or measure). Class. = classification (between, within, or mixed).

inferential statistic to use. The within subjects designs would be analyzed using the correlated or paired samples *t* test or repeated measures ANOVA (if there are more than two levels or measures of the dependent variable), as dis-

cussed in chapter 15. The single factor between groups designs would be analyzed with an independent samples *t* test or one-way ANOVA, as discussed in
chapter 14, and the two-factor Solomon four-group design would be analyzed
with a two-way ANOVA, as discussed in chapter 17.

SUMMARY

This chapter described the general design classifications of between groups,
within subjects, and mixed designs. Remember that in *between groups designs*, each participant is in only one group or condition. In *within subjects or
repeated measures designs,* on the other hand, each participant receives all the
conditions or levels of the independent variable. In *mixed designs,* there is at
least one between groups independent variable and at least one within subjects
independent *variable.* In classifying the design, do not consider the dependent
variable(s).

The diagrams, classifications, and descriptions presented in this chapter are
for difference questions that use the randomized experimental,
quasi-experimental, and comparative approaches to research. Appropriate
classification and description of the design is crucial for choosing the appropriate inferential statistic, usually some type of analysis of variance.

STUDY AIDS

Concepts

- Between groups designs
- Carryover effects
- Change over time
- Matching
- Mixed designs
- Solomon four-group design
- Within subjects designs

Distinctions

- Active versus attribute versus within subjects versus mixed designs
- Between groups designs versus within subjects designs versus mixed de-
  signs
- Single factor versus factorial designs

Application Problems

1. Explain why the independent variable(s) for a within subjects design are
not usually attribute independent variables.

2. Within subjects designs usually employ one of two types of independent
variables. One type is the active independent variable. What is the other type,
and how is it used?

3. Give an example of a within subjects (repeated measure) design, and diagram it.

For questions 4–7 answer the following:

    a. Identify the independent variable(s). For each, state whether it is active, attribute, or change over time.

    b. Identify the dependent variable(s).

    c. Diagram the design.

    d. Identify the design classification (e.g., 4 × 4 factorial).

4. A researcher wanted to know if type of exercise and type of individual influences a person's willingness to stay in an exercise program. The researcher recruited 300 participants. The study included people considered young (20–35), middle-aged (36–50) and above middle-aged (51–70). The study also included 150 men and 150 women. Additionally, of the 300 participants, 100 were African American, 100 were white/Non-Hispanic, and 100 were Hispanic. The participants were randomly assigned to three different exercise regimes: running in circles around a track, swimming laps at an indoor pool, or riding a bike in the Rocky Mountains. The regimes lasted for 2 months. At the end of the 2 months, the participants all completed the Willingness to Continue Exercising Regime Scale.

5. A humanities professor who was going to lead a year-long study-abroad program wondered if travel experience had any impact on students' ability to understand and embrace diversity in others. At the beginning of the school year the professor gave all the students the Morgan Multicultural Acceptance Scale. This scale was also given at the end of the year when the students returned from abroad.

6. A dog trainer was interested in knowing whether her new aversive approach to obedience training was effective. She divided her new clientele into three different groups. The first group received traditional dog training, wherein good behavior is rewarded with praise and treats. The second group received the new aversive training, wherein nonconforming behavior was punished with removed water and food, slaps on the nose, and loud yelling by the trainer and the owner. The third group was the control and did not get any training for their dogs. Before the training and three months later, the trainer rated the dogs from all three groups on a dog obedience scale.

7. An investigator was interested in two different cues that might be used in the reproduction of movement: (a) the initial position of the movement and same or different, (b) the speed of the movement, fast or slow. In addition, she was also interested in how age affects reproduction of movement. Three groups of participants (40 participants per group) were in the study. These three groups were either 7 year olds, 11 year olds, or adults. Within each group subjects were randomly assigned to one of four conditions. These conditions were a fast movement with the initial position the same, a slow movement with the initial position the same, a fast movement with the initial position different, and a slow movement with the initial condition different. The researcher measured the distance error from the target and the angle error.

CHAPTER

13

Selection of Statistical Methods

Choosing the proper statistical analysis may seem like a difficult task, considering the large number of possible choices. However, this task should be easier because you are now familiar with independent and dependent variables, research approaches, design classifications, and scales or levels of measurement. This chapter presents a series of decision steps and four tables that will help you choose an appropriate inferential statistic. However, before presenting the decision tree and describing how to use the statistical selection tables, we review the concepts that are necessary for selecting inferential statistics.

REVIEW OF CONCEPTS NECESSARY FOR SELECTING INFERENTIAL STATISTICS

Research Approaches and Questions

In chapter 5, we discussed five research approaches and three types of research questions. Figure 13.1 (which is the same as Fig. 5.3) is the key figure that presents the relationships among the five specific approaches, the three types of research questions, and the three types of statistics: difference inferential, associational inferential, and descriptive.

Difference Questions. The first three approaches (randomized experimental, quasi-experimental, and comparative) all compare groups and test difference questions or hypotheses, as in our women graduate students' exercise and heart rate example (chap. 11). These three approaches usually use the same types of statistics, which we called difference inferential statistics. Remember that difference statistics and questions are used to compare a few groups (e.g., males versus females, experimental versus control, or three curriculums) for each group's average scores on the dependent variable (e.g., an achievement measure).

Associational Questions. We hope you remember that associational questions use the associational approach to research and what we call associational inferential statistics. The statistics in this group examine the association or correlation between two or more *variables*. If there is a positive association, persons who have high scores on one variable tend to have high scores on the second variable; those with low scores tend to be low on both variables. That is, high scores are associated with high scores, low with low, and medium with medium. On the other hand, if there is a negative association between the two variables, those with *low* scores on the first variable tend to have *high* scores on the second variable and vice versa. That is, low scores are associated with high scores. If there is no association, you cannot predict a person's score on the second variable from knowing the first. People who score high on the first variable might be high, or low, or medium on the second variable.

Descriptive questions and statistics were discussed in chapter 9, so will not be discussed in this chapter. It is worth noting that in several cases there may be more than one appropriate statistical analysis. One might assume, because the statistical formulas are precise mathematically, that this same precision generalizes to the choice of a statistical test. As we shall see, unfortunately, this is not always true.

Independent and Dependent Variables

We discussed variables in depth in chapter 4. Remember that the independent variable is a *presumed* cause of changes in the dependent variable, although the moderate and weak quasi-experimental, comparative, and associational approaches do not provide good evidence about causes. We distinguished, in chapter 4, between active or manipulated independent variables and attribute independent variables. Although this distinction is important for deciding whether the independent variable is a cause, it is not relevant for deciding which inferential statistic to use. Thus, we will not mention active and attribute independent variables again in this chapter. What *is* relevant for selecting statistics is the number of variables, especially the number of independent variables and levels within these independent variables.

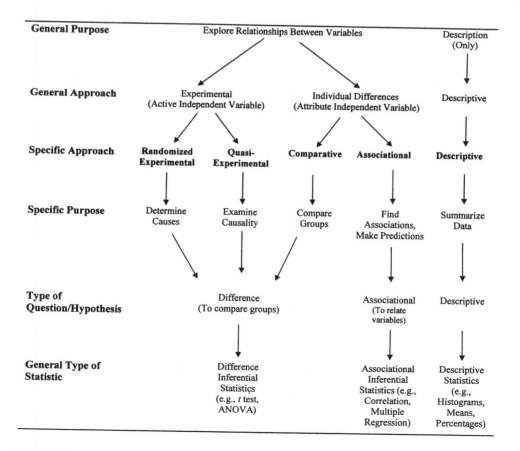

FIG. 13.1.   Schematic diagram showing how the general type of statistic and hypotheses or question used in a study corresponds to the purposes and the approach.

Number of Independent Variables.   First you need to decide whether for *this* research question there is one, or more than one, independent variable. If there is only one, we call the design *basic* (or *single factor* design, if answering a difference question). If there is more than one independent variable, the statistics are called *complex* (or *factorial* in the case of difference questions).

Number of Levels of the Independent Variable.   A difference question is indicated when the independent variable has a few (i.e., two to four) levels. That is, do males and females or experimental and control groups differ on the dependent variable? However, if the independent variable has more than four *unordered* (nominal) levels, one would usually still ask a difference question and compare the groups. For example, do six ethnic groups differ? Remember that there have to be at least two levels or there is not a variable; rather, there is a constant.

When the independent variable has five or more *ordered* levels, you usually ask an associational question and use associational inferential statistics. Thus, if the independent variable is continuous (an infinite number of ordered levels within a range) or approximates a continuous variable (our rule of thumb is five or more ordered levels), associational statistics are used. However, one can also ask an associational question when the independent variable is nominal. It should be noted that the two variable associational inferential statistics (e.g., Pearson correlation) are bidirectional, so statisticians would say that there is no independent variable. However, because researchers usually have a causal relationship in mind, we suggest identifying one of the variables as the independent variable.

The dependent variable is also important for the appropriate choice of an inferential statistic. The primary issue is the level of measurement of the dependent variable, which we discuss following.

Design Classifications

Our discussion of design classifications in chapter 12 is important background for selecting an appropriate statistic. The key issue for selecting an appropriate statistic is whether the classification is between, within, or mixed. These classifications apply only to the randomized experimental, quasi-experimental, and comparative approaches (i.e., to difference questions).

Between Groups Versus Within Subjects Single Factor Designs.   With one independent variable, the design must be either between or within because it takes at least two independent variables to have a mixed design. To use basic difference statistics, you need to know whether the two or more groups or levels of the independent variable are independent of each other (a between groups design) or related (a within subjects or repeated measures design).[1] In

---

[1]Note that in this sentence the word independent has two different meanings. The second usage, meaning separate from, not related to, or not influenced by, is a key term in statistics and is an assumption of many statistical tests. Appendix A contrasts the several meanings of terms like independent, random, and validity, whose meanings, unfortunately, depend on the context. We have tried to be clear about the context.

between groups designs, each participant is in only one group, and participants are neither matched in pairs, triads, and so on, nor related as couples, mother and child(ren), or teacher and student(s). In within subjects or repeated measures designs, the participants are either assessed two or more times (repeated measures), or else two (or even three or more) of them are matched or paired up in a meaningful way. For statistical purposes, their scores are not independent (i.e., they are said to be related or correlated samples). These within subjects designs use different statistics than the between groups designs, as we will see.

Classification in Factorial Designs.   When you have two or more independent variables, there are three possible design classifications: all between groups, all within subjects, and mixed (between and within). Thus, to choose the appropriate complex difference statistic, you have to understand this distinction. In between groups designs, the groups are independent; each participant is assessed only once on any given dependent variable. In within subjects designs, each person is assessed in every condition and so has a score in every cell in the design. In mixed designs, such as the pretest–posttest control group design, there is at least one between groups variable and at least one within subjects variable.

Levels or Scales of Measurement

For appropriate statistical selection, level of measurement is also important. Remember that *normally distributed* data was the highest level discussed in chapter 9. It is also an assumption of parametric statistics such as the *t* test, ANOVA, and Pearson correlation. *Ordinal* data have three or more levels ordered from low to high (often ranks), but with unequal spaces between levels and, more importantly for statistical selection, they are not normally distributed. In contrast, *nominal* data have three or more unordered levels or categories.

For difference statistics, the variable whose level of measurement matters is the dependent variable. The independent variable can be nominal (e.g., ethnic groups) or ordered (e.g., low, medium, and high), but usually has fewer than five ordered levels. For associational statistics, the level of measurement for both or all variables needs to be determined.

Dichotomous variables form a special case, as discussed in chapter 9. Remember that although dichotomous variables are in many ways like nominal variables, they can be used, especially as independent or predictor variables in multiple regression, as if they were normally distributed variables.

Other Assumptions

Every statistical test is based on certain assumptions. In general, the parametric statistics (*t* test, ANOVA, Pearson correlation, multiple regression) have more assumptions. The parametric statistics have normality of a distribution as one of the assumptions. Often, this assumption can be violated quite a bit before the results are distorted; thus, the variables used in parametric analyses only have to be approximately normally distributed.

Equality of variances is another common assumption of parametric tests. Again, this can be violated to a degree, and some statistical programs (e.g., SPSS) have built-in corrections for some parametric statistics. However, if one or both of these or other assumptions are markedly violated, then the equivalent ordinal nonparametric test should be used.

It should be apparent from the preceding discussion (and that to follow) that selection of an appropriate statistic is, to some extent, a matter of judgment and best practice. Even so, there are several guidelines that must be followed. We will point these out as we encounter them.

The assumption of independence was mentioned earlier under Design Classifications. This assumption must not be violated, for example, by using a between groups statistic when your data are really within subjects.

SELECTION OF APPROPRIATE INFERENTIAL STATISTICS

How to Use the Statistical Selection Tables

Figure 13.2, as well as the following text, will help to organize your thinking when selecting an appropriate statistical test. First, decide whether your research question or hypothesis is a *difference* one (i.e., compares groups) or an *associational* one (relates variables). Our rule of thumb is that if the independent or predictor variable has five or more *ordered* levels or categories, the question should be considered an associational one.[2] If the independent variable has two to four categories it is usually better to treat the question as a difference one. The latter leads you to Tables 13.1 or 13.3 and the former to Tables 13.2 or 13.4.

Second, decide how many variables there are in your question. If there is only one independent variable, use Table 13.1 or 13.2, depending on how you answered the first question. If there is more than one independent (or dependent) variable to be used in this analysis, use Tables 13.3 or 13.4, depending on whether the research question is a difference or associational question.

Basic Difference Statistics.   If your question involves a *basic, single factor, difference question*, use Table 13.1. To do so you must determine (a) the level of measurement of the *dependent* variable and whether assumptions are markedly violated, (b) how many levels or groups or samples there are in your independent variable, and (c) whether the design is between groups or within subjects. The answers to these questions lead to a specific location and statistic in Table 13.1. Notice that you are asked to decide whether the independent variable has two versus two or more levels of the independent variable. You might ask why we bother to have a separate category for two levels when "two or more" includes two. One part of the answer is that the popular *t* test can only be used when there are two levels; the second part is that the *t* test can be used with a directional (one-tailed) hypothesis, whereas the alternative statistic,

---

[2]The exception is that if you want to assess the *strength* of the association between two nominal variables (or ordered variables with a few levels, you would use the appropriate nominal associational statistic (i.e., Phi or Cramer's V).

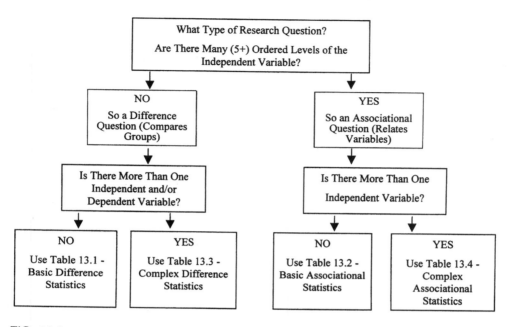

What Type of Research Question?

Are There Many (5+) Ordered Levels of the Independent Variable?

NO

So a Difference Question (Compares Groups)

YES

So an Associational Question (Relates Variables)

Is There More Than One Independent and/or Dependent Variable?

Is There More Than One

Independent Variable?

NO

Use Table 13.1 - Basic Difference Statistics

YES

Use Table 13.3 - Complex Difference Statistics

NO

Use Table 13.2 - Basic Associational Statistics

YES

Use Table 13.4 - Complex Associational Statistics

FIG. 13.2.   A decision tree to decide how to select the appropriate statistic.

one-way ANOVA, is always two-tailed. There is more on this topic in chapter 14. All the statistics in Table 13.1 are discussed in chapters 14 and 15.

Remember that if assumptions of the parametric test are markedly violated one should use the equivalent, ordinal nonparametric statistic (e.g., Mann–Whitney instead of the independent samples t test). These ordinal, nonparametric alternatives are listed right below the parametric test. Little power is lost in using these tests, so it is probably wise to use them when assumptions are markedly violated. It would also be legitimate to use the statistics in the bottom row (e.g., chi-square) if one had ordinal or normal data, but there is a major loss of power in doing that, so it is not a good practice. A principle in using Tables 13.1 and 13.2 is that it is acceptable to use a statistic farther down a given column. You lose a little power going from the top to the second (ordinal) row, but you lose a lot of power going from the second to the third row in the column. It is a serious error to use the wrong column, that is, within instead of between or vice versa. Another absolute violation that will produce meaningless results is to use a statistic from the top two rows in Tables 13.1 and 13.2 (e.g., a t test or Mann–Whitney U) when one has a nominal dependent variable. That is definitely wrong!

Basic Associational Statistics.   If you ask a *basic,* two variable, *associational question,* use Table 13.2. Which row you use depends on *both* variables. If both are at least approximately normally distributed (and other assumptions met), you would use the Pearson product moment correlation. If both variables are at least ordered and parametric assumptions are markedly violated,

TABLE 13.1

Selection of an Appropriate Inferential Statistic for Basic, Single Factor, Difference Questions or Hypotheses (for Experimental, Quasi-Experimental, and Comparative Approaches)

Scale of Measurement of Dependent Variable	Compare	One Factor or Independent Variable With 2 Categories or Levels/Groups/Samples		One Independent Variable 2 or More Categories or Levels or Groups	
		Independent Samples or Groups (Between)	Repeated Measures or Related Samples (Within)	Independent Samples or Groups (Between)	Repeated Measures or Related Samples (Within)
Parametric Statistics Dependent variable approximates normal distribution data and assumptions not markedly violated	Means	Independent samples t test or One-way ANOVA Chap 14	Paired samples t test Chap 15	One-way ANOVA Chap 14	Repeated measures ANOVA Chap 15
Non Parametric Statistics Dependent variables clearly ordinal (ranked) data or assumptions markedly violated	Medians or ranks	Mann–Whitney Chap 14	Wilcoxon or sign test Chap 15	Kruskal–Wallis Chap 14	Friedman Chap 15
Dependent variable nominal (categorical) data	Counts	Chi-Square or Fisher exact test Chap 14	McNemar Chap 15	Chi-Square Chap 14	Cochran Q test Chap 15

Note. To select the appropriate statistic, locate a box based on a) the type of question, b) the design, and c) the scale of measurement. It is acceptable to use statistics that are in the box(es) below the appropriate statistic, but there is usually loss of information and power. It is not acceptable to use statistics above the appropriate box.

• Related samples designs are also called repeated measures, matched or paired groups, and within subjects.

• Chi-Square: Instead of difference questions, chi-square tests for the independence of two variables. Frequency data or counts of the number of Ss in each cell or category are used rather than raw scores and means.

• ANOVA is Analysis of Variance or F.

TABLE 13.2
Selection of an Appropriate Inferential Statistic for Basic, Two Variable, Associational Questions or Hypotheses (for Associational Approach)

Level (scale) of Measurement of Both Variables	Relate	Two Variables or Scores for the Same or Related Subjects
Variables are both normal data and other assumptions not markedly violated	Scores	Pearson (r) Chap 16
Both variables at least ordinal data	Ranks	Spearman (rho) Chap 16
One or both variables are nominal data	Counts	Phi or Cramer's V Chap 16

TABLE 13.3
Selection of the Appropriate Complex (More than One Independent and/or Dependent Variable) Statistic to Answer Difference Questions or Hypotheses (for the Experimental, Quasi-Experimental, and/or Comparative Approaches)

Dependent Variable(s) ↓	Two or More Independent Variables		
	All Between Groups	All Within Subjects	Mixed (Between & Within)
One normally distributed dependent variable	Factorial ANOVA Chap 17	Factorial ANOVA with repeated measures on all factors	Factorial ANOVA with repeated measures on last or last 2 factors Chap 18
Ordinal dependent variable	None common	None common	None common
Nominal dependent variable	Log linear	None common	None common
Several normally distributed dependent variables	MANOVA Chap 19	MANOVA with repeated measures on all factors	MANOVA with repeated measures on last or last several factors Chap 19

TABLE 13.4
Selection of the Appropriate Complex Associational Statistic for the Purpose of Predicting a Single Dependent or Outcome Variable from Several Independent Variables

One Dependent Variable ↓	Several Independent Variables		
	All Normally Distributed	Some Normal Some Dichotomous	All Dichotomous
Normally distributed (continuous)	Multiple regression Chap 19	Multiple regression Chap 19	Multiple regression Chap 19
Dichotomous	Discriminant analysis Chap 19	Logistic regression Chap 19	Logistic regression Chap 19

use the Spearman rank order correlation, Rho. If one or both of the variables are nominal, use Phi (if both variables have two levels, a 2 × 2 cross-tabulation) or Cramer's V for a larger cross-tabulation. Table 13.2 shows only two (Phi and Cramer's V) of many associational statistics that ask about the strength of the association between two variables, when one or both are nominal variables, for example, ethnic group and voting preference. The use of these statistics is relatively uncommon in the literature so we do not discuss them in detail, but Phi and Cramer's V are discussed briefly in chapter 16. The Pearson and Spearman correlations also are discussed in chapter 16.

Complex Difference Statistics. If you ask a *complex difference question* (three or more variables), appropriate statistics are identified in Table 13.3. To select the appropriate statistic, you first decide whether the design classification is between groups, within subjects, or mixed. Then if there is one dependent variable, and it is approximately normally distributed, you are led to one of three factorial ANOVAs. These ANOVAs are similar but have different formulas, so it is important to know which one to do. The between groups factorial ANOVA is discussed in chapter 17, and the mixed ANOVA is discussed in chapter 18, along with the analysis of covariance (ANCOVA). We do not discuss the two-factor repeated measures ANOVA, because it is not common in education or in the allied health disciplines.

Notice that, unfortunately, there are no common ordinal statistics that are equivalent to the factorial ANOVAs. Log linear analysis is sometimes seen in the literature, but is not discussed in this book. It is similar to a factorial ANOVA for nominal or categorical data and is similar to a complex chi-square.

The bottom row of Table 13.3 shows three multivariate analyses of variance (MANOVAs) that parallel the three factorial ANOVAs but are used when one wants to analyze several normally distributed dependent variables together instead of one at a time. MANOVA can also be used instead of several one-way ANOVAs when there is one independent variable (single factor design) and several dependent variables that you want to analyze in one analysis rather than separately. Chapter 19 has a brief discussion of MANOVA, its use, and assumptions.

Complex Associational Statistics. If you ask a *complex associational question* (two or more independent variables), appropriate statistics are identified in Table 13.4. These and other complex associational statistics are discussed in chapter 19. Notice that the left-hand column of Table 13.4 is different from the other three tables in that ordinal and nominal levels of measurement are not listed. There are no common ordinal statistics similar to these, but, discriminant analyses can be used with a nominal (three unordered levels) dependent variable. That makes interpretation much more complex. The top row lists multiple regression, which is used for cases in which two or more independent variables predict a normally distributed dependent variable. Notice that multiple regression can be used when the dependent variables are normally distributed and when they are dichotomous. Actually, the assumption of normality for multiple regression is more complex than indicated. When to use discriminant analysis and logistic regression is indicated in Table 13.4.

Occasionally you will see a research article in which a dichotomous dependent variable was used in a *t* test, ANOVA, or Pearson correlation. Because of the special nature of dichotomous variables, this is not wrong, as would be the use of a nominal (three or more unordered levels) dependent variable with these parametric statistics. However, we think that it is a better practice to use the same statistics with dichotomous variables that you would use with nominal variables. The exception is that it is appropriate to use dichotomous (dummy) independent variables in multiple regression and logistic regression (see Table 13.4).

Not shown are four complex associational statistics that you may see in the literature. The most common is *factor analysis*, which is usually used to reduce a relatively large number of variables to a smaller number of groups of variables. These new composite variables are called factors or components. Factor analysis is discussed briefly in chapter 19 and also in chapter 20.

Because they are very advanced statistics, the other three are not discussed in this book, but they are mentioned here. *Canonical correlation* is a correlation of a linear combination of several independent variables with a linear combination of several dependent variables. *Path analysis* is a multivariate analysis in which "causal" relationships among several variables are represented by figures showing the "paths" among them. *Structural equation models* (SEM) are models that describe causal relationships among latent (unobserved) variables. Path analysis and SEM are related; both provide tests of the accuracy of the proposed model and both are said by proponents to provide evidence of causal linkages from nonexperimental designs. However, the APA Task Force on Statistical Inference states that "the use of complicated 'causal modeling' software rarely yields results that have any interpretation as causal effects" (Wilkinson & The Task Force on Statistical Inference, 1999, p. 600).

The General Linear Model

Something that is not obvious from Tables 13.1 and 13.2 is that the broad question of whether there is a relationship between variables X and Y can be answered two ways. If both the independent variable and dependent variable provide approximately normally distributed data with five or more levels, the obvious statistic to use (from Fig. 13.1 and Table 13.2) is the Pearson correlation, and that would be our recommendation. However, some researchers choose to divide the independent variable into two or several categories or groups such as low, medium, and high and then do a one-way ANOVA. Conversely, others who start with an independent variable that has a few categories (say two through four ordered categories) may choose to do a correlation instead of a one-way ANOVA. Although these choices are not wrong, we do not think they are the best practice. We say this because, in the first example, information is lost by dividing a continuous independent variable into a few categories. In the second example, there would be a restricted range, which tends to decrease the size of the correlation coefficient.

In the preceding examples, we recommended one of the choices, but the fact that there *are* two choices raises a bigger and more complex issue that we have hinted at in earlier chapters. Statisticians point out, and can prove mathematically, that the distinction between difference and associational statistics is an artificial one and that one-way ANOVA and Pearson correlation are mathematically the same, as are factorial ANOVA and multiple regression. Thus, the full range of methods used to analyze one continuous dependent variable and one or more independent variables, either continuous or categorical, are mathematically related (Keppel & Zedeck, 1989). The model on which this is based is called the *General Linear Model*; it is "general" in that the kind of independent variable is not specified. The idea is that the relationship between the independent and dependent variables can be expressed by an equation with terms for the weighted values of each of the independent or predictor variables plus an error term.

What this means is that if you have a continuous, normally distributed dependent or outcome variable and five or so levels of a normally distributed independent variable (not derived by dividing a continuous variable), it would be appropriate to analyze it with either a correlation or a one-way ANOVA. You should get the same answer for the significance level. However, you would need a large sample to have enough participants in each group for the ANOVA comparisons if you have many more than four levels of the independent variable.

Although we recognize that our distinction between difference and associational parametric statistics is a simplification, we still think it is useful heuristically. We hope that this glimpse of an advanced topic is clear and helpful. If not, you can probably skip this section and still have a good basic understanding of how to choose appropriate inferential statistics.

SUMMARY

This chapter serves as an introduction to the selection of appropriate statistical methods. In the next six chapters we discuss conceptually, and in more depth, the statistical methods shown in Tables 13.1 to 13.4. We take examples from journals that publish research in applied settings and demonstrate why the author(s) selected a particular statistical method. Our approach shows that the choice of a particular statistical method is directly related to the general design classification, and the level of measurement. In addition, we discuss how the results of the statistical method were interpreted.

Selection of an appropriate statistic requires judgment as well as following the decision rules. This process can be tough, but this overview should have given you a good foundation. You should review this chapter when you need to decide on a statistic to use. If you do so, you will have a good grasp of how the various statistics fit together and when to use them.

STUDY AIDS

Concepts

- General linear model
- Normality or normally distributed
- Statistical assumptions
- Statistical independence

Distinctions

- Basic (two variables) versus complex (three or more variables) inferential statistics
- Compare groups versus associate variables
- Dichotomous versus nominal versus ordinal versus normal level of measurement
- Difference questions versus associational questions
- Number of independent variables versus number of levels of the variable
- Parametric versus nonparametric statistics
- Within subjects versus between groups versus mixed design classification

Application Problems

1. How should you decide if your research is a difference question or an associational question?

2. How should you determine if you should use basic or complex statistical analyses?

3. A decision to compare means, medians or counts is based on?

For problems 4 to 10, create an example and then use the tables in chapter 13 to arrive at the proper statistical analysis.

4. One independent variable, three levels, between groups, one ordinal non-normally distributed dependent variable.

5. Two between groups independent variables, each with three levels, one normally distributed dependent variable.

6. One between groups independent variable, one repeated measures independent variable, each with two levels, one normally distributed dependent variable.

7. One independent variable, two levels, repeated measures, one nominal dependent variable.

8. One independent variable, four levels, between groups, one nominal dependent variable.

9. Three normally distributed and one dichotomous independent variables, one normally distributed dependent variable.

10. A teacher ranked the 25 students in her Algebra 1 class from 1 = highest to 25 = lowest in terms of their grades on several tests. After the next semester, she checked the school records to see what grade the students received from their Algebra 2 teacher. The teacher wanted to know if her final ranking of the students in Algebra 1 had influenced their grade in Algebra 2.

Integrating Designs and Analyses: Interpreting Results

14

Single Factor
Between Groups Designs:
Analysis and Interpretation

Study Aids
Concepts
Distinctions
Application Problems

OVERVIEW

The examples of analyses for this chapter include statistical tests that are used for a design with one independent variable that has two or more levels, and all participants are in one and only one condition (between groups). The single factor design would include studies that use the *quantitative* randomized experimental, quasi-experimental, and comparative approaches. It is important to remember (see Fig. 5.2) that the appropriate statistical test is the same for each of these quantitative approaches. For example, consider three different quantitative approaches.

The randomized experimental approach uses a design where participants are randomly assigned to intervention and control groups. The intervention group receives a form of treatment, and the control group either receives no treatment, or a traditional treatment. At the end of the intervention period, both groups are measured and compared on a dependent variable(s). In this design, there is one independent variable with two levels. Participants are in one and only one condition or group.

Now consider the quasi-experimental approach that uses a design where participants self-assign themselves into the intervention group, and a separate control group is selected. At the end of the intervention period, both groups are measured and compared on a dependent variable(s). Again, there is one independent variable with two levels and participants are in one and only one condition of the study.

A third example is the comparative approach that compares participants on an attribute independent variable. One could compare a group of physically handicapped participants with a group of participants who are not physically handicapped on a motor skill dependent variable. Again, there is one independent variable with two levels and participants are in one and only one condition of the study.

All three of these examples of quantitative approaches fall under the heading of single factor designs. The interpretation of the results from each of these examples would be different because the rigor (relative *internal validity*) of each design, but the statistical analysis would be the same, because each example was a single factor between groups design with two levels. Although the previous examples had only two conditions, single factor designs also include approaches with one independent variable and *more* than two levels. Therefore, any of the above examples could have had three or more levels and still be classified as a single factor design. For example, a study with two treatment conditions and a control condition is still a single factor design.

We have divided this chapter into analyses that apply to single factor designs that use parametric statistics and single factor designs that use nonparametric statistics. For the most part, the decision is made from the level of the dependent variable. Parametric statistics are appropriately applied to data from studies where the dependent variable is normally distributed (see chap. 9). Nonparametric statistics are usually applied to data from studies where the assumptions for using parametric statistics are violated, or the scale of the dependent variable is ordinal or nominal.

ANALYZING SINGLE FACTOR DESIGNS WITH PARAMETRIC STATISTICS

We start our analyses with single factor, between groups designs performed on dependent variables that are interval, or ratio scale (i.e., use parametric statistics), or both. Figure 14.1 demonstrates the decision tree for these analyses. We discuss the independent samples *t* test first and then the single factor, or one-way, analysis of variance (ANOVA).

t Test for Independent Samples

Does the method of questioning in class affect how students prepare for class? McDougall and Granby (1996) conducted a study to determine if students who

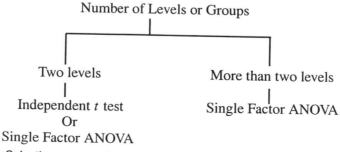

FIG. 14.1   Selecting parametric statistics for single factor between groups designs.

were called on in class randomly would prepare for class in a different manner than students whose participation was strictly voluntary. The researchers conducted the study in an undergraduate statistics class with 40 participants. The mode of participation in the class was voluntary until the middle of the semester. Then, approximately half of the class (intervention condition) was randomly assigned to a condition of random oral-questioning ($n = 18$). The other half of the class (control condition) continued in the voluntary participation mode ($n = 22$). At the end of the next class, all students were asked to complete a 12-item instrument that made up the dependent variables. For our purposes, we will look at one of the dependent variables: completion of assigned reading. This measure was defined as the number of pages from the assigned chapter that students had read prior to coming to class. The design for this study was a posttest-only control group design, because participants were randomly assigned to one and only one group, and measured just once. Thus, the research approach would be characterized as randomized experimental. The results of the study can be seen in Table 14.1.

McDougall and Granby performed a *t* test for independent samples to determine if the two conditions differed significantly on the measure of number of assigned pages read. A *t* test was selected to analyze the data for the following reasons (Fig. 14.1). First, there was just one independent variable, type of intervention. Second, there were only two levels, random participation and voluntary participation. Third, the dependent variable, number of pages of the assigned chapter read, was ratio data. The results of the *t* test were expressed as, "The differences between group means attained statistical significance: *t* (38) = 2.67, p < .02. " (p. 49). What does this mean?

Conceptual View of the t Test and Other Parametric Tests.   The *t* test (and the different analyses of variance [F test]) is a ratio of the variance between groups or conditions to the variance within the groups or conditions:

$$t = \frac{Variance_{between}}{Variance_{within}}$$

If this ratio is large (i.e., the variance between groups is several times greater than the variance within groups), then it is likely that the result will be statistically significant. What do we mean by the variance between groups and the variance within groups? In the *t* test, the variance between groups is determined from the difference between the mean of the intervention group and the

TABLE 14.1

Descriptive Statistics for the McDougall and Granby (1996) Study

Sample Description	Intervention Condition	Control Condition
Number of participants	18	22
Mean	16.47	9.84
Standard deviation	5.82	9.09

mean of the control group. In the McDougall and Granby (1996)study, the mean of the intervention group was 16.47 pages read, and the mean of the control group was 9.84 pages read. Therefore, the difference between the means was 6.63 pages in favor of the intervention condition. One would expect this difference between the two means to be large if in fact the intervention was effective. Between groups variance is often referred to as *treatment variance*. The variance within groups or conditions is the variability or differences among the individual participants within each group. One would expect there to be differences among participants within groups because they are different individuals. Other differences might be due to errors made in measurement. The size of the variance within groups can be estimated by calculating the standard deviation within each group. The standard deviations are used as part of the calculation of the within groups variance, as seen in Equation 1 following. If there are large differences among participants, the standard deviation will be large. On the other hand, if there are small differences, the standard deviation will be small. Variance within groups is often referred to as *error variance*. McDougall and Granby reported the standard deviations for both of their conditions (Table 14.1).

We stated that the *t* statistic is a ratio of between groups variance to within group variance. However, we have a specific equation for this statistic. Notice that in the numerator of Equation 1, the mean of the control group is subtracted from the mean of the intervention group, yielding a difference between means. This is an expression of between groups or treatment variance. In the denominator of the equation, each standard deviation is divided by the sample size, and then summed, yielding a term called the *standard error of the difference between means*. This is an expression of error or within groups variance.

The equation for the *t* statistic when sample sizes are *equal* is:

$$t = \frac{\overline{X}_I - \overline{X}_C}{\sqrt{\dfrac{s_I^2}{n_I} + \dfrac{s_C^2}{n_C}}} \tag{1}$$

and when the sample sizes are *equal or not equal* is:

$$t = \frac{\overline{X}_A - \overline{X}_B}{\sqrt{\left(\dfrac{(n_A - 1)s_A^2 + (n_B - 1)s_B^2}{n_A + n_B - 2}\right)\left(\dfrac{1}{n_A} + \dfrac{1}{n_B}\right)}} \; . \tag{2}$$

McDougall and Granby (1996) reported the value of *t* in their study as 2.67. They arrived at this value by using Equation 2 because the sample sizes in their two conditions were not equal (the intervention condition had 18 participants and the control condition had 22 participants):

$$t = \frac{16.47 - 9.84}{\sqrt{(\frac{(18-1)(5.82)^2 + (22-1)(9.09)^2}{(18+22)-2})(\frac{1}{18} + \frac{1}{22})}} = 2.67 \ .$$

What does a t value of 2.67 mean? How do they know the result is statistically significant? To answer this question, we need to understand what we mean by statistical significance. When we use hypothesis testing, we phrase our outcome in terms of the null hypothesis. Specifically, we state, *If the null hypothesis were true, what is the likelihood that this outcome could happen?* If the likelihood is small, less than 5 times in 100 for example, we would reject the null hypothesis and accept the alternative, or research hypothesis.

Understanding the t Value.   What if McDougall and Granby had randomly assigned their participants to the two different conditions, but had not intervened in the treatment condition? The two groups would be receiving the same conditions. Now, suppose they performed a t test on the data. We would not expect to see a significant difference between the two groups. We would expect the value of t to be zero in this situation, because nothing different has been done to the intervention group to separate it from the control group and the groups should be equivalent in all respects as a result of the random assignment. Therefore, we would expect the means of the two groups to be equal, and if we compute the difference between them (as in the numerator of the t equation), a value of zero would be expected. However, any time we compare means from two different groups, even though the groups are equivalent and we have done nothing to either group, the means probably will not be exactly equal because there are individual differences among the participants. Thus, when we calculate any t statistic, the outcome will be a value different from zero, but usually close to zero (usually less than one). When nothing is done to either group, the probability is high that the t value will be close to zero, supporting the null hypothesis of no difference. However, when a t value is large, such as that found in the McDougall and Granby study, the probability is *low* that there was nothing done to either group. In this case, the probability was less than .02. Placed in statistical jargon, the probability is less than .02 that the outcome of the McDougall and Granby study could happen if the null hypothesis were actually true. Therefore, they rejected the null hypothesis.

Degrees of Freedom.   Remember, McDougall and Granby (1996) stated their result as $t(38) = 2.67$, $p < .02$. The number in parentheses, 38, was the degrees of freedom. Degrees of freedom refers to the number of independent pieces of information from the data collected in the study. In the t test, we find the degrees of freedom from the number of participants in each group minus 1. In the intervention group, there were 18 participants, so we subtract 1 from 18 to get 17 degrees of freedom. In the control group, there were 22 participants, so we subtract 1 from 22 to get 21 degrees of freedom. Then, we add 17 and 21 to get 38 degrees of freedom, as stated in the study.

Why do we subtract one from the number of participants in each group to arrive at degrees of freedom? Degrees of freedom are independent pieces of information. In each group, each participant's score is an independent piece of information. The data collected from one participant are not dependent on the data collected from a second participant. The data from the two participants are independent. Therefore, in the McDougall and Granby study, it appears that we have 40 independent pieces of information. However, when we compute the *t* value, as in Equation 1 or Equation 2, we use the information from the standard deviation of each group (chap. 9). To compute the standard deviation, we subtract the mean of each group from each individual score in the group. This gives us a deviation score (deviation from the mean). If we were to add these scores, they would equal zero. Because the deviation scores add to zero, if we know the mean of a group, and all but one of the scores in that group, we could figure out the value of that missing score. When we use the *t* test to calculate a *t* value, one of the scores in each group is not independent. Therefore, we subtract 1 from the sample size in each group to determine our degrees of freedom (Equation 3), following:

$$df = (n_A - 1) + (n_B - 1). \qquad (3)$$

Describing the Results of the t Test.   McDougall and Granby (1996) concluded from the results of their study that the independent variable (method of in-class questioning) affects the dependent variable (preparation for class). Specifically, they noted that "students who expected random oral questioning also reported completing more of the assigned readings before class" (p. 51). Although they used a strong experimental design, the authors did not refer to cause in their discussion, but they could have, as we discussed in chapters 5 and 7.

Assumptions Underlying the t Test.   There are three major assumptions underlying the use of the *t* test for independent samples. These three assumptions also apply to the between groups ANOVA. Other assumptions will be added when we discuss repeated measures designs.

1. *Normality*: The dependent variable should be normally distributed for each of the populations from which the samples were selected.
2. *Homogeneity of variance*: The variances of the dependent variables of the populations (σ_A^2 and σ_B^2) underlying the samples should be equal.
3. *Independence*: Measures recorded from participants *must* be independent of each other. In other words, the performance of one participant is not affected by the performance of another participant.

How important are these assumptions for use of parametric statistics such as *t* and *F* tests? Although there is some disagreement among authors in the field of statistics, we tend to agree with Kerlinger (1986, p. 267), who suggested that violation of the assumptions of normality and homogeneity of variance are overrated. Violation of the independence assumption is serious and should not be tolerated, because independence underlies the rationale of most statistical tests. In fact, many researchers appear to pay little attention to these violations. When the first two assumptions underlying parametric tests are moderately violated, the researcher can ignore the violations because *t* and *F* are "robust" (i.e., not affected by violations). However, if these assumptions are markedly violated, you should select a nonparametric test or make an adjustment. One problem with choosing a nonparametric test is that these tests are less flexible and generally less powerful than their parametric equivalents. *Power* is defined as the probability of rejecting a false null hypothesis, which is what we hope to do.

A Second Example of Selecting an Independent Samples t Test.   Does chronic disability affect memory performance? Tun, Tun, and Wingfield (1997) conducted a study by using young and old adults with long-term spinal cord injury (SCI). The authors used both objective and subjective measures to assess memory performance. One of the subjective measures was the Divided Attention Questionnaire (DAQ). On this questionnaire, participants rated from 1 (very easy) to 5 (very difficult) their ability to divide attention between concurrent activities. There were 15 combinations of activities. The participants rated each activity on difficulty, change, and frequency. We will look at the difficulty part of the scale. Forty-six participants with spinal cord injury were included in the study. Tun et al. (1997) divided the participants, according to age, into two groups of 23 participants each. The mean of the younger group was 39.9 years, and the mean of the older group was 67.1 years. The data for the difficulty measure of the DAQ for this study can be seen in Table 14.2.

Tun et al. (1997) selected a *t* test for independent samples to analyze their data. The rationale behind this decision (see Fig. 14.1) was that the study involved one between groups independent variable with two levels. The dependent variable was scaled at the interval level. Notice that this study would fit into the category of the comparative research approach because the independent variable, age, was an attribute independent variable. However, even though this study used the comparative approach and the McDougall and Granby (1996) study used a randomized experimental approach, both studies were analyzed with an independent samples *t* test. Tun et al. used the formula for the *t* test for independent samples with equal sample sizes (see Equation 1):

TABLE 14.2
Descriptive Statistics for the Tun et al. (1997) Study

Sample Description	Young SCI Participants	Old SCI Participants
Number of participants	23	23
Mean difficulty rating	2.3	2.5
Standard deviation	1.0	.7

$$t = \frac{2.3 - 2.5}{\sqrt{\dfrac{(1)^2}{23} + \dfrac{(.7)^2}{23}}} = -.79 \ .$$

Tun et al. (1997) reported, "There was no age difference in scores...on the Difficulty Scale of the Divided Attention Questionnaire, $t(44) < 1$, indicating that older adults were not more concerned than the young ...with problems in dividing attention" (p. 171).

Confidence Intervals

Recall the study by McDougall and Granby (1996). The data obtained from that study were subjected to analysis by a t test for independent samples. The t test demonstrated that the null hypothesis should be rejected. Statistically speaking, we could say that the two groups came from populations with different means, one a population of people who received the random oral-questioning condition and the other a population of people who received the voluntary participation mode. Practically speaking, we might say that we can be confident that those in the random oral-questioning condition read more pages of the chapter outside of class than did those in the voluntary participation condition.

When we speak of something as being significantly different from something else, or one group performing significantly better than another group, there is a danger from an interpretation standpoint that significance indicates all or nothing or a large difference. Furthermore, we often forget about the actual data and how much of a difference actually exists. The use of statistics implies probabilities. When the null hypothesis is rejected at an α level of .05, we are saying that the probability is less than 5 times in 100, given a true null hypothesis that this could have happened by chance. Rejecting the null hypothesis does not mean the difference could not have happened by chance. Rather than expressing the results of a study as a significance statement (i.e., rejecting or not rejecting the null hypothesis), statisticians often express results as a *confidence interval* around the difference between sample means. Rather than saying that we reject the null hypothesis, we say that with 95% confidence the true population mean difference is within the confidence interval. What this tells us is that if we were to select 100 samples, and establish a confidence interval for each of the samples, the true population mean difference would be in 95 of the confidence intervals but would not be in 5 of the confidence intervals.

We can use the data from McDougall and Granby (1996) to establish a 95% confidence interval. We can construct this interval by using information provided to us from performing the t test. To construct confidence intervals we need to know the difference between the sample means (numerator of the t equation), the estimated standard error of the difference between means (denominator of the t equation), and the t value associated with the two-tailed significance level that we have selected at $\alpha = .05$ (this value is often referred to as the critical t value and is obtained from a t table). All of the information needed for determining confidence intervals (with the exception of the two-tailed significance level) was obtained from performing the t test. The 95% confidence interval for the McDougall and Granby (1996) study is between 1.6 pages and 11.6 pages. Practically speaking, we can be confident that the random participation technique will increase students' reading outside of class by between 1.6 and 11.6 pages.

Single Factor Analysis of Variance (ANOVA)

In our previous examples, we had one independent variable with two levels. We now introduce the single factor analysis of variance (ANOVA). This analysis is mostly used in between group designs with one independent variable and more than two levels. It should be noted, however, that the single factor analysis of variance also can be used in single factor between groups designs with only two levels, similar to the t test (Fig. 14.1). The data should be scaled at the interval or ratio level. One normally would choose the t test if a directional hypothesis is made, because t gives the researcher more power (probability of rejecting a false null hypothesis). If a nondirectional hypothesis is selected for this design, then either a t test or a single factor ANOVA could be used because $t^2 = F$ when there are only two levels. Our presentation of the single factor ANOVA will be with more than two levels or groups.

One of two studies performed by Tuckman (1996) investigated incentive motivation in college students. Tuckman compared an incentive motivation condition to a learning strategy condition to determine if incentive motivation would increase performance on a 50-item multiple choice test that measured comprehension rather than recall. Tuckman used three different educational psychology classes composed of junior and senior students who wanted to become teachers. Tuckman determined that the three classes were not different with respect to age, gender, and scores on a reading subtest. Then he randomly assigned the classes to one of three conditions (a strong quasi-experimental design). The three conditions were an incentive motivation condition that involved taking a quiz prior to each class session. The quiz grades would count as part of their grade for the class. The second condition was a learning strategy condition. For this condition, the students performed homework assignments to identify key terms in the textbook. The third class was a control group. They received strictly lectures on the chapters. At the end of 5 weeks, the students took the 50-item multiple choice test. The dependent variable was the percentage of correct responses on the test. This measure was scaled at the interval or ratio level. Tuckman analyzed the data by using a single factor analysis of variance. The reason for this choice (Fig. 14.1) was that there was one independent variable with more than two levels. The independent variable was a between groups independent variable. The dependent variable was scaled at the interval or ratio level.

Multiple t Tests?   How should we proceed if we have a between groups design, a dependent variable that is scaled at the interval or ratio level, and one independent variable with three levels? This situation is not uncommon in research. Actually, we infrequently have two levels within one independent variable. One answer to the analysis question could be to perform three *t* tests. We could compare the incentive motivation group to the learning strategy group, the learning strategy group to the control group, and the incentive motivation group to the control group. All possible comparisons would be considered. The problem is that the three *t* tests are *not* independent from each other. In other words, once we determine that the incentive motivation group is greater than the learning strategy group, and the learning strategy group is greater than the control group, then the third piece of information, that the incentive motivation group is greater than the control group, is already known. In the field of statistics, independence is held in high regard. The result of doing multiple *t* tests is that the probability of a type I error, which is set at .05 for each hypothesis, increases substantially.

When we examine the single factor analysis of variance, we are comparing the variability between groups (numerator) to the variability within groups (denominator). Previously, when discussing the *t* test, our variability within groups had been expressed in standard deviation units (estimated standard error of the difference between means), and our variability between groups had been expressed as a difference between means. Now we are going to work with variances. (Remember that variance is the square of the standard deviation.) The ANOVA is used to compare the variability between groups (treatment variance + error) to variability within groups (error).

Source Table for the One-Way ANOVA.   Although the results of a *t* test are usually summarized in one sentence as previously reported, it is common for the results of an ANOVA to be summarized in a source table. We start with the summary or source table (Table 14.3). This table shows how the variance and degrees of freedom are assigned in the analysis of variance. It also demonstrates how the *F* statistic is determined. The *F* statistic is the summary statistic for all of the analyses of variance. For the degrees of freedom, $k =$ the number of levels (groups) of the independent variable, and $N =$ total number of participants.

The procedure for calculating the *F* for the single factor analysis of variance is to calculate a total variance for the study. This variance is then divided into variance that results from the treatment, referred to as *between groups vari-*

TABLE 14.3
Analysis of Variance Source Table

Source of Variation	Sums of Squares (SS)	Degrees of Freedom (df)	Mean Squares (MS)	F
Between groups	$SS_{between\ groups}$	$k-1$	$MS_{between\ groups}$	$\dfrac{MS_{between\ groups}}{MS_{within\ subjects}}$
Within subjects	$SS_{within\ subjects}$	$N-k$	$MS_{within\ subjects}$	
Total	SS_{Total}	$N-1$		

ance, and variance that results from error, referred to as *within subjects variance*. To make the calculations easier, *sums of squares* are calculated first. Then this value is divided by the degrees of freedom. The new values, *mean squares*, are the variance estimates for between groups and within subjects. The *mean square between groups* is then divided by the *mean square within subjects*, yielding the *F* value. Let's examine the source table of a single factor analysis of variance before returning to the Tuckman (1996) study.

Durr, Guglielmino, and Guglielmino (1995) were interested in the relationship between different occupational categories at a large manufacturing firm and readiness for self-directed learning. They measured readiness for self-directed learning using the Self-Directed Learning Readiness Scale (SDLRS), a 58-item summated Likert scale. There were nine occupational categories at the factory. This is an example of the comparative research methodology, because the independent variable, type of occupational category, is an attribute independent variable. These categories, the number of participants in each category, and the mean score on the SDLRS for each category can be seen in Table 14.4.

Durr et al. (1995) performed a single factor analysis of variance on the data because they had one independent variable, type of occupational category, with nine levels. The design was between groups because participants could be classified into one occupational category only. The dependent variable, in the form of a Likert scale, was assumed to be scaled at the interval level. The results of this analysis can be seen in Table 14.5.

TABLE 14.4
Means and Sample Sizes for the Durr et al. (1995) Study

Occupational Category	Number of Participants	Mean Score on SDLRS
Manufacturing/factory	16	220
Clerical/administration	107	223
Engineers	114	233
Sales	98	242
Support professionals	43	231
Manufacturing managers	9	237
Support managers	63	238
Engineering managers	81	236
Sales managers	44	246

TABLE 14.5
Source Table for Comparison of Nine Occupational Categories in the Durr et al. (1995) Study

Source of Variation	Sums of Squares (SS)	Degrees of Freedom (df)	Mean Squares (MS)	F
Between groups	28,855	8	3,607	6.39
Within subjects	325,045	576	564	
Total	353,901	584		

The sums of squares for both between groups and within subjects are calculated first. Then the degrees of freedom are determined. Notice that there are 8 degrees of freedom associated with the between groups variance. This is because there were nine groups in the study, and from Table 14.3, degrees of freedom for between groups variance are determined by subtracting the number of groups minus one. The degrees of freedom for within subjects variance are determined by subtracting the number of groups from the total number of participants. There were 585 participants and nine groups, which yields 576 degrees of freedom. The mean squares are determined by dividing each sums of squares by the accompanying degrees of freedom. The last step is to determine the F value by dividing the mean square between groups (treatment variance) by the mean square within subjects (error variance). This yields an F value of 6.39.

Interpreting the F Value.   What does an F of 6.39 mean? Durr et al. (1995) found this value to be significant at a probability of .000. In other words, the probability that the outcome of the study (the nine different mean values) could happen by chance, assuming a true null hypothesis is less than 1 in 1,000, or highly unlikely. Therefore, Durr et al. rejected the null hypothesis of no difference among sample means. They concluded that, because the highest scores in the management category were those of sales managers, these scores were significantly higher than all of the other categories. This conclusion is not necessarily correct statistically. A significant F value from an analysis of variance only tells you that there is at least one significant difference among all of the levels or groups. It does not inform the researcher whether there are other significant differences. To determine which groups or conditions are significantly different from each other following a significant F, a post hoc test must be done. The only exception to this rule is a design with one independent variable and only two levels or groups.

There are numerous post hoc test alternatives from which to choose. Some of the most common are Fisher's least significant difference test (*LSD*) (R. A. Fisher, 1935), Tukey's honestly significant difference test (*HSD*) (Tukey, 1953), Newman–Keuls test (see Kirk, 1982), Scheffe's test for all comparisons (Scheffe, 1953), and Dunnett's test (Dunnett, 1955). Huck, Cormier, and Bounds (1974) rank post hoc comparisons from liberal to conservative, depending on how difficult it is to find a significant difference between sample means. The Fisher *LSD* test is the most liberal, whereas the Scheffe test is the most conservative. We recommend *against* using the *LSD* test (is this the sixties?), as it is too liberal (increased probability of making a type I error). The Tukey *HSD* test and the Newman–Keuls test are considered middle-of-the-road tests between liberal and conservative. The Dunnett test (Dunnett, 1955) is a post hoc test to be used when comparing a control group to each of the other treatment groups. Figure 14.2 shows the steps to be followed in deciding whether a post hoc test is needed.

Example of a Post Hoc Test Following a Single Factor ANOVA.   Let us return to the Tuckman (1996) study. There were three groups in this study, an incentive motivation group, a learning strategy group, and a control group. The

dependent variable was the percentage of items correct on a 50-item achievement test. The data for this study can be seen in Table 14.6.

Tuckman (1996) performed a single factor ANOVA on the data from his
study and reported the outcome from this analysis as, "The analysis of variance
(ANOVA) for the difference between the three group means yielded $F(2, 106)$
$= 21.69, p < .001$ " (p. 202). First, notice that Tuckman did not present a source
table, but reported his analysis in the text of the article. This is common, especially when reporting the results from a single factor ANOVA. In his statement,
the degrees of freedom are in parentheses, similar to the reporting of the t test,
except there are two different degrees of freedom for the single factor ANOVA.
In the current study, there were two degrees of freedom for the between groups
variance (number of groups in the study minus one) and 106 degrees of freedom for the within subjects variance (number of participants in the study minus the number of groups). The result was significant at a probability of less
than .001, indicating a very low likelihood that this result could happen by

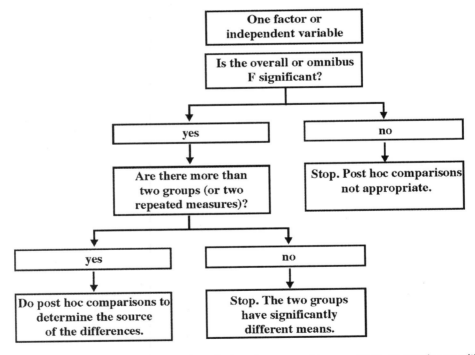

FIG. 14.2.   Schematic representation of when to use post hoc multiple comparisons with
a one-way ANOVA.

TABLE 14.6
Descriptive Statistics for the Tuckman (1995) Study

Sample Description	Incentive Motivation	Learning Strategy	Control
Number of participants	36	35	38
Mean	82.8%	71.6%	66.9%
Standard deviation	9.3	9.4	12.6

chance. A significant F indicates that there is at least one significant difference among the groups in the study. However, to determine which groups were significantly different, a post hoc test must be performed.

Tuckman (1996) performed a post hoc test by using a Newman–Keuls procedure. The results of this test revealed that the incentive motivation group performed significantly better than either the learning strategy group or the control group, but the learning strategy group was not significantly different from the control group.

ANALYZING SINGLE FACTOR DESIGNS WITH NONPARAMETRIC STATISTICS

Mann–Whitney U Test for Independent Samples

The Mann–Whitney U test, a nonparametric test, is done when the design is a between groups design with one independent variable and two levels. However, either there has been a violation of the assumptions underlying the t test, most often the assumption of normality, or the data are ordinal and not normally distributed. Nonparametric analyses often are referred to as distribution-free analyses. Parametric tests such as the t and the F require that the data be normally distributed. Nonparametric tests are free of the normal distribution. Actually, each nonparametric analysis has its own sampling distribution. The word *nonparametric* indicates that the analyses do not use the parameters μ and σ (population mean and standard deviation) from the normal distribution.

In education, allied health, and applied social sciences, there are numerous examples of scales, such as independence scales, where it would be presumptuous to assume that the data are interval. For example, if we rate independence on a scale from 1 to 3, and describe a score of 1 as being able to perform no activities, a score of 2 as being able to perform a few activities, and a score of 3 as being able to perform a lot of activities, the intervals between 1 and 2, and 2 and 3 do not seem to be equal. Therefore, it would be more appropriate to use nonparametric analyses. The one situation where a nonparametric test should *never* be used is when a parametric test already has been used and the outcome has failed to lead to a decision to reject the null hypothesis. The use of a nonparametric test in place of a parametric test will not increase power, or the probability of rejecting a false null hypothesis. Nonparametric tests, like parametric tests, have their proper place, but typically they are not as powerful.

Although we do not go into detail about the nonparametric tests that we mention (see Siegel and Castellan, 1988), most of the tests use a ranking procedure for the data and then apply a particular formula to the data. To perform the ranking procedure, all of the data from all of the groups are converted to ranks, by ordering from the smallest number to the largest number, regardless of the particular group or condition. Once the data are ranked, the *rankings* can be used in an equation. Usually this entails summing the rankings from each group. As one might expect, if the sums of the rankings are very different between or among groups, then they are probably significantly different. We can look up the result of the equations in a table and draw a conclusion by using the same logic as the t test.

Examples of the Mann–Whitney U Test. A common situation where the Mann–Whitney U test is applied occurs when there are a small number of participants, and the sample sizes are not equal. Janelle (1992) studied the locus of control in 13 nondisabled and 8 congenitally disabled adolescents by using the Nowicki–Strickland Locus of Control Scale for Children. The type of quantitative approach for this study was comparative, because the independent variable, presence of a disability, would be considered an attribute independent variable. The design for this study had one independent variable, presence of disability, with two levels. Also, it was a between groups design. Therefore, a t test for independent samples or a Mann–Whitney U test could have been selected because the data were interval. Janelle selected a nonparametric test, presumably as a result of the small sample size and the unequal sizes of the two groups (Fig. 14.3). She reported her findings as, "The Mann–Whitney U test ($U = 58.50$, p = .635), however did not indicate a statistically significant difference between the two groups" (p. 337). Janelle concluded that disability is not a significant factor in externality in adolescents.

The Mann–Whitney U test is also used when the dependent variable data do not appear to be normally distributed. Czerniecki, Deitz, Crowe, and Booth (1993) compared boys with girls aged 18 to 23 months on four measures of attending behavior, total time attending, total number of activities attended to, average attending time per activity, and longest time attending to one activity. Again, this study is an example of the comparative quantitative approach because there was one attribute independent variable, gender, with two levels. The authors stated that, "because visual inspection of the resulting tables and graphs revealed that much of the data were not normally distributed, the Mann–Whitney U, a nonparametric statistic, was employed to test the hypothesis" (p. 712). Of interest in this study was that a second hypothesis was also tested, comparing children 18 to 20 months with those 21 to 23 months. Again, a Mann–Whitney U test was selected.

Kruskal–Wallis One-Way Analysis of Variance by Ranks

The Kruskal–Wallis One-Way Analysis of variance by ranks is the nonparametric analogue of the single factor between groups ANOVA with three or more levels. It is used when there is one independent variable with more than two levels; participants are in one and only one group; and either there has been

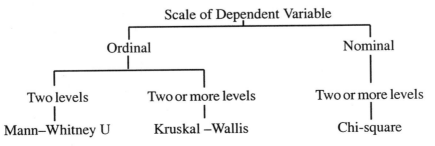

FIG. 14.3. Selection of the appropriate nonparametric statistic for a single factor between groups design with an ordinal or nominal dependent variable.

a violation of the assumptions for parametric statistics, or the data are ordinal and not normally distributed, or both. The preliminary steps in the Kruskal–Wallis analysis of variance are similar to that of the Mann–Whitney U test. Data are ranked from smallest to largest without respect to group. Then the groups are summed and applied to the equation. Similar to a single factor ANOVA, a significant Kruskal–Wallis test must be followed by a post hoc test because there are at least three levels.

The logic underlying the Kruskal–Wallis ANOVA is that if you had three identical distributions of scores and you selected three groups at random, one from each distribution, you would expect their ranks to be distributed equally under the null hypothesis. However, if the ranks are very different for at least one of the groups, then the null hypothesis would be rejected.

Examples of the Kruskal–Wallis Analysis of Variance by Ranks.   Morgan and Griego (1998) provide an example from the "high school and beyond" data of the relationship between fathers' education and mathematics achievement scores (p. 196). There were three levels of fathers' education (high school graduate or less, some college, or Bachelor of Science degree or more). The scale of the dependent variable, mathematics achievement, was considered to be ratio. Therefore, the design was a single factor design with three levels. The data can be seen in Table 14.7.

Normally, the correct statistical selection would be a single factor analysis of variance (Fig. 14.1). Notice, however, that the sample sizes are different. The standard deviations also are different, with those in the *Bachelor of Science degree condition* having a standard deviation almost twice that of those in the *some college condition.* Morgan and Griego (1998) determined that the data violated the assumption of homogeneity of variance by using a procedure called Levene's test. Therefore, they performed a Kruskal–Wallis One-Way Analysis of Variance by Ranks, and found the results to be statistically significant ($p = .001$).

Although it is more common to use the Kruskal–Wallis statistical test because at least one of the assumptions underlying parametric tests is violated, the test also can be used when the data for a single factor design are ordinal. Tate (1997) conducted a study to determine if peppermint oil reduced postoperative nausea in gynecological surgical patients; 18 patients who underwent major surgery were assigned to one of three groups, a control group that received no treatment, a placebo group, and a peppermint oil group. Each participant filled out a scale that the authors described as a "standardized descriptive ordinal scale to collect the subjective patient self-reported data" (p. 545). The

TABLE 14.7

Comparison of Math Achievement Scores for Three Fathers' Education Groups

Sample Description	High School Graduate or Less	Some College	Bachelor of Science Degree or More
Number of participants	38	16	19
Mean	10.09	14.40	16.35
Standard deviation	5.61	4.66	7.41

scale can be seen in Fig. 14.4. Note that many researchers would consider this rating scale to be at least approximately interval because the categories (0–4) are not only ordered, but at least approximately equally spaced. If so, the appropriate statistic would have been a one-way ANOVA. However, Kruskall–Wallis is a reasonable and conservative choice.

The authors found a statistically significant difference among the three groups ($p = .048$). The authors performed a post hoc test to determine where these differences occurred, as must also be done in a significant single factor analysis of variance with more than two levels. They used the Mann–Whitney U test for the three post hoc comparisons and found that the significant differences were between the peppermint oil group and the placebo group. The Mann–Whitney is appropriate as a post hoc test but is also liberal, being analogous to the Fisher *LSD* test mentioned earlier.

Chi-square (χ^2) Test for Independence With Nominal Data

In this part of the chapter we are working with categorical data. Specifically, we are determining how many people (the frequency count) fall into a particular category, relative to a different category. We examine data (nominal data) that identifies a person as belonging to a particular group. For example, we may be interested in the relation between gender and political affiliation. One participant may be female and belong to the Democratic Party. The next participant may be male and belong to the Democratic Party. The next participant may be female and belong to the Republican Party. In these examples, it was determined through measurement that no person had more or less of something than another person. Each participant was only identified as belonging to a particular group or combination of groups.

When measuring at the nominal or categorical level, the amount of information gained is less than when measuring at the interval or ordinal levels. For example, suppose that you are taking a course, Statistics 1A, at the university and you (with the instructor's approval) decide to be graded pass (P) or fail (F). Let's assume that you passed the class. Now, suppose that a review committee examines a transcript of your course work. Because they are interested in your background in statistics, they look for a statistics course on your transcript. The grade of P only shows that you passed the course. You could have done A, B, C, or D work. Therefore, even if you did A-level work, that information has not been transmitted. The finer the gradations on the measurement scale, the more information that is transmitted. We recommend that you not divide your

0	1	2	3	4
I am not experiencing any nausea	I feel slightly nauseated	I feel moderately nauseated	I feel extremely nauseated	I am so nauseated I feel I am about to vomit

FIG. 14.4.   An ordinal rating scale. From "Peppermint Oil: A Treatment for Postoperative Nausea," by S. Tate, 1997, *Journal of Advanced Nursing, 26*, p. 545. Copyright 1997 by Blackwell Sciences Ltd. Adapted with Permission.

data into two or a few categories if the data are continuous or have a number of ordered categories. However, sometimes your data on both the independent and dependent variables are nominal or can best be represented by a few categories. That is when you use a *chi-square test*.

The chi-square test for independence tests the *association* between two variables, an independent variable and a dependent variable. Testing a relationship between an independent variable and a dependent variable is no different when using a chi-square test than it is when using a *t* test, except that the dependent variable is categorical rather than continuous. Under the null hypothesis, the independent and dependent variables are assumed to be independent of each other.

The requirements for a chi-square test of independence are one independent variable with at least two levels or categories and one dependent variable that is also categorical. The data (frequencies) are measured at the nominal or categorical level. The design is between groups so that each participant can be in only one group.

Gliner, Haber, and Weise (1999) evaluated a curriculum change in occupational therapy (OT) designed to increase awareness about appropriate employment placement for persons with developmental disabilities by using a comparative quantitative methodology. Gliner et al. (1999) compared professional program OT students with pre-OT students and business students by using vignettes. The students were given descriptions of a person with a developmental disability and descriptions of different types of employment. Each student could "hire" the person with a developmental disability and "assign" that person to a segregated work, supported work, or competitive work setting. The dependent variable was the number of students (frequency) who selected a particular type of work. Gliner et al. (1999) selected a chi-square test because there was one between groups independent variable, type of student, with three levels, and the data were nominal (Fig. 14.3). The data are shown in Table 14.8. The equation for the chi-square test of independence is as follows:

$$\chi^2 = \sum_{i=1}^{k} \frac{(O_i - E_i)^2}{E_i}.$$

The equation looks a lot worse than it is because summation signs always scare people. For each of the nine cells in Table 14.8, we must subtract the expected frequencies from our observed frequencies (our actual data), square this num-

TABLE 14.8

Cross-tabulation Table of Frequency Data from the Gliner et al. (1999) Study

Group	Segregated Work	Supported Work	Competitive Work	Totals
Business students	20	42	14	76
Pre OT students	6	43	6	55
OT students	2	49	17	68
Totals	28	134	37	199

ber, and then divide this number by our expected frequencies. The expected frequencies are the frequencies we would expect if the independent variable was not related to the dependent variable. We use this same equation for each of the cells (rows times columns) in the study and then add the number for each cell to obtain our chi-square value. In our present example, we have nine cells, so we will need to carry out this procedure nine times.

Notice that in Table 14.8 we have included the totals for the rows and the columns. These are called *marginal totals*. In addition, we have the total for all of the participants ($N = 199$). We perform the analysis by using Equation 4. To obtain our expected frequencies, we must multiply the marginals associated with each cell and divide by N.

We start by finding the expected frequency for each cell. There are nine cells. We do this by multiplying the corresponding total for each row and column, and dividing by the total.

For our example, the expected frequency for the cell business students by segregated work is:

$$\frac{76 \times 28}{199} = 10.7.$$

The expected frequency for the cell OT students by supported work is:

$$\frac{68 \times 134}{199} = 45.78.$$

We do this for all nine cells. Then we use the chi-square equation to make the calculations, which are as follows:

$$\chi^2 = \frac{(20-10.69)^2}{10.69} + \frac{(6-7.74)^2}{7.74} + \frac{(2-9.57)^2}{9.57} + \frac{(42-51.17)^2}{51.17} + \ldots \frac{(17-12.64)^2}{12.64}$$

$$\chi^2 = 18.79.$$

Gliner et al. (1999) reported, "A chi-square test of independence demonstrated a significant relationship between the two variables of employment decision and class, $\chi^2(4) = 18.79, p = .001$." The degrees of freedom for this example are four, as stated in the parentheses. This was determined by using Equation 5, as follows:

$$df = (r-1)\ (c-1), \tag{5}$$

where r = number of rows, and
where c = number of columns.

There were three levels in the independent variable from the Gliner et al. (1999) study. To determine which of the groups were different, Gliner et al. performed follow-up chi-square tests to more precisely estimate differences among conditions. They found that the significant difference was between the professional OT students and the business students.

Similar to the requirements discussed for the *t* test and single factor analysis of variance, there are two requirements that should be met to satisfy the assumptions for any chi-square analysis: Yates correction and minimum expected frequencies.[1]

Sometimes it is difficult to decide which variable is the independent variable. For example, consider two variables, attitude toward gun control and political affiliation. One might ask which variable seems to cause or predict the other. Davis (1985) has specified rules of causal order that are helpful in determining which variable is the causal variable. For the most part, these rules are based on the independent variable preceding the dependent variable in time. However, although some researchers see the chi-square test as a method of testing the relationship between two variables without specifying which variable is the independent variable, we think that researchers should have in mind a position about which is the independent (presumed cause) and dependent (outcome or result) variable prior to the study.

SUMMARY

In this chapter we discussed the selection and application of appropriate statistical methods used in single factor between groups designs. We divided the chapter into a selection of appropriate parametric and nonparametric statistics from the scale of the dependent variable and depending on certain assumptions had been satisfied. In the section on parametric statistics, we discussed the *t* test for independent samples and the single factor analysis of variance with accompanying post hoc tests. The *t* test is more commonly used when there is one independent variable with two levels because it gives the researcher the option of testing a directional hypothesis. When the independent variable has more than two levels, the single factor ANOVA is the procedure of choice.

The nonparametric tests for single factor, between groups designs that we discussed were the Mann–Whitney *U* test, the Kruskal–Wallis analysis of variance by ranks, and the chi-square test. The Mann–Whitney *U* test and the Kruskal–Wallis test are used with ordinal data that are not normally distributed, or to convert interval data to ranks because of violation of assumptions underlying parametric tests. The chi-square test is used with nominal data and can be used with two or more than two conditions or levels. Nonparametric

---

[1]Statistical opinion on meeting either of these requirements for a chi-square test is not unanimous. Camilli and Hopkins (1978) used computer-generated replications and found that the chi-square test was robust with expected frequencies less than five. In addition, they recommended not using Yates correction, because it decreased the type I error rate to far lower than the value of alpha, hence decreasing power. Bradley, Bradley, McGrath, and Cutcomb (1979) also found that using expected frequencies of less than five did not increase type I error.

tests are used less frequently than parametric analyses and usually are less powerful.

Study Aids

Concepts

- Chi-square test
- Degrees of freedom
- Homogeneity of variance
- Independence
- Kruskal–Wallis analysis of variance by ranks
- Mann–Whitney U test
- Normality
- Post hoc comparisons
- Single factor ANOVA
- Source table
- t test

Distinctions

- Parametric versus nonparametric statistics
- t test versus single factor ANOVA
- t test versus Mann–Whitney U test versus χ^2 test
- Single factor ANOVA versus Kruskal–Wallis ANOVA versus χ^2 test

Application Problems

Questions 1 to 4. For the following passages select the proper statistical analysis based on (a) whether the design is between groups, within subjects, or mixed; (b) number of levels of the independent variable(s); (c) the scale-level of measurement of the dependent variable(s); and (d) whether assumptions underlying parametric tests are violated.

1. A therapist was interested in determining the effectiveness of a new treatment for children with cerebral palsy. The therapist had 40 such children in her clinic. She randomly assigned participants to one of two groups (20 in each group). The treatment group received the new treatment therapy. The control group received a traditional therapy. After four months, all 40 children performed a motor coordination task. If the child completed the task, treatment was considered to be successful. If the child was unable to complete the task, treatment was considered to be unsuccessful.

2. A professor who taught statistics was curious to know about different methods of calculating the Pearson Product Moment Correlation Coefficient. Specifically, he wondered which way was quicker, *the deviation method* or *the raw score* method. It just so happened that he had a class of 31 graduate students. He randomly assigned 16 students to the deviation method, and 15 students to the raw score method, and asked the students to keep track of how long it took (to the nearest minute) to determine the correlation coefficient for the problem.

3. At a clinic in the Rocky Mountains, a hand therapist was interested in determining the functional recovery of joint replacement surgery as opposed to two other more conservative treatments, steroids and splinting, on persons with rheumatoid arthritis. Thirty participants were randomly selected from a population of hand therapy patients. The participants were randomly assigned to one of three groups (10 participants in each). The groups were the surgery condition, drug condition, and the splint condition. After 6 months, all three groups were measured on a subtest of the Gliner Occupational Hand Recovery Index, an interval scale.

4. An investigator is interested in comparing successful employment due to different service delivery systems for persons with traumatic brain injury. One system (n = 10) was referred to as the cognitive delivery system (C). A second system (n = 10) was the emotional delivery system (E). A third system (n = 10) was the case management delivery system (CM). The investigator ranked the 30 subjects from 1 to 30 on how successful they were on their first job after recovery.

5. A therapist wanted to know if his special splint would increase the range of motion (ROM) in the wrist after a traumatic injury. He had eight patients wear the special splint, and eight patients wear the standard splint. He predicted that his special splint would increase ROM (in degrees) at the end of the recovery period. He performed a t test for independent samples on the data and found a t value of 1.82. He went to a t table and found that this value was greater than the critical value for a t with 14 degrees of freedom (one-tailed). He concluded that his special splint was statistically significantly better than the standard splint. What did he mean by statistical significance?

6. You have three independent groups, with 10 participants in each group (n = 30). These groups are labeled A_1, A_2, and A_3. The means of the three groups are 10, 14, and 20 respectively. You wonder if there is a significant difference for any of the possible comparisons.

   a. How many comparisons are there?

   b. If you use a t test to test each comparison, what danger do you run into?

   c. You decide to perform an analysis of variance on the data. The results are as follows, fill in the rest of the table:

Source of variation	SS	df	MS	F
Between groups	320	k-1		
Within subjects	1080	n-k		

   d. You find that the F is statistically significant. How do you determine which of the groups are different from each other?

7. The design is a single factor (between groups) design with two levels. The data are normally distributed. There are two analyses that can be performed.

   What are the two different types of analyses that can be used in this situation?

   When should each analysis be used, and why?

15

Single Factor
Within Subjects Designs:
Analysis and Interpretation

Overview

The analyses that are discussed in this chapter are used in a design with one independent variable and two or more levels or conditions, and participants are measured under all conditions. These designs are referred to as within subjects, dependent samples, or repeated measures designs. This means that participants undergo all conditions of the study or participants are matched on a variable related to the dependent variable, indicating that the two groups are related.

Similar to the approaches described in the previous chapter, the type of research approaches used with single factor within subjects (repeated measures) designs are randomized experimental, quasi-experimental, and comparative. For example, Rumrill and Garnette (1997) studied an intervention designed to increase consumer participation in the Americans with Disabilities Act (ADA) Title I accommodation request process. There were 36 participants in the study. They divided these 36 participants into 18 matched pairs based on gender, occupational status, and age. Then they randomly assigned one member of each pair to an intervention condition and the other member of each pair to a control condition. The design for this study is described as a single factor repeated measures design with two levels. This is an example of the randomized experimental approach applied to situations with repeated measures.

Another example of the randomized experimental approach that applies to repeated measures situations is a study by Hsieh, Nelson, Smith, and Peterson (1996). They were interested in the effect of purposeful activity on balance for people with hemiplegia. They had 21 participants who underwent all three conditions of the study. Because they randomly assigned participants to one of three different *orders* of experiencing the conditions, the approach was randomized experimental. The design for this study was a single factor repeated measures design with three levels.

Single factor repeated measures designs also can fit into the quasi-experimental approach. Consider a study by Luft and Pizzini (1998), who were interested in the influence of visiting a Problem Solving Demonstration Classroom (PSDC) on a problem solving model (Search, Solve, Create, and Share Problem Model). They had seven teachers in their study. Prior to visiting the demonstration classroom, the teachers collected data from their classrooms with an assessment instrument that was developed to measure changes in behavior of both students and teachers related to problem solving implementation. These changes were measured on a one (highest) to five (lowest) score. Examples of categories measured included time in cooperative groups, group cohesiveness, and students' actively participating. After four visits to the PSDC, data were collected again by using the same instrument. The specific design for this study was a single group pretest–posttest design. The general design classification is a single factor repeated measures design with two levels, pretest and posttest.

King et al. (1997) used a similar repeated measures approach to study social skills training. They studied a 10-week social skills training program for children with physical disabilities. These students were measured on a School Social Skills scale prior to the intervention (pretest), after training (posttest), and 24 weeks after the end of training (follow-up). The design for this study is a

:sign with three levels. Because all partici-
ime), the approach is quasi-experimental.
used with repeated measures designs. For ex-
on (1997) examined the effects of disordered
verbal working memory, and letter knowl-
ldren with phonologic impairment with 15
ie basis of mental age and gender. Phonology
) the approach is comparative. The design for
neasures design with two levels.

hin subjects or repeated measures, design
n the study. This saves time in recruitment
ants have certain characteristics that are
n. However, a more important reason for
ι is that variability among participants is
:he statistical analysis of between groups
;is of variance, where we are comparing
.......oიιιιy υeτween groups (treatment variance) to the variability within
groups (error variance). When we perform a repeated measures design, each
participant is undergoing all of the conditions. Therefore, it is expected that
any changes from condition to condition result from the nature of a particular
condition (treatment), and not variability among participants (error), because
the same participant is experiencing each of the conditions. This reduction in
error variance increases the size of the t or F ratio and results in a greater probability of finding a statistically significant difference if one is actually there.

Disadvantages of Within Subjects Designs

Although within subjects or repeated measures, designs are advantageous in
reducing error variance, there are two distinct disadvantages of using repeated
measures designs. The first disadvantage is that repeated measures designs
cannot be used in situations where a lasting effect might take place within any
of the conditions. This problem is referred to as *carryover effects*. For example,
if an investigator is interested in the effect of a treatment or intervention, she
could not use a repeated measures design, because once participants experienced the treatment condition, they could not be expected to "unlearn" the
treatment and then undergo a control condition. Because of carryover effects,
repeated measures designs are considered less flexible than between groups
designs and are seen less frequently in the literature, especially in journals em-
phasizing applied research. One method of circumventing carryover effects
and still gaining the advantage of reducing error variance is to use a *matching
procedure*. In a matching procedure, participants are grouped into pairs
(dyads) or triplets (triads) based on a characteristic that should be related to the
dependent variable. An example might be intelligence. After participants are
grouped, they are assigned (randomly is optimum) to groups and then the study
is carried out. Conceptually, the idea of matching is to make each member of

the pair or triad as though he or she were the same participant undergoing all conditions. Therefore, designs that use matching are considered to be repeated measures designs and use similar statistical procedures.

A second disadvantage of repeated measures designs is that the degrees of freedom in the study is reduced. If one did a repeated measures study with two conditions, it would take half as many participants to gather the same amount of data, because each person was measured twice. Although a reduced number of participants may make it easier to conduct the study, it also reduces statistical power. For example, consider a study that compares an intervention condition to a control condition, where there are 20 participants in each condition. If a between groups design is used to complete the study, there are 40 participants, or 38 degrees of freedom (remember $df = [n-1] + [n-1]$ for an independent samples t test). On the other hand, suppose that a repeated measures design was used to carry out the study. There would be 20 participants in each condition, but because each participant undergoes both conditions, there would only be 20 participants in the study. The degrees of freedom would be $n - 1$, or 19. Therefore, statistical power would be reduced. The decision to use either a between groups design or a repeated measures design stems from the issue of an increased sample size versus a reduction in error variance.

ANALYZING SINGLE FACTOR WITHIN SUBJECTS DESIGNS WITH PARAMETRIC STATISTICS

We will discuss two different statistics that are used with single factor within subjects or repeated measures, designs. These two statistics are the t test for correlated samples and the single factor repeated measures analysis of variance. When these statistics should be selected is depicted in Fig. 15.1.

t Test for Paired or Related Samples

The t test for related or paired samples is used when there is one independent variable, with two levels, and the participants undergo both conditions, or pairs of participants have been matched on a relevant variable. The dependent vari-

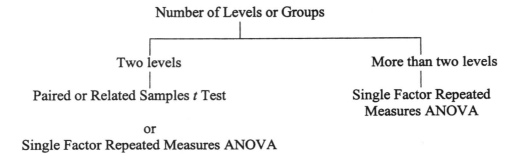

FIG. 15.1.   Decision tree for selecting the appropriate parametric single factor within subjects (repeated measures) statistic.

able must be interval or ratio data. The advantage of this statistical test over the single factor analysis of variance with repeated measures is the option to use a directional hypothesis, when appropriate.

An example of a study that used the *t* test for related samples is the study by Webster et al. (1997) mentioned earlier. They matched 15 children diagnosed as phonologically impaired with 15 children with normal phonology on mental age and gender. Then they measured the children on dependent variables of sentence memory, rhyme, alliteration, pseudo-word segmentation, and letter identification. We examine one analysis of the dependent variable, sentence memory. Participants had to repeat sentences that ranged in word length from 3 to 13 words. A percentage correct score was computed. Table 15.1 shows the data from the Webster et al. (1997) study.

Webster et al. used a *t* test for paired or correlated samples to compare the performance of the matched pairs on sentence memory. This test was selected because there was one independent variable with repeated measures (the groups were matched), two levels, and the dependent variable was a ratio level scale.

The equation for the *t* test for correlated samples is shown in Equation 1:

$$t = \frac{\overline{D}}{S_{\overline{D}}} , \qquad (1)$$

$$\text{where } S_{\overline{D}} = \frac{S_D}{\sqrt{n}}.$$

The formula for the *t* test for correlated samples is different from the *t* test for independent samples (chap. 14), and much easier to use. We do not need to compute the means, standard deviations, and standard errors for *each* group. Instead, for each pair of participants, we subtract the phonologically impaired score from the phonologically normal score, yielding a difference or change score for each pair of participants. Then, we obtain the mean, standard deviation, and standard error of the difference between means on these change scores. Thus, once we have obtained the change scores, we perform these statistical calculations on only one group of scores. The *t* test for correlated samples can be demonstrated with the data from Table 15.1 (Webster et al., 1997):

TABLE 15.1

**Means and Standard Deviations from the Webster et al. (1997)
Study for the Variable of Sentence Memory**

Sample Description	Phonologically Normal		Phonologically Impaired
Number of participants	15		15
Mean	84.50		62.00
Standard deviation	11.92		21.38
Difference between means		22.50	
Standard deviation of the difference between means		25.39	

$$t = \frac{22.5}{6.56} = 3.43 ,$$

$$\text{where} \quad s_{\overline{D}} = \frac{25.39}{\sqrt{15}} = 6.56 .$$

Webster et al. (1997) concluded that "children with normal phonology outperformed those with impaired phonology on sentence memory, $t(14) = 3.43$, $p < .004$." (p. 369). Notice that the number in parentheses, 14, is the degrees of freedom for this study. As we pointed out previously, the mean and standard deviation are performed on only one set of scores, the difference scores. There are 15 difference scores and only one degree of freedom is lost from redundancy. Therefore, the degrees of freedom for this study is 14. The notation $p < .004$ indicates that the probability that this outcome results from chance, assuming a true null hypothesis, is less than 4 times in 1,000, a rare event. The null hypothesis of no difference between conditions is rejected.

Single Factor Analysis of Variance With Repeated Measures

The most common situation where the single factor analysis of variance with repeated measures is performed occurs where there is one independent variable, two or more levels; the dependent variable is interval or ratio level; and the participants undergo all conditions or levels of the study. We previously mentioned a study by Hsieh et al. (1996), who investigated the effect of purposeful activity on balance for people with hemiplegia. All of their participants underwent three different conditions, although the order of undergoing each condition was randomly assigned. The design for their study was a single factor repeated measures design with three levels. The dependent variables, frequency and duration of exercise, were ratio. Hsieh et al. (1996) performed a single factor analysis of variance with repeated measures to determine if there were differences among the three conditions (see Fig. 15.1).

A second situation where the single factor repeated measures analysis of variance is performed occurs when matching has occurred as a part of the design of the study. When participants are matched, the design becomes a repeated measures design. Gliner and Sample (1993) conducted a study to gather baseline data on quality of life among three different groups prior to further intervention. The three groups were a sheltered work group (SW), a supported employment group (SE), and a job-matched control group (JM). Participants were matched from supported employment to sheltered work on IQ and age, and from supported employment to job-matched control on place of work and age. These matches resulted in 18 triads from 54 subjects. The dependent variable was Environmental Control, a subscale of the Quality of Life Index (Schalock, Keith, Hoffman, & Karan, 1989).

Like all analysis of variance statistics, the results from a single factor repeated measures or within subjects analysis of variance are reported in a source table (see Table 15.2). Notice that because our design is a repeated measures or within subjects design, there is no between groups component. The treatment effect comes from the within subjects component. This is different from the single factor between groups design that we discussed in chapter 14 (see Table 15.3).

The first source of variation reported in the source table of the single factor repeated measures analysis of variance is the between subjects sums of squares. This source of variation is determined from the differences among participants. If the participants differ among each other on the dependent variable, then this source of variation will be relatively large. If, on the other hand, there are small differences among participants on the dependent variable, then the between subjects sums of squares will be small. The larger the between subjects sums of squares, the larger the reduction in error variance; therefore, it is desirable for participants to differ on the dependent variable in a repeated measures design. Once the between subjects sums of squares is computed, it is subtracted from the total sums of squares. The difference is the within subjects sums of squares. From here, the calculations are identical to the single factor between groups analysis of variance discussed in chapter 14. The result is a treatment mean squares and an error or residual mean squares. It is important to remember that there is a trade-off when using any repeated measures analysis of variance. This trade-off is between the reduction in error variance from the participants being different on the dependent variable, and the reduction in degrees of freedom because the design is repeated measures. If participants are not different on the dependent variable, then power will be lost, because degrees of freedom are less than for a between groups design.

Let's return to the Gliner and Sample (1993) study. The data can be seen in Table 15.4. Gliner and Sample (1993) selected a single factor analysis repeated measures analysis of variance to determine differences among the three employment conditions in this comparative research approach. The rationale for selection of this analysis was that there was one independent variable with three levels; the participants were matched, forming triads; and the dependent

TABLE 15.2
Source Table for a Single-Factor Within Subjects Design

Source	SS	df	MS	F
Between subjects		$n-1$		
Within subjects				
Treatment		$k-1$		$\dfrac{MS_{Treatment}}{MS_{Residual}}$
Residual or Error		$(n-1)(k-1)$		

TABLE 15.3
Source Table for a Single-Factor Between Groups Design

Source of Variation	Sums of Squares (SS)	Degrees of Freedom (df)	Mean Squares (MS)	F
Between groups		$k-1$	$MS_{between\ groups}$	$\dfrac{MS_{between\ groups}}{MS_{within\ subjects}}$
Within subjects		$N-k$	$MS_{within\ subjects}$	

variable was interval level. The source table that demonstrates the results from the Gliner and Sample study can be seen in Table 15.5.

Gliner and Sample reported their results as follows. A significant difference was observed among the three employment conditions on the measure of environmental control, $F(2,34) = 19.21$, $p < .001$. Therefore, the probability of this result occurring by chance, assuming a true null hypothesis, is less than 1 in 1,000. Therefore, Gliner and Sample rejected the null hypothesis of no difference among groups. However, finding a significant F after performing an analysis of variance with *more than two groups* only tells you that at least two of the groups are significantly different. It does not tell you which two are different or if there is more than one pair of groups that are different. Therefore, Gliner and Sample performed a Tukey *HSD* post hoc test to determine where differences existed. The results from that test showed that the job-matched control was significantly greater on environmental control than both the sheltered work and supported employment conditions. In addition, the supported employment condition was significantly higher on environmental control than the sheltered work condition.

The example that we provided for the single factor ANOVA with repeated measures used matching instead of repeated measures on the same participants. The reason for the former is that there are few instances where a repeated measures design with one independent variable could be used in an internally valid study. Can you think of an example?

ANALYZING SINGLE FACTOR WITHIN SUBJECTS DESIGNS WITH NONPARAMETRIC STATISTICS

Nonparametric statistics are used with within subjects, or repeated measures, designs as with between groups designs, when the data are scaled at the ordinal (and not normally distributed) or nominal level, or one of the assumptions underlying use of parametric statistics has been violated. We discuss briefly four

TABLE 15.4

Descriptive Statistics for the Gliner and Sample (1993) Study

Employment Condition	Number of Participants	Mean Score on Environmental Control
Sheltered work	18	33
Supported employment	18	37.11
Job matched control	18	42

TABLE 15.5.

Source Table for the Gliner and Sample (1993) Study

Source	SS	df	MS	F
Between subjects	595	17	35	
Within subjects				
Treatment	730	2	365	19.21
Residual	646	34	19	

different nonparametric statistics to be used with single factor repeated measures designs (see Fig. 15.2). It should be noted that the use of these statistics in applied settings are relatively rare compared to their parametric counterparts discussed previously.

Wilcoxon Matched Pairs Test

The Wilcoxon matched pairs test is to be used in a design where there is one independent variable, with two levels, and the participants undergo both conditions, or pairs of participants have been matched on a relevant variable. The dependent variable data are ordinal (and not normally distributed) or there have been violations of assumptions of the *t* test for correlated samples.

As was the case in other nonparametric tests that we discussed, in the Wilcoxon test we convert the scores to ranks and then use a specific equation to determine statistical significance. In the nonparametric procedures for between groups designs, the ranking of scores takes place within each group. In the Wilcoxon test, differences between conditions for each participant (or pair if participants are matched) are obtained first (maintaining the positive or negative sign) and then these differences are ranked. Next, the ranks are totaled. The farther the sum of the ranks is from zero, the higher the probability of a significant difference between conditions.

Chiara, Carlos, Martin, Miller, and Nadeau (1998) used a Wilcoxon test as part of a set of analyses to determine how patients with multiple sclerosis (MS) would react to a cold treatment. Fourteen participants diagnosed with MS underwent two treatments, rest at room temperature and rest in a cold water bath. Chiara et al. describe the design as "a repeated measures design with random assignment of (the order of) experimental and control conditions" (p. 523). Therefore, this research approach is randomized experimental. The general

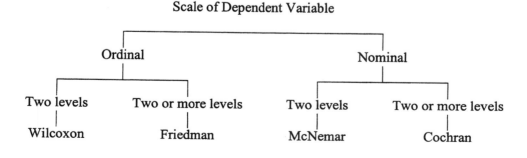

FIG. 15.2.   Decision tree for selecting the appropriate nonparametric single factor within subjects statistic.

classification of design is a single factor repeated measures design with two levels. One of the dependent variables selected by Chiara et al. was level of spasticity, as measured by the Modified Ashworth Scale, an ordinal level scale. A Wilcoxon test was used to examine the spasticity data because there was one repeated measures independent variable with two levels, and the dependent variable was measured on an ordinal scale. They found a significant difference between conditions and reported their results as, "spasticity was significantly lower $(Z = -2.309, p < .05)$ immediately after AT (room temperature) than after CT (cold temperature bath)." Chiara et al. concluded, "Our finding of a CT-induced increase in spasticity does not agree with other studies, which have reported a decrease. The reasons for this discrepancy are unclear, but may include the use of lower bath temperatures in other studies or the use of subjective measures of spasticity in previous studies" (p. 527).

Friedman Two-Way Analysis of Variance by Ranks[1]

The Friedman test is used in a repeated measures design when there is *one* independent variable, three or more levels, and the dependent variable is scaled at the ordinal level (and not normally distributed) or the data are interval but violations of assumptions have occurred, especially those of normality. The Friedman test is similar to the Wilcoxon sign ranks test in that scores are obtained for each participant across conditions and then converted to ranks. In the Wilcoxon test, differences were obtained between the two conditions and then ranked, whereas in the Friedman test, scores are *summed* across conditions prior to converting to ranks.

Studies had demonstrated that running on natural or off-road surfaces demanded more energy than running on road. Creagh, Reilly, and Lees (1998) were interested if this running off road caused biomechanical alterations to stride characteristics. They set up a study that used a repeated measures design to test their hypothesis in nine female runners. The runners were randomly assigned to the order of experiencing three different terrain conditions. These conditions were a path (control condition), short grass, and long grass. The runners were videotaped while experiencing each of these conditions. Creagh et al. measured 10 different stride characteristics. Although all of these measures were scaled at the ratio level, not all were believed to be normally distributed. According to Creagh et al., "Those variables shown to be non-parametric (maximum upper leg angle and maximum flexion angular velocity of knee) were compared using Friedman's test" (p. 1031). The rationale for selecting Friedman's test is one repeated measures independent variable, with more than two levels, and the dependent variable was not assumed to be normally distributed. Creagh et al. proposed post hoc tests by using the Wilcoxon test to determine specific differences among groups if the Friedman test was statistically significant. Note, however, that using the Wilcoxon test after the Friedman test is analogous to using the Fisher *LSD* test after an ANOVA; it is somewhat "liberal."

---

[1]Note, part of the name (two-way) of this analysis is misleading because, in our conceptualization, there is only one independent variable in this analysis. The second F is for "between subjects" (see Source Table 15.2), but we are not interested in that F.

McNemar Test

The McNemar test is used in a design where there is one independent variable, with two levels, and the participants undergo both conditions, or pairs of participants have been matched on a relevant variable. The dependent variable is nominal or categorical data. The McNemar test is similar to the chi-square test in that frequencies are the unit of measurement, and they can be visualized in a cross-tabulation table.[2] Furthermore, a chi-square table is used to determine statistical significance. However, because each participant undergoes both conditions of the study, there are important differences from the chi-square test for independence.

Cochran Q Test

The Cochran Q test is used in a design where there is one independent variable, with three or more levels, and the participants undergo all conditions, or participants have been matched on a relevant variable. The dependent variable is nominal or categorical data and can have *only two* categories. The Cochran test is an extension of the McNemar test in that frequencies are the unit of measurement, but in this test the participants undergo more than two conditions. A chi-square table is used to determine statistical significance.

A study by Tarr and Bishop (1992) provides examples for the use of both the McNemar test and the Cochran Q test. They were interested in the different instructional approaches to increase motor performance in children with developmental disabilities. The three instructional approaches were cooperative, competitive, and individualistic. The participants were five boys with developmental disabilities enrolled in a remedial motor behavior program. The participants underwent six observational periods for each instructional approach. The *order* of instructional approaches was randomly assigned, so this is considered to be a randomized experiment. During each observation period, each child performed three motor skills in a randomly assigned order. The dependent variable was the frequency of successful motor performance by the participants for each instructional approach. This is a dichotomous nominal dependent variable, where the participant is judged as successful or not successful. Tarr and Bishop selected a Cochran Q test to analyze the differences among groups. This analysis was selected because there was one repeated measures independent variable (type of instruction), there were more than two conditions, and the dependent variable was nominal and dichotomous. The authors reported, "Even though the magnitude of the difference between the competitive, cooperative, and individualistic approaches is small, the Cochran Q test yielded a significant difference between the instructional approaches, (Cochran Q [2] = 9.418, $p < .05$)" (p. 20). The Cochran Q test, similar to other analyses that compare more than two groups or conditions, only indicates at least one significant difference. An additional test needs to be performed to determine specific differences among conditions.

---

[2]If the expected frequencies are less than five per cell, the binomial test is recommended (Siegel & Castellan, 1988).

Tarr and Bishop (1992) selected the McNemar test as a follow-up test for the significant Cochran Q test. The reason a McNemar test was selected was that the follow-up comparisons would be between the conditions of competitive versus cooperative, cooperative versus individualistic, and competitive versus individualistic. For each of these comparisons, there is one repeated measures independent variable, two levels, and a nominal dependent variable. After performing the McNemar test for each of the three comparisons, Tarr and Bishop concluded, "Based on the McNemar test, there was a significant difference between the competitive and the individualistic approaches (χ^2 [1, $N = 5$] = 7.018, $p < .05$); the competitive approach was more effective in producing successful motor performance" (p. 20). Neither of the other comparisons was statistically significant.

SUMMARY

In this chapter, we discussed the selection of appropriate statistical tests for single factor within subjects (repeated measures) designs and provided examples from the literature. As we did in the preceding chapter, we divided the analyses into parametric and nonparametric tests. The parametric tests that we discussed for single factor repeated measures designs were the t test for correlated samples and the single factor repeated measures ANOVA. While both analyses can be used in single factor repeated measures designs with two levels, the t test should be selected if the researcher plans on testing a directional hypothesis. When the design is repeated measures, but has more than two levels, the single factor repeated measures analysis of variance should be used and followed by appropriate post hoc procedures, if the F is significant.

We also introduced four nonparametric tests to be used in single factor within subjects or repeated measures, designs. The Wilcoxon test (applied when there are two levels of the independent variable) and the Friedman test (applied when there are more than two levels of the independent variable) are used with ordinal data, or to convert interval data to ranks because of violation of assumptions underlying parametric tests. The Wilcoxon test also may be used as a post hoc test to a significant Friedman test, but is more liberal than the Tukey test. The McNemar test (applied when there are two levels of the independent variable) and the Cochran Q test (applied when there are more than two levels of the independent variable) are used with nominal data. The McNemar test may be used as a post hoc test following a significant Cochran Q test, but it, too, is liberal. Nonparametric statistical procedures are relatively rare in the literature for single factor repeated measures designs.

STUDY AIDS

Concepts

- Carryover effects
- Cochran Q test

- Friedman test
- Matching
- McNemar test
- Single factor repeated measures ANOVA
- t test for paired samples
- Wilcoxon matched pairs test

Distinctions

- Between groups designs versus within subjects designs
- Single factor repeated measures ANOVA versus Friedman test versus Cochran Q test
- Matching versus within subjects designs
- t test for paired samples versus single factor repeated measures ANOVA
- t test for paired samples versus Wilcoxon matched pairs test versus McNemar test

Application Problems

For the following six passages select the proper statistical analysis based on (a) whether the design is between groups or within subjects, (b) number of levels of the independent variable(s), (c) scale of measurement of the dependent variable(s), and (d) whether assumptions underlying parametric tests are violated.

1. A graduate seminar class has 10 students. The students are exposed to four different instructors, each instructor representing a different teaching style. At the end of the semester, each student is asked to rank the four instructors from one to four on class challenge. Are there significant differences among teaching styles?

2. A researcher hypothesized that applying splints over a 3-month period would significantly increase range of motion in patients who were quadriplegic. A random sample of 16 patients with this disability was selected. The patients were then matched on initial range of motion to form eight pairs. Then one participant of each pair was randomly assigned to the intervention group ($n = 8$), and the other randomly assigned to the control group ($n = 8$). The intervention group was splinted for 3 months, while the control group was not splinted. After 3 months, range of motion (which was normally distributed) was measured for each group and they were compared.

3. An educator is interested in cooperative learning groups. She wonders if active participation increases if groups are facilitated by someone in this area. A study is conducted during two different class periods. In one class period, participants engage in cooperative groups without a facilitator. During a second class period she introduces a facilitator into the groups. One member of each group, unknown to other members, keeps track of active participation. After each class, participants are divided into whether they actively participated or did not actively participate.

4. A study is carried out to determine if a hands-on entrepreneurial curriculum for high school students will increase entrepreneurial skills. Twenty stu-

dents were matched into ten pairs based on gender and previous high school grades. One member of each pair was assigned to the intervention condition, the hands-on entrepreneurial curriculum. The other member of the pair was assigned to the traditional business class, where most of the activities were students reading simulations and class discussions. At the end of the semester, each student was given an entrepreneurial skill score, on a one to five scale, with five being always, four being most of the time, three being sometimes, two being rarely, and one being never.

5. A researcher was interested in determining how to get people with arthritis to use joint protection techniques. She observed 20 people with arthritis in their home for one morning and found that 6 out of 20 used joint protection techniques. She then gave a demonstration on joint protection to each participant. One month later she observed each of the participants again for one morning. She found that 16 out of 20 people used joint protection techniques.

6. A graduate seminar class has 10 students. The students are exposed to four different instructors, each instructor representing a different teaching style. At the end of the semester, each student is asked to judge each teaching style as challenging or not challenging. Are there significant differences among teaching styles?

7. As described in this chapter, Webster et al. (1997) performed a study that matched participants in pairs and then performed a *t* test for paired samples. What are the advantages and disadvantages of matching in this situation (Hint: consider degrees of freedom)?

8. As described in this chapter, Gliner and Sample (1993) performed a repeated measures ANOVA to compare three matched groups. They also performed a Tukey HSD post-hoc test in the study. Explain why.

CHAPTER
16

Basic Associational Designs: Analysis and Interpretation

In this chapter we examine the association between two variables, an independent variable and a dependent variable, but in this case, both variables are continuous or at least have many ordered levels and, thus, may be approximately continuous. Many methodologists choose to describe a correlation, such as that resulting from a Pearson product–moment correlation, as a relation between two variables without designating one as the independent variable and one as the dependent variable. Others choose to describe the relation as occurring between two dependent variables. Our emphasis on designating one variable as the independent variable and the other variable as the dependent variable follows from the previous chapters on design and the natural lead into linear regression. We discuss the Pearson product–moment correlation, (r), the nonparametric equivalent, Spearman rank–order correlation (r_s), and also introduce linear regression. In our previous discussion of statistical analyses in chapters 14 and 15, the independent variable has been categorical, and typically not more than three or four categories. The analyses that we discussed conformed to the research approaches of randomized experimental, quasi-experimental, and comparative. Now we would like you to consider an independent variable that is continuous. A continuous independent variable is almost always an attribute independent variable. Therefore, when the independent variable and the dependent variable are continuous, the research approach is associational.

ANALYZING CONTINUOUS SINGLE FACTOR DESIGNS WITH PARAMETRIC STATISTICS

Pearson Product–Moment Correlation

Atler and Gliner (1989) were interested in the relationship between certain psychosocial variables and poststroke activity. They hypothesized that different marital relationship characteristics, attitudes expressed toward disability, and social support networks of spouses of stroke patients would result in different activity levels and different satisfaction of activity levels. The independent variables in this study were marital relationship characteristics, attitudes expressed toward disability, and social support networks of spouses. The dependent variables were activity levels and satisfaction with activity levels. In this study, both the independent variables and the dependent variables were measured by using different scales that resulted in continuous measures. For example, to test one of the hypotheses of this study, Atler and Gliner examined the relationship between the independent variable of social support and the dependent variable of satisfaction of activity level. Atler and Gliner selected a Pearson product–moment correlation to test the relationship because there was one independent variable, level of social support; the independent variable had numerous levels (considered to be approximately continuous); and the dependent variable was scaled at the interval level.

The Pearson product–moment correlation tests the association or relationship between two continuous variables. We describe it in the present context to test the relationship between a continuous independent variable and a continuous dependent variable, as described in the associational approach. However, the Pearson product–moment correlation is also widely used in other areas, especially measurement reliability and validity (chap. 20), where one might test the relationship between two administrations of the same instrument (test–retest reliability) or the relationship between an instrument and some external criterion (predictive validity).

The Pearson product–moment correlation is expressed as a coefficient, r, which gives the association, or relationship, between the two variables. This coefficient has a range of -1 to $+1$. Pearson r values that are close to $+1$, such as values above .7, are considered to be strong positive relationships between the two variables. A positive relationship means that as scores on one variable increase, scores on the other variable also increase. On the other hand, r values that are close to -1, such as values below $-.7$, are considered to be strong negative, or inverse, relationships between the two variables. An inverse relationship means that high scores on one of the variables are associated with low scores for the same person on the other variable, and vice versa. When the r value is near zero, it indicates that there is no relationship between the two variables. An example of no relationship occurs when high scores on the independent variable are associated with high, medium, and low scores on the dependent variable. A low correlation means that you cannot predict the dependent variable by knowing the scores on the independent variable.

When reporting the results of a study that uses a Pearson product–moment correlation, the value of r is expressed along with the degrees of freedom and the significance level. For example, Atler and Gliner (1989) reported that "a positive correlation between social support scores and satisfaction was found ... ($r = .32$, $df = 28$, $p < .05$)" (p. 21). The r value of .32 from this study is considered to be a relatively weak positive relationship. The degrees of freedom of 28 indicate that there were 30 participants in the study, because the degrees of freedom for a Pearson correlation coefficient is the number of participants in the study minus two.

Statistical Significance and the Pearson Product–Moment Correlation.   As with any inferential statistic, one must be cautious about the interpretation of statistically significant correlation coefficients. There is an inverse relationship between the number of participants in the study, and the size of the coefficient needed to obtain statistical significance. In other words, studies with a large number of participants might find statistically significant correlation coefficients, but they may be trivial. If we examine a table of critical values for the Pearson product–moment correlation, we will find that, if there are 100 participants in a study, a correlation of about .20 is all that is needed to obtain statistical significance, given a nondirectional hypothesis. Therefore, it is useful with correlation coefficients to obtain an index of effect size.

A statistically significant outcome gives an indication of the probability that the result could have happened by chance. It does not describe the strength of the relationship between the independent and dependent variables. An effect size describes the *strength* of a relationship between an independent and a dependent variable, in other words, how much of the outcome can be predicted from the independent variable. One can calculate an effect size for every statistic. It is especially easy to perform this operation for a Pearson product–moment correlation because one measure of the effect size is r^2. This describes the amount of shared variance or overlap between the independent and dependent variables. For example, a study might show that the relationship between high school achievement test (ACT) scores (independent variable) and first-year college grades (dependent variable) was $r = .7$. The r^2 would equal .49. This would indicate that approximately half of the variance between the two measures was common to both, such as intelligence. On the other hand, half of the variance is unexplained.

Although many investigators do not report the effect size with their results, most journals are now requiring some index of the size of effect in addition to a determination of statistical significance. For example, in the Atler and Gliner (1989) study, they reported that the shared variance (r^2) between social support scores and activity levels was only 9.6%. Therefore, even though they obtained a significant correlation between the two measures, the "effect" of the independent variable was small.

Correlation Matrix.   It is relatively rare to see a single correlation coefficient or even two or three correlation coefficients in a study such as that found in Atler and Gliner (1989). Instead, it is much more common to report a *correlation matrix*. A correlation matrix is a table of correlation coefficients that shows how all variables are related to each other. For example, Kirchner and Holm (1997) conducted a study to predict academic and clinical performance of occupational therapy students. In their study, they had six independent variables (undergraduate grade point average [GPA], GRE- (Grad Record Examination) verbal, GRE-quantitative, GRE-analytic, a score from three reference letters, and a score from a student essay) and three dependent variables (graduate GPA, client attendance, and client outcomes). Table 16.1 shows the correlation matrix for their study.

TABLE 16.1

Intercorrelations Between Dependent and Independent Variables

Variables	1	2	3	4	5	6	7	8	9
1. Undergraduate GPA	—	.18	.08	.11	.15	.10	.24	.16	−.02
2. GRE - verbal		—	.27	.48	−.02	.10	.23	−.20	−.16
3. GRE - quantitative			—	.49	−.09	.08	.34	−.25	−.19
4. GRE - analytical				—	−.04	.00	.25	−.17	−.23
5. Reference					—	.20	.14	−.09	−.12
6. Essay						—	.24	−.27	−.15
7. GPA in O.T. courses							—	−.17	−.12
8. Client outcomes								—	.28
9. Client attendance									—

Note. $|r| \geq .20, p \leq .05$
$|r| \geq .27, p \leq .01$

A table displaying a correlation matrix has the variables ordered horizontally across the top row of the table, and vertically down the first column of the table. Notice that all of the correlation coefficients are in the upper right corner of the table. The values also could be in the lower left corner of the table, but this would be redundant because the same values would be present. Notice that in each row there is one cell with an underline. This denotes that a variable is being correlated with itself. All of the underlines taken together are referred to as the diagonal. To interpret a correlation matrix, one reads down the first column to find the variable of interest. Next, you proceed across to find the other variable of interest. Where these two variables intersect is the correlation coefficient for the two variables. For example, if we are interested in the relationship between the independent variable undergraduate GPA and the dependent variable client outcomes, we proceed across the row marked undergraduate GPA until it intersects the number 8, which is client outcomes. The correlation coefficient for this relationship is .16, indicating a weak, not statistically significant, positive relationship. Below the table, we have noted the critical values that a correlation coefficient must exceed to be significant at .05 or .01. We have placed these critical values within an absolute values sign. This means that a correlation coefficient of .20 or −.20 is significant at the .05 level.

It is common to see correlation matrices in studies that are interested in the relationship among many variables. However, for many of these studies, the correlation matrix is just the first step in the data analysis. In these studies, a multiple regression will be done. We discuss this common multivariate procedure in chapter 19. Whenever a correlation matrix is the first step in a more complex analysis, the correlation coefficients that are displayed in the matrix are referred to as *zero order correlations*.

USING NONPARAMETRIC ASSOCIATIONAL STATISTICS TO ANALYZE SINGLE FACTOR DESIGNS

Spearman Rank–Order Correlation

Similar to single factor designs discussed in chapters 14 and 15, the single factor design with many ordered levels should be analyzed with a nonparametric statistic if either the independent or dependent variables are measured on an ordinal scale (and not normally distributed) or the measurement of one of the variables violates the assumptions underlying parametric statistics. The nonparametric statistic most commonly used when assessing the relationship between ordered independent and dependent variables is the Spearman rank–order correlation (*rho*).

Murphy and Gliner (1988) were interested in the perceptual and motor processes of children who had difficulty learning motor skills. They felt that poor motor skills (dependent variable) were due to problems in perception (independent variable). To conduct this study, they measured 38 students on perceptual skills and then correlated these results with measures of motor skills. The approach to this study was associational because both the independent and dependent variables had many ordered levels and the independent variable was an attribute variable. However, according to Murphy and Gliner, "For analysis purposes, the data were conceived of as representing an ordinal scale, suggesting the use of nonparametric statistics" (p. 96). Furthermore, they pointed out, "The purpose of these analyses was to determine whether there was a *monotonic* relationship between the scores obtained on the motor tasks and the scores obtained on the perceptual tasks" (p. 98). Notice that the authors refer to the relationship between the two variables as monotonic, which indicates that as one variable increases, the other variable also increases, but not necessarily by the same amount. Had this been a Pearson product–moment correlation, the relationship would have been described as linear. However, with a Spearman correlation, the relationship between the two variables will not be linear because the data are ordinal. An example of ordinal data in this study is as follows. Scoring on one of the measures of motor skills was two or more errors: in the sequence = 0 points, one card out of sequence = 1 point, all cards in sequence = 2 points. Murphy and Gliner selected the Spearman *rho* correlation to analyze the data because there was one continuous independent variable, one multilevel ordered dependent variable, and the data were considered to be ordinal on at least one of the two variables.

Burleigh, Farber, and Gillard (1998) performed a study to determine if there is a relationship between community integration and life satisfaction after traumatic brain injury. Using the associational approach, Burleigh et al. correlated community integration (an attribute independent variable) and life satisfaction with the Spearman correlation. A Spearman correlation was selected because the instruments used to measure the independent and dependent variables were ordinal scales. They correlated life satisfaction with total community integration, and its subscales, home integration, social integration, and productivity integration. The results of their analyses appear in Table 16.2. They concluded, "Spearman rank–order correlations used to analyze the relationship of life satisfaction to home, social, and productivity integration showed a low, but significant, correlation only between social integration and life satisfaction (*rho* = .37, *p* = .047)" (p. 48).

Phi and Cramer's V

When the independent and dependent variables are nominal, the appropriate associational inferential statistic is Phi or Cramer's V. These statistics describe

TABLE 16.2

Correlation of Life Satisfaction Index-A With Total Community Integration Questionnaire and Its Subscales

Community Integration Questionnaire	*Life Satisfaction Index-A*	
	rho	*p*
Total community integration	−.06	.77
Home integration	−.16	.39
Social integration	.37	.047
Productivity integration	−.28	.13

Note.   *N* = 30.

the *strength* of the association or relationship between two nominal variables. They begin with a cross-tabulation table that is the same as the tables we presented in chapter 14 when discussing chi-square. Phi is the appropriate statistic for a 2 × 2 table, that is, when the independent and dependent variables each have two levels. Cramer's V is used when there are more than two levels of one or both variables.

LINEAR REGRESSION

Not only is it important to know that there is a relation between two variables, but if this relation is sufficiently strong, it allows us to predict one variable from another variable. When we discuss prediction, we are attempting to predict the dependent variable from the independent variable. This is why we have discussed the associational approach in terms of independent and dependent variables. When we have just two variables, an independent variable and a dependent variable, and we attempt to predict one from the other, this is called *linear regression*. It should be noted that there are many different types of regression, but here we are talking about using data obtained from the Pearson product–moment correlation.

If we know the correlation coefficient (r) between an independent variable (X) and a dependent variable (Y), and also know the mean and standard deviation of each of the variables, we can create an equation which allows us to predict the dependent variable from the independent variable. Often when discussing linear regression, the independent variable is referred to as the *predictor variable* and the dependent variable is referred to as the *criterion variable*. The linear regression equation is used to determine a straight line and is expressed as follows:

Start with the equation $Y' = a + bX$ (the equation for a straight line), where $Y' = Y$ value predicted from a particular X value.
$a = Y$ coordinate of the point at which the regression line intersects the Y axis.
$b =$ Slope of the regression line.

Let's start with an example. Frone (1998) was interested in predicting work injuries among employed adolescents. Frone selected a number of independent or predictor variables that would best predict the dependent variable work injuries. Some of these predictor variables were demographic variables, such as age or gender. Other predictor variables were job related, such as job tenure, physical hazards, and supervisor monitoring. In his study, Frone actually had 20 predictor variables. This was because he was attempting to determine the best combination of these variables to predict work injuries. This procedure is called *multiple regression*, and we discuss its use in chapter 19. However, for our example we will select just one of Frone's predictor variables, work hazards, and his dependent variable, work injuries to establish a linear regression equation. Frone defined physical hazards as, "the extent to which individuals are exposed to dangerous equipment, unsafe working conditions, and poor environmental controls" (pp. 569–570). The independent variable, physical hazards, was measured from the average of seven items. The dependent variable, work injuries, was assessed from a self-report of seven types of work injuries experienced during the previous 9 months. The data for the two variables can be seen in Table 16.3. The correlation coefficient, r, between the two variables was .50.

The slope, b, is found as follows:

$$b = r \frac{s_y}{s_x}$$

$$b = (.50)\frac{.70}{.78}$$

$$b = .45 \quad .$$

The y intercept, a, is found as follows:

$$a = \overline{Y} - b\overline{X}$$

$$a = 1.62 - (.45)(2.02)$$

$$a = .71$$

$$Y' = .71 + .45X.$$

Therefore, if we know a particular X value, we can predict the Y value. Or, if we know a participant's physical hazards, we can predict work injuries. For example, if a participant had a physical hazard rating of three, we would predict that he would have an injury rating of

$$Y' = .71 + .45X$$
$$Y' = .71 + .45(3)$$
$$Y' = 2.06 \text{ injury rating.}$$

On the other hand, if our participant had a physical hazard rating of one, we would predict that he would have an injury rating of

$$Y' = .71 + .45(1)$$
$$Y' = 1.16 \text{ injury rating.}$$

We could also graph our results (Fig. 16.1).

TABLE 16.3

Descriptive Statistics from the Frone (1998) Study

Sample Description	Physical Hazards	Work Injuries
Number of participants	319	319
Mean	2.02	1.62
Standard deviation	.78	.70

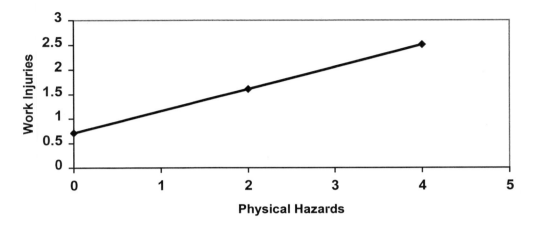

FIG. 16.1.   Linear regression of physical hazards and injury rating.

To display the regression line, we substitute into our equation to find at least three points, and draw a line between the points. For our example, the equation is as follows:

$$Y' = .71 + .45(X).$$

We substitute three values for X. The first value should be 0. Therefore, when X = 0, Y' = .73. Then we plot those two coordinates. The second value might be 2. When X = 2, Y' = 1.61. Then we plot these two coordinates. The third value might be 4. When X = 4, Y' = 2.51. Then we plot these two coordinates. Now we draw a line through the three points. We must be cautious when applying any linear regression equation because the correlation coefficient, r, is never going to be 1.0. In our present example, r was only .5. Therefore, r^2, which is an index of the strength of the relationship between the two variables, is only 25%. This means that 75% of the variance between the two variables is unexplained. Had we graphed the actual data points from the 319 participants in the study for the two variables, most of the points would not fit along our line. The farther the points are away from the line, the lower the value of the correlation coefficient.

Sometimes, we are interested in applying a linear regression equation that was obtained from another study. A second reason to be cautious when applying a linear regression equation obtained from another study is that the sample from which the equation was obtained must be similar to your participants of interest. We return to linear regression in chapter 19, when we address multiple regression and other multivariate methods.

SUMMARY

In this chapter we discussed the selection and application of appropriate statistical methods used in the associational research approach. These statistical methods are usually used in single factor designs with many ordered levels of the independent variable. The most common correlation coefficient used to describe the relationship between a continuous independent and a dependent variable is the Pearson product–moment correlation, r. This value can be squared to determine the effect size of a correlation coefficient. When the measurement of the independent variable is not at the interval level, or there are violations precluding the use of parametric statistics, the Spearman correlation is most often applied. We also demonstrated linear regression as a method to predict the dependent variable when there is a relationship between the independent and dependent variables.

Study Aids

Concepts

- Correlation matrix
- Cramer's V
- Linear regression
- Pearson product–moment correlation
- Phi coefficient
- Spearman rank–order correlation
- Squared correlation coefficient

Distinctions

- Correlation coefficient versus squared correlation coefficient
- Correlation versus linear regression
- Pearson product–moment correlation versus Spearman rank–order correlation

Application Problems

1. A therapist was interested in predicting success on the job following therapy. The therapist felt that a good outcome measure of therapy at discharge was the number of hours a person could spend in a simulated work task. The best measure of success on the job was number of months in current employment. The therapist gathered data from files of previous patients. The data were as follows:

S#	Hours Simulated Task	Months Current Employment
1	8	12
2	7.5	10
3	7	9
4	6	10
5	6	9
6	5	6
7	4.5	7
8	3	6
9	2	5
10	2	4

Three patients have just been discharged. Their work simulation results were 3.5, 6.5, and 7 respectively. How long would you predict each person will work, assuming an r of 0.94 from the above data?

2. A study was performed to determine if high school teaching performance in the classroom could be predicted from scores on a licensure examination. Both measurement tools are scaled at the interval level. The correlation, r, between teaching performance and licensure examination was 0.5. What problems might result in predicting this teaching performance?

3. Is there a relationship between teaching evaluations and course grades. The hypothesis was tested in a graduate seminar with 10 students. The students' grades in the course ranged from C (2) to A (4). The course evaluations ranged from neutral (3) to very good (5). What analysis should be performed to test this relationship, and why?

4. An investigator performs a study for an insurance company to determine the relationship, if any, between hand strength after surgery and length of time in treatment. The investigator measures each patient after surgery to determine hand strength. Then she divides the patients into low, medium, and high length-of-time each patient spent in treatment. In order to determine if there are differences among the three groups, she performs a single factor ANOVA with hand strength as the dependent variable. How could she use the associational approach in this study? What would be the advantages?

CHAPTER

17

Adding Independent Variables— Complex Between Groups Designs: Analysis and Interpretation

OVERVIEW

The three previous chapters discussed the design and analyses of single factor studies, where there was only one independent variable. However, it is uncommon to find in current literature the case where only one independent variable is present. In this chapter we introduce a second between groups independent variable, discuss the advantages of having more than one independent variable, and demonstrate how these designs (complex designs) are analyzed and interpreted. In chapter 18, we continue our discussion on complex designs by introducing a repeated measures independent variable as the second independent variable, creating a mixed design. Remember, that in chapter 12, we discussed the three general design classifications (between groups, within subjects, and mixed) and noted that they determine the specific statistics to use in data analysis. Although we are adding a second independent variable in the current chapter, the designs are still between groups because both independent variables are between groups independent variables. However, most of the experimental designs in chapter 18 are mixed designs, which by definition have at least two independent variables, one *between groups* and one *within subjects (repeated measures)*. These mixed, two-factor designs are often those with a pretest and a posttest (within subjects) *and* with experimental and control groups (between groups).

Reasons for Adding a Second (or More) Independent Variable(s)

There are two major reasons for adding a second independent variable in a study. The first reason is that adding a second independent variable gives the researcher more information. When we have two independent variables in a single study, we can determine how each independent variable works by itself and determine how the two independent variables work together or interact. How an independent variable works by itself is referred to as a *main effect*. How two independent variables interact in a study is referred to as an *interaction effect*. In a study with two independent variables, there will be two main effects (one for each independent variable) and an interaction effect. We would like to emphasize that the term *effect* can be misleading because it seems to imply a causal relationship. As noted in earlier chapters, this inference is not justified if the independent variable is an attribute, and may not be justified even if the independent variable is active. Thus you should be cautious when interpreting results.

Consider a study by Robinson, Katayama, Dubois, and Devaney (1998), who were interested in the effects of two independent variables on concept application. The two independent variables were (a) whether the students reviewed information immediately or delayed doing so, and (b) the use of a study aid (text only, text plus outline, text plus graphic organizer). In this study, there was one main effect for when students reviewed the information, and a second main effect for the use of a study aid. There was also an interaction effect between the review of information and the use of a study aid. Robinson et al. randomly assigned students to all conditions, thus both independent variables were active.

It is important to recognize that when independent variables are added to increase information, the main effects of both independent variables are usually of interest. Therefore, these independent variables are usually active.

The second reason for using a two-factor design instead of two single-factor designs is that *error variance is more precisely estimated*. To explain this conceptually, the nature of error variance must be understood. Error variance is variability that is attributed to individual differences among participants. Sometimes these differences are due to the fact that tests often do not measure a particular construct reliably. Other times these differences are due to things such as age or gender differences among participants. It is the latter type of error that we are trying to remove. If we can introduce a second independent variable, such as age or gender, then the part of the error variance that resulted from these attributes would be removed and distributed as a second independent variable. The error variance would be significantly reduced. Gliner et al. (1999) conducted a study to investigate hiring decisions among undergraduate students. Specifically, Gliner et al. were interested in the employability ratings students would give to hiring a person into either a segregated employment setting, a supportive employment setting, or a competitive employment setting. Employment setting was the independent variable of interest, and students were randomly assigned to rate one of the three employment settings. Gliner et al. selected students from a preoccupational therapy program, an occupational therapy program, and a business program. Therefore, the second independent variable, student program, was an attribute independent variable. Similar to those in the Robinson et al. (1998) study mentioned earlier, there were two main effects and an interaction effect in the Gliner et al. study. These effects were type of employment condition (main effect), type of student program (main effect), and employment condition by student program (interaction effect). What is especially important about this study was that Gliner et al. were primarily interested in the active independent variable, type of employment setting. The other independent variable, student program, was not important by itself (main effect), but if it was significant, it could reduce the variability in the study. Therefore, when attempting to reduce error by adding a second independent variable, the second independent variable is usually an attribute independent variable.

TWO-FACTOR DESIGNS AND QUANTITATIVE RESEARCH APPROACHES

Two-factor designs imply that both independent variables are between groups independent variables. In addition, we outlined different quantitative approaches, including randomized experimental, quasi-experimental, comparative, associational, and descriptive. These quantitative approaches were based, for the most part, on characteristics of the independent variable. When we add a second independent variable in a study, do we still have the same quantitative approaches? The answer to this question is yes. We base our answer on the characteristics of the primary independent variable in the study.

We start with the example of the study by Robinson et al. (1998), described earlier. This study has two active independent variables, with participants randomly assigned to the conditions of both independent variables. Therefore, this study would fit the randomized experimental approach. Now consider a study by Bergin (1994), who was interested in the type of goal situation on a number of learning indices. Specifically, he investigated the difference between a mastery goal situation and a competitive goal situation on interest, learning strategies, test achievement, and free recall achievement. He randomly assigned students to either the mastery goal situation or the competitive goal situation. A second independent variable was also introduced in the study, student GPA. This second independent variable had two levels, low or high. We also classify this study into the quantitative research approach of randomized experimental, because the primary independent variable was active and students were randomly assigned to conditions. The Gliner et al. (1999) study would also fit into the randomized experimental approach, because the independent variable of primary interest was active and participants were randomly assigned to conditions.

A study by Tuckman (1995, Experiment 2) provides an example of a two-factor design that fits the quasi-experimental approach. In this study, Tuckman was interested in comparing an incentive motivation condition with a learning strategy condition on three different achievement tests and all three tests combined (four dependent variables). The learning strategy condition was provided to one intact class and the incentive motivation condition was provided to a second intact class. A second independent variable, student grade point average (GPA) with three levels (low, medium, and high), was also added, similar to the Bergin (1995) study. This study is considered to be a quasi-experimental approach because the primary independent variable was active, but participants were not randomly assigned to classrooms. Instead, the classrooms were selected from the method used by the instructor, making a medium-level quasi-experimental approach.

A study by Richardson and Fergus (1993) demonstrates the two-factor complex comparative approach. They were interested in whether high school students who were judged to be of higher ability differed from those who were judged to be of lower ability on learning style, as measured by the Inventory of Learning Processes. In addition, Richardson and Fergus were interested in whether the independent variable gender also influenced learning style. Notice that in this study both independent variables are attribute independent variables, so the quantitative approach is comparative.[1]

Main Effects in More Detail

To set the stage for the two-factor analysis of variance, we need to examine main effects and interaction effects in more detail. Therefore, we return to the study by

---

[1]Although this example of two attribute independent variables fits our comparative approach, caution must be taken when analyzing the data from this type of study. The problem is that when both independent variables are attribute independent variables, the possibility that the two independent variables are correlated is high. If this is the case, the outcome from the analysis will be biased (see Pedhazur & Schmelkin, 1991, pp. 537–538.)

Tuckman (1996, Experiment 2). Recall that Tuckman had a 2 × 3 factorial design. The two levels of the first independent variable were incentive motivation versus learning strategy. The three levels of the second independent variable were GPA: low, medium, and high. We will use just one of his dependent variables, the first achievement test, which was a 65-item multiple choice examination. The average scores on the first achievement test (percent correct) can be seen in Table 17.1. Notice that we have included, along with the average test scores for each of the six groups, column averages, row averages, and an overall average. These column and row averages are helpful when examining main effects. For example, in the Tuckman study, the design was a 3 × 2 factorial design. Because there were two independent variables, there were two main effects, one for each independent variable. One main effect is the type of condition, incentive motivation or learning strategy. Notice that the mean for the incentive motivation condition is 72.9 (row 1) and the mean for the learning strategy condition is 72.5 (row 2). When we analyze our data for this study by using a two-factor analysis of variance, one of the questions that will be answered is whether the main effect for type of condition is statistically significant. To determine this answer, the mean for incentive motivation condition (72.9) will be compared with the mean of the learning strategy condition (72.5). The second main effect for this study was grade point average. To determine this main effect, we will compare the average for the high GPA (76.8), with the average for the medium GPA (72.4), with the average of the low GPA (68.8).

Interaction Effects in More Detail

In addition to determining if each main effect is statistically significant, we are also interested in determining if the interaction effect is statistically significant. The interaction effect is determined by examining the individual means within the cells of Table 17.1. To understand an interaction effect, we need to examine patterns among these individual cells. For example, if we look across the three cells of row one (incentive motivation condition) of Table 17.1, we see that the three means are almost equal (73.7, 72.2, 72.7). On the other hand, if we look across the three cells of row two (learning strategy condition) of Table 17.1, we see that the means are decreasing from high GPA (79.9) to medium GPA (72.6) to low GPA (64.9).

The first step in the examination of complex studies, where more than one independent variable is involved, is to graph the data. When setting up any graph, always place the dependent variable on the Y (vertical) axis. When there are two independent variables involved, a rule of thumb is to place the attribute independent variable on the X (horizontal) axis, and graph the active independ-

TABLE 17.1

Average Test Scores for Test 1, Experiment 2 From Tuckman (1995) Study

Condition	High GPA	Medium GPA	Low GPA	Average
Incentive motivation	73.7	72.2	72.7	72.9
Learning strategy	79.9	72.6	64.9	72.5
Average	76.8	72.4	68.8	72.7

ent variable with separate lines, as we have done in Fig. 17.1. Figure 17.1 demonstrates a *disordinal* interaction. In a disordinal interaction, the lines on the graph cross. If we had not included the low GPA condition, but only the medium and high GPA conditions, the interaction would be called *ordinal*. An interaction is said to be ordinal if the lines are clearly not parallel but do not cross within the graph. When there is no interaction, the lines usually run parallel to each other. Sometimes it is helpful to use bar graphs to examine information from two-factor experiments. Figure 17.2 is an example of the same data plotted as a bar graph. For the high GPA group, we see that the learning strategy condition is about 6 percentage points higher than the incentive motivation condition. When we look at the medium GPA group, we see that the two conditions have almost the same percentage points. On the other hand, when we look at the low GPA group, we see a reverse of the high GPA group. The incentive motivation condition is almost eight percentage points higher than the learning strategy condition. According to Kerlinger (1986), "Interaction occurs when an independent variable has different effects on a dependent vari-

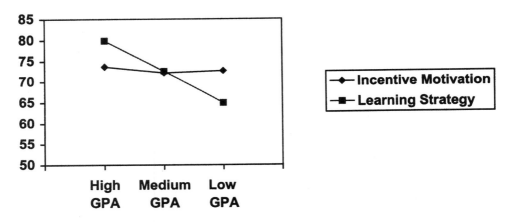

FIG. 17.1.   Plot of the interaction of condition with grade point average (GPA).

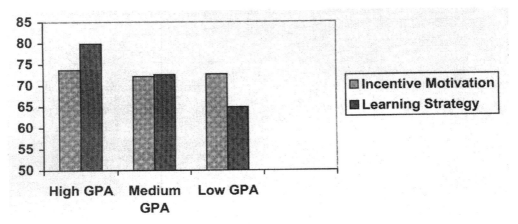

FIG. 17.2.   Bar graph of the interaction of condition with grade point average (GPA).

able at different levels of another independent variable" (p. 230). What this means is that when we observe a significant interaction effect, we will notice that at one level of an independent variable, medium GPA in our example, there is no significant difference between the two conditions of the other independent variable incentive motivation $\bar{X} = 72.2$ versus learning strategy ($\bar{X} = 72.6$). On the other hand, at another level of this same independent variable, there should be a significant difference between the two conditions of the other independent variable. This can be seen in either the high GPA level, where the learning strategy condition ($\bar{X} = 79.9$) is higher than the incentive motivation condition ($\bar{X}$ 73.7) or in the low GPA level, where the incentive motivation condition ($\bar{X} = 72.7$) is higher than the learning strategy condition ($\bar{X} = 64.9$). Although we have examined the data visually, the only way to know which conditions are different statistically is to perform the proper analysis, which for the present example is a two-factor ANOVA, with appropriate follow-up tests if needed.

ANALYSIS OF TWO-FACTOR DESIGNS

Regardless of the type of quantitative research approach, two-factor designs are analyzed by two-factor analysis of variance as long as both independent variables are between groups independent variables, and the data approximate an interval scale and other ANOVA assumptions (see chap. 14) are not markedly violated. For those studies with two independent variables that have data that are ordinal or categorical, there are not many options. These studies are frequently analyzed by nonparametric techniques applied to one independent variable at a time, but the interaction effect is lost. There are more sophisticated techniques, such as log linear analysis, which are beyond the scope of this text.

Source Table for a Two-Factor Analysis of Variance.   In chapter 14 we discussed the single factor analysis of variance. All analysis of variance procedures have an accompanying source table. In chapter 14, this source table was depicted in Table 14.3. For the single factor analysis of variance, the variance is divided into that due to treatment, usually referred to as between groups, and that due to error, usually described as within subjects. The generalized source table for the two-factor ANOVA is presented in Table 17.2. Similar to the one-way ANOVA, the two-way ANOVA starts by dividing the sums of squares into a treatment component and an error component. Next, the treatment component is divided into a sums of squares for independent variable A, a sums of squares for independent variable B, and the remainder is the interaction sums of squares $A \times B$. Each of these sums of squares is divided by degrees of freedom to obtain mean squares. There will be four mean squares. The degrees of freedom for independent variable A are q (the number of levels of independent variable A) minus one. The degrees of freedom for independent variable B are r (the number of levels of independent variable B) minus one. The interaction degrees of freedom are computed by multiplying the degrees of freedom for independent variable A times the degrees of freedom of independent variable B. The degrees of freedom for the error term are computed by multiplying the number of levels of independent variable A times the number of levels of independent variable B times the sample size for any cell (n) minus one. There will be four mean squares (MS) in the source table: a mean square for independent variable A, a mean square for independent variable B, a mean square interaction $A \times B$, and a mean square error. Once the mean squares have been calculated, the F values are obtained.

Remember that in a two-factor ANOVA there are three Fs and three questions that we can answer, one about each main effect and the interaction. Each of the three F values is obtained by dividing the MS for that source of variation by the MS for error, as seen in the last column in Table 17.2.

To understand the role of the source table in a two-way ANOVA, let's examine the data from the study by Tuckman (1995, Experiment 2). Earlier we described the means for each of the groups in this study in Table 17.1. Now we examine the source table from that study in Table 17.3.

Questions Answered in the Two-Factor Analysis of Variance.   In a one-way or single factor design, one hypothesis is tested, the effect of that independent variable, for example, the treatment. In this two-way or two-factor design, three hypotheses were tested: (a) there is a difference between the two conditions of independent variable A (incentive motivation versus learning strategy); (b) there is a difference among the three GPA groupings of independent variable B; and (c) there is an interaction of independent variables A and B. In this example, the first hypothesis was not supported. There was no significant difference between the incentive motivation condition and the learning strategy condition, as evidenced by a very small F value of .40. The second hypothesis was supported. There was a significant difference among the three GPA groupings, with an F value of 4.71, which was significant at the .05 level. The third hypothesis, the interaction between the two independent variables, also was supported. The F value of 3.46 was significant at the .05 level.

Describing the Results in the Text.   Although we have presented the data from the Tuckman (1995, Experiment 2) two-way ANOVA in a source table, it is not uncommon for many journals to have authors report their results in text form to save space. The data from Table 17.3 would be reported as follows.

TABLE 17.2
Two-Factor Analysis of Variance Source Table

Source of Variation	SS	df	MS	F
Independent variable A		$q-1$		$\dfrac{MS_A}{Ms_{error}}$
Independent variable B		$r-1$		$\dfrac{MS_B}{Ms_{error}}$
Interaction $A \times B$		$(q-1)(r-1)$		$\dfrac{MS_{AB}}{MS_{error}}$
Error or within subjects		$qr(n-1)$		

There was no significant difference between the incentive motivation condition and the learning strategy condition, $F(1, 109) = .40$, *NS*. There was a significant main effect for GPA, $F(2,109) = 4.71$, $p < .05$. There also was a significant interaction effect, $F(2,109) = 3.46$, $p < .05$. When presenting the results in text form, the degrees of freedom are placed in parentheses. The degrees of freedom reported are those for the particular source of variation, such as a particular main effect, divided by the degrees of freedom of the error term. If the outcome is not significant, the abbreviation *NS* is often reported. However, because most analyses these days are performed by a statistical package on a computer, the actual p value should be reported.

Interpretation of the Results From a Two-Factor ANOVA Source Table

Table 17.3 demonstrated that there was a significant main effect for GPA and a significant interaction effect between the two conditions and GPA. When there is a statistically significant interaction effect, it should be interpreted first, before any significant main effect. The reason for giving more weight to interpreting the interaction effect is that it provides the simplest (most parsimonious) explanation. It also gives more accurate, less potentially misleading information. In the example earlier, the main effect suggests that there are significant differences among the three GPA groups. However, a closer examination of the means provided in Table 17.1 shows that these differences are primarily due to the learning strategy condition. In fact, the differences among the three GPA groups for the incentive motivation condition are small. There is a second reason for interpreting a significant interaction effect before a significant main effect in the present study. The author was not particularly interested in GPA by itself. As we mentioned earlier, often when the second independent variable is an attribute independent variable, the purpose is to reduce error variation. In the present study, Tuckman (1996) referred to GPA as a moderator variable. In other words, GPA would affect the incentive motivation condition differently than the learning strategy condition.

The information provided in the source table, that there is a significant interaction effect, is not sufficient for interpretation of that interaction effect. Instead, follow-up statistical procedures need to be performed to pinpoint the interaction effect.

TABLE 17.3
**Two-Factor ANOVA Source Table from Tuckman (1995, Experiment 2)
Using the First Test Data Scores as the Dependent Variable**

Source	SS	df	MS	F
Condition	4.82	1	4.82	.40
GPA	112.46	2	56.23	4.71*
Condition × GPA	82.62	2	41.31	3.46*
Within subjects (error)	1302.55	109	11.95	

*$p < .05$.

Statistical Procedures for Interpretation of an Interaction Effect.   Whenever a significant interaction effect is obtained, further statistical procedures must be implemented. These statistical procedures are referred to as simple main effects analyses and post hoc comparisons. Simple main effects analysis is a statistical procedure that takes advantage of the information already compiled from computing the two-factor ANOVA. Performing simple main effects is similar to performing single factor ANOVAs on either the rows or the columns in Table 17.1.[2] If simple main effects were performed for the column conditions, there would be three simple main effects, high GPA, medium GPA, and low GPA. Each simple main effect would be tested to determine if there was a significant difference. In the present study, it appeared that there was no significant simple main effect for the high GPA condition or the medium GPA condition, but there was a significant simple main effect for the low GPA condition. Tuckman (1996) concluded, "Each significant interaction resulted from low-GPA students doing much better in the incentive motivation condition than in the learning strategy condition, whereas middle-GPA and high-GPA students did equally well in each treatment condition" (p. 204).

Simple main effects analysis could have been performed for the two row conditions instead of the three column conditions. However, if there were statistically significant differences for either of the row conditions, follow up post hoc analyses would have to be performed, similar to a one-way ANOVA (chap. 14) because there are three levels in each of the row conditions.

Statistical Procedures for Interpretation of Significant Main Effects.   Earlier, we stated that interpretation of a significant interaction effect should always precede interpretation of significant main effects. However, it is not uncommon to find studies where there are no significant interaction effects, but one or both main effects are significant. Table 17.4 shows data from Tuckman (1996, Experiment 2) for his third test (dependent variable). A two-factor ANOVA performed on the data revealed the following source table (Table 17.5).

Notice that whereas both main effects are statistically significant, the interaction effect is not significant. The follow-up statistical procedures for interpretation of main effects are straightforward. If the main effect is significant and has only *two* levels, then no further analysis is needed. Because there is a significant difference, the difference must be between the means of the two conditions. Examination of the means should reveal which condition performed better. This is evidenced by the main effect for condition, which tests the difference between the incentive motivation condition and the learning strategy condition. Data from Table 17.4 demonstrate that students performed significantly better in the incentive motivation condition ($\overline{X} = 76.1$) compared to the learning strategy condition ($\overline{X} = 71.7$). A significant main effect also was found for GPA. However, because there were *three* conditions of GPA, a follow-up or post hoc test, such as a Tukey *HSD*, needs to be performed to determine where the three GPA conditions are different.

---

[2]Although it is possible to perform simple main effects on both the rows and the columns, the information from performing both is, for the most part, redundant.

TABLE 17.4

Average Test Scores for Test 3, Experiment 2, From the Tuckman (1995) Study

Condition	High GPA	Medium GPA	Low GPA	Average
Incentive motivation	80.2	72.7	75.4	76.1
Learning strategy	78.7	70.9	65.5	71.7
Average	79.4	71.8	70.5	73.9

TABLE 17.5

Two-Factor ANOVA Source Table From Tuckman (1996, Experiment 2) Third Test Data

Source	SS	df	MS	F
Condition	51.91	1	51.91	4.03*
GPA	182.80	2	91.40	7.10**
Condition × GPA	34.42	2	17.21	1.34
Within subjects (error)	1403.92	109	12.88	

$*p < .05. **p < .01$

Summary

We introduced complex designs in this chapter, starting with complex between groups designs, or more specifically, two-factor designs. Complex designs are designs with more than one independent variable. The two major reasons for adding a second independent variable in a study are to provide the researcher with more information and to reduce error variance. Even though the designs are complex, they still fall into one of the quantitative approaches described in chapter 5. We described main effects and interaction effects and provided examples of each. The two-factor analysis of variance was introduced as the proper analysis for the two-factor design. This analysis answers three different questions, one for each main effect in the study and one for the interaction effect. Follow-up post hoc tests following significant main effects were described. Simple main effects analysis following significant interaction effects were explained. Emphasis was placed on the proper interpretation of interaction effects.

Study Aids

Concepts

- Disordinal interaction
- Interaction effects
- Main effects
- Ordinal interaction

- Simple effects
- Two-factor ANOVA

Distinctions

- Main effects versus interaction effects
- Ordinal versus disordinal interaction
- Simple effects versus post hoc comparisons

Application Problems

1. What is a factorial design? Why would you use a factorial design?
2. What is the difference between a main effect and an interaction effect?
3. Why would you do one analysis (factorial ANOVA) instead of two separate analyses (e.g., t tests) when you have two independent variables?
4. Why is it important to look first at interaction effects?
5. A faculty member conducted a study to determine who performed better in his research class, those students in education or those students in occupational therapy. In addition, he felt that gender could also make a contribution. Therefore, he conducted a retrospective study (i.e., went back into previous records) and formed the following four groups of ten students in each group: Male education (ME), female education (FE), male OT (MOT), female OT (FOT). Dr. G then calculated the mean test scores for each group; they were as follows:
   - ME = 81
   - FE = 93
   - MOT = 89
   - FOT = 84
   a. Graph the above data.
   b. The sums of squares for the results are in the following source table. Complete it.
   c. If an F of 4.11 is required for statistical significance, interpret the results.

Source Table

Source	SS	df	MS	F
Major	420			
Gender	250			
Major by gender	600			
Within subjects (error)	5200			

6. An investigator was interested in the effect of teaching style on students' perception of credibility of their instructor. One style of interest was the participatory action style in which the students took responsibility for much of the class material. The other style of interest was labeled the traditional style, in which delivery of material was by lecture. Two instructors from the same de-

partment taught the same class; one instructor was skilled in the participatory learning style, while the other was skilled in the traditional style. The investigator also thought that the age of students might affect this research project due to different expectations among students. The investigator decided to select three different age groups for the project: young, middle, and older. The investigator performs a two-factor ANOVA. What should the investigator do under each of the following situations:

    a. The investigator finds a significant main effect for teaching style, but no significant main effect for age, or teaching style by age interaction.

    b. The investigator finds a significant main effect for age, but no significant main effect for teaching style and no teaching style by age interaction.

    c. The investigator finds no significant main effects for teaching style or age, but a significant teaching style by age interaction.

    d. The investigator finds significant main effects for teaching style and age, and a teaching style by age interaction.

18

Mixed Factorial Designs: Analysis and Interpretation

INTRODUCTION

In this chapter we discuss how to analyze and interpret the mixed factorial design. Previously, we defined the mixed design as a design that has a minimum of two independent variables. One of the independent variables must be a between groups independent variable. The other independent variable must be a within subjects independent variable. Sometimes mixed designs have more than two independent variables. For example, a mixed design might have three independent variables, with two between groups independent variables and one within subjects independent variable. Or, a mixed design might have three independent variables, with one between groups independent variable and two within subjects independent variables. However, the minimum requirement still holds: there must be at least one between groups independent variable and one within subjects independent variable for the design to be a mixed design. Because mixed designs are the most complex designs that we have covered, we limit our discussion to the simplest mixed design, a design with one between groups independent variable and one within subjects independent variable. This design is often referred to as a two-factor design with repeated measures on the second factor.

Similar to the approaches for the other designs that we have discussed previously, the different quantitative approaches apply to the mixed design. For the most part, these approaches are randomized experimental and quasi-experimental. Comparative approaches that use the mixed design are less common, but do occur. We label the design as one of these three approaches, depending on the highest approach used, usually noted from the between groups independent variable. For example, if participants were randomly assigned on one of the independent variables, then the approach is randomized experimental. Jongbloed et al. (1989) randomly assigned participants who had experienced a stroke to two different treatment conditions (between groups independent variable), and then measured them over time (within subjects independent variable). Lan and Repman (1995) had two between groups independent variables, modeling and grade level, and one within subjects independent variable, context. Because participants were randomly assigned to one of the independent variables, modeling, the approach is considered to be randomized experimental.

Louth, McAllister, and McAllister (1992) were interested in the effects of collaborative writing techniques (active independent variable) on freshman writing. Students were already in sections of freshman composition (intact groups) so the approach was quasi-experimental. Sections were randomly assigned to one of three writing conditions (between groups independent variable) and measured over time (within subjects independent variable). Because the between groups independent variable involved random assignment of treatments to intact groups, the study was considered to be a strong quasi-experimental approach. Gilfoyle and Gliner (1985) were interested in the impact of an education program on attitudes toward handicapped children. Three schools participated in the study. Two schools received the intervention and the third school served as the control condition. Students in the schools were assessed over time. The quantitative approach for the study was considered to be quasi-experimental of medium strength because students were in intact groups (schools) rather than being randomly assigned to the intervention or the control condition, and the treatment was not randomly assigned to the groups.

A mixed design example that used the comparative approach can be seen in a study by Chambers (1994). Chambers was interested in assessing different types of leaders in the field of education. He sent a questionnaire to three different types of leaders in education. They were student affairs leadership educators, academic affairs leadership educators, and community-based leadership educators. These leadership types formed the between groups independent variable with three levels. This independent variable was an attribute independent variable. Each participant in the study rated the importance in evaluating college student leadership programs on the criteria of program structuring, methodology, program administration, and consequences. Thus, the second independent variable, a within subjects independent variable, was labeled evaluation category with four levels. Therefore, the design for the Chambers study was a mixed design, and because both independent variables were attributes, the research approach was considered to be comparative.

For our discussion, we divide mixed designs into two different categories. One category we refer to as true mixed designs. In this category, the between groups independent variable may be active (usually) or attribute, but the within subjects independent variable must be active. We label our second category of mixed designs pretest–posttest designs. Again, the between groups independent variable is usually active, but could be an attribute independent variable. However, the within subjects independent variable in pretest–posttest designs is neither active nor attribute, but referred to as change over time. While this is a special circumstance, it is common in all areas of applied research. When we describe either category of design, the term mixed or two-factor design with repeated measures on the second factor applies to both. However, although the analysis of the true mixed design is almost always a two-factor ANOVA with repeated measures on the second factor, there are at least three different methods to analyze the pretest–posttest design.

THE TRUE MIXED DESIGN

The true mixed design has one between groups independent variable that is almost always active and one within subjects variable that is always active.

Analyzing the True Mixed Design

To analyze data from a design with at least one between groups independent variable and one within subjects independent variable, the proper analysis is a mixed analysis of variance (ANOVA). In the present chapter, for explanatory purposes, we only discuss mixed designs with one between groups independent variable and one within subjects independent variable. Therefore, when we are referring to the mixed ANOVA in this chapter, it could also be called a two-factor ANOVA with repeated measures on the second factor. The mixed ANOVA answers the same three questions that were answered by a two-factor

ANOVA discussed in chapter 17. The three questions are (a) Is there a significant main effect for the first independent variable (in this case, the between groups independent variable)? (b) Is there a significant main effect for the second independent variable (in this case, the within subjects independent variable)? and (c) Is there a significant interaction effect between the two independent variables? While the questions asked in the two-factor mixed ANOVA are similar to those of the two-factor ANOVA, the actual analysis is different. We see this when we show the source table. Let's start with an example of a true mixed design about children's persistence.

Lan and Repman (1995) were interested in elementary school aged children's responses to success and failure on a mathematics task. Specifically, they investigated the independent variables of modeling, collaboration, and grade level on the dependent variable, persistence. To simplify our discussion, we will leave out the independent variable, grade level. The between groups independent variable was the modeling condition, with two levels, modeling and no modeling. In the modeling condition, participants read a story on a computer prior to problem selection about a boy who, even though experiencing failure, chose difficult mathematics problems and improved in mathematics achievement. The nonmodeling condition participants did not receive the story. The repeated measures independent variable was collaboration, with two levels, performing individually, and performing collaboratively with another participant. The order of participation in these two conditions was randomly assigned. Therefore, the design for the study by Lan and Repman (as we report it) is a two-by-two factorial design with repeated measures on the second factor. One of the dependent variables for the study was persistence, which was determined by the participants' choice of level of problems after failing a problem at a particular level. This score ranged from 0 to 2. Table 18.1 shows the average persistence data for the study.

Source Table for Mixed ANOVA.   Table 18.2 shows the source table for the two-factor ANOVA with repeated measures on the second factor. Notice, in the last column, that three different F values are obtained, similar to those obtained in the two-factor ANOVA. Furthermore, each F value answers questions similar to those in the two-factor ANOVA. For example, there is an F value computed for the main effect for independent variable A. In the present case, independent variable A is always the between groups independent variable. There is also an F value for independent variable B, which, in the mixed ANOVA, is always the repeated measures independent variable. Last, there is an F value for the interaction between the two independent variables. The ma-

TABLE 18.1

Data From the Lan and Repman (1995) Study

Condition	Individual	Collaborative	Average
Modeling	1.25	1.16	1.21
No Modeling	1.11	1.23	1.17
Average	1.18	1.20	1.19

jor difference between the two-factor ANOVA and the two-factor ANOVA with repeated measures on the second factor (mixed ANOVA) is that the F values are calculated differently. In the mixed ANOVA, there are two error terms, one for the between groups independent variable (called A error), and one for the repeated measures independent variable (called B error). The between groups independent variable F is determined by using the error term from the between groups part of the analysis. The repeated measures independent variable F and the interaction effect F are determined by using the repeated measures error term.

Example Source Table.   Let's look at the source table from the Lan and Repman (1995) study on persistence data. We have modified their source table from the original article because we left out the third independent variable, grade level. The source table can be seen in Table 18.3. The data described in the source table from the Lan and Repman (1995) study reveal no significant main effects for the independent variables of modeling, $F(1,136) = 1.08, p = .30$; or context, $F(1,136) = .29, p = .57$, but a there is significant modeling by context interaction effect, $F(1,136) = 10.43, p < .01$. Figure 18.1 demonstrates the modeling by context interaction effect.

TABLE 18.2
Source Table for the Mixed ANOVA

Source of Variation	SS	df	MS	F
Between groups				
A		$(q-1)$		$\dfrac{MS_A}{MS_{A\,error}}$
A error		$q(n-1)$		
Within subjects				
B		$(r-1)$		$\dfrac{MS_B}{MS_{B\,error}}$
AB		$(q-1)(r-1)$		$\dfrac{MS_{AB}}{MS_{B\,error}}$
B error		$q(n-1)(r-1)$		

TABLE 18.3
Modified Source Table on Persistence Data From Lan and Repman (1995)

Source of Variation	SS	df	MS	F
Between subjects				
Modeling	.14	1	.14	1.08
Error$_{between}$	17.98	136	.13	
Within subjects				
Context	.02	1	.02	.29
Modeling × context	.73	1	.73	10.43*
Error$_{within}$	8.93	136	.07	

*p < .01.

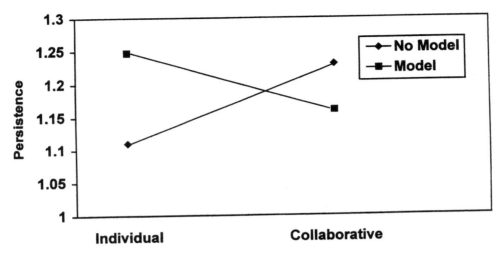

FIG. 18.1. Plot of an interaction drawn from the data in Lan and Repman (1995).

The interaction effect is interpreted as follows. When participants perform in the individual condition, those in the modeling group are more persistent than those in the no modeling group. On the other hand, when participants are in the collaboration condition, those in the modeling group seem to perform worse than those in the no modeling condition. Lan and Repman (1995) tested this interpretation of the interaction effect by using simple effects analysis (chap. 17). Interestingly, they found significant differences between the modeling and no modeling groups when the participants performed the task in the individual situation. However, when participants performed the task in the collaborative situation, there were no significant differences between the modeling and no modeling groups. This study shows the need to follow up significant interaction effects from any factorial ANOVA with simple main effects analysis. Thus, even though the graph of the data appeared to demonstrate significant differences under *both* conditions, statistical analysis revealed significant differences under only one of the conditions.

THE PRETEST–POSTTEST DESIGN

Analyzing the Pretest–Posttest Design

Because of the extensive use of the pretest–posttest design, where type of intervention is the between groups independent variable and change over time is the repeated measures factor (mixed design), much has been written on the analysis (Huck & McLean, 1975; Reichardt, 1979). We discuss three different methods used to analyze the mixed design, *the mixed ANOVA approach*, *the gain score approach*, and the *analysis of covariance (ANCOVA) approach*. As an example for the three different approaches, consider the study by Louth et al. (1992), who examined the effects of collaborative writing techniques on freshman writing and attitudes. There were three treatment groups in this study, consisting of six sections of freshman composition students. Two sections were instructed to write interactively, two sections were instructed to use group writing, and two sections were instructed to write independently. The design for the study was a 3×2 factorial design with repeated measures on the second factor. This is a mixed design. The between groups independent variable is treatment, with the three writing conditions as the three levels. The within subjects or repeated measures independent variable is change over time, with two levels, pretest and posttest. The different sections were randomly assigned to the treatment conditions (strong quasi-experimental approach). All students wrote a 50-minute pretest essay before the study began. After 8 weeks, all students were given a posttest by using the same essay instructions as in the pretest. English faculty scored both pretests and posttests naïve to the treatment conditions of the students. The essays were scored on a 6-point scale. The data for the study can be seen in Table 18.4 and is also graphed in Fig. 18.2.

The Mixed ANOVA Approach.   We discussed the mixed ANOVA in detail earlier in this chapter. When used with the pretest–posttest design, the analysis is the same, generating the same source table. Like any two-factor analysis of variance, the outcome results in answers to three separate questions. Are there

TABLE 18.4
Mean Writing Scores From Louth et al., 1992

Intervention	n	Test Time	
		Pretest	*Posttest*
Independent	44	3.00	3.07
Interactive	45	2.37	3.01
Group	47	2.27	2.84

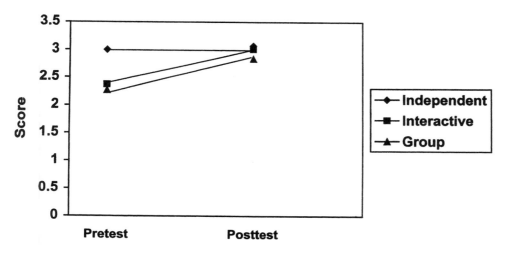

FIG. 18.2.   Pretest-Posttest plot drawn from the Louth et al. (1992) data.

significant differences among the levels of the first independent variable (main effect for the between groups independent variable)? Are there significant differences between the levels of the repeated measures independent variable (main effect for the within subjects independent variable)? Are there significant interaction effects as a result of the two independent variables? Let's examine the mixed ANOVA approach for the example demonstrated in Fig. 18.2.

When we examine the example in Fig. 18.2, we see that the only question of interest to us is the results of the interaction effect. Why? First, think about the main effect for the between groups independent variable, type of writing condition. What would a significant main effect for writing condition tell us? It would mean that there is at least one difference among the three writing conditions, averaged across the pretest and the posttest measurement periods. In other words, it would not demonstrate which intervention condition actually worked because the pretest scores are combined with the posttest scores. Therefore, the between groups main effect in the mixed ANOVA approach to analysis of the pretest–posttest design provides little meaningful information. Now let's examine the second main effect, the within subjects main effect. What would a significant difference tell us? A significant main effect for time tells us that there is a change from pretest scores to posttest scores averaged across all three groups. It does not tell us which groups changed significantly, only that, on the average, all three groups or conditions changed. It should be noted that this is not uncommon in therapeutic interventions, where patients are apt to get better over time, regardless of treatment. This is often referred to as the internal validity threat of maturation. Thus, a significant within subjects main effect, time, also does not provide us with the information of interest. Now we will examine the meaning of a significant interaction effect in the pretest–posttest design.

If we study Fig. 18.2, we see that the trends of the three different interventions from pretest to posttest are not similar. The sections that were required to write independently remain almost the same from pretest to posttest. On the other hand, the interactive writing sections and the group writing sections increased from pretest to posttest. Louth et al. (1992) found a statistically significant interaction between the writing conditions and time, which they reported as, "There was a significant main effect for test time, $F(1,133) = 23.33$, $p < .001$, which was qualified by a significant test time × condition interaction, $F(2, 133) = 4.50$, $p < .013$" (p. 219). To interpret the significant interaction effect, simple main effects analysis must be performed, as described in our discussion in chapter 17. Louth et al. performed simple main effects analysis and reported their findings as, "I tested the simple effect of test time within each condition. As expected, there was a significant increase from pretest to posttest for both the interactive condition, $F(1,133) = 12.65$, $p < .001$, and the group condition, $F(1, 133) = 20.26$, $p < .001$. However, there was no significant increase for the independent group, $F(1,133) = .14$, $p < .710$" (pp. 219).

One of the problems with performing a mixed ANOVA to analyze the pretest–posttest design is the interpretation of the interaction effect. The problem results from the interaction of the treatment and the pretest. Logically, it is difficult to comprehend how this could be possible, because the treatment is not introduced until after the pretest has been given. In a pretest–posttest design, the treatment can only interact with the posttest (Huck & McLean, 1975).

In summary, the mixed ANOVA approach to analysis of the pretest–posttest design is dependent on a significant interaction effect between the treatment conditions and time. If the interaction effect is statistically significant, tests of simple main effects must be performed, similar to those done by Louth et al. (1992), to interpret the outcome.

The Gain Score Approach. The gain score approach to the analysis of the pretest–posttest design is a simpler method than the mixed ANOVA approach. The gain score approach reduces the mixed design to a single factor design. To understand the gain score approach, let's reexamine the example of the study by Louth et al. (1992). The first step in the gain score approach is to subtract pretest scores from posttest scores for every participant in the study. Therefore, in the Louth et al. study, we would start by subtracting the pretest score from the posttest score for each of the 44 participants in the independent writing condition. This would give us 44 gain scores for the writing condition. We would do the same for each of the 45 participants in the interactive writing condition and the 47 participants in the group writing condition. The result is seen in Table 18.5. Notice that the design has been changed from a mixed design (two-factor design with repeated measures on the second factor) to a single factor design with three levels. The three levels, or conditions, are the independent writing condition, the interactive writing condition, and the group writing condition. The dependent variable is no longer the scores on a 6-point scale, but *it is the difference in these scores from pretest to posttest.* Because the design is now a single factor design with three levels, the appropriate analysis is the single factor ANOVA, as discussed in chapter 14. If a single factor ANOVA is performed on these data, and the result is statistically significant, a post hoc test would be performed to interpret the differences among conditions.

What information is obtained from performing a gain score analysis for a mixed design? The gain score analysis determines differences in the amount gained (or lost) among the three conditions. This is usually the information that one is interested in when implementing a study using the pretest–posttest design. Let's take a look at the three conditions in the Louth et al. (1992) study. The independent writing condition is really a control condition, because this is what has been in existence previously. Like typical control groups in a pretest–posttest design, this control group may not stay the same over a period of time, and could change as a result of practice or other variables. However, what

TABLE 18.5

Mean Gain Scores From Louth et al., 1992

Intervention	n	Average Gain Score
Independent	44	.07
Interactive	45	.64
Group	47	.57

is important is that the other two conditions of the study must be compared to the control group to determine the effectiveness of their interventions. The gain score approach provides the gain or effectiveness of each condition over time. By comparing the gain scores of the interactive writing condition and the group writing condition with the independent writing condition, a conclusion can be reached concerning the effectiveness of each condition. We mentioned previously that applying the mixed ANOVA to the pretest–posttest design presented problems because of the interpretation of the interaction effect. Interestingly, the F value for the interaction effect in the mixed ANOVA is identical to the F value of a single factor ANOVA performed on the gain scores (or t^2 if a t test is performed).

A weakness of the gain score approach is that it does not provide information about differences prior to the intervention (pretest scores). For example, in the Louth et al. (1992) study, it appeared that the independent writing condition was greater than the other two conditions prior to the intervention. In fact, Louth et al. confirmed this finding by using simple effects analysis in their mixed ANOVA approach. The gain score approach only demonstrates changes from pretest to posttest, but does not provide information about the pretest scores.

The Analysis of Covariance Approach.   The analysis of covariance (ANCOVA) is a statistical method used to reduce error variance. When used in the analysis of the pretest–posttest design, the ANCOVA also changes the design from a mixed design to a single factor design. Therefore, in this case, the ANCOVA is a *single factor* ANCOVA. However, the ANCOVA makes use of differences in the pretest scores among conditions to adjust the posttest scores. Once these adjustments have been made on the posttest scores, then the analysis is applied only to the posttest scores.[1]

Again, let's look at the Louth et al. (1992) study to apply the ANCOVA approach. Figure 18.2 shows the data from this study. Notice that the pretest scores are different among the three conditions, especially for the independent writing condition. The ANCOVA approach takes these pretest score differences into account by adjusting the *posttest* scores from these differences. How are these adjustments made? The ANCOVA procedure takes into account the correlation between the pretest and posttest scores for each group. One of the assumptions of the ANCOVA is that the relationship between the covariate (pretest scores) and the dependent variable (posttest scores) is significant and linear. The posttest scores are adjusted by using the average linear regression (chap. 16) between pretest scores and posttest scores for all conditions of the study. A second assumption of the analysis of covariance is that the regression slopes for each covariate (pretest)–variate (posttest) relationship must be parallel.

What type of adjustment would be made to the Louth et al. (1992) data? Although we do not have the original data from the Louth et al. study, we can generate data that would give us the same pretest and posttest means. We will make up data for 10 participants from each of the three conditions. The three groups

---

[1]Another use of the single factor ANCOVA in the pretest–posttest design is to use the pretest scores as the covariate, but use the gain scores, rather than the posttest scores, as the dependent variable.

of 10 participants in each group have the same pretest and posttest means, as seen in Table 18.4. The single factor ANCOVA does two things. First, it adjusts the posttest scores from pretest differences. Table 18.6 demonstrates this adjustment of posttest scores. Notice the differences between the posttest means and the *adjusted posttest means*. As we expected, the independent writing condition was adjusted much lower, whereas the other two conditions were adjusted higher. In addition to adjusting posttest scores, the single factor ANCOVA also performs a statistical analysis similar to the single factor ANOVA. In fact, the source table for the single factor ANCOVA is almost the same as the single factor ANOVA, except that in the ANCOVA, one degree of freedom is lost in the error source of variation. Thus, power is decreased slightly when an ANCOVA is performed. Table 18.7 shows the source table for the single factor ANCOVA for our made-up data. The results of our ANCOVA show a significant difference among the three groups, $F(3,26) = 7.23$, $p < .01$. Therefore, we performed a Tukey *HSD* post hoc test to interpret the results. We found that the adjusted posttest means were significantly higher for both the interactive writing condition and the group condition when compared to the independent writing condition, but they did not differ from each other.

The advantage of using a single factor ANCOVA to analyze data from the pretest–posttest design is that it is easier to understand than the mixed ANOVA and often more precise than the gain score method. The single factor ANCOVA simplifies the analysis by converting the mixed design into a single factor design, as does the gain score analysis. There are two disadvantages of the ANCOVA approach to the analysis of the pretest–posttest design. The first disadvantage is that to use the ANCOVA, the assumptions of linearity and parallel slopes should be satisfied. Because the pretest scores and the posttest scores are from the same people, these assumptions are usually met. The second, and perhaps more important, caution when applying the single factor ANCOVA to the analysis of the pretest–posttest design is the issue of type of

Table 18.6

Posttest Score Adjustment for Mean Writing Scores from Made-Up Data

| Intervention | n | Test Time | | Adjusted Posttest |
		Pretest	Posttest	
Independent	10	3.00	3.07	2.653
Interactive	10	2.37	3.01	3.177
Group	10	2.27	2.84	3.09

TABLE 18.7

Source Table for Single-Factor ANCOVA

Source of Variation	SS	df	MS	F
Writing conditions	.693	2	.347	7.23*
Error$_{between}$	1.238	26	.048	

*$p < .01$.

quantitative approach. If participants are randomly assigned to conditions prior to the study (randomized experimental design) then the ANCOVA is the recommended analysis. On the other hand, when participants are not randomly assigned to conditions, as in the quasi-experimental and comparative approaches, then one must be cautious when using the ANCOVA to analyze the pretest–posttest design. Reichardt (1979) discusses extensively the positives and negatives of using ANCOVA to adjust posttest scores from pretest differences as a result of groups that were intact prior to the introduction of the treatment. For the most part, ANCOVA is the proper analysis. However, the precision of ANCOVA in this situation is almost always less than in the situation where participants have been randomly assigned to groups.

In conclusion, when the mixed design has only *two* levels of the within subjects independent variable, such as pretest and posttest, the following should apply. We strongly recommend the use of the single factor ANCOVA to analyze the pretest–posttest design when participants have been randomly assigned to conditions prior to the study. However, when participants are already in intact groups, the gain score approach may be just as sensitive. We do not recommend the mixed ANOVA approach to the analysis of the pretest–posttest design because, for the most part, the gain score approach provides the same information and is clearer. However, when the within subjects independent variable has more than two levels, the mixed ANOVA approach may be the best choice, although the analysis of covariance can also be used in this situation. As in the Louth et al. (1992) example, the results of the three methods often turn out to produce the same general interpretation.

A NOTE ON THE GENERAL USE OF ANCOVA

We have discussed the ANCOVA as a statistical procedure to analyze the pretest-posttest design. However, the ANCOVA procedure has many uses with other types of designs, especially single and two-factor between groups designs. ANCOVA is commonly used in situations when the investigator suspects that a third variable may be responsible for the relationship between the independent and dependent variables. One way to eliminate the "third" variable problem is to match participants on that variable. In chapter 14, we discussed an example by Gliner and Sample (1993) that matched participants on a number of variables, including intelligence. Instead of matching, these authors could have used intelligence as a covariate and performed a single factor ANCOVA. This would eliminate the possible confounding that intelligence level has on environmental control. Used in this example, the ANCOVA procedure would adjust scores on the dependent variable, environmental control, on the basis of the relationship between this variable and the covariate, intelligence. For an in-depth examination of ANCOVA see Keppel (1991).

SUMMARY

In this chapter, we defined the mixed design as having at least one between groups independent variable and one within subjects independent variable.

The mixed design may have different quantitative approaches, usually randomized experimental or quasi-experimental. We divided the mixed design into two categories, the true mixed design and the pretest–posttest design. The true mixed design is analyzed by using a mixed ANOVA. The pretest–posttest design may be analyzed by three different statistical methods: the mixed ANOVA analysis, the gain score analysis, and the analysis of covariance. We pointed out the strengths and weaknesses of each of these methods, and where they are most appropriate.

STUDY AIDS

Concepts

- ANCOVA
- Gain scores analysis
- Mixed ANOVA
- Pretest–posttest design
- True mixed design

Distinctions

- Mixed ANOVA versus gain scores analysis versus ANCOVA
- True mixed design versus pretest–posttest design

Application Problems

1. Some researchers argue that ANCOVA is the most appropriate statistic to use with pretest-posttest data. Explain.

2. A researcher was interested in the effects of different treatments for back injury on return to work. Specifically, she was interested in whether those people who were treated for back injury noninvasively, for example rest and exercise, would perform differently from those who were treated through surgery. To model the back to work experience, a vibration machine was used to simulate driving of large machinery. A person who suffered a back injury might be able to sit for long periods of time if there was no vibration, but not under conditions of vibration. Therefore, each participant in the study underwent three conditions, driving with vibration, driving without vibration, and just sitting. There were eight patients in the exercise group and eight patients in the surgery group. The dependent variable was pain perception, a 10 point scale where 1 was no pain and 10 was intolerable pain. The means were as follows:

Treatment	Condition		
	Sitting	*Driving without vibration*	*Driving with vibration*
Exercise	.33	1.33	3
Surgery	.33	3.67	6

a. Describe the design (e.g., 2 × 2 factorial).

b. Graph the above data.

The source table is as follows:

Source of Variation	SS	df	MS	F
Between Subjects				
Treatment	28			
Error (between)	6			
Within Subjects				
Condition	80			
Treatment by	30			
Condition Error (within)	15			

c. Complete the source table.

3. A physics professor was interested in demonstrating that his new method of teaching was superior to the traditional teaching method in changing the attitude of students toward physics. Prior to the start of the semester, students were randomly assigned to one of two beginning physics sections, the new method and the old method. During the first day of class, all students took the Attitude Toward Physics test. At the end of the semester the students took this test again. For each of the following analyses, explain what outcome would be used to support the professor's argument.

a. Mixed ANOVA

b. Gain score *t* test

c. Analysis of covariance

19

Interpretation of Complex Associational Analyses and MANOVA

Concepts
Distinctions
Application Problems

Most of the methods presented briefly in this chapter are complex and need to be performed with a computer, yet you probably will encounter some of them in your readings. In fact, in research by our graduate students, all of these methods have been used. A major limiting requirement of these methods is that a large number of participants is needed relative to the number of variables selected.

All of the methods we have discussed in previous chapters are considered to be univariate statistics because there is only one dependent variable in the analysis. Generally, statistics are called multivariate if they have more than one dependent variable. However, most books on multivariate statistics include other complex or multiple variable statistics, such as multiple regression, because there is not a consensus about how the term multivariate should be used (see Grimm & Yarnold, 1994). In this chapter, we discuss five multiple variable (more than one independent variable, or dependent variable, or both) methods that are usually included in multivariate statistics books. We start with the multivariate analysis of variance (MANOVA), because the designs that are used for this procedure are similar to many of the univariate designs that we already have discussed in chapters 14, 15, 17, and 18.

ANALYSES BASED ON THE COMPLEX DIFFERENCE QUESTIONS

Multivariate Analysis of Variance (MANOVA)

Purpose.   MANOVA compares two or more groups by means of a linear composite dependent variable. The term MANOVA appears frequently when reading journal articles. MANOVA can be used with any of the ANOVAs that we have discussed in chapters 14, 15, 17, and 18 when there are multiple dependent variables or measures. For example, Stone, Lemanek, Fishel, Fernandez, and Altemeier (1990) were interested in differences among children with certain disabilities on play behavior and motor imitation. They had five different groups of children in their study: autistic, hearing impaired, language impaired, mentally retarded, and nonhandicapped. They observed each child through a one-way mirror in a free-play situation for 8 minutes and then in a one-on-one imitation assessment for 5 minutes. There were five dependent variables in the study: number of toys used, percent of time playing with toys, percent of time playing appropriately with toys, number of functional play acts, and imitation score. The design for this study was a single factor design with five levels. The independent variable was the type of disability group. The five levels were the five different groups studied. Because the independent variable was an attribute independent variable, the quantitative approach was considered to be comparative.

Notice that there were five different dependent variables in the Stone et al. (1990) study. As we increase the number of dependent variables, the probability that these dependent variables are related increases, especially because we are often trying to use multiple measures of a single construct. The danger is that if we were to apply a separate F test for each of the dependent variables, and in fact they were related, we might get significant outcomes for each dependent variable. However, it is probable that the redundant information shared among the dependent variables contributes to statistical significance. If we use multiple dependent variables that are related in designs typically analyzed by t or F statistics, the MANOVA is the appropriate choice. Therefore, Stone et al. decided to perform a single factor MANOVA on the data.

The MANOVA combines the several dependent variables in such a way that a new variable (linear composite) is formed. The multivariate F tests to see if the groups (based on the independent variable) differ for this new composite variable. Thus, MANOVA provides additional information not available from computing several separate ANOVAs. There is more than one significance test statistic for the MANOVA. The most common statistics are Wilk's lambda, and Hotelling T^2. Other test statistics for the MANOVA seen, for example, on an SPSS printout, are Pillai's trace and Roy's largest root. All of these statistics are converted to an F statistic to determine statistical significance (see J. Stevens, 1986 for more information about choice of a particular multivariate statistic). If the MANOVA is statistically significant, then appropriate follow-up procedures are performed, similar to post hoc tests after a significant F. These follow-up procedures are often selected for the purpose of the study. For example, if the purpose of the study is to determine the relative contributions of the different dependent variables to the independent variable, then a discriminant analysis could be used. In this case, each of the dependent variables would be used as a predictor variable and the independent variable would be used as the criterion variable. The discriminant analysis would yield the best linear combination of variables (dependent variables) that would predict the independent variable. Stone et al. (1990) performed a discriminant analysis as a follow-up procedure in their study. For a conceptual view of other MANOVA follow-up procedures, see Weinfurt (1997).

One might ask if a MANOVA should be performed if more than one dependent variable is included in the study, but the dependent variables are not related. Previously, it was thought that using a MANOVA would protect against making a type I error, which could occur if one were to perform multiple ANOVAs or *t* tests. In other words, it was thought that MANOVA would keep the type I error at the same level and not inflate it from the multiple comparisons (similar to performing multiple *t* tests). Therefore, it was common practice to first perform a MANOVA, and then, if a statistically significant result was found, to perform univariate ANOVAs or *t* tests. However, it appears that MANOVA does not protect against making a type I error for multiple dependent variables. Current thinking is that if more than one dependent variable is included in the study, and these dependent variables are not related, do not do MANOVA. Instead, do several ANOVAs or *t* tests but divide the significance level by the number of dependent variables to protect against a type I error (Dunn, 1961).

Conditions for Use of MANOVA
1. One or a few categorical independent variables.
2. Two or more approximately normally distributed dependent variables.
3. The dependent variables must be correlated.

COMPLEX ANALYSES BASED ON THE ASSOCIATIONAL APPROACH

The first three data analysis methods in this section are used to predict a dependent or criterion variable from several independent or predictor variables. The first statistic we discuss, *multiple regression*, includes several different forms or types of analyses. The most common of these is simultaneous multiple (linear) regression. Other types of multiple regression include hierarchical multiple regression and stepwise multiple regression. In multiple regression analysis, the criterion variable should be approximately normally distributed, usually having many ordered values. Two other methods used to predict a criterion variable from several predictor variables are discriminant analysis and logistic regression. However, in these latter two methods, the criterion variable is categorical. The fourth complex analysis that is based on the associational approach, factor analysis, also appears frequently in the research literature. The most common purpose of factor analysis is to reduce large numbers of dependent variables to a smaller number called *factors*.

Multiple Regression Analysis

Purpose.   Multiple regression is used to predict a normally distributed criterion (dependent) variable from a combination of several normally distributed, or dichotomous predictors (independent variables), or both.

Previously (chap. 16), we discussed (a) the relation between two variables, (b) how this relation could be calculated with a Pearson product–moment correlation coefficient, and (c) how this relation could be used to form an equation to predict one variable by knowing the other (regression). If we were to determine the relation between GRE scores and graduate student performance, as measured by grades in graduate school, you might find a Pearson product–moment correlation, r, of 0.30. An additional step might be to form an equation so that you could predict future success in graduate school (as measured by GPA) from current GRE scores. Therefore, if you knew a student's average GRE score, you could predict performance in graduate school. How well? The r^2 gives one indication. The r^2 in this example would be 0.09. How do we interpret r^2 in this situation?

The r^2 is the amount of shared variance between the two variables. We could say that there is an underlying variable of cognitive ability that is common to both GRE scores and grades in graduate school, such as brain power or IQ, that explains about 9% of the variance. Another way of looking at the problem is to focus on the Y variable or grades in graduate school. We call Y the dependent variable, or for this purpose, the *criterion* variable. GRE scores before entering graduate school could now be referred to as the independent variable or *predictor* variable. From our data, we can conclude that GRE scores account for about 9% of the variance of grades in graduate school. Looking at it from another direction, we could say that 91% of the variance in predicting grades in graduate school is unexplained. How can we improve our prediction? This leads us to multiple regression.

To compute multiple regression, we start by constructing a correlation matrix among all of the variables, including the dependent variable. (This matrix is used for almost all multiple regression and multivariate procedures.) A correlation matrix is just a table of all possible correlations among variables. Then, operations similar to linear regression analysis (chap. 16) are performed. We arrive at an equation to predict Y'. This equation is the best linear combination of independent or predictor variables to predict the criterion variable. Each variable in the equation has a weight assigned to it to maximize prediction. These weights are called *partial regression coefficients*. Partial regression coefficients, taken by themselves, demonstrate how much of an individual contribution each variable is making to the prediction of the dependent or criterion variable. Statistical significance is determined for each of these partial regression coefficients. The significance statement determines whether a particular predictor variable is significantly different from zero. If these regression coefficients are standardized by converting them to z scores (beta weights), then the coefficients can be compared to determine the relative strength among each of the variables. In addition, a variance explained measure, R^2, is used to determine the total variance accounted for in the criterion variable by the combination of predictor variables. It should be noted that just because a predictor variable is not statistically significant does not mean that variable should be dropped from the equation. The variable could still be making a contribution to the overall R^2. Furthermore, it is possible, but not common, to have a significant R^2, even if none of the individual predictor variables are statistically significant.

Simultaneous Multiple Regression.   The most common method of multiple regression is called simultaneous multiple regression. In this method, all of the predictor variables are entered simultaneously. The best linear combination of variables is determined by using a least squares fit similar to linear regression discussed in chapter 16. An example of a simultaneous multiple regression is as follows. Morgan and Griego (1998) wanted to determine how well mathematics achievement could be predicted from a combination of seven variables: motivation, competence, pleasure, grades in high school, father's and mother's education revised, and gender. Table 19.1 shows the multiple R and R^2 values for the simultaneous multiple regression. The multiple R tells us that a strong relationship exists between the predictor variables and the criterion variable, mathematics achievement. The adjusted R^2 indicates that 38% of the variance in mathematics achievement was predicted from the combination of predictor variables. Table 19.2 shows the coefficients for the same simultaneous multiple regression problem. Table 19.2 shows, for each variable in the multiple regression, the raw (unstandardized) coefficients, the standardized coefficients (beta weights), the t values, and the significance level for each of the variables. Note that both grades in high school and gender were considered to be statistically significant, assuming an alpha level of .05. In addition, we could form the equation for prediction of mathematics achievement from the unstandardized coefficients as follows:

$$Y' = -4.293 = 1.684X_1 + .117X_2 + .874X_3 + 1.762X_4 + 1.477X_5 + 1.027X_6 - 3.359X_7.$$

TABLE 19.1

Multiple Correlation and Adjusted R²

R	Adjusted R^2
.666	.379

TABLE 19.2

Multiple Regression Coefficients

Variables	Unstandardized Coefficients		Standardized Coefficients (Beta)	t
	ß	S.E.		
Constant	−4.293	5.15		−.833
Motivation scale	1.684	1.23	.158	1.373
Competence scale	.117	1.41	.011	.083
Pleasure scale	.874	1.78	.083	.742
Grades in high school	1.762	.48	.416	3.680**
Father's education revised	1.477	1.03	.186	1.439
Mother's education revised	1.027	1.27	.104	.810
Gender	−3.359	1.39	−.253	−2.409*

**p < .01. *p < .05.

This equation then could be used in the future to predict mathematics achievement of individual students, assuming a similar sample of participants. The Xs correspond to an individual's score on each of the predictor variables; i.e., X_1 = motivation scale score, X_2 = competence, and so forth.

Hierarchical Multiple Regression.   This multiple regression procedure has recently become popular. Conceptually, it has similarities to the stepwise linear regression approach, described in the next section. Variables are entered in steps, and the change in R^2 is examined at each step. However, in hierarchical regression, the order to enter each variable into the equation is decided ahead of time by the investigator. Usually these decisions are based on a careful conceptualization of the problem and result in the testing of particular hypotheses. Hierarchical multiple regression also allows the researcher to control for or eliminate the effects of a particular variable by entering that variable into the equation first. Also, more than one variable can be entered into the equation at once. The probability of committing a type I error is usually reduced in hierarchical regression because fewer steps are used to enter variables into the equation. Table 19.3 (Morgan & Griego, 1998) shows the hierarchical multiple regression analysis from the same example as that used for the simultaneous multiple regression. In this example, the variable gender was entered first to control for its effects. All of the other predictor variables were entered next in a block. Gender accounted for approximately 6% of the variance. The addition of the other predictor variables accounted for about 32% of the variance.

Stepwise Regression.   The stepwise approach is similar to hierarchical multiple regression, but the computer decides the order and how many of the potential predictors are used. The stepwise regression procedure describes how much more each independent or predictor variable has contributed to the prediction from the preceding predictor variable(s). The conceptual view of stepwise linear regression is as follows.

Each phase of the procedure is called a step. At Step 0, a correlation matrix is formed among all variables including the criterion or dependent variable. At Step 1, the predictor variable that correlates the highest with the criterion variable is entered into the equation. (Note: At this step, and any following step, the size of the correlation must reach a designated significance level for the predictor variable to be entered.) At Step 2, the predictor variable that adds the most new variance to the first predictor variable is entered into the equation. At Step 3, the predictor variable that adds the most to the two predictor variables already selected is entered into the equation. This continues until either all variables are entered into the equation or significance is not reached for any of the remaining variables.

Table 19.3
Multiple Correlation and R^2 for Hierarchical Multiple Regression

Variables	R	R^2	Adjusted R^2	Standard Error of the Estimate
Gender	.272	.074	.060	6.46
All other variables	.666	.443	.379	5.25

While stepwise linear regression makes a lot of sense conceptually, there are several problems that have been associated with this approach, and one should probably use this approach only as an exploratory procedure (see Thompson, 1995, for a critical review of this procedure). One of the problems with this approach is that because of the potentially large number of predictor variables that could be entered into the equation, the probability of a type I error is considerably larger than the usual alpha of .05. The second, and perhaps more important, objection with the stepwise approach is that the computer, rather than the researcher, makes the decision about which variables should be included in the equation. This is especially the case when one enters a large number of predictor variables into the stepwise analysis with little thought given to particular hypotheses or theory. Many statisticians associate this approach with the terms "data mining" or "snooping." Third, the approach takes advantage of possible small differences when entering variables and, thus, is likely not to replicate with another sample.

Conditions for Use of Multiple Regression Analysis
1. The dependent variable should be normally distributed data.
2. The independent variables, for the most part, also must be normally distributed data. If the independent variables represent either ordinal (non-normal) or nominal (categorical) data, then dichotomous "dummy" variables must be created by recoding.

Discriminant Analysis

Purpose.   Discriminant analysis is used to predict a categorical criterion variable from a combination of several normally distributed independent variables. Specifically, the method can be used to predict group participation, for example, pass or fail.

Discriminant function analysis is used in situations similar to multiple regression analysis, except that the criterion variable is categorical rather than continuous. A discriminant function prediction equation is derived in a similar way as the equation on multiple regression. However, there are two other important differences between discriminant function analysis and multiple regression analysis. The first difference is that the coefficients (weights) in the discriminant function analysis are selected from how well they classify participants into groups. The second difference between discriminant function analysis and multiple regression analysis is that if the criterion variable in discriminant function analysis has more than two categories, then more than one discriminant function equation is likely.

A use of discriminant function analysis would be if our criterion variable representing graduate student success was divided into students who graduated or not, rather than being based on their grade point average. Likewise, in an employability example, if success versus failure, rather than degree of success, was the dependent variable, discriminant analysis would be appropriate. You may read articles that use multiple regression with a dichotomous dependent variable. Such an analysis is not necessarily wrong, but we would argue that it is not the most appropriate for a data set with a dichotomous criterion.

An example of the use of discriminant function analysis is taken from Morgan and Griego (1998). In this example, predictor variables of motivation, competence, pleasure, father's and mother's education revised, and gender were used to predict if students would take algebra 2. Table 19.4 shows the discriminant function coefficients. These coefficients, or weights, produce the best linear combination of the variables that maximally discriminates or differentiates those who took algebra 2 from those who did not. The discriminant function equation for the above predictor variables is written as:

$$Z = .577X_1 + .330X_2 - .197X_3 + .151X_4 - .320X_5 + .530X_6.$$

It could be used to predict in a new sample whether a student would take algebra 2.

Table 19.5 demonstrates the classification results for the current sample from the discriminant function equation. The classification table describes how well the discriminant function equation predicts group membership (taken algebra 2 or not). In this example, the overall correct classification was 72.5% and was statistically significant.

Earlier in this chapter, we mentioned that the discriminant analysis is a common follow-up procedure for a statistically significant MANOVA. The study by Stone et al. (1990) provides an example of this follow-up procedure. Recall that they had one independent variable (type of handicap condition) with five levels. There were five dependent variables. Following a significant MANOVA, they performed a discriminant analysis, by using the dependent variables as the predictor variables. Because they were primarily interested in discriminating between autistic children and other children, their criterion variable was dichotomous, either autistic children or the other handicapping

TABLE 19.4
Standardized Canonical Discriminant Function Coefficients

Predictor Variables	Function
Father's education revised	.577
Mother's education revised	.330
Gender	−.197
Motivation scale	.151
Pleasure scale	−.320
Competence scale	.530

TABLE 19.5
Discriminant Analysis Classification Table

Sample Description	Algebra 2 in High School	Predicted Group Membership		Total
		Not Taken	Taken	
Frequency	Not taken	28	8	36
	Taken	11	22	33
Percent	Not taken	77.8	22.2	100
	Taken	33.3	66.7	100

conditions, excluding the nonhandicapped group. They found that three of the predictor variables, appropriate toy play, functional play, and imitation, combined to significantly discriminate between the two groups (autistic and nonautistic). Furthermore, they reported that 82% of the autistic children and 100% of the nonautistic children were classified correctly.

Conditions for Use of Discriminant Analysis
1. The dependent variable must be categorical. It may have more than two categories but that makes the interpretation much more complex.
2. The independent variables must be normally distributed. If nominal independent variables must be used, a logistic regression would be the appropriate analysis (Grimm & Yarnold, 1994). Thus, in the Morgan and Griego (1998) example, it would have been better to omit the gender variable or to use logistic regression.

Logistic Regression Analysis

Purpose.   Logistic regression is used to predict a dichotomous criterion variable from a combination of several independent variables.

Logistic regression also involves a situation where the criterion variable is categorical; however, for this analysis, the criterion variable may have *only* two categories. In addition, logistic regression analysis is considered to be a nonlinear analysis. Therefore, if you suspect that the relation between your predictors and the criterion variable is not linear, logistic regression is a good choice, assuming you have a two-category criterion variable. In addition, logistic regression analysis is used when some or all of the predictor variables are categorical.

For example, one might be interested in predicting which students would drop out versus finish or graduate from a training program on the basis of a combination of gender and ethnic group (nominal or categorical predictor variables) and a test (a continuous or interval predictor variable).

Conditions for Use of Logistic Regression Analysis
1. The criterion variable must be categorical and is limited to only two categories; that is, it must be dichotomous.
2. The predictor variables can be dichotomous or normally distributed.

Factor Analysis

Purpose.   Factor analysis is most often used to combine a number of items or variables to form a smaller number of composite variables or factors. It is also used to look for latent or unobservable variables or constructs from observed variables.

Factor analysis is perhaps the oldest and best known of the multivariate methods. Factor analysis has been used by our graduate students primarily to reduce the number of variables in a study by examining which variables are closely related. Once the original variables are reduced to a smaller number of composite variables (called *factors* or *components*), other analyses may be performed. Factor analysis, like other multivariate methods, begins with a correlation matrix. The purpose of this matrix is to identify which variables (often test- or rating-scale items) correlate with each other but do not correlate with other variables or items. The idea is to identify a limited number of factors that are relatively independent of each other. If you are developing a test, you might start with 25 questions. However, there is a strong possibility that all 25 questions are not independent of each other. A factor analysis could be used in the exploratory sense to determine underlying clusters or groupings of questions that could be explained by a few factors. Each cluster or factor should be tested with Cronbach's alpha to be sure that internal consistency reliability is adequate (see chap. 20).

In addition, a factor analysis could be used to confirm conceptualizations that have already been postulated but not fully tested. In this use, factor analysis is one of the methods of demonstrating construct validity and is sometimes called *factorial validity* (see chap. 20).

A study by Robnett and Gliner (1995) demonstrates the use of factor analysis to reduce the number of dependent variables in a study to a smaller number of factors. Robnett and Gliner were interested in the quality of life of persons with disabilities. Specifically, they were interested in the quality of life of people with disability conditions that were progressive and disability conditions that were stable. They selected multiple sclerosis (MS), as an example of the former, and for the latter, spinal cord injury (SCI). As a comparison group, they added occupational therapists (OT). To determine quality of life, they developed a quality-of-life inventory. There were 80 questions in this inventory. After the inventory had been given to participants from all three groups (MS, SCI, and OT), the researchers performed a factor analysis to reduce the number of questions to a few factors. There were 405 participants who returned the quality-of-life instrument. Table 19.6 demonstrates a portion of the results of the factor analysis (the actual factor analysis had seven factors). Table 19.6 shows how each of the questions relates (loads) on each of the factors. In this table, all factor loadings that were less than .30 were omitted and displayed as dashes to make it easier to visualize the results. To interpret this table, start with Factor 1. Notice that Questions 22, 11, 16, and 18 all have relatively high loadings on Factor 1 and low loadings on Factors 2 and 3. However, Question 20 had loadings on both Factors 1 and 2. This means that question 20 was related to both factors. Because Robnett and Gliner were interested in using the factors for further comparison, this item was dropped from the study. Questions 61 and 34 also had multiple factor loadings and were eliminated from the study. Factors 2 and 3 were examined in the same manner; the researchers looked for questions that loaded high on each of those factors, but low on the other two factors.

Factor analysis does not name the factors, and it is up to the investigators to come up with names for the factors that would be agreed on by others in the field. In the Robnett and Gliner (1995) study, the first three factors were called *closeness to others*, *self-achievement*, and *health/activity level*. When performing factor analysis, it is important to describe how much of the total variance is accounted for by each factor. Table 19.7 provides the names of the seven factors from the Robnett and Gliner (1995) study and their percentage

TABLE 19.6

Factor Loading Patterns for First Three Factors in Robnett and Gliner (1995) Study

Question	Factor 1	Factor 2	Factor 3
22	.759	——	——
11	.699	——	——
16	.695	——	——
18	.633	——	——
20	.593	.376	——
19	.580	——	——
24	.524	——	——
59	——	.666	——
65	——	.588	——
61	——	.571	.316
60	——	.562	——
34	——	.522	.346
30	——	——	.761
27	——	——	.704
25	——	——	.630
26	——	——	.619
14	——	——	.552
7	——	——	−.543
1	——	——	.515

TABLE 19.7

Factor Names and Percentage Variance from Robnett and Gliner (1995)

Factor	Factor Name	Percentage Variance
1	Closeness to others	7.7
2	Self-achievement	6.8
3	Health/Activity level	6.5
4	Positive feelings	6.3
5	Outlook	5.3
6	Spiritual life	3.1
7	Routine behavior	2.3

variance. There are numerous procedures for determining how many factors should be retained from the factor analysis. These methods are often referred to as *stopping rules* (see Grimm & Yarnold, 1997). However, it is important to remember that there should be theoretical reasoning involved in the development of the instrument, and subsequent factor retention should be, at least in part, based on this reasoning.

Robnett and Gliner (1995) used the seven factors as dependent variables for further comparisons, which involved seven single factor (one-way) ANOVAs, to determine if there were differences in quality of life among the three groups in their study on each of these composite variables. Note that the term *factor* has two different meanings in the preceding sentence. Both terms refer to variables, but single factor ANOVA refers to the number of independent variables in the study (in this case one, type of person: MS, SCI, or OT). The seven factors from the factor analysis are the dependent variables in this case.

Conditions for Use of Factor Analysis
1. A number of normally distributed variables, usually dependent variables.
2. It is arbitrary and depends on the study as to whether these variables are independent (predictors) or dependent (criterion) variables.

SUMMARY OF MULTIPLE VARIABLE STATISTICAL METHODS

Table 19.8 is provided as a summary of the five statistical methods we have presented in this chapter. The table provides the purpose and information about the number and scale or type of independent and dependent variables for each of the methods. We also have added, at the bottom of the table, factorial ANOVA (see chap. 17 and 18) because it fits within the group of methods that we have called complex or multiple variable (i.e., those with more than one independent variable, or dependent variable, or both) even though it is not usually considered to be a "multivariate statistic."

Study Aids

Concepts

- Discriminant analysis
- Factor analysis
- Logistic regression
- MANOVA
- Multiple regression

Distinctions

- Factor analysis versus factorial ANOVA
- MANOVA versus univariate ANOVAs
- Multiple regression versus discriminant analysis versus logistic regression
- Simultaneous regression versus hierarchical regression versus stepwise regression

Application Problems

1. The Director of Special Education in a suburban school district wanted to compare two schools in terms of how English as a Second Language (ESL) students were performing in their respective schools. The independent variable was school, with several levels. Dependent variables included ESL stu-

TABLE 19.8

Summary of the Purposes and Conditions for Use of Six Multiple Variable Statistics

Complex Associational or Relational Questions

Purpose: Predict a criterion or dependent variable from several independent variables. Look for a combination of independent variables to optimally predict the dependent variable.

Statistic	Independent Variable Number and Type	Dependent Variable Number and Type
Multiple regression	Several	One
	Normal and/or dichotomous	Normally distributed
Discriminant	Several	One
	Normal	Categorical
Logistic regression	Several	One
	Normal and/or dichotomous	Dichotomous

Purpose: Reduce the number of variables to a smaller number of composite variables or factors. Also look for latent variables.

Statistic	Independent Variable	Dependent Variable
Factor analysis	None (however, sometimes the several variables are independent variables)	Several normally distributed

Complex Difference or Group Comparison Questions

Purpose: Look for significant differences among the levels of each independent variable and for a significant interaction.

Statistic	Independent Variable	Dependent Variable
Factorial ANOVA	Two or a few	One (at a time)
	categorical	normally distributed

Purpose: Compare group means (i.e., look for significant differences) on a linear combination of the dependentvariables and also each dependent variable separately.

Statistic	Independent Variable	Dependent Variable
MANOVA	One or a few	Two or more
	categorical	normally distributed

Note.   Categorical variables can be unordered (nominal) or ordered, but usually have a small number of levels or values. Adapted from Tabachnick & Fidell (1989).

dents' standardized national test scores in each of the four subject areas. What type of statistic should be used in this study and why?

2.   A consortium of researchers wants to look at some of the impacts of welfare reform on individuals and families who have not received public assistance for two years. They have a large multi-state sample. For each case an *economic well-being* score was computed as the *outcome variable*. The researchers were interested in their ability to predict economic well-being from prior level of education, years of work experience, transportation availability, training received while on welfare, and the relative health of the local economy (all dichotomous or interval scale measures).

a.   What type of analysis would be appropriate? Explain.

b. The researchers wanted to know what combination of the above factors predicted whether a former welfare recipient will have been employed or not since leaving welfare. What analytical approach should they use?
For questions 3 to 6, match the analysis with the particular and explain why.
   a. Multivariate analysis of variance
   b. Multiple regression
   c. Factor analysis
   d. Discriminant analysis

3. You have a pretest-posttest control group design. Your dependent variable is a 50 item questionnaire which was given to 250 participants in the intervention group and 250 participants in the nonintervention group. Your next step is to reduce the number of questions to a smaller number composite/summated variables.

4. You are interested in predicting if people are successful or unsuccessful when they return to work. Your predictor variables are strength, range of motion, I.Q., and the Gliner Greed Scale.

5. You have one independent variable with three levels. You have five dependent variables that could be related.

6. You are trying to predict grade point average in graduate school in an English department. Your predictor variables are undergraduate GPA, GRE verbal scores, score on an interest inventory, and age.

Measurement, Instruments, and Procedures

20

Measurement Reliability and Validity

In this chapter we discuss two important concepts for performing applied research. These concepts, measurement reliability and measurement validity, are part of overall research validity, or the quality of the whole study. In chapters 6 and 10, we gave a brief overview of the four components of research validity. Those four components were internal validity, measurement reliability and statistics, measurement validity and the generalizability of the constructs, and external validity. Measurement reliability is a component of measurement reliability and statistics. Measurement validity is a component of measurement validity and the generalizability of the constructs. We discuss measurement reliability and validity in depth in this chapter. Then, in chapter 23, we discuss how both are part of research validity.

MEASUREMENT RELIABILITY

What is reliability? When a person is said to be reliable, we have certain conceptions about that person. For example, the person always shows up for meetings on time; therefore, he is a reliable person. Or, the person always gets the job done; therefore, she is a reliable person. When we use tests or other instruments to measure outcomes, we also need to make sure that these instruments are reliable. Cronbach (1960) said that reliability "always refers to consistency throughout a series of measurements" (p. 127). The importance of reliability for research methods cannot be overstated. If our outcome measure is not reliable, then we cannot accurately assess the results of our study. Hence, our study will be worthless.

An Example

To understand the importance of measurement reliability and its underpinnings, it is best to start with an example. A researcher is interested in determining if quality of life for persons with cognitive disabilities can be increased through a recreational support program. To determine if the intervention (recreational support program) works, he designs a randomized experiment by using a pretest–posttest control group design, where one group receives the intervention (X) for 6 months, and the other group does not receive the intervention (~X). Both groups receive the pretest with an instrument that measures quality of life, and then after the 6-month period, they receive the same instrument on the posttest. As in earlier chapters, the design can be shown as follows:

$$R \quad O_1 \quad X \quad O_2$$
$$R \quad O_1 \quad {\sim}X \quad O_2$$

The researcher will measure quality of life with a particular measurement tool (dependent variable), which we will call the Quality of Life (QOL) inventory. He will measure both the intervention and control groups prior to the intervention on the QOL and then again after the period of the intervention. Therefore, each participant in the study will obtain a score on the QOL prior to the intervention and after the intervention period. If the QOL inventory has a range between 0 and 100, then each participant will receive both a pretest score and a posttest score within this range. The researcher hopes that the posttest scores in the intervention group are higher than those of the control group. Because of the random assignment, the groups should be equivalent initially. As we have seen in chapters 6 and 7, this design is a strong one in terms of internal validity. However, it is possible that the study is weak in other respects. For example, population external validity could be low if the participants were unrepresentative of the theoretical population. The issue here is whether the QOL inventory will measure quality of life consistently (reliably) in this study with this group of participants.

Test Scores

We call any score that we obtain from any individual on a particular instrument, an *observed score*. If Jones scores 49 on the pretest of the QOL, then Jones' observed score is 49. If we were to give Jones the QOL a second time, his observed score probably will be different from 49. It might be 53 or 43. If we gave the QOL to Jones a third time, the score probably will be different from either of the scores received from previous administrations of the test. Because Jones' score will not be the same each time we give the QOL, and because we must give Jones a second QOL after the intervention, how will we know if the change in Jones' score from pretest to posttest is due to the intervention, or perhaps due to something else? Stated another way, how do we know whether the change in Jones' score is due to systematic variation (variation as a result of the intervention) or unsystematic variation (variation as a result of other factors). To understand our problem, we must consider classical test theory, and true and error scores.

According to classical test theory, an *observed* score consists of a *true score* and *error*. If we could subtract the true score from the observed score, we could determine how much of the score is due to error. We never actually know the amount of the observed score that is due to the true score, and the amount of the observed score that is due to error. If we were to measure the person thousands of times, and take the average of all of those measurements, then the average score would be very close to the individual's true score. Unfortunately, we rarely measure a person more than a couple of times on any given instrument.

Because we rarely measure a person multiple times with any instrument, the researcher may have trouble with his study. Again, the problem is that if he is trying to assess the change that results from his intervention, he will need to measure each participant more than one time. Suppose Jones is in the intervention condition, and his QOL score increases from 49 (pretest) to 53 (posttest). How do we know whether this increase is due to an increase in Jones' true score (systematic variation) or merely due to error (unsystematic variation)? The solution to the problem is to choose a test with high reliability. We have not considered specific methods of determining reliability at this point, but we have stated that reliability is a measure of consistency. How does reliability relate to observed scores and true scores? Measurement reliability is expressed as a coefficient. The *reliability coefficient* is the ratio of the variance of true scores to the variance of observed scores (Ghiselli, Campbell, & Zedeck, 1981). In other words, the higher the reliability of an instrument, the closer that true scores will be to observed scores for that instrument. Now, given what we know about observed scores, true scores, and error, we should consider correlation coefficients.

Correlation Coefficient

We can discuss reliability conceptually as a form of consistency. However, when evaluating instruments, it is important to be able to express reliability in a numerical form. This allows us to compare different instruments on properties of reliability. The measure most often selected to evaluate reliability is referred to as a *correlation coefficient*. As discussed in chapter 16, a correlation coefficient is usually expressed as the letter *r*, and indicates the strength of a relation. The values of *r* range between −1 and +1. A value of 0 is viewed as no relation between two variables or scores, whereas values close to −1 or +1 are viewed as very strong relationships between two variables. A strong negative relationship, often referred to as an inverse relationship, indicates that the *higher* the score is on one variable or test, the *lower* the score is on a second variable or test. On the other hand, a strong positive relationship indicates that people who score high on one test also will score high on a second test. Although the correlation coefficient *r* can vary from −1 to +1, to say that a measurement is reliable, one would expect a coefficient between +.7 and +1.0. Others have suggested even stricter criteria. Anastasi (1988), when discussing a reliability coefficient of .72 stated, "Nevertheless, the obtained correlation is somewhat lower than is desirable for reliability coefficients which usually fall in the .80s and .90s" (p. 115). Nunnally (1978) stated that reliability coefficients of .8 are acceptable for research, but that .9 is necessary for measures that will be used to make decisions about individuals, by using instruments such as IQ tests, GREs, SATs (Scholastic Aptitude Tests), and those for personnel decisions. However, it is common to see published journal articles in which one or a few reliability coefficients are below .7, usually .6 or above. Note that, although correlations of −.7 to −1.0 indicate a strong (negative) correlation, they are totally unacceptable for reliability. Such a high negative correlation would indicate that persons who initially score high on the measure later score low and vice versa. A negative reliability coefficient probably indicates a computational error or terrible inconsistency.

METHODS TO ASSESS RELIABILITY

Test–Retest Reliability

Test–retest reliability is one of the most common forms of reliability (Daniel & Witta, 1997). Cronbach (1960) refers to this coefficient as a coefficient of stability. Test–retest reliability is easy to understand. If a test is reliable, and if it is given more than once to the same person, that person's scores should be very close to one another, if not equal. If the researcher wants to obtain test–retest reliability on his QOL instrument, he would find a sample of persons who were not participants in the experiment but who would fit his target population. He would administer the QOL to this sample, and at a later date (at a date that would approximate the interval of the intervention), he would administer the QOL to the same sample. Then he would determine the reliability coefficient from the scores of the two administrations by using a correlation between the sets of scores. If the reliability coefficient is relatively high, for example above .80, he would be satisfied that the QOL has good test–retest reliability. On the other hand, if the reliability coefficient is below .70, then he may need to reconsider the QOL as a reliable measure of quality of life.

Certain considerations must be taken into account to determine test–retest reliability. The first point is that test–retest reliability is not established during a study. The reliability coefficient must be established ahead of time, prior to the study, by using a period of time when little related to the substance of the instrument should be happening between the two administrations of the instrument.[1] In most cases, test–retest reliability has already been established for the instrument of choice, so the investigator need not worry about having to determine reliability for the study. In many cases, more than one reliability coefficient has been obtained for a particular instrument. However, the investigator needs to make sure of the following criteria when selecting the instrument:

1. The reliability of the instrument is high (e.g., above .80) or at least marginally acceptable (e.g., above .60).

---

[1]This is especially important for experiments and for areas such as child development, where rapid growth during the interval between the two administrations of the instrument could alter test–retest reliability.

2. The length of time that had been used to establish the test–retest reliability is similar to the length of time to be used in the study. It should be noted that as the length of time increases between administrations, the reliability decreases.
3. The sample that had been used to determine reliability of the instrument is similar to the sample that will be used in the current study.

Parallel Forms Reliability

One of the problems of using the same instrument for the pretest and the posttest of a study is that participants may use the knowledge gained on the pretest to alter the posttest score. This problem, often referred to as testing (or carryover) effects, creates significant problems for the investigator because it becomes impossible to determine if the change in scores is due to the intervention or to knowledge obtained on the pretest. One way of avoiding the pretest problem is to create a design without a pretest, for example, the posttest-only control group design. However, that design only can be used if the investigator can randomly assign participants to groups. A quasi-experimental approach is more likely in applied settings, where the investigator will need to use a pretest.

To counteract the testing problem, some tests have a second or parallel form that could be used as a posttest in place of the instrument used for the pretest. Parallel forms reliability (coefficient of equivalence, Cronbach, 1960) involves establishing the relationship between the two forms of the same test. This type of reliability is easy to establish, because it involves having a sample of participants take the two forms of the same instrument with very little time elapsed between the two administrations. Then a correlation coefficient is determined for the two sets of scores, similar to that done in test–retest reliability. Again, a reliability coefficient of at least .80 would be expected for good parallel forms reliability.

Internal Consistency Reliability

Often, in addition to obtaining test–retest reliability, or parallel forms reliability, the researcher wants to know that the instrument is consistent among the items, that is, the instrument is measuring a single concept, or construct. Rather than correlate different administrations of the same instrument, the investigator can use the results of a single administration of the instrument to determine internal consistency. The most common methods of determining internal consistency are the split-half method, the Kuder–Richardson (K–R 20) method, and Cronbach's alpha. The last two methods are often referred to as interitem reliability. All three can be used only when one has data from several items that are combined to make a composite score.

Split-Half Methods.   These methods of obtaining internal consistency reliability involve correlating two halves of the same test. The term *split-half* is a general term to describe a number of different methods of correlating one half of the test with the second half of the test. For example, one could correlate the first half of the test with the second half of the test, or correlate the odd items with the even items. A third, and highly recommended method, is to randomly sample half of the items of the test and correlate them with the remaining items.

One of the problems with obtaining split-half reliability is that when dividing the test into two halves, the number of items is reduced by 50%, compared to a test–retest reliability or alternative forms reliability. This reduction in size means that the resulting correlation coefficient will probably underestimate reliability (Suen, 1990). Therefore, once the reliability coefficient is established by calculating the correlation coefficient, r, it is necessary to adjust the size of the r by using the Spearman–Brown formula,[2] as follows:

$$reliability = \frac{I_{ratio}\, r}{1 + (I_{ratio} - 1)r}$$

where I_{ratio} = the ratio of the number of items in the desired test divided by the number of items in the original test, and

r = the correlation coefficient of the two halves of the test.

However, because we are using the Spearman–Brown formula in a specific instance, split-half reliability, I_{ratio} will always be 2 (twice the size of the split test). Therefore, the formula for adjusting the reliability coefficient for split-half reliability is as follows:

$$reliability = \frac{2r}{1 + r}$$

Therefore, if you compute the correlation coefficient between the first and second halves of your test, and find that it equals .7, the Spearman–Brown formula adjustment would change the r from .7 to .82.

Kuder–Richardson 20.   If the instrument that you are using is intended to measure a single theme or trait, you may wish to determine how all of the items are related to each other. If each item is scored dichotomously, such as pass/fail, true/false, right/wrong, then *K–R 20* is the appropriate method of determining interitem reliability. To use this method, the following equation is used:

$$reliability = \frac{I}{I-1}\left(\frac{s^2 - \Sigma_{pq}}{s^2}\right),$$

where I = total number of items on the test, s^2 = total variance of the test scores, p = proportion of participants who pass an item, and q = proportion of participants who do not pass an item.

---

[2] The Spearman–Brown formula is most commonly used to determine reliability of a test if more items are to be added or subtracted.

Cronbach's Alpha.   If each item on the test has multiple choices, such as a Likert scale, then *Cronbach's alpha* is the method of choice to determine interitem reliability. Cronbach's alpha currently is the most commonly used index of reliability in the area of educational and psychological research (Daniel & Witta, 1997). To complete Cronbach's alpha the following equation is applied:

$$\alpha = (\frac{I}{I-1})(\frac{s^2 - \Sigma s^2}{s^2}) \, ,$$

where I = total number of items on the test, s^2 = total variance of the test scores, and Σs^2 = sum of the variances for each item.

It should be noted that measures of interitem reliability, especially Cronbach's alpha, are often seen when reading a research article. The reason for this, as stated earlier, is that it takes only one administration of the instrument. More important, though, is that alpha is related to construct validity. One of the problems with Cronbach's alpha is that, although it is a measure of internal consistency, it does not necessarily measure homogeneity, or unidimensionality. In other words, people often determine Cronbach's alpha, and assume that because it is at a high level, for example, .85, the test is measuring only one concept or construct. Unfortunately, as pointed out by Schmitt (1996b) and Spector (1992), even though the overall item correlations may be relatively high, they could be measuring more than one factor or dimension. This can lead to problems, because one of the assumptions of using Cronbach's alpha as an index of reliability is that it is measuring only one construct. We caution that, when reporting reliability, if only Cronbach's α is provided without information indicating that there is only one underlying dimension, or another index of reliability, then reliability has not been adequately assessed.

Standard Error of Measurement

When selecting a test, one of the most important questions to ask, in addition to reliability and validity information, is what type of variability of performance might we expect. In the previous chapter, we discussed the standard deviation as an index of variability and also introduced the normal curve. We will need both, in addition to information on reliability, when we consider the standard error of measurement. The standard error of measurement allows us to establish a range of scores (confidence interval) within which should lie a performer's true score. First, let's look at the equation for the standard error of measurement; then we provide an example to help explain the concept. The equation for the standard error of measurement is as follows:

$$s_m = s\sqrt{1-r} \, ,$$

where s = standard deviation of the test, and r = the reliability coefficient.

Suppose that you have an intelligence test like the Wechsler Adult Intelligence Scale (WAIS), that has a known standard deviation of 15. Let's say that the reliability coefficient is, on average, .92. What will be the standard error of measurement? Fitting these numbers into the equation, the standard error of measurement (s_m) = 4.24. A given individual takes the test and scores 110. From our earlier introduction to classical test theory, this *observed score* is equal to a *true score* plus *error.* We do not know (nor will we ever know) the individual's true score. Therefore, we must estimate the true score from a single test. To do this, we use the standard error of measurement, and set a confidence interval around the observed score. The size of this confidence interval will depend on how sure we want to be that the true score fits within this interval. In most cases, we want to be at least 95% sure (two standard deviations). Therefore, we set up a 95% confidence interval around the observed score. To do this, we multiply our standard error of measurement times the z score that represents two standard deviations from the mean on a normal curve. This z value is 1.96 (see Fig. 9.2). Therefore, 4.24 times 1.96 gives us a value of 8.32. We can conclude that our true score falls within the 95% confidence interval of 110 ± 8.32 or between 101.68 and 118.32. Or, if the person took the test 100 times, 95 times the true score would fall within that interval.

The standard error of measurement illustrates the importance of the reliability coefficient. Suppose that in this example, our reliability coefficient was .65 instead of .92. Our standard error of measurement would now be 12.09. We multiply this value times 1.96 to establish our confidence interval. Our confidence interval is 110 ± 23.70 or between 86.3 and 133.7. The precision of our estimate of the true score has decreased substantially as a result of a low reliability coefficient.

Interrater (Interobserver) Reliability

The previous methods to establish reliability were accomplished by examining scores on an instrument. However, sometimes the measurement tool is observation performed by judges (usually the case with qualitative research). When observation is the instrument, then reliability must be established among the judges to maintain consistency. This type of reliability is referred to as *interrater reliability.* Although there are numerous ways to determine this form of reliability, the common theme is that two or more judges (observers) score certain episodes of behavior and a form of correlation is performed to determine the level of agreement among the judges.

Percentage Agreement Methods.   These methods involve having two or more raters, prior to the study, observe a sample of behaviors that will be similar to what would be observed in the study. Suppose that rater *A* observes 8 occurrences of a particular behavior and rater *B* observes 10 occurrences of the same behavior. A percentage is then computed by dividing the smaller number of observations by the larger number of observations of the specific behavior. In this case, the percentage is 80. One of the problems with this method is that, although both observers may agree that a behavior was elicited a particular number of times, this does not mean that each time the behavior occurred both judges agreed. For example, suppose that the behavior of cooperation was the dependent variable for a study. Prior to the study, two judges were to observe a classroom of students for particular instances of cooperation. One observer (judge) said that there were 8 examples of cooperation. A second observer said that there were 10 examples of cooperation. The percentage agreement would be 8 divided by 10 or 80%. However, it is possible that the 8 instances observed by one judge were not the same instances observed by the second judge. The percentage would be inflated in this particular instance. Ottenbacher (1986) suggested using a point-by-point basis of establishing interrater reliability. In this method, each behavior would be rated as an agreement or disagreement between judges. The point-by-point method would be easiest to perform if the behavior is on a tape that could be played for the judges. To calculate percentage agreement in the point-by-point method, the number of agreements between the two judges would be divided by the total number of responses (agreements plus disagreements). A problem with this method is that it ignores chance agreements when few categories are used (Bartko & Carpenter, 1976). An additional problem with these percentage agreement methods is that they are most suited to situations with only two raters.

Intraclass Correlation Coefficients (ICC).   Often, when performing a study by using observations of behavior as the dependent variable, more than two observers are needed. Intraclass correlation coefficients allow the researcher to calculate a reliability coefficient with two or more judges. (For an excellent review of ICC-type methods, including Kappa, see Bartko & Carpenter, 1976.) One criterion that must be satisfied to use the intraclass correlation coefficient is that the behavior to be rated must be scaled at an interval level. For example, each rater might be rating instances of cooperation on a 1–5 scale. These ICCs are computed by using analysis of variance methods with repeated measures to analyze interrater reliability.[3] (We discussed repeated measures analysis of variance in chap. 15.) A second advantage of the ICC method of computing interrater reliability is that if the judges are selected randomly, then the researcher can generalize the interrater reliability beyond the sample of judges who took part in the reliability study.

Kappa.   A method of calculating intraclass correlation coefficients when the data are nominal is the Kappa statistic. Similar to ICC, Kappa can be computed with two or more raters. Kappa also corrects for chance agreement. Although the data for using Kappa are often dichotomous, for example, present or absent, it is not uncommon to have more than two nominal categories.

---

[3]Although it appears that intraclass correlation coefficients are used most commonly for interrater reliability, especially in rehabilitation literature, these methods can be used for test–retest reliability and internal consistency reliability (Shavelson, 1988).

Summary of Reliability Methods

We have discussed different methods of assessing reliability. Although each method provides a measure of consistency, not all provide the same measure of consistency. It is up to the consumer to be aware of how reliability was established before using a particular instrument. To say that an instrument is reliable has relatively little meaning. Each statement of reliability must specify the type of reliability and the strength of the reliability coefficient.

Typically, if one does not create the instrument, but uses an instrument already published, then reliability indices should have been established. The most common places to find studies of the reliability of the instrument are in the instrument manual, which is often referred to in the original journal publication that introduced the instrument. The instrumentation section of any research article that used the particular instrument should also provide information about the reliability of that instrument.

MEASUREMENT VALIDITY

Early in this chapter, we mentioned that measurement reliability and measurement validity were part of the overall concept of research validity. Measurement validity is part of the component that we have labeled measurement validity and generalizability of the constructs.

The current view of validity is that it is an evaluation of scores on a particular test and of how these scores will be interpreted. Thus, when we address the issue of validity for a particular test, we are addressing the issue of the validity of the scores on that test for a particular purpose, and not the validity of the test or instrument per se. Therefore, any particular test might be used for a number of purposes. For example, specialty area scores on the graduate record examination might be used to predict first-year success in graduate school. However, they also could be used as a method to assess current status in a particular undergraduate major. Although the same test is used in both instances, the purpose of the test is completely different for each situation. Or, as a colleague has pointed out, a chain saw is "valid" for tree surgery but not brain surgery. Therefore, prior to using the test, validity would need to be determined for each purpose or use.

Validity, or, perhaps more importantly, the evaluation of validity, is concerned with establishing evidence for the use of a particular instrument in a particular setting. In the next section we illustrate different methods of gathering evidence to support validity. It should be noted that only one type of evidence, no matter how strong, is insufficient for establishing validity. Instead, all of the different methods should be applied toward evaluation of the validity of a particular test or instrument.

Even though an instrument may be consistent (high reliability), it may not be valid. For example, one could construct a device for measuring a length of 12 inches. However, suppose that the device actually measures 13 inches. The device will be consistent but not valid because it does not measure what it is supposed to measure. Although the correlation coefficient is most often used to describe measurement reliability, there is no one type of statistic to describe measurement validity. However, the correlation coefficient is used to describe one type of measurement validity, criterion validity. When one reads a research article, there is usually more information about the reliability of the instrument than about the validity of the instrument. The reason for this is that measurement validity is usually more difficult to obtain. We discuss four different types of evidence for validity: face validity, content validity, criterion validity, and construct validity. Note, however, that many researchers do not consider face validity to be a scientifically recognized type of measurement validity.

Face Validity

An instrument is said to have face validity if the content appears to be appropriate for the purpose of the instrument. The key word is *appears*. Face validity does not actually describe the content. For example, faculty are often deluged by book salespersons trying to get them to use their text for a class. Sometimes, the instructor will select the book from the table of contents, because the topics appear to be covered, even though the instructor has no idea how well the topics are covered. Similarly, suppose an instructor is teaching a class in statistics. The midterm exam contains questions that appear to be about statistics that were covered in class. Students may feel that this test has good face validity (at least before the midterm), even though the problems are not solvable and, thus, not a good measure of statistics knowledge. So face validity is not enough, but if nothing else, face validity is a selling point for an instrument.

Content Validity

Content validity, as opposed to face validity, refers to the actual content of the instrument. Specifically, one asks if the content that comprises the instrument is representative of the concept that one is attempting to measure. For example, A. G. Fisher (1995) has constructed an instrument called the Assessment of Motor and Process Skills (AMPs). One of the most important contributions of the instrument is that it has ecological soundness. Fisher has participants choose to perform everyday tasks from a list of possible tasks that require motor and process skills. If Fisher asked participants to stack blocks or perform other artificial types of motor tasks, then her test would not have strong content validity, even though the artificial tasks involved motor activity. Her test has strong content validity because the tasks not only involve motor and process activity, but also because they are representative of the types of tasks that a person would do in everyday life.

There is no statistic that demonstrates content validity. Instead, the process of establishing content validity usually starts with a definition of the concept that the investigator is attempting to measure. A second step to content validity is a literature search to see how this concept is represented in the literature. Next, items are generated that might measure this concept. Gradually, this list of items is reduced to form the test. One of the methods of reducing items is to form a panel of experts to review the items for representativeness of the concept.

Criterion-Related Validity

When people mention measurement validity, they are usually referring to criterion validity. Criterion validity refers to validating the instrument against some form of external criterion. This validation procedure usually involves establishing a correlation coefficient between the instrument and the external or outside criterion. The key to criterion validity is being able to establish an outside criterion that is measurable. Common examples of criterion validity involve instruments that are intended to select participants for a school or a profession. There are two types of evidence for criterion validity: predictive evidence and concurrent evidence.

Predictive Evidence.   When we try to determine how someone will do in the future on the basis of a particular instrument, we are usually referring to predictive evidence. Tests such as the Scholastic Aptitude Test, the Graduate Record Examination, and the Law School Aptitude Test are examples of instruments that are used to predict future performance. For example, the Scholastic Aptitude Test (SAT) is often required for students attempting to enter college. If the SAT has good predictive evidence, then students who score high on this test will perform better in college than those who do not score high. The criterion in this case would be a measure of how well the student performs in college, usually grades during the first year.

To establish predictive evidence in this example, high school students would take the SAT. Then, when they are finished with their freshman year of college, correlations would be established between their high school SAT scores and college grades. If the correlation is high, then predictive evidence is good. If the correlation is low, then the test has problems for prediction of future performance. A problem with predictive evidence is that often not all of the participants who were evaluated on the original instrument can be evaluated on the criterion variable. This is especially the case in selection studies. For example, we may have SAT scores for a wide range of high school students. However, not all of these students will attend college. Therefore, our criterion variable of first semester college GPA will not only have fewer participants than our predictor variable, but will represent a more homogeneous group (those selected into college). Therefore, the range of scores of those who could participate in the study on both the predictor and criterion variables is restricted, leading to a smaller correlation coefficient (Anastasi, 1988).

A second drawback with predictive evidence is that, to establish validity, the researcher must wait until those who were tested initially can be measured on the criterion. Sometimes this wait could take years. Therefore, a second type of criterion validity was developed to deal with this problem.

Concurrent Evidence.   Similar to predictive evidence, concurrent evidence also examines the relationship between an instrument and an outside criterion. However, as mentioned earlier, sometimes it is too expensive to wait between the time that the test was taken and the measurement of the criterion. For example, suppose that we were interested to see if the SAT taken in high school was a good predictor of freshman grades in college. However, we do not wish to wait the time it takes for the high school students to become freshmen. To determine concurrent evidence, we could take current freshmen and have them take the SAT and see if it correlates with their grades (present grades because they are now freshmen). If there is a high correlation, we can have confidence in using the instrument as a predictor for success in college. However, concurrent evidence is not the same as predictive evidence, and one may not wish to place as much confidence in this procedure. Also, restricted range problems similar to those pointed out under predictive evidence are present. In this example, we must make the assumption that there was little change between high school students and college students, because the target for the SAT is high school students. If there are large changes between high school and college, the validity of the instrument should be questioned. The best situation would be to obtain both predictive and concurrent evidence, although Cronbach (1960) suggests that this rarely occurs.

Concurrent evidence also can be obtained by substituting another instrument for the criterion, especially if it is difficult to measure the criterion. For example, the Assessment of Motor and Process Skills (A. G. Fisher, 1995) (discussed earlier) was compared to the Scales of Independent Behavior in adults with developmental disabilities (Bryze, 1991). However, Cromack (1989) points out that the instrument that is substituted for the criterion can never be more valid than the criterion. One must be cautious when substituting an instrument for a criterion, because in many cases the substituted instrument has not been validated against the criterion of interest. This is often the case with therapeutic or educational outcomes. Perhaps more important, if another instrument is substituted for the criterion, what size correlation would be expected? If the correlation coefficient is quite high, for example, .8 or .9, then your instrument is not providing different information from the criterion instrument. If the correlation is too low, then your instrument is measuring a different construct than the criterion instrument.

The major drawback to criterion validity is the problem of finding a suitable criterion and then being able to measure that criterion. For example, gaining admission to occupational and physical therapy programs in the United States is very difficult because of the high number of applicants for the limited number of positions. To select the successful applicants, criteria such as grades and achievement tests are often used. Students (especially those who are not admitted) often complain that high grades do not make the person a good therapist. Could one create an admission test that would predict becoming a good therapist? Consider the problems of defining and measuring the criterion of "what makes a good occupational or physical therapist?"

Construct Validity

The last type of measurement validity, and certainly the most complex, is construct validity. Constructs are hypothetical concepts that cannot be observed directly. Intelligence, achievement, and anxiety are all constructs. Although we cannot observe a construct directly, most of us agree that these constructs exist through different observable behaviors. For example, we cannot directly observe anxiety, but under certain circumstances we may observe anxious behaviors such as sweating or pacing that are specific to a particular context, such as immediately before an important examination. Therefore, it is common to create instruments to measure particular constructs, such as a test that measures state anxiety, or a test that measures intelligence.

When applying construct validity to an instrument, there is a requirement that the construct that the instrument is measuring is guided by an underlying theory. Often, especially in applied disciplines, there is little underlying theory to support the construct. As Cronbach (1960) points out, "Sometimes the test is used for a long time before any theory is developed around it" (p. 121). Construct validation is a (relatively slow) process where the investigator conducts studies to attempt to demonstrate that the instrument is measuring a construct. Three processes that are important for achieving construct validity are convergent evidence, discriminant evidence, and factorial evidence.

Convergent Evidence.   This is determined by obtaining relatively high correlations between your scale and other measures that the theory suggests would be related. To demonstrate construct validity, one develops hypotheses about what the instrument should predict (*convergent evidence*, or *validity*) if it is actually measuring the construct.

Discriminant Evidence.   This is provided by obtaining relatively low correlations between your scale and measures that the theory suggests should not be related to it (Lord & Novick, 1968). Discriminant evidence can also be obtained by comparing groups that should differ on your scale and finding that they do, in fact, differ.

Factorial Evidence.   This type of evidence is provided when a construct is complex, and several aspects (or factors) of it are measured. If the clustering of items (usually done with factor analysis) supports the theory-based grouping of items, factorial evidence is provided (see chap. 19 for a brief discussion of factor analysis).

Examples.   The first example, from the area of rehabilitation, demonstrates these points. Harvey et al. (1992) developed an instrument called the Patient Evaluation and Conference System (PECS) to predict clinically based admission decisions. They predicted that their instrument, the PECS, could *discriminate* among patients in hospital, intermediate, and day programs in terms of the functional independence and impairment. They found that, overall, their instrument correctly classified 75% of the patients for each of the categories. This same group of investigators also provided further evidence of construct validity by performing *factor analysis* to reduce items that were either redundant or not related to the construct (Silverstein et al., 1992).

A second example concerns the Assessment of Motor and Process Skills (AMPs) instrument developed by A. G. Fisher (1995). Bernspang and A. G. Fisher (1995) predicted that AMPs scores would differ significantly between persons with Cerebral Vascular Accident (CVA) when compared to a nondisabled age group control. On the other hand, they also predicted that there would be no differences between persons who had a CVA in the left hemisphere compared to those who had a CVA in the right hemisphere. This last prediction is very important for the AMPs, because the tasks performed for this instrument are those done every day. The results supported Bernspang and Fisher's predictions and provided both *discriminant* and *convergent* evidence for the validity of the AMPs.

A third example is from the mastery motivation literature (Morgan et al., 1993). The Dimensions of Mastery questionnaire (DMQ) was designed to measure five aspects or domains of mastery motivation: persistence at object-related tasks, gross motor tasks, social mastery motivation with peers, social mastery motivation with adults, and mastery pleasure. Factor analysis supported the grouping of items into these five clusters and provided *factorial* evidence.

Construct validity is never actually achieved. It is a continuing process of experimentation and modification leading to the refinement of the instrument that measures the construct.

SUMMARY

Measurement reliability and validity are exceptionally important issues for research in applied settings. Many of the issues are beyond the scope of the present text. For those interested in measurement reliability and validity in more depth, especially for constructing an instrument, we recommend the texts of Anastasi (1988), Cronbach (1970), and Ghiselli et al. (1981). Table 20.1 provides a summary of the concepts covered in the preceding sections.

TABLE 20.1
Measurement Reliability and Validity

Stability or Consistency	*Correctness or Accuracy*
The participant gets the same or very similar score from a test, observation, or rating. There is reliability of the following:	The score accurately reflects or measures what it was designed or intended to measure.
a. Participants' responses	a. Face validity—the items look valid.
1. Test–retest reliability-stability over time.	b. Content validity—all aspects of the construct are represented in appropriate proportions.
2. Parallel forms reliability - consistency across presumably equivalent versions of the instrument.	c. Criterion-related validity 1. Predictive—the test predicts some criterion in the future. 2. Concurrent—test and criterion are measured at the same time.
3. Internal consistency - items that are to be combined are related to each other.	
b. Observers' responses	d. Construct validity
1. Interrater reliability - different observers or raters give similar scores.	1. Convergent—based on theory, variables predicted to be related are related.
	2. Discriminant—variables predicted not to be related are not related.
	3. Factorial—factor analysis yields a theoretically meaningful solution.

STUDY AIDS

Concepts

- Cronbach's alpha
- Correlation coefficient
- Error
- Intraclass correlation coefficients
- Kappa statistics
- Kuder–Richardson 20
- Observed score
- Percentage agreement methods
- Split-half reliability
- Standard error of measurement
- True score

Distinctions

- Convergent versus discriminant versus factorial evidence for construct measurement validity
- Face versus content versus criterion versus construct evidence for measurement validity
- Predictive versus concurrent evidence for criterion-related measurement validity
- Measurement reliability versus measurement validity
- Measurement validity versus research validity
- Test–retest versus parallel forms versus interval consistency versus interrater evidence for measurement reliability

Application Problems

1. A researcher is interested in determining if therapists interrupt female clients more than male clients. He has obtained videotapes of 30 therapy sessions, and plans to count the number of times the therapist interrupts female and male clients. The researcher hires a graduate student to count the occurrence of interruptions on all the tapes. The researcher then hires another graduate student to count the occurrence of interruptions on 12 of the tapes. Why did the researcher hire the second graduate student? What type of evidence for validity or reliability is the researcher concerned with? What statistical procedure might the researcher best use to determine this type of reliability or validity?

2. A researcher is interested in the influence of marital equality on marital satisfaction. In reading the literature, she learns that many variables (or factors) have been used to operationally define equality, such as shared decision-making power between spouses, fair division of labor, and equal access to

finances. She decides to include several of these factors in her measure of equality. Is the researcher concerned with reliability or validity as she makes decisions about the best way to measure equality? What kind of reliability or validity is she principally concerned with? In analyzing her data, how might she determine if the variables she measured were related to her independent variable?

3. A researcher has developed a measure of anxiety. She plans to use the measure for the first time to determine if learning about stress reduction techniques will influence anxiety levels. She gives her anxiety measure to her undergraduate psychology class, and teaches them stress reduction techniques. The next day, she gives her anxiety measure again. She is excited to report that her test-retest reliability is very high (0.98). You realize that she does not understand test-retest reliability fully. What recommendations would you make to her about how to appropriately establish test-retest reliability?

4. What is the appropriate method (if any) for determining internal consistency reliability for the following measures.

   a. A 10-item measure of locus of control scored with True or False.

   b. An 80-item measure of intimacy scored with a 5-point Likert scale.

   c. A one-item measure ("Whose career is given more priority between you and your spouse?") of relative career priority between spouses.

5. Researchers at a large elementary school in Colorado would like to measure change in aptitude on scientific concepts for all fifth graders before and after a new experiential science curriculum has been introduced. An exam would be given as a pretest measure. However, researchers are concerned about carry-over effects, so will use another form of their instrument as their posttest. What is the coefficient of equivalence? Explain how they will check the reliability of their instruments.

6. Researchers are presented with a new form of intelligence test to use with elementary age children in the United States. The test has been pilot tested with great excitement in several western states. Colorado researchers would like to have more information before piloting the instrument. They have been informed that the standard deviation is 15 and the reliability coefficient is 0.74, on the average. What is the standard error of measurement? Why is it useful to know this? How would this be measured?

7. An Instrument of Support was used to measure perceived support from co-workers in a mental health institution. Participants responded to four items on a 7-point Likert-like scale. Cronbach's alpha for the (support) scale was 0.79. What does this mean?

8. Gliner has developed a multiple-choice test called, "I want to get into grad school real bad," to make the selection process easier. (Also, if enough other schools are interested, he might make some money.) First he wants to determine evidence for reliability. Describe at least three methods that he could use to assess reliability.

   a. After studies on reliability have been performed, Gliner concludes, "The 'I want to get into grad school real bad' test is reliable." What, if anything is wrong with this statement?

b. Next, Gliner conducts a predictive validity study. He gives his test to all students admitted to the graduate program in the year 1988. Five years later, he sends each student a one-item questionnaire. The question asked, "How much money do you make per year?" The correlation between score on the Gliner test and salary level was 0.70. Therefore, Gliner suggested that the test be used in the future for applicants.

c. What are some of the problems encountered with the way Gliner established validity evidence?

d. How could Gliner have obtained validity information using concurrent validity?

e. When compared to predictive validity, what are the advantages and disadvantages of concurrent validity?

21

Types of Data Collection Techniques

Distinctions
Application Problems

OVERVIEW

There are many types of techniques and instruments used to collect data. Some research methods books have a number of chapters, each focusing on a different technique or tool such as interview, questionnaire, projective techniques, tests, or observations. Because this book focuses on research design and the resulting data analysis, we have chosen to de-emphasize our treatment of data collection techniques. In addition, this book is designed for a broad audience of students in the many disciplines related to education, applied health sciences, and applied social sciences. Because each of these fields has its preferred data collection techniques, we have focused on what is common across these disciplines, namely design and analysis. What we do in this chapter is provide a broad context for thinking about data collection techniques and sources where you may go to learn more about the specifics of developing or evaluating a questionnaire, interview, or other data collection technique.

As pointed out in chapter 1, we conceptualize the research approaches and designs as being approximately orthogonal to the techniques of data collection, and thus, in theory at least, any type of data collection technique could be used with any approach to research. It is true that some types of data collection are more commonly used with the randomized experimental or quasi-experimental approaches. Others are more common with comparative or associational approaches, and still others are more common in qualitative research.

Table 21.1 approximates how common each of several data collection techniques are within each of these three major groups of research approaches (listed on the left-hand side of the table). Note that we have ordered the data collection techniques along a dimension from observer report to self-report

TABLE 21.1

Data Collection Techniques Used by Specific Research Approaches
(Symbols in the table indicate likelihood of use)

	Research Approach		
	Quantitative Research		Qualitative Research
Data Collection Techniques	Experiments & Quasi-Experiments	Comparative, Associational, & Descriptive Approaches	
Researcher report measures			
Physiological recordings	++	+	-
Physical trace measures	+	-	+
Coded observations	++	++	+
Narrative observations	-	+	++
Participant observations	-	+	++
Other measures			
Standardized tests	+	++	-
Archival measures or documents	-	+	++
Content analysis	-	+	++
Self-report measures			
Summated attitude scales	+	++	-
Standardized personality scales	+	++	-
Questionnaires or surveys	+	++	-
Interviews	+	++	+
Focus groups	-	+	++

++ Quite likely
+ Possibly
- Not likely

measures. The observer report end includes observations and physiological recordings that are assumed to be less influenced by the participants' desire to look good or to answer in a socially desirable way. Of course, even these measures are not free of the effects of such factors if, as is usually the case, the participants realize that they are being observed or recorded. At the other end of the scale are measures based on self-reports of the participants, such as interviews, questionnaires, focus groups, and attitude and personality scales. In these cases, the responses are clearly filtered through the participants' eyes and are probably heavily influenced by factors such as social desirability and answering in acceptable ways. In the middle, we have put several types of measures that are undoubtedly influenced by the participants' conscious or unconscious need to look good but are, perhaps, less susceptible to such factors because the idea (in standardized achievement and aptitude tests, for instance) is for people to do as well as they can in figuring out the correct answer. With archival documents and content analysis, the data are gathered from records made for another purpose so there may be less built-in bias.

The concern about the filtering of participants' answers through perhaps faulty memories or in terms of socially desirable responses has led quantitative researchers, especially those who tend to use the randomized experimental and quasi-experimental approaches, to be suspicious about the validity of the self-report instruments. Thus, when using self-report measures, you should always be prepared to provide evidence supporting their validity, as discussed in the previous chapter. Of course, some self-report information, such as gender and other simple questions of fact that are not sensitive or controversial, are usually accepted at face value. On the other hand, observer reports are not necessarily valid measures of what they are intended to assess. One issue that is often pointed out by qualitative researchers is that cultural biases may lead observers to interpret their observations in inappropriate or ethnocentric ways.

Recommendations for further reading about data collection techniques are provided in the references. In general, it is advisable to select instruments that have been used in other studies if they have been shown to be reliable and valid with the types of participants and for the purpose that you have in mind. *Tests* (1991) and *Tests in Print* (1994) provide references to thousands of published educational, psychological, and business instruments that are available for purchase or use. The *Mental Measurements Yearbooks* provide summaries and reviews of a large number of published instruments, including aptitude, intelligence, and achievement tests, and also personality and vocational inventories or scales. Similarly, *Test Critiques* annually publishes norms, reliability, and validity data, and practical applications in a user-friendly style. It covers the most frequently used psychological, educational, and business-related instruments. Note that the use of the term *tests* in those books is broader than the way it is used in this book. *Tests*, as in *Test Critiques*, refer to a broad range of data collection techniques, not just those with correct answers, and are similar to our term *standardized*. Textbooks on testing and measurement (e.g., Anastasi, 1988; Thorndike & Hagen, 1991) also provide information on a wide variety of types of standardized instruments. The relevant research literature and ERIC are other good sources for instruments that one might use.

Of course, you may not be able to find an instrument that suits the goals of your research. This is especially likely if you are interested in attitudes, or knowledge, or both about a specific topic, issue, or program. In this case, you may decide to construct a questionnaire or interview to assess what your participants know about, or how they perceive the topic, or both. Dillman (1978), Fowler (1993), Salant and Dillman (1994), and Sudman and Bradburn (1989) provide useful advice about developing and using interviews and questionnaires.

TYPES OF DATA COLLECTION TECHNIQUES

Direct Observation

As noted earlier, many researchers prefer systematic, direct observation of behavior as the most accurate and desirable method of recording behavior, especially the behavior of children. The following discussion of observations deals with what is often called *direct observation* in which the investigator trains observers to observe and record the behaviors of the participants in the study. Indirect observations are used when the investigator interviews or otherwise questions untrained observers, such as parents or teachers, about participants (e.g., children) that they know well. Indirect observation could also include questionnaires or interviews because the participants often are asked to report about their own behavior. Now we will discuss several other dimensions on which observational techniques vary.

Naturalness of the Setting.   The setting for the observations can vary from natural environments (such as a school, playground, park, or home) through more controlled settings (such as a laboratory playroom that is designed to look like a living room) to highly artificial laboratory settings (such as used in a hospital or physiological laboratory). In chapter 10, we discussed the issue of ecological validity, one aspect of which was the naturalness of the setting. Although natural settings have ecological validity, they usually sacrifice a degree of control and the opportunity to present stimuli in a systematic way. Furthermore, equipment such as video cameras and computer-based observational aides are much more difficult to use in a natural setting. Note that qualitative researchers observe almost exclusively in natural settings. Quantitative researchers use the whole range of settings, but some prefer laboratory settings.

Degree of Observer Participation.   This dimension varies from situations in which the observer is a participant (preferred by qualitative researchers) to situations such as public places in which the observer is entirely unobtrusive. Most observations, however, are done in situations where the participants know that the observer is observing them and have agreed to it. It is common for such observers to attempt to be as unobtrusive as possible by sitting off to one side or observing from behind a one-way mirror in a laboratory.

Amount of Detail.   Observations also vary on this dimension, which goes from global summary information (such as overall ratings based on the whole observation period) to moment-by-moment records of the observed behaviors. Obviously, the latter provides more detail, and it requires considerable preparation and training of observers. Moment-by-moment observations may use codes for various behaviors that can be recorded either with paper-and-pencil or with some aid, such as a computer or dictating machine. Detailed records also can be narrative records in which the observer dictates or attempts to write down everything that happens in sequential order.

Breadth of Coverage.   This dimension varies from observational schemes that attempt to record many things that are going on in a person's environment to very specific observations of one or a few types of behavior, such as aggressive incidents or task-directed behaviors.

Standardized Versus Investigator-Developed (One Study) Instruments

Standardized instruments are those that have resulted from careful preparation and cover topics of broad interest to a number of investigators. They are usually published and, thus, are described and reviewed in the *Mental Measurement*

Yearbook or *Test Critiques*. These instruments usually have a manual that includes norms used to make comparisons with a broader sample than is usually used in a single study, and they have information about reliability and validity.

Investigator-developed measures are those developed by a researcher for use in one or a few studies. Such instruments also should be carefully developed, and they should provide at least basic evidence of reliability and validity in the article or report of the study in which they were used. However, there usually is no separate manual or materials available for others to buy or use.

The next several sections use this distinction. Although some tests, personality measures and attitude measures, for instance, are developed by investigators or teachers for one-time use in a specific study, there are many standardized measures available and, in general, it is wise to use them if they have good reported reliability and validity and cover the concept that you intend to measure. Questionnaires and interviews are usually developed by an investigator for one-time use in a particular study on a specific topic. However, some questionnaires and interviews are used in several studies, often to assess the same issue at different times; for example, there is an annual survey of entering college freshmen that has asked many of the same questions for a number of years.

Standardized Tests

Although the term *test* is often used broadly to refer to a wide range of aptitude, personality, and attitude measures, we define the term more narrowly. By a test, we mean a set of problems with right or wrong answers. The score is based on the number of correct answers that the person had. In standardized tests, the scores are usually translated into a normed score that can be used to compare the participants with others who have taken the test. These tests are referred to as *norm referenced tests*. The scores may be in terms of percentile ranks or a well-established metric in which the mean and standard deviation are known. For example, the Graduate Record Exam (GRE) scores were originally normed so that 500 would be the mean and 100 would be the standard deviation. IQ tests were normed so that 100 was the mean and 15 was the standard deviation. An alternative to norm referenced tests is *criterion referenced tests*. These tests examine how well the student or participant has learned a specific skill (the criterion). Such tests measure a student's achievement without comparing it to the scores of other students. This kind of test is often used in schools, but is less commonly used in research.

Most standardized tests are said to be objective because there is little disagreement about the scores obtained from them. There may be disagreement about how to interpret the results, but if a machine or an untrained assistant can score the test or other measure, the measure is said to be objective. Multiple choice tests and rating scales are said to be objective; essay tests and projective techniques are less objective because the scores are influenced by the judgment of the scorers.

Achievement Tests.   Most research about the effectiveness of instructional methods uses achievement as the dependent or outcome variable. Thus, achievement tests are widely used in educational research as well as in schools. Such tests measure the mastery or achievement of students in an area related to what they should have learned in school. Achievement tests are available for individual school subjects such as biology or history, and they are also available in comprehensive batteries that measure broad areas of achievement such as verbal or quantitative achievement. For example, the California Achievement Test (CAT) contains tests in the area of reading, language, and arithmetic. You need to be careful when selecting an achievement test that it is reliable and appropriate for measuring the aspect of achievement in which you are interested. The test also must show reliability and validity evidence for the participants to be included in the study. Thus, if you are using a particular ethnic group or students with developmental delays, you need to be sure that the test is appropriate for that sample. If these criteria are met, then there are advantages in the use of a standardized instrument. In addition to saving time and effort, the results of your study can be compared to those of others by using the same instrument.

When the available standardized tests are not appropriate for the objectives of your study, you may have to construct your own test. It is better to do so than to use an inappropriate standardized test just because it is available. If you do develop your own test, you should be careful in preparing it so that you determine its reliability and validity before using it. Refer to the books on tests and measurement mentioned earlier (e.g., Thorndike & Hagen, 1991) if you decide to develop your own achievement test.

Performance and Authentic Assessments.   Although most common achievement tests are paper-and-pencil tests of the type just described, a researcher may want to measure actual performance, that is, what an individual can do rather than what he or she knows. *Performance assessment* has become a popular alternative to traditional tests. In such an assessment, the investigator observes an individual's performance on a certain task and then judges the product on the basis of certain criteria. Performance assessments are common in such areas as art, music, or science, where the individual is expected to be able to do or produce something such as a painting, a recital, or a research report.

Some performance assessments are referred to as *authentic assessments,* but not all performance assessments are authentic in the sense that they are "real life" assessments. To be considered authentic, the tasks should be high on ecological validity, as discussed in chapter 10, that is, they might include such things as an actual job interview, an individual or group research project, or a report. Performance and authentic assessments provide a way to measure abilities and skills that are not easily assessed by paper-and-pencil tests. However, they take much more time and expense to administer and score.

Aptitude Tests.   Aptitude tests in the past were often called *intelligence tests,* but this term is less often used now because of controversy about the definition of intelligence and to what extent it is inherited. Performance on such aptitude tests is partly dependent on genetic background and partly on environment and schooling. Aptitude tests, in contrast to achievement tests, are intended to measure more general performance or problem-solving ability. These tests attempt to measure the participant's ability to solve problems and apply knowledge in a variety of situations. Researchers and educators have found aptitude tests to be generally useful for the purpose of predicting school success and as an independent variable that must be controlled in educational studies. The many aptitude tests that are available can be divided into those that must be administered individually and those that can be used with groups.

The most widely used individual intelligence tests are the Stanford–Binet and the Wechsler tests. The Stanford–Binet test produces an *intelligence quotient* (IQ), which is derived by dividing the obtained mental age (MA) by the person's actual or chronological age (CA). The Stanford–Binet gives a general measure of intelligence and provides measures of separate abilities. There are several age versions of the Wechsler intelligence scales; each provides two scores for each person, verbal and nonverbal IQ. A trained psychometrician must give these individual intelligence tests to one person at a time, which is expensive in both time and money.

Group aptitude tests, on the other hand, are more practical for use in school systems and in research where group averages are to be used. There are now many group aptitude tests available, identified in the *Mental Measurements Yearbook* or *Test Critiques*.

Standardized Personality Inventories

Personality inventories present the participant with a collection of statements describing behaviors or patterns of behaviors. The participants are then asked to indicate whether the statement is characteristic of their behavior, by checking yes or no or by indicating how typical it is of them. Usually there are a number of statements for each characteristic measured by the instrument. Some of these inventories assess only one trait; for example, authoritarianism is measured by the *California F Scale* and anxiety is measured by the *State Trait Anxiety Scales*. Other personality inventories, such as *Cattell's 16 Personality Factor Questionnaire,* measure a number of traits. Some inventories measure characteristics that one might not strictly consider to be personality. For example, the *Strong Interest Inventory* is used primarily to assess vocational interests. Other inventories measure temperament (e.g., *Child Temperament Inventory*), behavior problems (e.g., *Child Behavior Checklist*), or motivation (e.g., *Dimensions of Mastery Questionnaire*). Notice that these personality instruments have various labels: scale, inventory, questionnaire, and checklist.

These measures are said to be standardized because they have been administered to a wide variety of respondents and information about these norm groups and about the reliability and validity evidence of the measures is usually provided in the manual for the inventory. It is also possible for an investigator to develop a measure of an aspect of personality specifically for a particular study. As with standardized measures, reliability and validity need to be addressed.

Paper-and-pencil inventories have the advantages of being relatively inexpensive to administer and objective to score. However, there are disadvantages mostly related to the problem of validity. We should mention here that the validity of a personality inventory depends not only on respondents' ability to read and understand the items but also on their understanding of themselves and their willingness to give frank and honest answers. Although personality inventories, especially the more carefully developed and standardized inventories, can provide useful information for research, there is clearly the possibility that they may be superficial or biased.

Another major type of personality assessment is the *projective technique.* These measures are not often used in educational and social science research, because they require an extensively trained person to administer and score. Thus, they are expensive. Projective techniques ask the participant to respond to unstructured stimuli like ink blots or ambiguous pictures. They are called projective because it is assumed that the respondent will project their personality or motivation into their interpretation of the stimulus.

Attitude Scales

Summated (Likert) Attitude Scales.   Many personality inventories use the same summated method to be described here, but Likert (1932) initially developed this method as a way of measuring attitudes about particular groups, institutions, or concepts. Researchers often develop their own scales for measuring attitudes or values, but there are also a number of standardized scales to measure certain kinds of attitudes like social responsibility. There are several approaches to measuring attitudes. We describe only the summated Likert scales and the semantic differential scales. The term *Likert scale* is used in two ways: for the summated scale to be discussed in this section and for the individual items or rating scales from which the summated scale is computed. Likert items are statements about a particular topic; and the participants are asked to indicate whether they strongly agree (SA), agree (A), are undecided (U), disagree (D), or strongly disagree (SD). The summated Likert scale is constructed by developing a number of statements about the topic, usually some of which are clearly favorable and some of which are unfavorable. These statements are intended to provide a representative sample of all possible opinions or attitudes about the subject. These statements are then presented to a group of participants who are asked to rate each statement from strongly disagree to strongly agree. To compute the summated scale score, each type of answer is given a numerical value or weighting, usually 1 for strongly disagree, up to 5 for strongly agree. When computing the summated scale, the negatively worded or unfavorable items need to be reversed in terms of the weighting. In this case, strongly disagree is given a weight of 5 and strongly agree is given a weight of 1. Consider the following three items from a social responsibility scale (Berkowitz & Lutterman, 1968):

1. Every person should give some of his time for the good of his town or country. SD   D   U   A   SA
2. Letting your friends down is not so bad because we can't do good all the time.   SD   D   U   A   SA
3. It is the duty of each person to do his job the very best he can.
   SD   D   U   A   SA

A person with a highly favorable attitude toward social responsibility might circle SA for the first item, SD for the second item, and A for the third item. His or her summated score would be 5 for the first item, 5 for the second item, and 4 for the third item, or 14. You should be able to see that the summated scores could range from 3 for someone who is very low on agreement with the attitude of social responsibility to a maximum of 15 for someone who is most highly positive in terms of this attitude.

Summated rating attitude scales, like all the other data collection tools discussed in this chapter, need to be investigated for reliability, as discussed in chapter 20. Internal consistency would be indicated if the various individual items correlate with each other, indicating that they belong together in assessing this attitude. Validity would be assessed in the ways detailed in chapter 20, by seeing if this summated scale can differentiate between groups thought to differ on this attitude or by correlations with other measures that are assumed to be related to this attitude. The construction of summated scales (for attitude or personality measurement) is discussed in depth by Spector (1992).

Semantic Differential Scales.   Another approach to measuring attitudes is the semantic differential scale developed by Osgood, Suci, and Tannenbaum (1957). This measure is based on the assumption that concepts or objects have what is called *connotative* in addition to *denotative* (or dictionary) meaning for individuals. Connotative meaning has to do with surplus meaning or what the concept or object suggests or connotes to the participant.

Semantic differential scales are adaptable and relatively easy to construct, if one wants to know how participants feel about concepts such as "site-based management," "ADA requirements," or "organized religion." Participants are asked to rate the concept on each of a set of bipolar adjective pairs, which Osgood et al. (1957) found formed three clusters or factors: *evaluative*, with adjective pairs such as good-bad or valuable-worthless; *potency* pairs such as strong-weak or large-small; and *activity* pairs such as active-passive or fast-slow. The evaluative cluster is used most often in research. The semantic differential scales are scored much like the summated rating scales just discussed. The rating for each item is given a score, usually from 1 to 7. If the positively connoted term is on the left, the score would be reversed. If the positive term is on the right, no reversal would be done. Then the score for each item on a scale (e.g., evaluative) would be added.

Questionnaires and Interviews

These two broad techniques are sometimes called *survey research methods*, but we think that is misleading because questionnaires and interviews are used in many studies that would not meet the definition of survey research. In survey research, a sample of participants is drawn (usually by using one of the probability sampling methods discussed in chap. 10) from a larger population. This sample is asked a series of questions related to a topic about which they should have some knowledge or attitude. The intent of surveys is to make inferences describing the whole population, so the sampling method and return rate are important considerations, as discussed in chapter 10.

Questionnaires and interviews used in surveys are usually developed by the investigator for one-time use in a particular study. However, sometimes the same or similar questions are asked on a number of occasions to assess changes in attitudes, product preferences, or voting preferences over time. *Questionnaires* are any group of written questions to which participants are asked to respond in writing, often by checking or circling responses. *Interviews* are a series of questions presented orally by an interviewer and are usually responded to orally by the participant. Both questionnaires and interviews can be highly structured with close-ended questions in which the possible answers are specified and the participants merely pick one of the provided responses. However, it is common for interviews to be more open ended, allowing the participant to provide detailed answers to questions that do not lend themselves to short answers.

Questionnaires

There are two basic ways to gather information with a questionnaire: mailed questionnaires and directly administered questionnaires.

Mailed Questionnaires.   In this case, names and addresses of persons in the population must be assembled. Then, a sample from this population is selected by using one of the techniques described in chapter 10. When the accessible population is small, all persons may be sampled. This group is then mailed a questionnaire with a cover letter and a stamped, return-addressed envelope. Reminder post cards, or duplicate copies of the questionnaire, or both are often sent to nonrespondents or, if respondents are not specifically identified, to all persons who initially received the questionnaire. Compared to interviews, mailed questionnaires are relatively cost effective because they require little time to administer on the part of the investigators and do not require the hiring of persons to administer the instrument. Information can be obtained relatively rapidly, that is, in a few weeks, but a poor response rate is often obtained because of the impersonality and likely lack of rapport with the investigator.

Directly Administered Questionnaires.   In this technique, the questionnaire is usually administered to a group of people who are assembled in a certain place for a specific purpose such as a class or a club meeting. It is also possible to directly administer a questionnaire in a one-to-one, face-to-face situation, such as giving a questionnaire to the mother of a young child while testing the child, but this is relatively uncommon. The main advantage of directly administered questionnaires is that a high response rate is usually obtained, especially if the participants are expected to be in that location anyway. On the other hand, the sample is unlikely to be a probability sample from a desired target population, in part because some percentage of potential participants probably will not attend the class or meeting. This can be a serious problem in college classrooms. This technique can be cost effective if it only requires one or few administrations of the questionnaire and if the administrator's time is not considered or does not have to be paid.

Types of Questionnaire Items.   Salant and Dillman (1994) provide an excellent source for persons who want to develop and conduct their own questionnaire or structured interview. They describe four types of question structure for questionnaire and interview items: open-ended, partially open-ended, close-ended unordered choices, and close-ended ordered responses. Each of these types of items has advantages and disadvantages, as discussed briefly in the following paragraphs.

Open-ended questions do not provide choices for the participants to select. Instead, each participant must formulate an answer in his or her own words. Although this type of question requires the least effort to write, it has several major drawbacks. Open-ended questions are demanding for the participants, especially if the responses have to be written out or are on issues that the person has not considered recently or at all. Open-ended questions tend to produce many different responses with only a few mentions of each topic. This type of question does not provide comparable information across a sample, because people who did not think to mention an answer might have done so if they had been given choices from which to select. Finally, the responses to open-ended questions require considerable time to code and prepare for entry into a computer. However, there are a number of advantages that make them useful in certain circumstances, especially if the investigator did not have enough knowledge before the study to make good close-ended questions. Sometimes open-ended questions require a simple straightforward answer such as the person's date of birth or favorite class. In these cases, developing a list of possible responses is wasteful of space. Open-ended questions are more often successfully used in interviews than in questionnaires.

Partially open-ended questions usually provide several possible answers and then have a space for other responses or comments. This can be useful, but our experience is that participants usually do not use the spaces, and not much additional information is provided.

Close-ended unordered items are commonly used when answers to a question fit nominal categories that do not fall on a continuum. Participants are asked to choose among these discrete categories and select which one best reflects their opinion or situation. In some cases, the person is allowed to check all categories that apply, but then the question actually becomes a series of yes/no questions with each response category being scored later as if it were a separate question. If it is not possible to have a complete list of possible answers, a partially open-ended question may be used.

Close-ended questions with ordered choices are common on questionnaires and are often similar to the individual items in a personality inventory or a summated attitude scale. These questions may in fact be single Likert-type items in which a statement is made and the respondent is asked to rate one or a series of items from strongly disagree to strongly agree. A number of other types of items with ordered choices are possible (see Salant & Dillman, 1994).

Interviews

Two main types of interviews are telephone and face-to-face. *Telephone interviews* are almost always structured and usually brief, that is, less than half an hour. This technique is commonly used by survey researchers to obtain a quick, geographically diverse or national sample. *Face-to-face interviews,* on the other hand, can vary from what amounts to a highly structured, oral questionnaire with close-ended answers to in-depth interviews, which are preferred by qualitative researchers who want to get detailed responses from the participants. Telephone and structured face-to-face interviews are usually coded on the spot. The categories are often close-ended so that the interviewer only needs to circle the chosen response or fill in a brief blank. In-depth interviews are usually tape-recorded and transcribed later so that the participant's comments can be coded later. All types of interviews are relatively expensive because of their one-to-one nature. In-depth interviews are even more expensive because of training, transcription, and coding costs.

Focus Groups

Focus groups are like interviews, but relatively small groups of 8 to 10 people are interviewed together. Such groups may stimulate peoples' thinking and elicit ideas about a specific topic. They have been used by businesses to learn how customers will react to new products, and have been used by political campaigns to test voter opinions about a topic. Nonprofit agencies may also use focus groups to identify the perceptions and ideas of potential or actual participants in a program or a service. Focus groups can provide an initial idea about what responses people will give to a certain type of question. This can be helpful in developing more structured questionnaires or interviews.

SUMMARY

This chapter provides an overview of many of the techniques used in the applied behavioral sciences to gather data from human participants. Most of the methods are used by both quantitative (positivist) and qualitative (constructivist) researchers but to different extents. Qualitative researchers also prefer more open-ended, less structured data collection techniques than do quantitative researchers, but this distinction is not absolute. Direct observation of participants by the researcher is common among experimental researchers and qualitative researchers; it is less common among so-called survey researchers who use self-report interviews and questionnaires extensively. It is important that investigators use instruments that are reliable and valid for the population and purpose for which they will be used. Standardized instruments have manuals providing norms and indexes of reliability and validity. However, if the populations and purposes on which these data are based are different from yours, it may be necessary for you to develop your own instrument or, at least, to provide new evidence of reliability and validity.

STUDY AIDS

Concepts

- Direct observation
- Focus group

- Naturalness of the setting
- Participant observation
- Performance and authentic assessment
- Reliability and validity of the measures
- Semantic differential scales
- Standardized tests
- Standardized personality inventories
- Summated (Likert) attitude scales

Distinctions

- Achievement tests versus aptitude tests
- Data collection techniques (methods) versus research approaches
- Norm referenced versus criterion referenced tests
- Open-ended versus closed-ended questions
- Questionnaire question or item versus research question
- Questionnaire versus interview
- Researcher report measures versus self-report or participant measures

Application Problems

1. A researcher designed a measure of work satisfaction. Part of this measure is included below.

Shown below are pairs of words that indicate how people feel about their work. Consider each of the word pairs and circle the number that best indicates how you feel about your job-work in general.

Boring	1	2	3	4	5	6	7	Interesting
Enjoyable	1	2	3	4	5	6	7	Miserable
Useless	1	2	3	4	5	6	7	Worthwhile

etc.

What kind of attitude scale is this? How would you score it if a person circled 5, 2, and 6?

2. Table 21.1 gives an approximation of how common each of the several data collection techniques are within each major grouping of research approaches. Why would physiological recordings be most common for experiments and quasi-experiments? Why would self-report measures be most commonly used with comparative, associational, and descriptive approaches? Why is it that standardized tests, summated attitude scales, and standard personality scales are unlikely to be used in qualitative research?

3. Indicate whether the following questions are open-ended, or partially open-ended, or close-ended ordered, or close-ended unordered items. Discuss the pros and cons of formatting questions as shown.

a. What is your date of birth? _____ .

b. Is there anyone for whom you provide special care due to illness, a handicap, or old age?

No_____

Yes_____

Please explain: _____

c. For which of the following areas of expenditure do you have the highest priority?

Defense _____

Education_____

Health and Welfare_____

Other. Please specify:_____

d. What type of work schedule best describes your work situation?

_____Standard full-time (8–5)

_____Flexible work hours

_____Compressed week

e. Which best describes the kind of building in which you live?

_____A mobile home

_____A one-family house detached from any other

_____A one-family house attached to at least one other house

_____An apartment building

f. Please describe the qualities of your favorite teacher.

4. Your colleague is interested in learning if parenting style influences adolescent delinquency. He asks for your opinion about whether he should use a questionnaire or interview format to collect his data. What do you tell him are the pros and cons of each?

5. A researcher is interested in the degree to which therapeutic alliance (or, the strength of the relationship between client and therapist) affects the therapeutic outcome (or, the success of therapy). If the researcher observes the sessions from behind a one-way mirror and rates therapeutic alliance on a Likert scale, what kind of measure is this? If the researcher asks the client to report their perception of alliance using a Likert scale, what kind of measure is this? What are the benefits and drawbacks of each?

6. What's the difference between a research question and a questionnaire or item? Provide two examples of each.

Steps in the Research Process: Practical and Ethical Issues

STEPS IN THE RESEARCH PROCESS

Throughout this book, we have been discussing the process of applied behavioral research. Now, we review these steps briefly with an emphasis on practical considerations and a discussion of a variety of ethical issues related to the various steps in the process of doing research.

Plan the Sample Selection

In chapter 10, we described the process of selecting a sample of potential participants from what is usually a much larger theoretical population. Several strategies for selecting the sample and several obstacles to obtaining a representative sample were discussed. We pointed out that external population validity depends on the representativeness of the accessible population and also on the representativeness of the actual sample of those participants who agreed to participate and completed the study.

Cooperating Agencies.   To obtain a broad and representative *accessible population*, it is often necessary to make arrangements with other agencies or institutions such as school districts or clinics. These organizations must be convinced of the importance and benefits of the research and that any potential risks are minimal. If it has an institutional review board (IRB), that IRB will need to review the project, or may decide to exempt it. If the organization does not have an IRB, a means to assure your own IRB that the project is acceptable to them is needed. For example, a person authorized to obligate the agency could write a letter to your IRB stating support for the project and the extent of any assistance. Developing and maintaining these contacts can be a time-consuming aspect of research that needs to be planned and budgeted. There are also ethical issues to be considered for collaborating agencies. What benefits will they and their students or clients gain? Will the agency benefit but the students or clients be exposed to a potential risk or loss of privacy? Your IRB will no doubt consider these issues and possible conflicts of interest.

A variant of this is what is called *brokered* data. In this case, the researcher lacks access to a given population and the broker (e.g., school principal or clinic director) may not allow the researcher to actually collect the data because of concern about privacy. The agency may be willing to collect the data for the researcher or at least to hand out anonymous questionnaires to their clients and ask them if they would be willing to respond. It is considered a breach of patient–provider confidentiality to allow an outside researcher full access to medical files or even a list of patients to contact directly. Contact or file review should be done by the health care provider or school. Because clinics and schools are busy, they may not have time to contact clients or review files. This has led to a fair amount of tension between the principles of recruitment ethics and the desire to obtain complete data and a representative sample. A low response rate and, likely, an unrepresentative sample will be created if the clinic or school announces the study and leaves it up to potential participants to contact the researcher.

Response Rate.   Another issue about response rate is the need to balance obtaining a high response rate with respect for persons who decide not to take part. It is acceptable to try to convince potential participants of the importance and value of their contribution; you may remind them that they forgot to answer a mailed survey. You can also offer incentives, but you must stop before becoming coercive or offensive. This may especially be a problem with telephone surveys, in part because hired interviewers may go too far unless properly trained. Remember that well-constructed short questionnaires are more likely to be responded to than poorly worded, long, or open-ended ones.

Dropouts.   In multisession and longitudinal research, there is the additional issue of maintaining the consent and cooperation of the participants. In these kinds of research, it is important that participants do not drop out of the study unnecessarily. Any coercion to continue is unacceptable. Therefore, develop-

ing good rapport and maintaining good sensitive relationships with the participants and their needs will often forestall such dropouts. If the participants are
to be rewarded for their participation, it may be possible to arrange prorated
payments toward the end of the study so that its completion is rewarded. However, the IRB will have to approve any such arrangements and they must not
seem coercive or unfair to participants who desire to leave the study midway.

Plan the Design and Analysis

It is important to carefully plan the research design and also the data analysis
before data collection begins. Statisticians are frequently frustrated when an
inexperienced researcher comes to them with a pile of data and asks for it to be
analyzed. All too often the design or instruments were not carefully planned
and, thus, the appropriate analysis cannot be performed.

On the other hand, qualitative researchers say that their design is emergent
rather than preplanned. We believe that this apparent dichotomy between qualitative and quantitative research paradigms is relative, more one of degree than
absolute. Qualitative researchers need to have a good idea about their research
questions and at least a good indication of the literature related to those questions. They would be unwise to embark on a major study without a good idea
about how they were going to analyze the data. It is true that after doing a few
interviews or observations they may discover that their original research questions were not the most interesting or did not elicit the information they sought.
Then they may decide to reformulate the questions to ask future participants.
This is also true, to a lesser extent, of quantitative research. All good research
should begin with pilot testing to ensure that the design and instruments are appropriate and will work well to answer the research questions. If it is discovered that the procedures or questions are not the most appropriate, a new
sample to assess the new questions should be obtained.

Deception.   Certain ethical issues are more likely to arise with some types of
design than with others. For example, deception is more likely to occur in experimental research, but, as we saw in chapter 3 (Humphreys, 1970), there can
be deception in qualitative and survey research if the participants are not fully
informed of the researcher's purposes and procedures. Deception involves a
misrepresentation of facts by commission, which occurs when the researcher
gives false information about the study. If the investigator does not fully inform the subjects about the important aspects of the study or its goals, omission or concealment has occurred.

Until recent years, social psychological research relied heavily on deception on the premise that information about certain topics, such as conformity or
obedience, would be unobtainable without deception because of participants'
defensiveness, embarrassment, or fear of reprisal. We discussed, in chapter 3,
the Milgram (1974) studies on obedience. There would be two problems with
repeating that research today. First, it's now typical for research participants,
especially college students, to assume that deception will occur and for them to
alter their behavior based on that assumption. Second, IRBs probably would
not allow it because deception should not involve participants in ways that they

would find unacceptable. Sieber (1992) states that "An indefensible rationale for deception is to trick people into research participation that they would have found unacceptable if they correctly understood it" (p. 64). IRBs emphasize truly informed consent and respect for autonomy.

Deception is allowable under certain circumstances but is restricted by IRBs recently. Are there alternatives to deception in research? Simulations, which are mock situations, are being used effectively to explore social behavior. Ethnographic or participant observation methods are used increasingly to study real behavior, often in a community-based setting. Ethical and practical considerations have led such researchers to provide fully informed consent procedures and to rely on rapport and trust rather than cleverness or deception as was the case in the Milgram (1974) obedience studies and the Humphreys (1970) tearoom sex study described in chapter 3. Also, the participants may be asked to consent to the researcher concealing important parts of the procedure. There is now evidence that most subjects will participate in research with the understanding that some details must be withheld until after the study. Of course, they are guaranteed a full debriefing. Often, after the debriefing, participants are offered an opportunity to withdraw their data from the study. If the participants trust the researcher to keep their data confidential, few are likely to withdraw at this point.

There are deep differences among the members of the research community about the ethics of deception. Some are strongly against it and others believe that it is the only viable way to study certain types of social behavior. Sieber (1992) makes two points on which she hopes all can agree. First, some important behaviors vanish under obvious scrutiny, and, thus, concealment or deception is sometimes necessary. Second, the more objectionable forms of deception are unnecessary and do not need to be used.

Debriefing.   Debriefing is a good practice for most studies and is almost always necessary for deception studies. In addition to discussing the goals of the study and reasons for the deception, it is desirable to provide evidence about the deception. In the case of false feedback about test performance, participants could be given their own unscored tests in a sealed envelope just as they had submitted them. It is important to try to eliminate any residue of generalized mistrust on the part of the participants. If the researcher detects any undesirable emotional results of the research, he or she should attempt to restore participants to a frame of mind at least as positive as that with which they entered the study.

However, there are certain cases where it might be better not to dehoax or debrief the participant because it may be harmful. For example, if a researcher were to study dishonesty, it may be better not to point out to participants that their behavior during the study was dishonest. At any rate, debriefing should be done without demeaning the participants' behavior or attitudes.

Experimental Research.   It is the nature of experimental designs (randomized experimental and quasi-experimental approaches) that some or all of the participants are given an intervention or treatment that may be medical, psychological, or educational. With these interventions, there is always the possibility of potential harm. Physical harm is much more likely with medical interventions than with educational or psychological interventions, but less tangible harm is possible with all interventions. For example, the participants in the new curriculum group may learn less than they would have if they had stayed in the traditional curriculum. Or certain kinds of training may require the participants in the intervention group to be more open and self-disclosing than they might otherwise prefer. If there is potential risk of harm as a result of the intervention, it should be as minor, reversible, of short duration, and negated as possible.

We have hinted at difficult issues about the control group in earlier chapters about experimental designs. For example, if a new treatment is found to be highly advantageous, it may be unethical to withhold it from the control group. It would be desirable to offer it to the control group. In some cases, this can be done by having a wait-list control group that receives the treatment after a period of delay presumably equal to the time that the intervention group was given the treatment. It may be necessary for an investigator to budget the costs of providing treatment to the control group at a later date.

In earlier chapters, we discussed the design advantages of having a no intervention or placebo control group. If a placebo control group were used, a "natural state argument" would need to be made to the IRB. The reasoning is that untreated participants are not being denied a benefit they already have, but are merely being left in their natural state. This argument is severely undercut if the control group has a disease or has come in for and does not receive treatment.

Nonexperimental and Qualitative Research.   As mentioned earlier, ethical problems are not confined to experimental research. For example, survey research has potential ethical issues related to coercing subjects to participate. In addition, certain types of information obtained from surveys could distress participants and be detrimental to them if they were identified by their employers or by other persons with power. So care must be taken. This issue applies to qualitative research as well. In fact, long quotes gathered in qualitative studies may be identifiable because they may include unique or personal information recognizable by others. In these cases, such information would have to be altered or deleted from the research report.

Animal Research.   There is a separate set of issues related to research with nonhuman animals. Because this book deals almost exclusively with human research, we only discuss animal research here briefly. It is important to note that the National Institutes of Health has published information about appropriate use of animals in research, and most universities have a separate IRB to consider use of animals in research. Principles in animal research involve: the training of the personnel conducting the research and handling the animals, the nature of the research and procedures, the facilities used to feed and house the animals, the methods used to transport them, and the justification for the number and species to be used. Clearly, experiments should be conducted in such a way as to avoid all unnecessary suffering and harm to the animals.

Select or Develop the Instruments

As discussed in the last chapter, it is necessary for a valid and ethical study to have high-quality data collection instruments. Therefore, selecting or developing instruments with strong evidence of reliability and validity data is both a practical and an ethical issue. In general, an inexperienced researcher should use already developed, standardized instruments whenever there are appropriate instruments available. Remember that reliability and validity do not reside in the instruments themselves, but in their use for certain purposes with certain types of participants. It may be necessary to question whether a commonly used instrument is appropriate if your population is an unusual or vulnerable one. Even well-established instruments should be pilot tested to be sure that the instrument is appropriate and does not raise ethical issues about privacy, for example.

Plan the Procedure for Data Collection

IRBs are sensitive to issues surrounding the procedure that is used for data collection. We have already discussed the issue of deception; it should be fully explained and justified if it is necessary. The procedure section of a proposal or a human research protocol should also describe the procedures that will be used to obtain consent from the participants. The IRB will want to see recruiting materials such as flyers or advertisements and also cover letters to be used as part of questionnaire research. If the participants are seen face-to-face or on the telephone, the IRB may want to see a copy of the script that you plan to use to introduce the project and inform participants about the procedures.

When planning the procedures for data collection, consider tokens of appreciation such as a toy for children or a pencil or a dollar for other participants. Such inducements are designed to increase the response rate, as are payments to participants.

Confidentiality. An important part of the procedure is to plan for ensuring confidentiality for each participant. This is a two part issue: a) only those on the research team can match the participants' identities with their response, if that is necessary, and b) the identity of specific participants, if known, is not revealed. This proscription applies not just to written reports but also means that the team will not talk about specific participants in public, for example, in the restroom, lunchroom, or hall. Focus groups pose special confidentiality problems because even though the researcher cautions other participants in the group about confidentiality, they may not heed it.

Confidentiality also may be important for the groups (e.g., school, hospital, company) from which the sample is drawn. It is common practice and often necessary that the identity of such groups be disguised in a report. In fact, some Native American tribes require that they only be referred to by general geographic region to avoid stigmatizing tribal members.

Usually the issue of confidentiality arises when the researcher is aware of the participants' identities and has agreed to keep them confidential. Certain procedures eliminate or minimize the link between identifiers and the data and, therefore, help to assure confidentiality. For example, one can assure that participants' names are not put on transcriptions of audiotape recordings, questionnaires, or data forms. Participants can be identified by a code (not their social security numbers) that is kept locked in a different place from the data. If vignettes or other descriptions are provided in a write-up, characteristics such as occupation, city, ethnic background, and so on should be changed. Audio or videotapes should be stored in a locked place and only viewed in places that provide privacy from unintended visitors. Tapes and master lists of names can be destroyed after the report has been accepted for publication or the thesis approved. The methods used to preserve confidentiality should be identified in the consent process so that the prospective participants can be assured that information will be kept confidential.

In cases where the research data are anonymous to the investigators, the issue is different. For example, if demographic or other potentially identifying data are obtained from an anonymous survey, the researcher needs to be careful that results are not presented in a way that someone familiar with the institutions from which participants were drawn would be able to deduce the identity of participants. For example, if a company had only one or a few minority workers, the confidentiality of their responses would be jeopardized if the average of their responses was presented in a report. Ensuring that the report does not unintentionally reveal identities is, of course, important in all research.

Obtain Approval from Institutional Review Board

IRBs and How They Work.   An institutional review board or human subjects committee is a committee that reviews proposals for studies with human participants before the research can begin. Sieber's (1992) book, *Planning Ethically Responsible Research: A Guide For Students and Internal Review Boards,* is a helpful guide on which we have based much of this section. The committee is mandated by federal regulations to protect human subjects and to decide whether the research plan has adequately dealt with ethical issues related to the project. IRBs were the result of the kinds of ethical problems that we mentioned in chapter 3. They consist of five or more members who have varying backgrounds; they include members of the broader community as well as scholars from a variety of areas within the university or research institution. The committee meets periodically, often monthly, to review research protocols for projects proposed by scholars and students at the institution.

All research at the institution that systematically collects data and is intended to develop generalizable knowledge must be reviewed, unless it meets the exemption criteria that some institutions allow. In practice, this means that any research project that is intended to be published in a journal or book, or, as a dissertation or thesis must be reviewed. Data gathered for administrative purposes and classroom demonstrations are not reviewed. Many institutions do not review research done for courses that is not intended to be published, but the instructor and student should follow the ethical principals described in this and chapter 3. The government also allows certain types of research, for example, anonymous questionnaires on noncontroversial topics and research dealing with methods of instruction in schools, to be exempt. However, many university IRBs require that all research be submitted to them and then they decide whether it will be exempt. Often, exempt status only means that there is a less intensive review, which will not have to wait until the next committee meeting, but the research protocol and periodic reports on progress may be required.

Usually *pilot testing,* which involves trying out procedures or fine-tuning a questionnaire with a few acquaintances or knowledgeable persons in the field does not require IRB review. However, *pilot studies* in which formal data are collected and analyzed do require IRB review.

IRBs have been controversial with some researchers who view them as obstacles to good scientific research. This is partly due to pressures to meet deadlines, which can lead to miscommunication and misunderstandings. It also might be due to an IRB that does not provide helpful assistance to researchers. The federal regulations require institutions to develop policies in keeping with the regulations, but which reflect community standards. Thus, it is likely that each institution may have different policies and could make different decisions about the same protocol. For these reasons, it is desirable for students to discuss their research with knowledgeable people at their institution, such as experts in the content area or other researchers, to be aware of potential ethical issues. It is also desirable to talk with people about the procedures of the local IRB and whether feedback can be obtained in advance. This may save considerable time and frustration. Students should be aware of policies and procedures of the IRB at their university. Often the administrator of the board is willing to discuss a project with the researcher before the protocol is submitted.

The Research Protocol.   The research protocol is a short version of your research proposal focusing on the research problem or objectives, the participants, procedures to be followed, risks, benefits, consent procedures, and confidentiality. The IRB probably will provide a detailed list of questions that they want to have answered as part of the protocol. Usually brief but specific answers to these questions will be the text of the protocol. Although some of the answers may be condensed versions of your proposal, others (e.g., statements of risks and benefits) may have to be expanded from what you have in your proposal. In addition, you will probably have to include several of the following attachments:

- Advertisements or posters
- Telephone scripts or other recruitment scripts
- Consent forms, including parental permission and child assent, or cover letters if written consent is not required. Most IRBs have a sample consent form, which indicates necessary and suggested wording
- Letter(s) of agreement or an IRB approval from cooperating organizations, perhaps on their letterhead with original signatures
- Instruments (evidence of permission for use may be required if the instrument is copyrighted)
- Debriefing materials
- Principal investigator's résumé
- A copy of the full research proposal or at least the method section

The protocol and attachments are submitted to the IRB for their consideration and, one hopes, approval. The protocol should remind the researcher of the elements that are essential to scientifically and ethically sound research.

Institutions are legally responsible for research conducted by faculty and students, and so are the researchers and advisors. Thus the protocol must reflect what is actually done in the research. If the researcher decides to change the procedure or the instruments, approval must be obtained from the IRB.

In addition to a complete discussion of the risks and benefits, including inducements, and an analysis of the risk/benefit ratio, there should be a complete discussion of the characteristics of the participants and the consent and confidentiality procedures. In terms of the participants, information about their ethnic background, gender, age, and state of health should be given and, if vulnerable populations are included, their use should be justified. If cooperating organizations or institutions are used to obtain participants, written approval must be obtained. It is desirable to provide a rationale for the number of participants to be included by using an analysis of power, as discussed in chapter 23.

The consent procedures and methods used to assure confidentiality need to be described in the protocol. The procedures should indicate how, where, and by whom informed consent will be negotiated and how debriefing will be conducted. The actual consent form should be attached to the protocol. If consent is implied by returning a mailed questionnaire or it is verbal, as in the case of a telephone interview, the cover letter or script detailing the procedures must be provided.

Potential Problems With Research Protocols.   Sieber (1992) discusses a number of problems that IRBs have encountered, and she provides tips on how to overcome them. Sometimes students or inexperienced researchers will not have adequate help in preparing the protocol. If that is your case, you should consult other experienced researchers, or the IRB administrator, or both. Watch for training classes that the institution might provide, and check other informational resources such as the IRB Web page.

Some protocols devote much space to the importance of the research but fail to describe the methods and procedures in enough detail or specificity. For example, the sampling procedure needs to be outlined clearly, as does the research design and the location of the research.

Some researchers play down or ignore risks that the IRB may identify. In addition to physical risks, there can be risks to employment, advancement, reputation, and financial standing. Emotional distress also can be a significant risk. Researchers need to be clear that they are sensitive to the issues of coercion and what is called dual-role relationships, when a researcher is also the teacher or supervisor of the potential participants. The researcher, whose intention is to help persons with a problem or handicap by using an intervention, also needs to be sensitive to the possibility that identifying them as participants in the intervention may in fact stigmatize them. Every effort should be made to be sensitive to this sort of situation and to insure the privacy of such individuals.

Collect, Analyze, and Interpret the Data

As with the other steps in the research process, a number of ethical issues arise during the data collection and analysis phases of research. Some of them involve the treatment of participants and have already been discussed, for example, sensitivity to participants' privacy concerns, confidentiality, and debriefing. Another set of ethical issues has to do with the integrity of the data collection, recording, and analysis. We turn now to these issues.

Integrity of the Data.   It should be obvious, as stated in *the Publication Manual of the American Psychological Association* (APA, 1994), that researchers "do not fabricate data or falsify results in their publications" (p. 293). And, if researchers discover significant errors in their published data, they correct them. Unfortunately, such scientific misconduct has occurred too often. Altman and Hernon (1997) describe over 60 publicly discussed cases of publications that involved fabricated, falsified, or plagiarized data. Altman and Hernon state that they discuss only a fraction of the cases in which scientific misconduct was determined. They note that although medicine has most cases, the problem is spread across many disciplines, including psychology, history, and chemistry, and that whole issues of journals in sociology, business, and medicine have been devoted to misconduct and professional ethics.

Fabrication (making up the data or results) and falsification (changing data or results) are clearly unacceptable but, one hopes, relatively rare. However, there are other behaviors that may result from carelessness, bias, or an unwise decision; these behaviors cause problems for the integrity of the data and the inferences that can be made. Some error in observing, recording, and entering data may be an inevitable by-product of using humans (versus electronic recording devices) in these roles, but good research minimizes such errors. Careful training of observers and other assistants can help. Checking data to be sure they are recorded and entered correctly can help as, in some cases, can the use of computers to reduce possible errors in transcribing data. Thus, carefulness is as important as honesty if the collected data are to be meaningful.

Qualitative researchers have argued, as discussed in chapter 2, Axiom 5, that inquiry is always value laden and is never completely objective. Thus, the perspectives that one brings to the research are bound to influence not only the selection of the problems, variables, and methods used, but also the coding or categorization of the data and how they are interpreted. Although this is true, much can and should be done to minimize the effects of the researcher's biases. First, one can acknowledge biases and try to figure out how they might influence the data collection, coding, and analysis. Checking the reliability of coding is desirable but not enough, especially if the other coders have similar biases or were trained by the researcher. Again, care to minimize the effects of avoidable bias may be as important as honesty for good research.

There are many choices to be made in conducting research. Financial and other constraints result in necessary choices that weaken a study in some way and strengthen it in other ways. For example, there is almost always a trade-off between internal and external validity; that is, good control tends to make things artificial. However, researchers also make unnecessary bad choices, some of which are ethically questionable. Meltzoff (1997) provides several examples of bad decisions that might occur during the data collection phase of the study. One example is the investigator who eliminates participants from the study for unexplained reasons. As we discussed earlier, participants must be given permission to withdraw at any time, so that it is a valid reason for the data to be excluded. But, if participants do not perform in the expected manner, that is not a valid reason. Another example would be changing the length of the study or overruling supposedly independent raters. Any such changes need to be justified and should not be caused by the data turning out the "wrong" way.

Integrity of Data Analysis.   A portion of this book has been about appropriate use and interpretation of statistics. It is important to point out that there are many legitimate disagreements among statisticians and researchers. We have noted some of these differences in earlier chapters. Clearly, altering the data or deliberately reporting an incorrect *p* value is unethical. We also have pointed out a number of things a researcher might do in analysis or interpretation that are wrong but not unethical, unless done to deceive deliberately. For example, using an inappropriate statistic, such as a *t* test, with a three or more category nominal dependent variable is wrong. Many other choices about statistics are not the best practice, often because the researcher is relatively inexperienced or unknowledgeable about statistics. For example, not testing for assumptions could lead to the wrong conclusions if the assumptions were markedly violated.

In other cases, reports of data analysis may at least raise suspicions of unethical behavior. Meltzoff (1997) provides several examples. One is the case in which participants seem to be divided arbitrarily after the fact into groups (such as high and low) when there was a continuous independent variable. Did the researcher try many cutoff points until finding one that was statistically significant? This concern is one reason we recommend using a correlation when the independent variable is continuous or has many ordered categories.

Many statisticians think that null hypothesis significance testing (NHST) is only appropriate when the researcher has one or a few well thought out hypotheses to test. They are skeptical of a study with many significance tests. However, most would support exploratory data analysis, without NHST (see Tukey, 1977).

Interpretation of the Results.   Authors need to be careful, in writing their results and discussion sections, to avoid distorting the findings or their implications. For example, in earlier chapters we discussed the mistake of inferring causation from comparative, associational, or even quasi-experimental studies. Therefore, care should be taken not to state that the independent variable "caused," "determined," or "impacted" the dependent variable unless the study was a well-controlled randomized experiment. In discussing results from nonexperimental studies, these terms should not be used or should only be used with qualifiers such as "may cause," or "appear to influence." Likewise, one should be careful about generalizations to broader populations from samples that may be unrepresentative of the population.

Disseminate the Results

Publishing is an essential part of the research process, which is not complete until the results are disseminated to other interested researchers. Publishing is the means by which the results are made public. Considerable detail is provided in the publication about the procedures and data analyses. This makes the researcher's work available for scrutiny by the scholarly community. This public scrutiny helps make science objective and is one reason why publishing is so important. Publications are also an important factor in the career of a researcher. They are used to evaluate the capability and performance of the researcher or professor, and are an important aspect of tenure and promotion at a university. Therefore, there is considerable pressure, especially on young faculty, which leads to a number of potential ethical problems.

Plagiarism.   Plagiarism is presenting a substantial portion of the work of another as if it were one's own. Paraphrasing, which involves summarizing and rearranging sentences, is acceptable if credit is given in the text. Plagiarism refers not just to words but also to the ideas and data of another person. Because literature reviews and textbooks are based heavily on the work of others, it is difficult to provide appropriate credit without overusing quotations. Also, it is often hard to know exactly which thoughts came from which source. Inexperienced writers and those for whom English is not their first language find it especially challenging to paraphrase because the original author may appear to have written things in the "best" way.

Multiple Publications.   The American Psychological Association's ethical principles (APA, 1992) states that researchers "do not publish, as original data, data that have been previously published. This does not preclude republishing data when they are accompanied by proper acknowledgment" APA, 1994 (p. 293). The APA publication manual (APA, 1994) goes on to say that duplicate publication distorts the knowledge base and wastes scarce resources, that is, journal pages. Authors must not submit to a journal a manuscript that has already been published in substantially the same form. Manuscripts previously included in the ERIC (Education Resources Information Centers) system, published as an abstract or summary, or circulated as a university or limited circulation document can be published in full later. However, manuscripts published in full in proceedings or in book chapters should not be published later in a journal. There is always an issue about how similar the current manuscript is to the original and the similarity of the audience. It is not uncommon, but perhaps ethically questionable, for researchers to rewrite a paper for a journal with a different audience. Journal articles are sometimes revised for publication as a chapter in a book. This is acceptable as long as the original source is cited and permission to adapt or reprint is obtained from the copyright holder. Problems of duplicate publication also may arise if the material is first published on the Internet or through the mass media.

Articles must not be submitted to more than one journal at a time. Only after rejection or withdrawal of the manuscript is it appropriate to submit the same article to another journal. The APA publication manual (APA, 1994) states:

the author must inform an editor of the existence of any similar manuscripts that have already been published or accepted for publication or that may be submitted for concurrent consideration to the same journal or elsewhere. The editor can then make an informed judgment as to whether the submitted manuscript includes sufficient new information to warrant consideration. (p. 296)

It is common, but in some ways undesirable, for several substantively different articles to be published from the same dissertation or large study. Pressures on authors to have a large number of publications and limitations by editors on space often lead to multiple publications from one study.

Authorship.   There has been considerable discussion in recent years about who should be listed as an author and even whether the whole concept of authorship should be scrapped in favor of some other system. For example, Rennie, Yank, and Emanuel (1997) have proposed that instead of authors each article provide a list of contributors indicating their specific contribution(s), for example, designed the statistical analyses, conceptualized the design, wrote the results and discussion. Part of the reason for this proposal is to identify responsibility or accountability for parts of the article. Another reason is that there have been disagreements about who should be an author and in what order.

A general, but not universally, agreed on policy is that authorship is reserved for those who make a substantial professional contribution to the study, and that order of authorship should be determined by the importance of their contribution. The APA publication manual (APA, 1994) states that "substantial professional contributions may include formulating the problem or hypothesis, structuring the experimental design, organizing and conducting the statistical analysis, interpreting the results, or writing a major portion of the paper" (p. 294). The manual goes on to say that lesser contributions, which may be acknowledged, include supporting functions such as designing the apparatus, conducting the statistical analysis, collecting or entering data, and recruiting participants. Note that these latter contributions are often those of undergraduate or graduate student volunteers or paid assistants, who may think that they deserve authorship.

Two types of problems result when determining authorship. On the one hand there are "guest" authors such as lab directors or colleagues who "need" another publication. They are persons who have not made a significant professional contribution to the project but are given authorship as a favor or as a "right" as a result of their status in a department or laboratory, or because with their names on an article the probability of acceptance is increased. On the other hand, there are "ghost" authors who did make a significant professional contribution but were not included as authors. These include junior researchers and students. Sometimes persons in power simply take advantage of less powerful or departed colleagues or students. However, the issues are not always clear. Often difficulties arise when a person loses interest or leaves the area after playing an important part in the initial aspects of the study. Perhaps the person even wrote a thesis that, in retrospect, turns out to be an early draft of the final accepted paper. The issue is what kind of credit should be given to such a person when an article is rejected, reanalyzed, and fully rewritten without the assistance of the initial contributor.

Fine and Kurdek (1993) present a number of examples of issues that can arise when faculty and students collaborate on research. The situation is frequently similar to the example in the previous paragraph; that is, the student's thesis or draft article is not adequate for publication, so the faculty member must revise it extensively. In general, we think that if an article is based on a student's thesis or dissertation, the student should definitely be an author, even if he or she does not participate in the revisions.[1] In most cases, *we* think the student should be the first author. However, Fine and Kurdek provide several examples in which they think it may not be appropriate for students to be the first author because they lost interest in the project and it was up to the advisor to reanalyze and rewrite the paper or to collect new data to make it publishable. Some scholars think that not taking the lead in writing up a dissertation for publication is indicative of poor scholarship on the part of the student and the paper should not be published.

Another issue is whether the faculty advisor should be co-author on a publication from a student's dissertation or thesis. The answer, it seems to us, is not unless the advisor made a significant contribution to the design of the study or to the writing of the final article. Reading and providing extensive feedback on a thesis or dissertation is what is expected of a faculty member and is not sufficient for authorship.

A good practice is for the collaborators to meet at the beginning of the project and agree on who should be authors and the order of authorship. It is also necessary for these authors to keep in contact and to renegotiate authorship if the circumstances change significantly. Each person's contribution should be documented and updated as necessary (see Rennie et al., 1997).

Finally, there are two other issues related to authorship. First, their consent should always be obtained before including someone as an author or, according to the APA publication manual (1994), even before including them in a note of acknowledgment. As a general rule, this recommendation seems extreme to us, but if it is stated or implied that the acknowledged person agrees with or supports the conclusions, their consent should surely be obtained. Second, all authors should review the manuscript before it is submitted because their names as authors imply that they take responsibility for the article. Some editors require that, when a paper is accepted, each author must sign a form accepting responsibility. However, with multiple authored articles it is probably unrealistic to assume that all authors are knowledgeable and should be responsible for all aspects of the paper. This was one of the reasons for the proposal by Rennie et al. (1997) to list specific contributions rather than authors.

Citing Publications in Your Résumé.   Students sometimes ask when and how to cite research papers in their curriculum vitae (C.V.) or résumé. This is an im-

---

[1]Note that the APA publication manual (APA, 1994) states that all authors should read and approve the final manuscript and accept responsibility for it. This could be difficult if the professor has lost contact with the student.

portant issue because incomplete citations can lead to concerns about sophistication and inaccurate citations can lead to accusations of misconduct. For the exact format of citations, you should consult the publication manual used in your discipline (e.g., APA, 1994). If there isn't such a manual, the format used by journals in your field is a good model to emulate. In all fields it is important to list all of the authors in the order that they appear in the publication, the date of publication, the exact title of the article, the publication title (if the article appears in a book or journal), the volume, if any, and the page numbers.

OTHER PRACTICAL AND ETHICAL ISSUES

Reviews and Reviewers

Most grant proposals and proposed journal articles are reviewed by peers who must be careful not to use the ideas of the original authors until they are published and then give them credit. Editors and reviewers must not quote proposals they have reviewed unless given explicit permission by the author.

The process requires a good deal of trust and integrity by the reviewers for it to work fairly and not be exploitative. Problems related to fairness of reviews are relatively common and most funding agencies and journals have specific policies to deal with them. Usually reviewers' identities are not revealed to the authors on the assumption that this will make reviews more candid and negative reviews less open to reprisal. However, on the other hand, others have argued that reviews might be more responsible and measured if the identity of the reviewer was known. In fact, in small fields, applicants can often guess the identity of the reviewer. A masked, formerly called blind, review occurs when the author's identity is not given to the reviewer. Information about the authors is removed from the manuscript. This type of review is common for manuscripts but is unusual for grant proposals. The argument for anonymous or masked review is that it gives a better chance to a new scholar because the work is judged solely on its merits rather than on the status of the authors. Again, in small fields, it may not be possible to disguise the manuscripts of well known researchers.

Once an article or book is published, a different kind of review takes place, not just in published book reviews but also in literature reviews and meta-analyses (see chap. 23). In meta-analyses, the reviewers often exclude studies judged not to be of high quality, even though published. Or the reviewer may decide to weight studies in terms of their merit, so some count more than others. Although these practices are a necessary part of the scientific process, they provide the opportunity for potential abuse and, at the least, hurt feelings.

Conflicts of Interest

Although scholars do their research for a variety of reasons, including curiosity and altruism, other factors, such as fame, fortune, and tenure are also motivators for doing research. A problem occurs when there is a real or apparent conflict between personal gain and obligations to the university or scientific community. One type of conflict is related to competition among scholars.

This could lead to reviewers treating their competitors unfairly or to the withholding of information from colleagues. Because originality and priority are so important, there is often an inherent conflict of interest that may restrict collaboration and cooperation. On the other hand, it is usually considered a conflict of interest to review grants or papers from close colleagues or persons from the same institution because of potential loyalty. Conflicts of interest are of concern in the writing stage as well as in earlier stages of the research and should be acknowledged. For example, if research on the effects or value of a product is funded by the producer of that product, the funding should be acknowledged in the notes to the article.

Conflicts of interest are not the same as misconduct but the latter can result from unacknowledged conflicts of interest, which need to be recognized and disclosed. The researcher needs to balance the priorities of collaboration and the search for truth with potential conflicts from personal gain, loyalty, and funding. Conflicts of interest are inevitable and not inherently bad, but not disclosing them is a problem. Even the appearance of conflicts should be disclosed.

Misconduct and the Structure of Science

In a controversial article, Woodward and Goodstein (1996), professors of philosophy and physics, make the argument that "many plausible-sounding rules for defining ethical conduct might be destructive to the aims of scientific inquiry" (p. 479). Examples of the types of plausible ethical principles or rules that they argue should not govern the behavior of scientists are as follows: scientists should never be motivated by personal gain, never believe dogmatically in an idea nor use exaggeration in promoting it, and scientists must lean over backwards to point out evidence contrary to their hypothesis. They ask the question of how fraud can be reduced without losing the positive effects of competition and reward.

Woodward and Goodstein (1996) argue that a certain amount of exaggeration of the value of one's approach and neglecting or playing down of contrary evidence may be necessary, especially in the early stages of a project. This is what psychologists call *belief-perseverance*. Given this, Woodward and Goodstein say that "an implicit code of conduct that encourages scientists to be a bit dogmatic and permits a certain measure of exaggeration…and that does not require an exhaustive discussion of its deficiencies may be perfectly sensible" (p. 485). They argue that part of the responsibility of scientists is to provide the best possible case for their ideas. It is up to others to point out defects and limitations. Woodward and Goodstein state that this is, in fact, what most scientists do. There are, of course, real limits here, and "exaggeration" is probably not the best word. Advocacy is appropriate, but any factual misstatement is unethical.

The typical research paper looks as if the writers had a much clearer conceptualization of the problem and results than is actually the case. Various blind alleys usually are not in the final publication. Although this may appear to be deceptive to the uninitiated and is clearly not in agreement with the principle of leaning over backwards to point out contrary evidence, "Nevertheless, the practice is virtually universal, because it is a much more efficient means of transmitting results than an accurate historical account" (Woodward & Goodstein, 1996, p. 488). Again, although a research report does not have to be historically accurate, it must not distort the results by leaving out important negative results or misstating what was found.

Woodward and Goodstein (1996) conclude by stating that they think each of the 15 reasonable-sounding principles or rules they listed is defective as a universal rule of scientific conduct. However, that "does not mean that it is impossible to recognize distinctive scientific misconduct" (p. 489). There is a difference between scientific misconduct and other types of misconduct, such as stealing or plagiarism that are serious misdeeds, which have established procedures for dealing with them. They argue that the types of misconduct that are specifically scientific misconduct require that a panel of peers assess the issue. Sometimes the issue involves stepping over the line between advocacy and deception. Fabrication and unwarranted manipulation of the data are examples of the kind of deception that cannot be tolerated. Expert judgment by peers is required to decide what types of data manipulation are unwarranted. The point here is that what may seem like simple, obvious rules about misconduct are often less clear in the specific case.

How is the student or new researcher to know what is acceptable advocacy and what crosses the line? We mentioned earlier in the sections on integrity of the data and in the analysis a few examples that appear to cross the line, as well as clear examples of misconduct. Peer judgment is required to decide whether a researcher's procedures for selecting particular participants or selectively discarding data are appropriate or involve misconduct. Junior researchers can learn about the complexities of appropriate behavior in their field best by observing and discussing issues with senior scholars or mentors in their field. However, you should be careful whom you emulate because, as pointed out in chapter 3 and earlier, not all senior researchers are good role models. We hope that this chapter has conveyed not only the complexity of the issues presented but also suggestions for action.

SUMMARY

This chapter extends the discussion in chapter 3 of ethical problems and principles. We moved step by step through the research process, discussing both practical and ethical issues that deal with sampling, planning the design and analysis, selecting instruments, planning the procedure, obtaining approval from the IRB, collecting and analyzing the data, and writing the report. In addition, we discussed issues about résumé citations, reviewers, conflicts of interest, and advocacy as contrasted to misconduct.

STUDY AIDS

Concepts

- Confidentiality
- Conflict of interest
- Consent forms
- Data fabrication and falsification
- Debriefing
- Deception
- Dropouts or attrition (also called experimental mortality)
- Ghost authors
- Guest authors
- IRB (Institutional Review Board)
- Masked (blind) review
- Multiple publications (of the same article)
- No intervention (or placebo group)
- Peer review
- Professional contribution (to a research project)
- Research protocol
- Response rate
- Scientific misconduct

Distinctions

- Confidential versus anonymous
- Pilot testing versus pilot studies
- Plagiarism versus paraphrasing

Application Problems

1. If you were writing a paper on data collection techniques and wanted to include the main idea from the following sentence from chapter 21 of this text, what are two ways that you might do so appropriately?

"The concern about the filtering of participants' answers through perhaps faulty memories or in terms of socially desirable responses has led quantitative researchers, especially those who tend to use the randomized experimental and quasi-experimental approaches, to be suspicious about the validity of self-report instruments." (p. 331–332)

2. A researcher has worked for several months to design her questionnaire, and wants to obtain feedback on the average time it takes to complete the questionnaire and if any questions are unclear. She asks several of her friends and colleagues to take the questionnaire, time themselves, and comment on anything that seemed unclear. What is this procedure called? Would the researcher be required to obtain Institutional Review Board (IRB) approval before giving the questionnaire to her friends and colleagues?

3. Another researcher wants to try her interview questions with teen parents who will not be in her study to assess the effectiveness of her interview questions. She recruits teen parents from her local community to interview. What is this called? Does this procedures require IRB approval?

4. A researcher interviewed individuals who had experienced a sexual assault. She assured her subjects that their identity would be kept confidential. How might she do this?

5. If a researcher wanted to assure participants that they would be anonymous, how might she collect her data?

6. Scientists are interested in the causes of violent behavior. Why do some individuals who appear to have experienced a normal childhood exhibit very violent behavior, with little or no remorse? The researchers hypothesized innate brain physiology differences. The warden agreed that all male prisoners from a high security prison in a southern state who had committed a violent crime and who had no evidence of childhood abuse or neglect would be included in the study. A demographically similar (age, ethnicity, family background, etc.) sample of males was selected from that state's population to serve as a comparison group, 40% of them agreed to participate (and were compensated $200). There were 28 individuals in the prisoner group and 30 in the non-criminal community group. Brain scans were done on all participants and then comparisons were made between the two groups.

    a. Discuss the ethical issues involved in the above study.

    b. Discuss population validity issues from the information provided.

    c. Discuss issues of ecological validity.

7. Bob has just completed a manuscript for publication. Although he had developed the rough outlines of the project on his own, he owes much to other individuals. The assistance he received includes the following:

    • A friend of his provided Bob with advice on how to obtain his sample.

    • The director of the stat lab gave Bob advice and also assisted in writing the results section.

    • A graduate student collected most of the structured interview data and did the computer data entry.

    a. What kind of attribution should be given to each of these individuals? For example, who should be recognized as an author and who should receive an acknowledgment in the paper? Who does not merit formal recognition? Explain.

    b. At what point in the process of one's research should decisions concerning authorship and acknowledgments be made?

    c. Are decisions concerning attribution entirely Bob's responsibility? Explain.

Research Validity, Replication, and Review

23

Research Validity
and Replication

TWO MORE DIMENSIONS OF RESEARCH VALIDITY

We now return to examine the last two dimensions of research validity. Remember research validity is the validity of a whole study in contrast to the validity of a single measure or instrument, which is what we discussed in chapter 20. In chapter 6 we discussed internal validity and in chapter 10 we discussed external validity, each with two main subdimensions and rating scales to use in evaluating the validity of a study.

MEASUREMENT RELIABILITY AND STATISTICS

Cook and Campbell (1979) called this dimension statistical conclusion validity, but we have modified the name to emphasize the importance of measurement reliability. We have concentrated on what we believe are the key issues. We think that there are four important *issues* underlying this dimension that students must keep in mind when designing or evaluating research. All of these issues should be considered when making the overall rating of this dimension a continuum from low through medium to high (see Fig. 23.1).

Reliability of Measures

The first issue is whether the variables (as a group) are measured reliably. A judgment is made based on the overall rating of the reliability of the instruments. A principle often emphasized in measurement classes is that a test or measure cannot be valid if it is not reliable. Likewise, a study's research validity is reduced considerably if one or more of the key variables is not measured reliably. Another consideration is whether several or all of the types of reliability were reported. Chapter 20 discussed measurement reliability in detail.

Appropriateness of Power

The Concept of Power.   Power from a statistical point of view relates to the probability of rejecting a false null hypothesis. Power implies a correct decision, so it should be maximized. In other words, if we set our alpha level at the

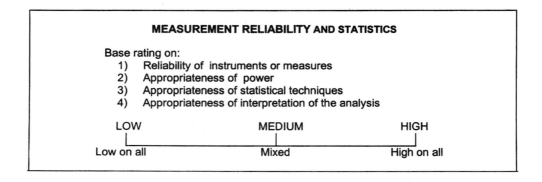

FIG. 23.1.   Evaluating the statistics and measurement reliability of the findings of a study.

conventional .05 or the less conventional .01, what is the probability of rejecting the null hypothesis, assuming it is false?

To get a better feel for this concept, study Fig. 23.2 (adapted from Loftus &
Loftus, 1982, p. 225). Figure 23.2 shows two normal curves representing the
population distribution if the null hypothesis (H_0) is true and the population distribution if the alternative hypothesis (H_1) is true (the null hypothesis is false).
The normal curve in the right of the figure, the population distribution assuming
that the null hypothesis is true, has an α level established at .05 or .01 (left tail of
this distribution). Remember that α is equal to the probability of a type I error, or
the probability of rejecting a true null hypothesis. Any outcome to the left of that
value (i.e., a t value exceeding the critical value established prior to the study)
will result in rejecting the null hypothesis and accepting the alternative hypothesis. Notice in the figure that at the cutoff point of $\alpha = .05$, the line is extended
through the alternative hypothesis distribution (the normal curve in the left of the
figure). The shaded area of the alternative hypothesis distribution (the normal
curve on the left) established by the cutoff point line at $\alpha = .05$ is the probability
of a type II error, or β (not rejecting the null hypothesis when it is false). The area
of the distribution of the alternative hypothesis that is *not shaded* is the probability of rejecting a false null hypothesis, or power $(1 - \beta)$. What most researchers
really want to know is how much power is in their study and how to increase
power. Ideally, power is set at a value of .80.[1]

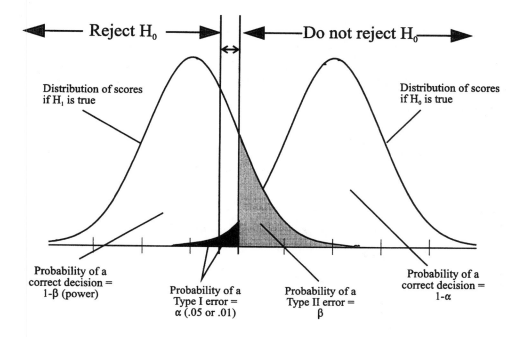

FIG. 23.2.   Relationships among α, β, and power. From Essence of Statistics (p. 225), by
G. R. Loftus and E. F. Loftus, 1982, Monterey, CA: Brooks/Cole. Adapted with permission.

---

[1]Keppel (1991) suggests that most methodologists in the behavioral sciences appear to agree on this
level of power, assuming that type I errors are more serious than type II errors. A value of .80 would yield a
type II error of .20, which is four times as large as a type I error of .05.

We can determine how much power $(1 - \beta)$ is present in a study by using power charts if we know the size of the sample, the significance level (α), and an estimate of the effect size of the study. For example, suppose a study is proposed to determine the effect of reform teaching on mathematics achievement in college students. A faculty member has volunteered to teach two different sections of linear algebra. She will teach one section in a reform manner and the other section in the traditional manner. The class size of the reform section is 24 students and the class size of the traditional section is 28 students. She sets her alpha level prior to the study at .05 for a directional hypothesis. Now she knows her sample size and alpha level. What is the estimated effect size of her study? Remember that earlier we discussed two different indices of effect size. Here we are interested in the effect size, d, in standard deviation units. We could estimate this effect size by using the following formula:

$$d = \frac{\overline{X}_1 - \overline{X}_c}{s_{pooled}} \ .$$

We would have to estimate both population means and the weighted average of the population standard deviation. Instead, the investigator can specify an effect size as small, medium, or large. For example, a small effect size would be around .2 standard deviations between the intervention and control means, a medium effect size would be around .5 standard deviations between the intervention and control means, and a large effect size would be about .8 standard deviations between the intervention and control means. How does the researcher know what effect size to estimate? The best estimate would be from previous studies in this area. If previous studies investigating the relationship between reform teaching and achievement demonstrate medium effect sizes, then an estimate of effect size for her study might be .5. Now that the researcher knows sample size, estimated effect size, and significance level for her study, she can use Fig. 23.3 to determine her power (from Lipsey, 1990). Notice that this particular power chart (Fig. 23.3) is for an independent t test with an α of .05 two-tailed (nondirectional hypothesis). On the X axis of Fig. 23.3 are the sample sizes for each group. Because our two groups are not equal, we will take the average of the two, which is 26. The closest value to 26 on the table is 25. We will use that as an estimate of our sample size in each group. On each of the curves is an effect size (ES). We locate the effect size curve of .5, the estimate of our predicted effect size. We find where the effect size curve of .5 crosses the sample size line of 25. At this point, we read the power on the Y axis. In our example, the power would be about .40. This is less than ideal power. How can the researcher increase power in her study?

How Can We Gain Power?   To increase power in our research situation, we need to decide which things we can control and which we cannot control. Control in this situation is relative rather than dichotomous. Our order of presentation of power is from what is usually least controllable to most controllable.

Our first element in gaining power is α. In Fig. 23.2 it can be seen that as alpha is set at a lower significance level, for example, .01 (the cutoff point is moved to the left), power is decreased. On the other hand, if α is set at a higher level, for example, .10, then power is increased. However, as we increase alpha, we also increase the probability of a type I error. More importantly, we really should not set alpha at a level higher than .05. The reason for this is mostly convention. Few research journals and, hence, our own colleagues will accept a research publication with alpha established higher than .05.

A second method to increase power involves formulation of hypotheses. Remember that when we use a t test, we have the option of formulating a directional or nondirectional hypothesis. Choice of a directional hypothesis will increase power because you are increasing the alpha level from, for example, .025 to .05. Similarly, when one has more than two groups in a single factor design, the option of using planned comparisons as opposed to a single factor analysis of variance is another way to increase power through the use of hypothesis formulation (see Keppel, 1991).

The next two elements important for increasing power can be clarified if we remember conceptually the formula for the t test. In the formula, variability between groups, referred to as treatment variance, is divided by variability within groups, referred to as error variance. If we decrease our error variance, and treatment variance remains the same, we will increase power.

One method of decreasing error variance and increasing power is to reduce the standard deviation, σ. Figure 23.4 (adapted from Shavelson, 1988, p. 301) demonstrates this concept. As you can see, reducing σ (right side of Fig. 23.4) changes the shape of the population distribution under the null and alternative hypothesis by making it narrower. If we reduce the value of the denominator

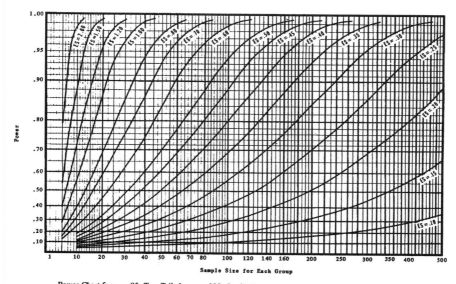

Power Chart for $\alpha = .05$, Two-Tailed or $\alpha = .025$, One-Tailed

FIG. 23.3.   Power table. From *Design Sensitivity: Statistical Power for Experimental Research* (p. 91), by M. W. Lipsey, 1990, Newbury Park, CA: Sage. Reprinted with permission.

(by reducing σ or *s*) in our *t* equation, and all other values remain the same, the value of *t* will increase. How do we decrease *s*? One strategy for decreasing *s* is to make sure that the groups are homogeneous. When working with special populations this is not always easy to achieve. For example, persons who have had cerebral vascular accidents are a very heterogeneous group. To reduce the heterogeneity of the participants, criteria need to be specified in advance. These criteria need to be relevant to the purpose of your study (e.g., Atler & Gliner, 1989; Dittmar & Gliner, 1987; Lafferty & Gliner, 1991).

A second strategy to decrease *s* is to make sure that the dependent measure has a high level of reliability. Whenever possible, use a measurement instrument that has been standardized and has shown evidence of good reliability. Measures that have low evidence of reliability increase within group variability, or *s*.

Finally, sample size is the element over which we have the most control toward increasing power. Again, an increase in sample size (*N*) reduces variability. Returning to our formula for *t*, the denominator involves dividing the standard error of the mean by the square root of the sample size, *N*. Therefore, the larger the value of *N*, the smaller the denominator will be. Returning to Fig. 23.3, our power chart, we can see that an increase in participants will increase power. If we double our sample size to 50 participants in each group, our power will be .70. It is important to remember all of the methods to increase power because there are many situations, such as program evaluations, where there are

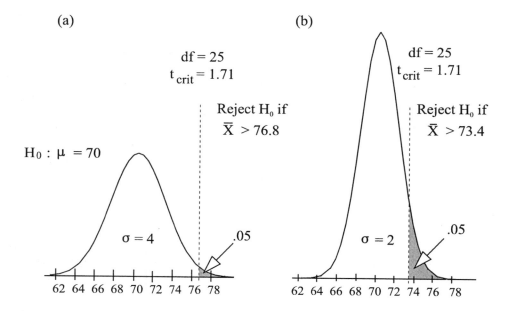

FIG. 23.4. Increasing power by decreasing variability. From *Statistical Reasoning For the Behavioral Sciences* (2nd ed.)(p. 301), by R. J. Shavelson, Copyright © 1988, Boston: Allyn and Bacon. Adapted with permission.

limits on obtaining participants. Also, there may be diminishing returns after a certain sample size is achieved.

Evaluating Power. The second issue in judging measurement reliability and statistics is whether power is appropriate. Power is the ability to detect a statistically significant difference or the ability to reject a false null hypothesis. We have defined power and discussed several methods of increasing power, but we focus here on sample size. A small sample may not produce enough power to detect a false null hypothesis, so it may be rated low on appropriateness of power. Cook and Campbell (1979) raise a second side to the issue of power that involves having too much power, especially with respect to the number of participants in a study. For the most part, the problem arises when an exceptionally large sample size (e.g., 1,000) yields a statistically significant, but very weak, relationship or a very small difference (i.e., one we can be almost certain was not due to chance but may lack practical importance).

Appropriateness of Statistical Techniques

A third issue underlying measurement reliability and statistics involves the selection of the proper statistical method to assess whether a relationship between the independent and dependent variable actually exists. In chapters 13 to 19, we examined in detail the appropriate choice of statistical procedures. We demonstrated different methods of selecting statistical procedures based primarily on the number of independent variables, the number of levels within the independent variable, the type of design, and the scale of measurement of the dependent variable. In addition, knowledge of assumptions underlying parametric analyses was also important for selection of alternatives to parametric statistics.

Sometimes researchers select the wrong statistic, such as a *t* test or a Pearson product–moment correlation with a nominal dependent variable. However, as Cook and Campbell (1979) pointed out, more often problems involve violation of assumptions underlying statistical tests or problems in making multiple comparisons without adjusting the alpha level. Such problems most often result in increasing the probability of making a type I error. Our own experience suggests that not adjusting the alpha level is more common than selection of an inappropriate statistic.

Appropriateness of Interpretation

The fourth issue underlying measurement reliability and statistics involves making the proper interpretation of the statistical analysis. Within each of our chapters on interpreting statistical methods (chap. 13–19), we spent time describing the proper interpretation of the results. Sometimes the correct statistic is selected, but the investigator misinterprets the findings, concluding more from the data than is actually given.

One common example is to interpret the results from a significant single factor ANOVA with at least three levels without performing the appropriate post hoc comparisons. Sometimes a conclusion follows that all groups or levels are significantly different from each other. A significant F implies only that there is a significant difference somewhere.

Failure to take into account the interaction effects and instead attending only to the main effects in a factorial ANOVA is a second example of improper interpretation of data analysis. Some researchers fail to acknowledge that in almost all factorial designs, a significant interaction between two independent variables almost always yields more information than results from either independent variable by itself.

The most common interpretation problem is the omission of an indication of the size of the effect. Most published studies have merely noted whether a result was statistically significant. As we discussed earlier, in the section of Appropriateness of Power, a statistically significant finding from a very large sample may be of little practical importance. A measure of effect size is necessary to know whether the effect was small, medium or large. Refer to chapter 11 or Cohen (1988) for a discussion of how to interpret size of the effect.

MEASUREMENT VALIDITY AND GENERALIZABILITY OF THE CONSTRUCTS

Cook and Campbell (1979) called this aspect of research validity *construct validity of putative causes and effects*, but we think that this label is confusing. What does *putative* mean? More importantly, this aspect of research validity relates to content and criterion-related validity as well as to construct validity. Thus, we suggest that a better label is *measurement validity and generalizability* of the constructs. This dimension has to do with whether the variables are appropriately defined and representative of the concepts or constructs under investigation. Research articles deal with this question piecemeal as test or measurement validity (see chap. 20 for an extended discussion). Here the task is to make an *overall judgment* of the measurement validity and the generalizability of the operational definitions of the several key constructs in the study (see Fig. 23.5.)

A key issue is whether these operational definitions are representative of the intended constructs. An example is an issue about the operational definition of mastery motivation used in several of the early studies on that concept. Young children were given a range of toys to play with freely. The assumption was that the amount of play or the number of different objects explored was a measure of mastery motivation. Others (e.g., Morgan et al., 1990) have argued that, although such behavior does reflect a type of motivation, it seems inappropriate to label it *mastery* motivation because in free play young children tend to play with toys and in ways that they have already mastered. Morgan et al. argued that some (moderate) degree of challenge should be a part of any definition and assessment of mastery motivation.

Consider another example where an investigator may be interested in testing the effects of two different teaching methods, traditional and reformed, on the development of self-confidence in students. To perform this study, the investigator must define the independent and dependent variables for the operations

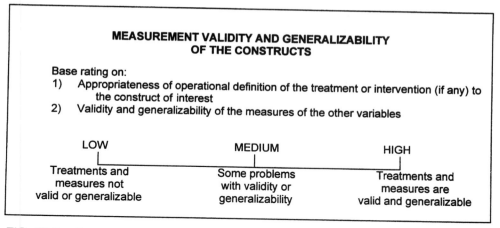

FIG. 23.5.   Evaluating the measurement validity and generalizability of a study.

needed to conduct the study. The traditional approach may be defined as a situation where the teacher lectures to the students and discussion or questions in class are discouraged. The reform approach might be defined as a situation where the students are actively involved in the learning process and take responsibility for learning. The dependent measure, self-confidence, could be defined as a score derived from self-reports on a particular psychometric inventory. The issue for measurement validity and generalizability of the constructs is whether these operational definitions are representative of the intended constructs. Unfortunately, often these operational definitions could be interpreted as measuring some other construct, which sets up a confounded study.

Cook and Campbell (1979) provide an excellent example of confounding by using the construct of supervision. In a study, supervision is operationally defined as the supervisor being 10 feet or less from the worker. However, the operational definition could also be relevant to the construct of stress because having a supervisor that close could lead to increased stress among workers. Therefore, are the investigators assessing the effects of supervision or the effects of stress?

RESEARCH VALIDITY: SUMMARY

This section reviews and summarizes the information on research validity from chapters 6, 10, 20, and this chapter. We have divided research validity into four main dimensions, each of which can be rated on a continuum from low through medium to high. The text of the chapters listed next to each dimension elaborates on how to use the dimensions to evaluate any study:

1. *Measurement Reliability and Statistics* (see chap. 20 and this chapter)
2. *Internal Validity* (see chap. 6)
   a. Equivalence of groups on participant characteristics
   b. Control of extraneous experience or environment variables
3. *Measurement Validity and Generalizability of the Constructs* (see chap. 20 and this chapter)

4. *External validity* (see chap. 10)
   a. Population validity
   b. Ecological validity

Note that internal and external validity each have two key dimensions. These dimensions, shown in Fig. 23.6 in the lower right-hand quadrant under research (or study) validity, provide a comprehensive evaluation of the validity of a whole study.

Figure 23.7 shows graphically the relationship among these concepts. It should be clear that the research validity of a study depends to some extent on the reliability of the specific instruments used in the study. That is why we have labeled one dimension of research validity *measurement reliability and statistics*. Furthermore, as stated earlier, measurement validity depends, in part, on the reliability of the measure and in turn research validity depends, in part, on the validity of the several measures used.

Reliability Stability or Consistency	**Validity** Accuracy or Representativeness
Measurement (or Test) Reliability The participant gets the same or a very similar score from a test, observation, rating, etc. Types of test reliability: a. Test-Retest Reliability b. Parallel Forms Reliability c. Internal Consistency Reliability d. Interrater Reliability	**Measurement (or Test) Validity** The score accurately reflects or measures what it was designed or intended to measure. Types of test validity: a. Face Validity b. Content Validity c. Criterion-related Validity d. Construct Validity

Research (or Study) Reliability
 If repeated, the study would produce similar results. This is called replication.
	Research (or Study) Validity
	 The results of the study are accurate and generalizable. Dimensions of the validity of the study:
	
	 a. Measurement Reliability & Statistics
	
	 b. Internal Validity
	
	   1. Equivalence of Groups on Participant Characteristics
	   2. Control of Extraneous Experience or Environment Variables
	
	 c. Measurement Validity and Generalizability of the Constructs
	
	 d. External Validity
	
	   1. Population Validity
	   2. Ecological Validity

FIG. 23.6.   Similarities and differences between measurement and research reliability and validity.

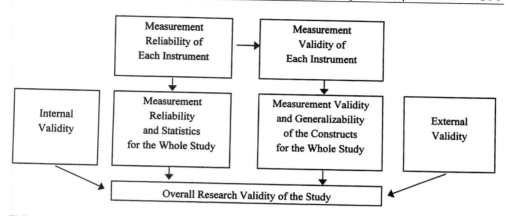

FIG. 23.7.   Schematic diagram showing how the overall validity of a study depends on the four major aspects or dimensions of research validity and in turn on the measurement reliability and validity of the several variables.

The Relative Importance of Different Validity Categories

It would appear impossible to achieve high ratings for each category of validity in a single study. Typically, something is sacrificed in one category to obtain strength in another category. For example, investigators who conduct studies in tightly controlled situations, often in a laboratory, are usually willing to sacrifice a measure of external validity in favor of strong internal validity. On the other hand, researchers who conduct studies "in the field" usually give up a degree of internal validity in favor of strong external validity, even if random assignment of participants to interventions is possible. Should a study be judged more or less harshly contingent on a weakness in a certain validity category?

Campbell and Stanley (1966) did comment on the problem. "Both types of criteria (internal and external validity) are obviously important, even though they are frequently at odds in that features increasing one may jeopardize the other. The selection of designs strong in both types of validity is obviously our ideal" (p. 5). We agree with Cook and Campbell's (1979) statement when planning research, "The art of designing causal studies is to minimize the need for trade-offs and to try to estimate in any particular instance the size of the gains and losses in internal and external validity that are involved in different trade-off options" (p. 90). We also think that in a study, the validity considerations are not random undertakings, but are constrained by other validity categories once certain priorities are selected.

Therefore, we think that all aspects of internal and external validity are important. None should be considered a priori as having more importance than others. Instead, we think that certain validity characteristics will be constrained by others, similar to the preceding example. We discuss this topic in more depth in chapter 24.

Finally, we would like to point out that the lower left side of Fig. 23.6 indicates that the reliability of the findings of a study is important. If the findings cannot be replicated by other researchers, the findings cannot be valid. This issue is dealt with, in part, in the remainder of this chapter under the topic of meta-analysis.

RESEARCH REPLICATION: META-ANALYSIS

Significance Testing Impedes the Goals of Science

Applied disciplines, like nonapplied disciplines, have the goal of accumulating knowledge. Most researchers would acknowledge that it is not proper to recommend an intervention or a treatment based on a single study. Instead, it is advisable to examine the cumulative effect of numerous studies before application. But how do we learn about the cumulative effects of a particular area of study? Usually this takes place by examining research that appears in journals of that particular discipline. Most of the articles that appear in discipline journals present statistically significant findings. However, not all studies result in statistically significant findings, and this creates a problem.

Often, when performing research in applied settings, the sample size is small. Sometimes this limitation applies to educational settings, such as working with intact classrooms, where classroom size is often small. Other examples might include clinical settings or working with persons with a particular disability. When the size of the sample is small, the probability of rejecting a false null hypothesis (power) is reduced. The lower probability of finding a statistically significant difference in your study when it is, in fact, there leads to many problems, the least important of which might be the commission of a type II error, and the most important (at least to most researchers) of which is the failure to publish the findings in a reputable, or perhaps not so reputable, journal. Most journal editors would have researchers in their various disciplines believe that any study that addresses a meaningful question, has the proper research design, analyzes the data correctly, and makes the proper conclusions, but fails to reject the null hypothesis has the same chance of being published as a study that did all of the above, but rejected the null hypothesis. This is simply not true. Studies have been performed that demonstrate a higher probability of acceptance of articles that present statistically significant differences (Rosenthal, 1979). What does all of this mean for applied disciplines in the future?

It means that when researchers search the literature to determine whether a particular therapy worked, or a particular classroom intervention was successful, the size of the effect will be overestimated. The reason is that, with the overemphasis on statistical significance by various journals, only those studies showing a relatively large difference will be published. Hence, if one were to average the size of the effects only from published studies, rather than from published and unpublished studies, a misleading result would occur.

Effect Size and Meta-Analysis

Previously we discussed one of the problems with null hypothesis significance testing (NHST), the mistake of equating a statistically significant relationship with the strength of that relationship. In fact, many statistically significant relationships are not very strong, but often are acquired with a large sample size. To examine the strength of a relationship, or specifically, the effect of the independent variable on the dependent variable, different statistical methods must be applied. These produce an index of the strength of the relationship between the independent and dependent variables, called an *effect size*. Effect sizes have been used for years; however, most researchers did not pay much attention to these indices because journals were most interested in statistically significant results.

Recently, effect size indices have become pervasive in all areas of research. To understand the rationale behind them, consider previous scholarly articles that focused on review of a research topic that might appear in a journal such as *Review of Educational Research Review* or *Psychological Bulletin*. In the past, these review articles would synthesize the literature by using a scorecard method to determine the number of studies that supported a particular finding and the number of studies that did not support a particular finding. The author of the article would attempt to rationalize the findings and make a legitimate conclusion. An example of this type of research might be the relationship between class size and student achievement. Suppose that those articles that demonstrate a statistically significant relationship between class size and student achievement form a category called support for student achievement, and those articles that do not show a statistically significant relationship form a category called no support. One either has to assume that there is a relationship between class size and student achievement or there is not a relationship.

Now, rather than examine whether or not a study demonstrated a statistically significant relationship, we decide to analyze each study for the effect size of the study, that is, the size of the relationship between class size and student achievement. This is done regardless of whether the study was statistically significant. In short, we take each study and calculate an effect size; then we average the effect sizes for all of the studies. This result gives us an overall index of the strength of the relationship between the independent variable and dependent variable, or in this case between class size and student achievement. This type of analysis is referred to as *meta-analysis*. A major strength of meta-analysis is that many studies that have been published previously have not demonstrated statistical significance because they have been underpowered, that is, the sample size was too small. However, the effect size of the study is relatively independent of sample size (as opposed to a judgment of statistical significance). Therefore, studies that did not result in statistical significance still can be included in the overall meta-analysis. (It should be noted that each effect size can be weighted for the number of participants in the study.) Furthermore, there is a greater chance for more studies that did not show statistical significance to be published because their usefulness in future meta-analysis would be considered. For an excellent treatment on this argument, see Schmitt (1996a).

If one believes that science is an accumulation of knowledge, then meta-analysis is the type of research that we can expect in the future. Since the earlier work by Glass and colleagues (Glass et al., 1981), there have been a number of texts in this area including two that we recommend: *Methods of Meta-analysis: Correcting Error and Bias in Research Findings* (Hunter & Schmidt, 1990); and *The Handbook of Research Synthesis* (Cooper & Hedges,

1994). In addition, journals such as those mentioned earlier now include a high proportion of articles that use the meta-analysis framework.

Issues With Using Meta-Analysis

Although meta-analysis has not been without critics, we will focus on three issues that are often encountered when using meta-analysis. The first issue for using this method is that content areas often are heterogeneous. For example, suppose that one is interested in demonstrating that reform- or inquiry-based teaching produces higher achievement than does traditional teaching. Assuming that we could label traditional teaching as a lecture method with little interchange between faculty and students, how would we determine reform teaching? There are many different methods of reform teaching. Some believe that reform teaching involves cooperative learning. Others believe that new technology may be the key to reform teaching. One might argue that any teaching method that is not lecture should be considered reform teaching. Therefore, the researcher is confronted with the decision of how exclusionary to be when considering what entails a reformed course. Along with a suitable definition of reform teaching is the issue of content areas. Should all reformed courses be included, or only those related to mathematics or science? The latter is still a heterogeneous category. Therefore, we can see that if there is difficulty in defining the independent or dependent variable, then the strength of the relationship between the two will be weakened and difficult to interpret. The more restrictive that we become in defining our variables, the higher the probability of demonstrating a large overall effect size. On the other hand, as we become more restrictive in our inclusion criteria for acceptable studies, we limit the generalizability of our findings.

A second issue that is often raised when applying meta-analysis concerns the type of methodological approach used to conduct each study. For example, suppose that in our meta-analysis, some studies used an experimental design, whereas other studies used either a quasi-experimental design or a comparative approach. Lipsey and Wilson (1993) found little difference in average effect sizes between randomized and nonrandomized studies. On the other hand, Heinsman and Shadish (1996) found that there were large differences between randomized and nonrandomized studies when investigating a number of different topics. Heinsman and Shadish (1996) suggested two ways to improve the design of nonrandomized studies for meta-analysis. The first concerns selection of participants into groups. They emphasized that whenever possible, participants should not be allowed to select themselves into groups. However, sometimes it is impossible to rule out self-selection bias of participants into certain settings, such as courses in a university. The other method to improve nonrandomized designs for meta-analysis suggested by Heinsman and Shadish (1996) is to reduce pretest differences between two groups through matching or analysis of covariance.

A third issue encountered in meta-analysis concerns the acceptable number of studies for a meta-analysis. Most meta-analyses include large numbers of studies. For example, in *Meta-Analysis for Explanation* (Cook et al.,

1992), all four content chapters involving meta-analysis included at least 150 studies. Journal articles that involve meta-analysis typically have fewer studies, but usually include at least 30 different studies. Is there a minimum number of studies for inclusion as a meta-analysis? Rosenthal (1985) points out that "meta-analytic procedures can be applied to as few as two studies; but when there are very few studies, the meta-analytic results are relatively unstable" (p. 185).

Performing a Meta-Analysis

Performing a meta-analysis involves a number of steps, similar to any methodological procedure. Although not all published articles using meta-analysis follow identical procedures, we will point out some of the more common steps:

    1. Literature search. The literature search would involve deciding what type of studies to include. For example, published articles, dissertation abstracts, and presentations at national meetings would meet the criteria for relevant literature. In addition, the type of literature searches might include Psychological Abstracts, Index Medicus, and various manual searches of particular journals.

    2. Inclusion criteria. The criteria for inclusion into the meta-analysis must be stated. For example, if one were considering the relationship between reform teaching and student achievement, some of the inclusion criteria might be (a) only mathematics courses, (b) standardized measures of achievement, (c) studies that were either experimental or quasi-experimental, and (d) studies where the comparison group used a traditional method of instruction.

    3. Coding of studies. Studies are then reviewed, and those which meet the criteria for inclusion into the meta-analysis are then coded on certain characteristics such as (a) demographics, (b) type of design, (c) method of reform teaching, (d) length of course, (e) type of achievement test, and so on.

    4. Computation and analysis of effect sizes. Effect sizes are then computed for each study, although one study may have more than one effect size. Each effect size is computed in terms of either an r value or a d value (see chap. 11). Effect sizes are then averaged, taking into account the number of participants in each study (weighted mean). If one is using r values for effect sizes, an overall effect size of .5 is considered large, an effect size of .3 is considered medium, and an effect size of .1 is considered small, if one is using d values, .2 is small, .5 is medium, and .8 is large (Cohen, 1988).

SUMMARY

This chapter was divided into two different topics, research validity and research replication. The two are not independent. We included two more dimensions of research validity under our general topic of research validity. These dimensions are measurement reliability and statistics, and measurement validity and generalizability of constructs. Under each dimension we pointed out the criteria that should be used to make a proper judgment when evaluating a research study. These two new dimensions, along with those previously introduced, internal validity and external validity, comprise the four dimensions of research validity. Although all four criteria are used to evaluate a research study, it is not likely that a study would be high on all four dimensions. Typically, something is sacrificed in one category to obtain strength in another category. We think that none of the dimensions should be considered a priori as having more importance than others. Under the topic of research replication, we discussed meta-analysis, and why it is needed. In addition, we pointed out how effect sizes are accumulated. Last, we introduced some of the important issues when using meta-analysis.

STUDY AIDS

Concepts

- Effect size
- Measurement reliability and statistics
- Measurement validity and generalizability of constructs
- Meta-analysis
- Reliability
- Research validity

Distinctions

- Measurement reliability versus measurement validity
- Measurement reliability versus research reliability
- Measurement validity versus research validity
- Meta-analysis versus research synthesis
- Research reliability versus research validity

Application Problems

For questions 1, 2, and 3 use Fig. 23.3.

1. A researcher feels that certain modifications to her treatment will result in added benefits to patients. A study is set up to compare the modified treatment (intervention group) to the original treatment (control group). Previous research using the original treatment has demonstrated effect sizes of about 0.70. The researcher is willing to accept power of 0.60. How many participants will she need in each group?

2. A colleague has just performed a study. A *t* test had failed to demonstrate a significant difference between his treatment and control groups. The effect size was 0.4. He had 15 participants in each group. How much power did he have in this study? What was the probability of a Type II Error?

3. A graduate student is planning her study. She has the cooperation of enough undergraduates to form two groups of 30 students in each group. She would like to have power of 0.70. In order to obtain a statistically significant outcome, how large of an effect size will she need?

4. One method of gaining power is to reduce error variance. How is this accomplished without increasing sample size?

5. You have been asked to evaluate a program that advocates joint protection techniques for persons with arthritis. The program is relatively small, and you only have 18 participants in each group. What reasonable steps should you take to maximize power without increasing sample size?

6. You are designing a study to demonstrate that nontraditional methods of instruction in mathematics produce better reasoning skills among high school juniors. You have access to one high school that appears representative of most high schools in your city. Should you design your study to focus on internal validity or external validity? Why?

7. It is often stated that research studies in the social sciences are underpowered? How can meta-analysis improve the situation?

Evaluating Empirical Research Studies: A Synthesis

OVERVIEW

In this chapter we review, step by step, the process of analyzing an article and then evaluating it by using the research validity scales described in earlier chapters. As we move through this process, we will mention key concepts and diagrams from earlier chapters that we have found useful in understanding research and the process of evaluating it. This evaluation is based on the answers to 16 questions (Table 24.1) that provide the information needed to analyze and evaluate the four aspects of research validity. The questions, and your critique, will focus on the method section of an article but will also include questions about the remainder of the article, including the title and conclusions. This evaluation draws on and synthesizes many parts of this book, so we will refer to the appropriate chapters.

Ideally, a study should be rated high on each criterion. However, there are always trade-offs and few, if any, studies are high on all criteria. Furthermore, the weight that researchers give to each of the criteria varies. For example, human and animal *experimental* researchers give more weight to internal validity, while *survey* and *qualitative* researchers give relatively more weight to aspects of external validity. Our experience indicates that studies usually compromise one or more aspects of external validity to achieve high internal validity or vice versa.

Peer Review

The evaluation begins with Question 1, which is about the source in which the study is presented or summarized. As a consumer of research, you will often read newspaper or newsletter articles summarizing research studies. These articles may not give much detail about the method used, but they will usually provide information about the source from which the summary article was taken. If the source is a scholarly journal, the chances are that the peer review was at least moderately extensive and strict. By peer review, we mean that the article was evaluated by other experts (peers) in the field, usually without them knowing who the author of the article was (masked review). If the association that publishes the journal consists primarily of practitioners who are only secondarily interested in research, the peer review of the design and analysis is likely to be less strict because practitioner reviews focus more on application and implications.

Presentations at professional meetings, even research-oriented meetings, are usually less strictly reviewed, especially if the judgment to accept was based on a summary or abstract of the paper. Furthermore, presentations to nonscholarly audiences or at events like press conferences are even less likely to be reviewed by independent scholars or researchers and, thus, do not have peer review. Finally, studies whose main or sole source is dissemination in a popular article or an article in a popular magazine or newspaper would not have had peer review. However, many newspaper articles are based on published peer-reviewed articles or presentations at professional meetings, so they have had some sort of peer review. But the journalist may have left out important details.

IDENTIFYING OR ANALYZING THE KEY VARIABLES AND DESIGN

Variables and Their Measurement Scales

The second question asks you to identify the key *independent variables*. For each, state (a) whether the variable is *active* (i.e., manipulated), *attribute*, or *change over time,* (b) the number of levels or categories, and (c) the scale of measurement of the independent variable. These distinctions are discussed in chapters 4, 9, and 12.

The third question asks you to identify the key *dependent variable(s)* and their levels of measurement. Figure 9.1 and Tables 9.1 and 9.2 should be useful in learning or remembering levels or scales of measurement. The level of measurement for the independent and, especially, the dependent variables helps determine the appropriateness of the statistics used in the study.

Research Hypotheses or Questions, Approaches, and Design

The fourth question asks you to identify the main research *hypotheses* or *questions*. Most studies have several questions or hypotheses, often outlined in the introduction, or the method section of the article, or both.

We believe that it is possible and useful to describe all studies as using one or more of the five research approaches (descriptive, associational, comparative, quasi-experimental, or randomized experimental, or a combination of these approaches), as described in Table 5.1 and in Fig. 5.1. Question 5 asks you to state which approaches were used in this study. Generally, each research question or hypothesis uses one of the approaches, so in a study with a number of questions, more than one approach may be used. It is common for a study to have several descriptive research questions, especially about the characteristics of the sample and, perhaps, about some of the dependent variables. Those parts of the method and results sections of an article use descriptive statistics and what we call the descriptive approach. However, almost all theses, dissertations, and papers published in quantitative journals go beyond the purely descriptive approach to compare groups, or relate variables, or both. Thus, most studies also will use one (or more) of the other four approaches. Identifying the research approach is important because it influences the internal validity of a study and what can be inferred about whether the independent variable *caused* any difference in the dependent variable. In general, the randomized experimental approach produces the best evidence for causation. Neither the comparative nor the associational approaches are well suited to providing evidence about causes. Quasi-experimentation is usually in between.

Question 6 states that if the study has experimental, quasi-experimental, or comparative research question(s), then one should identify the design classification (see chap. 12). This requires knowing (a) the number of *factors* (independent variables), (b) the number of levels or values of each factor, and (c) whether the design is *between groups*, *within subjects* (repeated measures), or *mixed*. For example, a design might be described as a 3 × 2 (mixed) factorial design with repeated measures on the second factor. This means that there are two independent variables, the first with three levels or groups and the second with two levels or, in this case, measured at two times because there are repeated measures. We think that this type of analysis of designs applies to not only the randomized experimental and quasi-experimental approaches (which is typical), but also to comparative approach questions, where there is no active or manipulated independent variable. Note that the above 3×2 design could be the typical experimental or quasi-experimental pretest–posttest design with three groups (e.g., two treatments and a control) or it could be a longitudinal (two ages) design comparing three types of participants (e.g., securely attached versus avoidant versus disorganized) over time.

Because the classification of the design, in this sense, could apply to comparative as well as experimental approaches, it does *not* provide information about causality. However, the design is critical to determining the appropriate statistical analysis, which, likewise, does not tell us about causation. We all know the phrase, "correlation does not indicate causation." However, the same is true for analysis of variance (ANOVA), if the approach was comparative; that is, the type of analysis or statistic does not determine causality. Thus, the typical ANOVA terminology of main "effects" can be misleading. In general, similar experimental, quasi-experimental, and comparative designs are all analyzed with the same type of analysis of variance (or t test). The specific type of data analysis depends on the design classification, and the level of measurement of the dependent variable as shown in Tables 13.1 and 13.3.

Question 7 asks you to name the specific randomized experimental or quasi-experimental design, if one was used. Table 7.2 provides a schematic diagram of most of the common designs and their names.

Note that if the research question or hypothesis and approach are associational, the analysis will usually be done with a correlation or multiple regression, and questions 6 and 7 are not applicable.

Measurement Reliability and Validity

Questions 8 and 9 require an evaluation based on the principle that in a good study each key variable should be measured reliably and validly. Therefore, we ask you to evaluate these aspects of *each* key variable separately (see chap. 20).

Question 8 asks *what types* of reliability (e.g., test–retest, internal consistency, interrater) were obtained and how strong is the evidence for the reliability of the measure? This was discussed in detail in chapter 20. Note that active independent variables seldom have information about measurement reliability (or validity). However, for attribute independent variables (except very objective or obvious ones like age and gender) and for dependent variables, the method section will usually report something on measurement reliability. Remember that a reliability coefficient of .70 or higher is usually considered necessary for a measure to have acceptable reliability, but in a complex study, a few reliability coefficients in the .60s are common. As indicated following, we view good measurement reliability as part of one aspect of research validity—the part we call measurement reliability and statistics. In evaluating information about reliability in an article, examine the method section. Were any reliability coefficients reported? Was more than one type reported for a measure? If the instruments had been used before, the author may only refer to another study and not provide actual coefficients.

Question 9 is about the validity of each measure. Again, you should comment both on what types of validity (i.e., face, content, criterion, construct) were reported and how strong the evidence was for validity. This was discussed in detail in chapter 20. Authors often only cite previous studies that used the instrument without providing details about the evidence for validity.

In summary, for each key measure or variable, one should comment about its reliability and validity.

EVALUATING RESEARCH VALIDITY

Now you are ready to evaluate the four key criteria for the validity of a study. These criteria are based on the writing (discussed in earlier chapters) of Campbell and Stanley (1966) and Cook and Campbell (1979), as modified by us. A high-quality study should have moderate to high ratings on each of the dimensions of research validity, as shown in Fig. 24.1 and Fig. 24.2. You are asked to rate the *study as a whole* on each of the scales, by using the criteria listed in the figures and discussed in the following sections.

Measurement Reliability and Statistics

The first dimension emphasizes the importance of measurement reliability. Question 10 requests an overall rating of the study from low through medium to high, that is based on all four of the following issues.

First, there is the issue of whether the variables as a group are measured reliably. You are asked in Question 10 to consider an overall rating of the reliability of all the instruments. A principle often emphasized in measurement classes is that a test or measure cannot be valid if it is not reliable. Likewise, a study's validity is reduced if one or more of the key measures are relatively unreliable.

Second, can a statistically significant relationship be detected, assuming that such a relationship exists? The ability to detect a statistically significant difference is most commonly referred to as *power* or the ability to reject a false null hypothesis. Although adequate power is based, in part, on having enough subjects in the study, there are other methods of increasing power (Lipsey, 1990). Some of these methods include decreasing variability and increasing reliability of the dependent variable or increasing the strength and consistency of administering the independent variable. Chapter 23 discusses these methods in more detail. Cook and Campbell (1979) raise a second side to the issue of power, which involves having too much power, especially for the number of participants in a study. For the most part, the problem arises when an exceptionally large sample size yields a statistically significant, but perhaps trivial, relationship. The trend toward estimating effect sizes in current research is one way of resolving this problem.

A third issue to consider involves the selection of the proper statistical method to assess whether a relationship between the independent and dependent variable actually exists. We have discussed selection and interpretation of

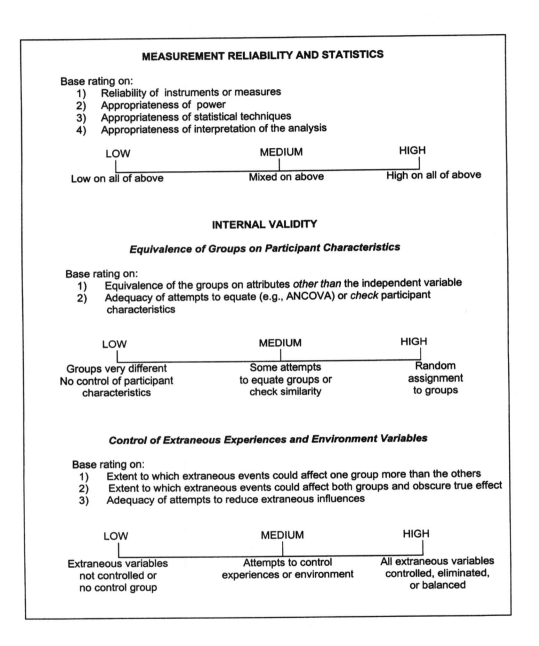

FIG. 24.1. Rating scales to evaluate the measurement reliability and statistics and the internal validity of the findings of a study.

MEASUREMENT VALIDITY AND GENERALIZABILITY OF THE CONSTRUCTS

Base rating on:
1) Appropriateness of operational definition of the treatment to the construct of interest
2) Validity and generalizability of the dependent variable measures

LOW	MEDIUM	HIGH
Treatments and measures not valid or generalizable	Some problems with validity or generalizability	Treatments and measures are valid and generalizable

EXTERNAL VALIDITY

Population

Base rating on:
1) Representativeness of accessible population vis-à-vis theoretical population
2) Adequacy of sampling method from accessible population
3) Adequacy response or return rate

LOW	MEDIUM	HIGH
Actual sample unrepresentative of the theoretical population	Some attempt to obtain good sample	Actual sample representative of theoretical population

Ecological

Base rating on:
1) Naturalness of setting or conditions
2) Adequacy of rapport with testers or observers.
3) Naturalness of procedures or tasks
4) Appropriateness of timing and length of treatment
5) Extent to which results are restricted to a specific time in history

LOW	MEDIUM	HIGH
Unnatural setting, tester, procedures, and time	Somewhat artificial (e.g., questionnaire)	Natural setting, tester, procedures, and time

FIG. 24.2. Rating scales to evaluate the measurement validity and generalizability of the constructs and the external validity of the findings of a study.

statistics in chapters 13 to 19. Sometimes researchers select the wrong statistic, such as a t test or correlation with a nominal dependent variable. As Cook and Campbell (1979) point out, more often problems involve violation of assumptions underlying statistical tests or problems in making multiple comparisons without adjusting the alpha level. Such problems may result in a type I or type II error. Our own experience suggests that not adjusting the alpha level is more common than selection of an inappropriate statistic.

The fourth issue to consider involves making the proper interpretation of the statistical analysis. Sometimes the correct statistic is selected, but the investigator misinterprets the findings, concluding more from the data than is actually given. For example, if one has a significant interaction from the analysis of a factorial ANOVA, one should examine the simple effects rather than the main effects, which may be misleading. These issues are discussed in more detail in chapters 13 to 19.

Internal Validity

Equivalence of Groups on Participant Characteristics. There are a number of specific threats to internal validity, several of which are subject factors, that could lead to a lack of equivalence of the participants in the two (or more) groups, and, thus, influence the dependent variable. You are asked in Question 11 to evaluate this aspect of internal validity.

In the randomized experimental, quasi-experimental, and comparative approaches, a key question is whether the groups that are compared are equivalent in all respects except the independent variable or variables, before the procedures of the study take place. The usual way to assure equivalence is by randomly assigning the participants to groups. Randomly assigning treatments to intact groups (strong quasi-experiments), matching, analysis of covariance, or checking for pretest equality of groups after the fact are all methods of achieving a medium level of this aspect of internal validity if random assignment is not possible.

Also included in this aspect of internal validity would be participant characteristics that appear to be equal initially, but lead to different developmental trajectories over time and, thus, group differences that are not due to the independent variable. Differences between groups in maturation rates, genetic predispositions, or in factors leading to subject attrition are examples. Regression to the mean of extreme groups is an example of where differences in participants, which were initially obvious, disappear over time because the initial score was not the true score.

If the approach is associational, there is only one group. In that case, this aspect of internal validity comes down to the question of whether participants who score high on the independent variable of interest are equivalent to those who score low, in terms of other attributes that may be correlated with the dependent variable. If it is likely that the high scorers are not equivalent to the low scorers for variables such as age, social status, education, and so forth, partialing out the variables on which the high and low subjects are unequal is one method of achieving a degree of this aspect of internal validity within the associational research approach. These issues are discussed in more detail in chapter 6.

Control of Extraneous Experience or Environment Variables.   Similarly, we have grouped several other "threats" to internal validity under a category that deals with the effects of extraneous (those variables not of interest in this study) experiences or environmental conditions during the study. Question 12 asks you to evaluate the internal validity scale control of extraneous experience and environment variables. The first aspect has to do with whether extraneous variables or events affect one group more than the other(s). In the associational approach, the issue is whether the experiences of the participants who are high on the independent variable are different from those who are low on the independent variable.

A second issue is whether something other than the independent variable is affecting the dependent variable for both or all groups. This problem is, of course, more likely to be serious when the treatment continues over an extended time period and in longitudinal research. Historical events and maturation could affect both groups equally, so group differences may not occur. However, the results could be misinterpreted if, for example, one concluded that significant pretest to posttest gains (or losses) in two experimental groups were due to the treatments rather than to an uncontrolled common (e.g., Hawthorne-type) experience or maturation. Of course, in longitudinal studies, maturation *is* the variable of interest. This issue is quite complex.

In randomized experimental designs, these experiential and environmental variables are usually well controlled, but in quasi-experimental designs, and especially in the comparative and associational approaches, such experiences may be inadequately controlled. In general, there is a trade-off between high control of extraneous variables and high ecological validity. It is hard to have both. If a study is rated low on these dimensions of internal validity, the authors should not use terms such as effect, impact, and determine that imply cause and effect. Phrases such as may affect, presumed cause, possible determinant seem appropriately cautious.

Measurement Validity and Generalizability of the Constructs

The rating requested in Question 13 has to do with whether the active independent variables (treatments), attribute independent variables, and dependent variables are measured validly and are appropriately defined so that they represent the concepts under investigation. You have been asked to deal with this question piecemeal in Question 9, above, on measurement validity, and we discussed it more fully in chapter 20. Now your task is to make an *overall judgment* of the validity and generalizability of the operational definitions of the several key variables in the study.

The issue is whether these operational definitions are representative of the intended concepts and constructs. In chapter 23, we provided three examples of problems for this dimension: mastery motivation in young children as measured by the amount of free play, the definitions of two different teaching methods (traditional and reform), and supervision as measured by being within 10 feet of the worker. The issue is whether these operational definitions are representative of the intended constructs. Unfortunately, often these operational definitions could be interpreted as measuring some other construct, which would set up a confounded study.

External Validity

Population Validity. This aspect of external validity is a participant selection problem that involves how participants were selected to be in the study. Were they randomly selected from a particular population, or were volunteers used? Most quantitative studies in the social sciences have not used random selection of participants, but the issue of population external validity is more complex than whether there was a random sample, as discussed in chapter 10 and presented in Fig. 10.1.

Question 14 asks for an overall rating of whether the actual sample of participants is representative of the theoretical or target population. To make this evaluation, first identify (a) the *theoretical population*, (b) the *accessible population*, (c) the *sampling design* and *selected sample*, and (d) the *actual sample* of participants who participated in the study. It is possible that the researcher could use a random or other probability sampling technique, but have an actual sample that is not representative of the theoretical population either because of a low response rate or because of the accessible population not being representative of the theoretical population. The latter problem seems almost universal, in part as a result of funding and travel limitations. Except in national survey research, we almost always start with an accessible population from the local school district, community, clinic, animal colony, and so on.

Figure 10.4 helps reinforce the important distinction between *random sampling* (or selection of subjects from the population), which influences population external validity, and *random assignment* (of subjects to groups), which influences the participant equivalence aspect of internal validity.

Ecological Validity. The second aspect of external validity, called *ecological validity*, has to do with the conditions or settings, testers, procedures, and times. Question 15 asks you to evaluate these aspects for how representative they are of real life, and, thus, whether the results can be generalized to real-life outcomes. Obviously, field research is more likely to be high on ecological external validity than laboratory procedures, especially if they are highly artificial. We would rate most of the self-report measures, especially questionnaires, to be artificial because they are not direct measures of the participant's actual behavior in a typical environment.

In chapter 10 we discussed two examples of problems with ecological validity. First, it was typical in the 1960s to test 6- to 12-month-old infants in an at least somewhat unnatural setting (lab playroom) with a male stranger who approached and quickly picked up the baby in a short series of predetermined steps. In the name of experimental control, no attempt was made to have the experimenter or stranger's behavior be contingent on the baby's. This procedure and even the existence of fear of strangers, was criticized as being low on ecological validity. The researcher had traded ecological validity for better control of the environment and the independent variable.

The other example involved an educator interested in the effect of a particular teaching style on student participation. To be high on ecological validity, the classroom should be similar to that of a normal classroom. Similarly, if the investigator asked students to come at night for the study, but these students normally attended class during the day, then there is a problem in ecological external validity. The investigator must ask if a representative method was used for selection of the setting and time, or was an unrepresentative method used?

ISSUES OF INTERPRETATION

Finally, the last question is a kind of summary question that asks you to evaluate the title and especially the discussion and conclusions for indications of inaccuracy or misleading statements, given your previous analysis of the study. Often in popular articles, the editor or writer will overstate the findings to make them more impressive or more easily understood by the public. Thus, in a popular article reporting on a study with relatively low internal validity because of lack of controls or lack of equivalence of groups, the writer may report or imply that the independent variable caused the dependent variable, had an impact on, or determined the outcome. These overstatements may not have been made in the actual article by the researcher, who may have presented the conclusions more cautiously and appropriately, given the internal validity of the study. Likewise, a study that involved rats or an unrepresentative sample of people or on one gender may be overgeneralized, perhaps without any mention of the types of subjects used, or implying that there is no problem in making more general statements. The astute consumer should become aware of these possible overinterpretations and evaluate the article appropriately.

AN EXAMPLE OF HOW TO USE THIS FRAMEWORK

To illustrate how to use this framework and Fig. 24.1 and 24.2 to evaluate research, consider a study by Gliner and Sample (1996). The purpose of the study was to increase quality of life for persons with developmental disabilities who were employed in sheltered work or supported employment, by using an intervention of community life options. The study attempted to achieve high internal validity by randomly assigning participants to either a community life options intervention or to their present situation. The study also attempted to achieve high external validity by carrying out the conditions in the actual setting. However, obtaining good research validity on all six dimensions could not be accomplished. A summary example of how a written evaluation of the six dimensions for the Gliner and Sample (1996) article might look is provided in the next two paragraphs.

Measurement reliability and statistics were judged overall to be medium high. Reliability of the measures was good. However, statistical power was constrained because there were a limited number of persons who fit the criteria to be in the study (persons with developmental disabilities who were employed in supported or sheltered work). Thus, the ability to detect a relationship was reduced. The choice of statistics and their interpretation was judged to be high.

Internal validity: equivalence of groups on participant characteristics was rated high because participants were randomly assigned to intervention conditions. However, a cautionary note could be raised because random assignment of participants to conditions may not make the groups equivalent with small numbers. *Control of extraneous experience* or *environment variables* was constrained by an emphasis on ecological validity so it was judged to be medium to low. In a community setting, where choice was experienced differently by different participants, it was difficult to insure that the experiences of each group were not influenced by outside variables.

In terms *of measurement validity and generalizability of the constructs*, the dependent variable, quality of life for persons with developmental disabilities, had been used several times with this population to measure quality of life among individuals who had moved out of institutionalized settings into community settings. However, the instrument may not have been appropriate for measuring changes following intervention in only one life area. In addition, the instrument may have been intended for lower functioning participants. In terms of the independent variable, the intervention seems appropriately named and generalizable. Overall this dimension was rated medium. *Population external validity* was considered to be medium low because the sample was limited to persons in one city, and there was not a random selection of appropriate participants even from that city. Instead, the sample was one of convenience. Thus, the accessible population might not represent all persons with developmental disabilities. Because the intervention was a real one and took place in an actual community setting, *ecological external validity* was judged to be high.

Concluding Comments

There are many other questions that could be asked about a research article, such as its readability, clarity, and so forth, but we believe that we have discussed the major dimensions and, thus, we have not tried to be totally comprehensive in our coverage.

SUMMARY

This chapter provides an integrated review of many of the important concepts made throughout the book. Thus, there are no new concepts or distinctions to present at the end of this chapter. Answers to the 16 questions presented in Table 24.1 provide a complete analysis and evaluation of a research study, especially of its method. To do such an analysis, you must identify the key variables and their characteristics (type and level of measurement). You must also identify the research questions, approaches, and design. In terms of evaluation, we have provided rating scales, and rubrics for rating them, to evaluate the four main dimensions of research validity. These dimensions are as follows:

1. Statistics and measurement reliability
2. Internal validity
   a. Equivalence of the groups on participant characteristics

TABLE 24.1

Analysis and Evaluation of Quantitative Research Studies

For each study, answer the following questions, focusing most of your evaluative comments on questions 8–16.

Evaluation of the Editorial Review

1. Rate the amount and strictness of the peer review from low to high. Explain.

Variables and Their Measurement Scales (see chapters 4 and 9). If there are many variables, pick 5–10 key or major ones, which may be composite variables.

2. Identify the key independent or antecedent or predictor variable(s). For each, state a) whether it is an active, attribute, or change-over-time independent variable, b) the number of levels or categories, and c) the level of measurement.
3. Name the key dependent or outcome variable(s) and their level(s) of measurement.

Research Questions, Approach(es), and Design (see chapters 5, 7, and 12)

4. Identify the main research questions or hypotheses.
5. Name the specific research approach (i.e., descriptive, associational, comparative, quasi-experimental, and/or randomized experimental) for each question (see chapter 5).
6. Identify the design classification (for example, 2 × 2 factorial with repeated measures on the second factor), if the approach is randomized experimental, quasi-experimental, or comparative (see chapter 12).
7. Identify the specific design name (e.g., posttest-only control group design) if the approach is randomized experimental or quasi-experimental (see chapter 7).

Measurement Reliability and Validity (see chapter 20). For the measure of each key variable, evaluate:

8. The reliability of the measure (not usually reported for demographics or active independent variables). What type(s) were done? Rate the strength of the evidence from low to high.
9. The validity of the measure (not usually reported for demographics or active independent variables). What type(s) were reported? Rate the strength of the evidence from low to high.

Evaluation of the Validity of the Findings of a Study (refer to Fig. 24.1 and Fig. 24.2)

10. Rate and comment on the measurement reliability and statistics overall (see chapters 20 and 23). Base your rating on:
    a) Reliability of the instruments or measures
    b) Appropriateness of power
    c) Appropriate choice or use of statistics
    d) Appropriate interpretation of statistical results.
11. Rate and comment on the equivalence of the groups on participant characteristics (see chapter 6).
12. Rate and comment on the control of extraneous experience or environment variables (see chapter 6).
13. Rate and comment on the measurement validity and generalizability of the constructs (see chapters 20 and 23).
14. Rate and comment on the population validity overall (see chapter 10). Before doing so, answer the following:
    a) Identify the theoretical, or target, and accessible populations and the selected and actual samples.
    b) How representative is the accessible population of the theoretical population?
    c) How representative is the selected sample of the accessible population?
    d) How representative is the actual sample vis-à-vis the selected sample? That is, how good was the response rate?
15. Rate and comment on each of the five aspects of the ecological validity (see chapter 10).

Evaluation of the Conclusions

16. Comment on whether the title, conclusions, and so forth were overstated or misleading, given your evaluation of the aspects.

      b. Control of (extraneous) experience/environment variables
3. Measurement validity and generalizability of the constructs
4. External validity
      a. Population validity
      b. Ecological validity

STUDY AIDS

Application Problems

For each of the following problems, evaluate the four aspects of research validity. If not enough information is provided, state what you would need to know to make an evaluation.

1. Researchers in a large metropolitan school district with a diverse multi-ethnic student population have implemented a study regarding the possible effects of type of curriculum and type of counselor on student leadership levels measured with an instrument using a summated Likert scale. The researchers were able to choose a random sample from the entire senior class. These students were then randomly assigned to two groups, either the experimental multi-ethnic or traditional leadership curriculum, taught by a counselor with extensive training in multi-cultural issues and a traditionally trained counselor, respectively. In other regards, these individuals are very similar in education and experience.

2. A researcher is interested in studying the effect of sleep deprivation on teenagers' math performance. He has a limited research budget, so he decides to study students at the local college. He obtained a list of all the students for each level (freshmen to senior). He randomly samples 10 students from each of the levels. All 40 agree to be in the study. They answer a questionnaire about the amount of sleep they had during finals week last semester and their SAT math scores.

3. A researcher plans to do a laboratory experimental study of sleep deprivation on math performance. He randomly assigns students from his sample to two groups of 20 each. One group is kept awake all night studying and given a math test in the morning. The other group is encouraged to sleep as long as they want before they take the math test in the morning.

4. A Ph.D. student asked a random sample of faculty at a college to answer a questionnaire; 50% responded. The faculty members classified their department heads as one of four types of leader (A, B, C, or D) based on answers to a brief leadership inventory. Faculty members were asked their own age, classified as younger (< 35), middle (35–49), or older (50+). The researcher wanted to know if the above characteristics seem to influence their job satisfaction, rated on a 9-point Likert scale.

5. A study was undertaken to determine the back to work effects of two types of treatment on post-surgical carpal tunnel syndrome patients. Treatment Full used splints on a full time basis, whereas treatment Part used splints on a part time basis. In addition, the investigator also was interested in whether patients who scored high on the personality variable of co-dependency would

do worse than patients who scored low on the variable of co-dependency. Five hundred post-surgical patients from a large metropolitan area volunteered for this study. All 500 patients were given the Gliner Co-dependency Personality Inventory (test-retest reliability $r = 0.88$; predictive validity $r = .66$). From this sample of 500 carpal tunnel syndrome patients, the 20 patients with the highest co-dependency scores (H) and the 20 patients with the lowest co-dependency scores (L) were selected to continue in the study. From these two groups, H and L, half of the patients were randomly assigned to the full time splint group F and half of the patients were randomly assigned to the part time splint group P. Prior to the interventions, all 40 participants were given the Gliner Carpal Tunnel Syndrome pain Inventory (not currently found in the *Buros Mental Measurements Yearbooks*). A high score on this inventory meant much pain and little success. After three months of intervention, all 40 participants were tested again on the Gliner Carpal Tunnel Syndrome pain Inventory.

APPENDIX

Confusing Terms[1] and Glossary

DIFFERENT TERMS FOR SIMILAR CONCEPTS

Variables

- Independent variable = antecedent = predictor = presumed cause = factor = _#_ -way
- Active independent variable = manipulated = intervention = treatment
- Attribute independent variable = measured variable = individual difference variable
- Dependent variable = outcome = criterion
- Levels (of a variable) = categories = values = groups = samples (from the variable)

Designs

- Between groups = independent samples = uncorrelated samples
- Within subjects = related samples = paired samples = repeated measures = matched groups = correlated samples
- Single factor design = one independent variable = basic
- Factorial design = two or more independent variables = complex design
- Random assignment to groups = how subjects get into groups = randomized design → high _internal_ validity

---

[1]The definitions of most "confusing" terms are found in the glossary.

- Randomized experiment = true experiment

Statistics

- Associate variables = relate = predict → correlation
- Compare groups = test differences → ANOVA
- ANOVA = *F* = analysis of variance
- Repeated measures ANOVA = within subjects ANOVA = randomized blocks ANOVA
- Mixed ANOVA = Split-plot ANOVA = (sometimes called repeated measures ANOVA)
- Mann–Whitney *U* test = Wilcoxon Mann–Whitney test

Sampling

- Random selection = random sampling → high *external* validity
- Theoretical population = target population
- Accessible population = sampling frame

Measurement

- Alternate forms = equivalent forms = parallel forms reliability
- Interval scale = numeric = continuous variable = quantitative = scale variable
- Nominal scale = categorical = unordered variable = qualitative = discrete variable
- Ordinal scale = unequal interval scale
- Normal = normally distributed variable = interval or ratio variable

Similar Terms for Different Concepts

- Measurement *validity* ≠ research *validity*
- *Random* assignment ≠ *random* selection ≠ *random order*
- *Random* assignment of participants to groups ≠ *random* assignment of treatments to groups
- *Cronbach's alpha* ≠ *alpha (significance) level*
- Random *samples* ≠ paired or related *samples* ≠ independent *samples*
- *Factorial design* ≠ *factorial evidence* for construct validity
- *Factor* (i.e., independent variable) ≠ *factor* analysis
- *Discriminant analysis* ≠ *discriminant* evidence for construct validity
- *Independent* samples ≠ *independent* variables
- Measurement *scale* ≠ a rating scale ≠ *summated or composite scale* ≠ semantic differential *scale*
- Research *question* ≠ *questionnaire question* or item
- *Theoretical* research ≠ *theoretical* population

KEY DISTINCTIONS

(see glossary and the indicated chapters)

Achievement tests versus aptitude tests (chap. 21)

Active versus attribute independent variable (chap. 4, 5)

Anonymous versus confidential (chap. 3)

Basic (two variables) versus complex (three or more variables) statistics (chap. 13)

Between groups designs versus within subjects designs versus mixed designs (chap. 12, 13, 15)

Compare groups versus associate variables (chap. 13)

Confidential versus anonymous (chap. 3, 22)

Control group versus comparision group (chap. 7)

Convergent versus discriminant versus factorial evidence for construct measurement validity (chap. 20)

Correlation coefficient versus squared correlation coefficient (chap. 16)

Correlation versus linear regression (chap. 16)

Data collection techniques (methods) versus research approaches (chap. 21)

Dichotomous versus nominal versus ordinal versus normal levels of measurement (chap. 9, 13)

Difference versus associational versus descriptive research questions and statistics (chap. 5, 6, 13)

Directional hypothesis versus nondirectional hypothesis (chap. 11)

Equivalence of groups on participant characteristics versus control of extraneous experience or environment variables

Experimental versus individual difference research approaches (chap. 5)

Face versus content versus criterion versus construct evidence for measurement validity (chap. 20)

Factor analysis versus factorial ANOVA (chap. 19)

Identifiable causes versus mutual simultaneous shaping (chap. 2)

Independent versus dependent versus extraneous variable (chap. 4)

Internal validity versus external validity (chap. 6, 10, 23, 24)

Laboratory versus field research (chap. 1)

Level versus mean level (chap. 8)

Level versus trend versus slope (chap. 8)

Levels of one variable versus a set or group of variables (chap. 4)

Main effects versus interaction effects (chap. 17)

MANOVA versus univariate ANOVAs (chap. 19)

Mean versus median versus mode (chap. 9)

Measurement reliability versus measurement validity (chap. 20, 23)

Measurement reliability versus research reliability (chap. 23)

Measurement validity versus research validity (chap. 20, 23)

Meta-analysis versus research synthesis (chap. 23)

Mixed ANOVA versus gain scores analysis versus ANCOVA (chap. 18)

Multiple baseline across subjects design versus multiple baseline across *behaviors* design versus multiple baseline across *settings* design (chap. 8)

Multiple regression versus discriminant analysis versus logistic regression (chap. 19)

Nominal versus ordinal versus interval/ratio scales of measurement (chap. 9)

Nomothetic/generalizable knowledge versus idiographic knowledge (chap. 2)

Norm referenced versus criterion referenced tests (chap. 21)

Null hypothesis versus alternative hypothesis (chap. 11)

Number of independent variables versus number of levels of the variable (chap. 13)

Open-ended versus closed-ended questions (chap. 21)

Ordered versus unordered or nominal variables (chap. 4, 9)

Ordinal versus disordinal interaction (chap. 17)

Parametric versus nonparametric statistics (chap. 13, 14)

Pearson product-moment correlation versus Spearman rank-order correlation (chap. 16)

Pilot testing versus pilot studies (chap. 22)

Plagiarism versus paraphrasing (chap. 22)

Poor quasi-experimental versus better quasi-experimental versus randomized experimental designs (chap. 7)

Population versus ecological external validity (chap. 10)

Population versus sample (chap. 10)

Positivist approach versus constructivist approach to research or paradigm or theoretical framework (chap. 1, 2)

Predictive versus concurrent evidence for criterion-related measurement validity (chap. 20)

Probability versus nonprobability sampling (chap. 10)

Producing knowledge versus understanding research as a consumer (chap. 1)

Quantitative versus qualitative data analysis (chap. 1)

Quantitative versus qualitative data and data collection (chap. 1)

Questionnaire question or item versus research question (chap. 21)

Questionnaire versus interview (chap. 21)

Quota versus purposive versus convenience sampling (chap. 10)

Random assignment of *participants* to groups versus random assignment of *treatments* to (intact) groups (chap. 5, 7)

Random *assignment* of participants to groups versus random *selection* or sampling of participants to be included in a study (chap. 5, 10)

Random assignment versus nonrandom assignment of participants to groups (chap. 7)

Randomized experimental versus quasi-experimental versus comparative versus associational versus descriptive approach to research (chap. 5)

Relationships between or among variables versus description of a variable (chap. 5)

Research problem versus personal or societal problem (chap. 4)

Research reliability versus research validity (chap. 23)

Researcher and participants are independent versus researcher and participants always influence each other (chap. 2)

Researcher report or observational measures versus self-report measures (chap. 1, 21)

Reversal designs versus multiple baseline designs (chap. 8)

Risks versus benefits (chap. 3)

Sample statistics versus population parameters (chap. 11)

Selected sample versus actual sample (chap. 10)

Simple effects versus post hoc comparisons (chap. 17)

Simple random versus systematic random versus stratified random versus cluster (random) sampling (chap. 10)

Simultaneous regression versus hierarchical regression versus stepwise regression (chap. 19)

Single factor ANOVA versus Kruskal–Wallis ANOVA versus χ^2 test (chap. 14)

Single factor repeated measures ANOVA versus Friedman test versus Cochran Q test (chap. 15)

Single factor designs versus factorial designs (chap. 12)

Single subject designs versus traditional group designs (chap. 8)

Single tangible reality versus multiple constructed realities (chap. 2)

Stratified sampling with equal versus differential proportions (chap. 10)

t test for paired samples versus single factor repeated measures ANOVA (chap. 15)

t test for paired samples versus Wilcoxon matched pairs test versus McNemar test (chap. 15)

t test versus Mann–Whitney U test versus χ^2 test (chap. 14)

t test versus single factor ANOVA (chap. 14)

Test-retest versus parallel forms versus interval consistency versus interrater evidence for measurement reliability (chap. 20)

Tests of significance versus confidence intervals (chap. 11)

The variable (itself) versus levels or categories of the variable (chap. 4)

Theoretical versus applied research (chap. 1)

Theoretical or target population versus accessible population (chap. 10)

True mixed design versus pretest–posttest design (chap. 18)

Type I versus Type II errors (chap. 11)

Value-free versus value-laden inquiry (chap. 2)

Weak quasi-experiments versus moderate strength quasi-experiments versus strong
   quasi-experiments (chap. 7)

GLOSSARY

Accessible Population   The group of participants to which the researcher has access.
   The accessible portion of the theoretical population often referred to as the survey
   population or sampling frame. See also convenience sample. (chap. 10)

Active Independent Variable   Sometimes called a manipulated variable. An intervention or manipulated independent variable as opposed to one that is an attribute of
   the participants or their ongoing environment. A variable one level of which is
   given to one group of participants but not to another, within a specified period of
   time. Thus, a pretest and posttest are possible but not always done. (chap. 4)

Actual Sample   The sample of subjects that complete the study and whose data are actually used in the data analysis and report of the study's results. (chap. 10)

Alternate Forms Reliability   Also called equivalent or parallel forms reliability. A
   measure of the consistency or correlation between two supposedly equivalent
   versions of a test or inventory. (chap. 20)

Alternative Hypothesis   A statement predicting that a relationship exists between the
   variables being researched. The converse of the null hypothesis. If the null hypothesis is rejected, the alternative hypothesis is supported. (chap. 11)

Analysis of Variance   (see ANOVA)

ANOVA   A statistical method that uses the sums of the squares of the deviations from
   the means to test the differences among two or more groups; in most cases it allows the total variance to be separated and attributed to defined sources; the simplest case ANOVA compares the variability between groups (treatment variance
   plus error) to variability within groups (error). (chap. 13, 14, 15, 17, 18)

Association   When the same or paired participants have scores on two variables, the
   strength of their association can be analyzed by using techniques such as correlation (for two variables) or multiple regression (for more than one independent
   variable) or canonical correlation (for more than one independent and more than
   one dependent variable). (chap. 5, 16, 19)

Associational Inferential Statistics   A group or type of statistics that analyzes the associations or relationships among variables and tests of the statistical significance
   of the relationships. Includes correlation and multiple regression. See also: association. (chap. 5)

Associational Research Approach   Sometimes called correlational approach. A single group of subjects or matched pairs are used to examine the relationship between an independent variable and a dependent variable. Usually variables
   measured are continuous or have five or more ordered levels; if so, correlation coefficient (Pearson's or Spearman's) showing the strength of the association or relationship between variables can be computed. If the independent and dependent
   variables are nominal, phi or Cramer's V (if more than two levels of either variable) is the appropriate measure of association. (chap. 5, 13, 16, 19)

Associational Research Hypotheses or Questions   A type of research question that attempts to assess the relation between variables, usually in a single group of subjects; the associational approach tests associational hypotheses or questions. (chap. 5)

Attribute Independent Variable   A variable that is a characteristic or a trait of a participant or of their ongoing environment, which the researchers did not manipulate but only measured. A variable that cannot be manipulated or given, yet is a major focus of the study, for example, gender, age, ethnic group or disability. (chap. 4)

Basic Associational Question   Used in studies that examine associations or relationships between two variables: one dependent variable and one independent variable. See also: complex associational question. (chap. 5, 13, 16)

Basic Difference Question   Used with randomized experimental, quasi-experimental, and comparative approaches; examines differences between groups or differences between two or more measures of the same participant (within subjects design). These questions have a single independent and a single dependent variable. (chap. 5, 13, 14, 15)

Between Groups Designs   Designs where each subject participating in the research is in one and only one condition or group. (chap. 12)

Bias   A consistent, nonrandom error in measurement with a predictable pattern across variables, which results in an over or under estimation of population values. (chap. 10)

Calculated Value   A value or number obtained after subjecting collected data to a statistical formula. (chap. 11)

Canonical Correlation   A correlation between linear composites formed from several independent and several dependent variables (chap. 13)

Cases   Persons, groups, or events that are of interest in a particular study. (chap. 10)

Categorical Variable   A variable that distinguishes among subjects by putting them into a limited number of levels, categories, or groups, indicating type or kind, as gender does by categorizing people into male or female. Also called discrete and nominal variable, but not all categorical variables have unordered categories. For example, low, medium, and high IQ is a categorical variable but not nominal. (chap. 4, 9)

Cause   When a change in one variable produces a change in another variable, the first variable is said to cause the second. There is much disagreement among researchers about how and even whether causes can be identified. (chap. 2, 5, 6)

Chi-square Test for Independence   A nonparametric, inferential statistical test that compares an expected frequency with a measured frequency (observed cases). Results show whether or not the results could have occurred by chance within the population. Used to determine a significant difference between two or more groups when there is one independent variable that is categorized on two or a few levels, and the dependent variable is also categorical. (chap. 13, 14)

Cluster   A collection or group (e.g., towns or schools) of potential subjects that do not overlap. Usually geographically grouped together. (chap. 4)

Cluster Sampling   Two-stage sampling procedure that first randomly selects specific groups (clusters) of subjects, and then selects all subjects (or a fixed proportion randomly) from those groups. (chap. 10)

Cochran Q Test   A nonparametric statistic used in a design where the independent variable has three or more levels and the participants undergo all conditions or have been matched on the relevant variable. The dependent variable is nominal or categorical. Frequencies are the unit of measurement. A chi-square distribution is used to determine statistical significance. (chap. 15)

Coefficient of Equivalence   Computed when testing for equivalent or parallel forms of reliability, establishing a relationship between the two forms of the same test. (chap. 20)

Coefficient of Stability   Computed when testing for test–retest reliability. (chap. 20)

Comparative Research Approach   Examines the difference between groups that are nonequivalent. Each group has differing characteristics but is the same in terms of some attribute independent variables. The number of groups corresponds to the number of levels of the attribute independent variable. There are always at least two and usually not more than four levels. The investigator cannot randomly assign subjects to groups because subjects are grouped according to one individual attribute that the investigator cannot alter or manipulate (e.g., gender, eye color, political affiliation). (chap. 5)

Comparison Group   A group of participants in a quasi-experiment who do not receive the treatment or intervention. Also a group in a randomized experiment that receives an alternative treatment. (chap. 7)

Complex Associational Question   Used in a study that examines relationships among variables within a single group. Has two or more independent variables used to predict one dependent variable. (chap. 13, 19)

Complex Associational Statistic   A statistic designed to predict a single dependent outcome variable from several independent variables. (chap. 13, 19)

Complex Difference Question   Used in random experimental, quasi-experimental, or comparative studies that examine differences between groups or between measures on the same group (*within subjects* designs). There are two or more independent variables. (chap. 13, 17, 18)

Concurrent Evidence for Criterion Validity   Also called concurrent validity. Examines the relationship between a measurement and an outside criterion, as does predictive validity, but assesses the test to be validated and the criterion at roughly the same time. (chap. 20)

Confidence Interval   A range of values within which there is a predetermined probability (95%) that the population parameters may fall. (chap. 14)

Construct   Something that exists theoretically but is not directly observable. A concept developed (constructed) for describing relations among phenomena or for other research purposes. (chap. 2)

Construct Validity   One aspect of measurement validity. A slow process where the investigator conducts studies to demonstrate that an instrument is measuring a construct (hypothetical concepts that cannot be directly observed). Three types of evidence are used to support construct validity: convergent, discriminant, and factorial. See also each type. (chap. 20)

Constructivist Paradigm   Asserts that reality and truth are subjective and dependent on each observer. Usually involves qualitative data collection and only descriptive or no statistical analyses. Frequently appropriate for human sciences research, which may involve consideration of variables that are difficult to quantify or to hold constant. Tends to be inductive in nature. Also called qualitative and naturalist paradigm. (chap. 1, 2)

Content Validity   An aspect of measurement validity. The content of the instrument is representative of the concept that is being measured. (chap. 20)

Continuous Variable   A variable that has an infinite (or very large) number of scores with a range. For example, height and grade point average are continuous variables. Person's heights could be 69.38 inches, 69.39 inches, or anything in between. (chap. 4)

Control Group   In randomized experimental research, a sample that receives no treatment to compare measurements with the sample that receives treatment. (chap. 5, 7)

Convenience Sample   A sample drawn from an approachable or easily obtainable subset of the general population. Participants are selected on the basis of convenience rather than making a serious attempt *beforehand* to select participants that are representative of the theoretical population. (chap. 10)

Convergent Evidence for Construct Validity   Other measures that are predicted theoretically to be related to the construct being validated are, in fact, related. One type of evidence to support construct validity. (chap. 20)

Correlation   A statistic that indicates the association or relationship between scores on two variables. Correlation may be positive, negative, or zero. Positive correlation reflects a direct relationship between two variables: as the value of one variable increases, the value of the other variable also increases. Negative correlation reflects an inverse relationship between two variables: As the value of one variable increases, the value of the other variable decreases. If no systematic relationship exists between two variables, the correlation is said to be zero. (chap. 16)

Correlation Coefficient   A number between -1.0 and $+1.0$ that expresses the strength of an association or relationship. Usually symbolized as r. (chap. 16)

Cramer's V   A statistical test used in associational research approaches where both the independent and dependent variables are nominal or categorical. (chap. 13, 16)

Credible   To be trustworthy or believable. Qualitative research frequently establishes credibility by relying on other researchers to reanalyze collected research data and corroborate the original research conclusions. (chap. 2)

Criterion-Related Validity   One aspect of measurement validity. Validating the instrument against a form of external criterion, usually involving computing a correlation coefficient between the instrument and the external or outside criterion, either concurrently or predictively. See also concurrent and predictive evidence for validity. (chap. 20)

Critical Value   The precise numerical values that define the limits of rejection for a null hypothesis. Values used in testing a statistic to determine if it is significant, that is, if it exceeds the parameters of the null hypothesis. (chap. 11)

Cronbach's Alpha   A method to determine interitem reliability or internal consistency for measures with several items (each with ordered responses) that will be summed to make a composite scale. (chap. 20)

Cross-Sectional Design   A design in which each participant is assessed at one age, but other younger or older persons are also tested to make age or maturation comparisons. See also longitudinal designs. (chap. 12)

Decision Trees   A pictorial method, resembling a flow chart, for breaking down the statistical selection process. (chap. 13, 14, 15, 17, 18)

Deductive Reasoning   Using the logic pattern of applying general principles to derive conclusions about specific cases. Used in quantitative studies to test a theory by deducing hypotheses, which are tested using statistics. (chap. 2)

Degrees of Freedom (df)   The number of data values that are free to vary when calculating a statistic. The number of observations (n) minus the number of restrictions placed on the data; *df* is used to look up critical values for many statistical tests. (chap. 11)

Dependent Variable   The dependent variable is the presumed outcome or criterion. It is assumed to measure or assess the effect of the independent variable. (chap. 4)

Descriptive Research Approach   This basic research approach considers only one variable at a time so that no comparisons or relationships are made. Descriptive research approaches use only descriptive statistics such as averages, percentages, histograms, and frequency distributions. (chap. 5)

Descriptive Statistics   Procedures for summarizing, organizing, graphing, and, in general, describing quantitative information. Often contrasted with inferential statistics, which are used to make inferences about a population based on information about a sample drawn from that population. (chap. 9)

Dichotomous Variable   Also called dummy variable. A variable with two levels or categories (e.g., male and female). Can be used in multiple regression analyses as an independent, predictor variable. (chap. 9, 19)

Difference Hypothesis or Questions   Predictive statements about the relationship between groups formed from the independent variables. Research questions are similar to hypotheses but are in question format. Difference hypotheses and questions are used when the research approach is randomized experimental, quasi-experimental, or comparative. (chap. 5)

Difference Inferential Statistics   Statistics that analyze the differences between two or more groups or levels of a variable. Used with randomized experimental, quasi-experimental, and comparative research approaches. Differences between two independent groups can be assessed using a two-sample *t* test (or the nonparametric Mann–Whitney or chi-square test). If the design is within subjects and there are two measures or conditions, use related samples *t* test (or the nonparametric Wilcoxon or McNemar tests). Differences between several independent groups formed from one independent variable can be tested using a one-way ANOVA. Several repeated assessments can be tested using repeated measures ANOVA. (chap. 5, 13)

Directional Hypothesis   A research hypothesis that predicts the direction of the relationship between variables. Because it bases rejection of the null hypothesis on a one-tailed test, it is a more statistically stringent measure than the nondirectional hypothesis. (chap. 11)

Disciplined Inquiry   A systematic investigation of a matter of public interest so that a logical argument can be carefully examined. Evidential tests and verification are valued. A dispassionate search for truth is valued over ideology. (chap. 1)

Discriminant Analysis   A complex associational statistic used to predict a categorical outcome (e.g., pass versus fail) from several normally distributed independent variables. Used to classify participants into groups. (chap. 19)

Discriminant Evidence for Construct Validity   Evidence to support construct validity is provided when groups that are predicted from theory or literature to differ on the measurement being validated. (chap. 20)

Disordinal Interaction   In graphing the results of a factorial ANOVA, when differences between cell means within a group are statistically significant, and when the lines that connect the cell mean (within-group differences) for two separate groups intersect, the interaction is disordinal. When they do not intersect but are significant, the interaction is ordinal. See also ordinal interaction. (chap. 17)

Dummy Variable   A dichotomous (two levels), variable (such as gender) that is assigned binary values for purposes of computation (i.e., male = 1, female = 2). See dichotomous variable. (chap. 9, 19)

Ecological External Validity   The extent to which the research is generalizable on the basis of whether the research environment is similar to the "real world" or natural environment. There are several aspects of ecological validity: naturalness of the setting and procedures, rapport with the researcher, and lack of time boundness to the questions or problem (chap. 10, 24)

Effect Size   Any of several measures of the strength of a relation. By contrast, tests of the null hypothesis only allow you to conclude that a relation is significantly larger than zero, but they do not tell you by how much. Thus, the effect size is an estimate of the degree to which a phenomenon is present in a population, or the extent to which the null hypothesis is false, or both. (chap. 11, 23)

Efficacy (of a technique or treatment)   In research, applies to evaluating the degree to which an experimental treatment or intervention has the desired or predicted effect. (chap. 6, 7)

Elements   Objects or persons of interest to be sampled in a particular study, usually the individual participants. (chap. 10)

Empirical Data   Information based on observations or experience. Often contrasted with theoretical information. (chap. 4)

Epistemology   Study or theory of how knowledge is attained and the limits, validity and reliability of knowledge. Variance exists in definitions of what knowledge is and how it is created or discovered. See chapter 2 for a discussion of two points of view: the positivist and constructivist.

Error Variance   In an ANOVA, the purpose of analyzing variance is to factor out the amount of variance between subjects within their own groups to more accurately determine the variance between groups. The amount of variance within the group is the error variance. (chap. 14, 15, 17, 18)

Experimental Approaches   Includes both randomized experimental and quasi-experimental research designs. They are generally strong in internal validity, so one can be more certain than with any other approaches about attributing cause to the independent variables. However, quasi-experimental designs vary greatly in strength and, thus, internal validity. (chap. 5, 7)

External Validity   This aspect of research validity, the validity of a whole study, deals with the question of generalizability. It has two aspects, population (sample representativeness) and ecological (naturalness of the research setting and process). (chap. 10, 24)

Extraneous Variables   These variables are not of interest in a particular study but they could influence the dependent variable, for example, environmental factors, time of day, and so on. (chap. 4)

F Statistic (F ratio)   In the ANOVA source of variation table, computing an *F* value is the final step. It is the variance between groups (treatment plus error) divided by the variance within each group (error). This ratio is used to assess whether a difference could have occurred by chance. (chap. 14, 15, 17, 18)

Face Validity   One aspect of measurement validity. The content of the instrument appears to be appropriate for the purpose of measuring the intended construct. Not accepted as a scientific method of validation, but often helpful in convincing the public. (chap. 20)

Factor   Another term for independent variable (e.g., single factor design = design with one independent variable). (chap. 14, 15)

Factor Analysis   A complex associational statistic used primarily to reduce a relatively large number of items or questions to a smaller number of composite variables. (chap.19)

Factorial ANOVA   An analysis of variance with two or more independent variables. See also factorial design. (chap. 17)

Factorial Design   A complex design with more than one independent variable. Designs with two variables are called two-factor or factorial designs. (chap. 17)

Factorial Evidence for Construct Validity   One type of evidence to support the measurement validity of a construct. Factor analysis supports the proposed theoretical organization of the aspects of a construct. (chap. 20)

Field   Study in a natural setting, not in a laboratory. An example is a school classroom. (chap. 1)

Frequency Distribution   Tabulation that indicates the number of times a given score or group of scores occurs. (chap. 9)

Frequency Polygons   A figure or chart that diagrams the frequency distribution and connects the points between ordered categories. (chap. 9)

Friedman Test   A nonparametric analysis of variance by using ranks when there is one independent variable with three or more levels, and a repeated measures or within subjects design. (chap. 13, 15)

Generalize   See external validity. (chap. 10, 24)

Hawthorne Effect   A specific kind of threat to research validity. The name is taken from the Hawthorne electric plant at which a team of researchers intended to experiment with how changes in the worker's environment (better lighting, more coffee breaks) might contribute to improved productivity. With these independent changes, productivity increased. The increase was attributed to the worker's knowledge that the treatment was intended to result in a positive response from the subjects. Ironically, subsequent studies in which a proposed treatment was hypothesized to decrease productivity (poorer lighting or fewer coffee breaks) also resulted in improved productivity. Thus the term is now used to describe any positive effect on a dependent variable that can be attributed to the participant's knowledge of the treatment, whether or not the treatment is implemented and whether or not the intended treatment is favorable. Opposite of "demoralization effect." (chap. 2, 6)

Homogeneity of Variance (Assumption of ...)   Although each sample will have individual members that differ from one another in their measured characteristics (variance), it is presumed that one sample does not have more variation in its members than does another sample of equal size. When the samples are equal, a *t* test of the difference between the means of the samples is an appropriate measure of comparison. When sample sizes differ between groups, this assumption is likely to be violated and an adjusted *t* test (Welch's) must be calculated to account for the differing sizes. This is one of the three underlying assumptions that must be met to use a *t* test or ANOVA. See also normality and independence. (chap. 13, 14, 15)

Hypothesis   A predictive statement about the relationship between two or more variables that a researcher intends to study. (chap. 4)

Independence (Assumption of ...)   Assumes that, within each sample, scores for the dependent variable are independent of each other. The performance of one participant is not affected by the performance of another participant. This is one of the three underlying assumptions that must be met to use a *t* test or ANOVA and many other statistical tests. See also homogeneity of variance and normality. (chap. 13, 14)

Independent Samples   Samples or groups that meet the assumption of independence. Thus, the two-sample *t* test is also called the independent samples *t* test. (chap. 14)

Independent Variable   The presumed cause in a study. Also a variable that can be used to predict the values of another variable. (chap. 4)

Inductive Reasoning   Using the logic of applying specific instances to derive general conclusions. Constructivist researchers argue that their approach is inductive in contrast to the deductive nature of the classical positivist scientific method. See also deductive reasoning. (chap. 2)

Inferential Statistics   Statistics that allow one to draw conclusions or inferences from data. Usually this means coming to conclusions about a population on the basis of data that describe a sample. (chap. 11)

Instrument Validity   See measurement validity. (chap. 20)

Instrumentation   A form or device used to collect data. Examples include interviews, questionnaires, and observations. (chap. 21, Appendix B)

Interaction Effect   Also called conditioning effect, joint effect, and moderating effect. The joint effect of two or more independent variables on a dependent variable. Interaction effects occur when independent variables have combined effects on a dependent variable. Interaction effects occur when the relation between two variables differs depending on the level of another variable. (chap. 17, 18)

Interitem Reliability   Also called internal consistency reliability. How all of the items of an instrument are related to each other. (chap. 20)

Internal Consistency Reliability   When the instrument is consistent among items. Cronbach's alpha is the most common measure of this type of reliability. (chap. 20)

Internal Validity   One aspect of research validity, the validity of a whole study. The extent to which the results of a study can be attributed to the treatments rather than to flaws in the research design. In other words, the degree to which one can draw valid conclusions about the causal effects of one variable on another. (chap. 6, 24)

Interrater (Interobserver) Reliability   The measure of reliability or consistency among judges (observers) in tools where observation is performed. Usually two or more judges score certain episodes of behavior; then the researcher computes a measure of agreement among judges (e.g., Cohen's Kappa, correlation, interclass correlation coefficient). (chap. 20)

Interval Scale of Measurement   Mutually exclusive categories that are ordered from high to low. The categories have equal intervals between them. (chap. 9)

Intervention   See treatment.

Interview   A data collection technique in which the researcher or interviewer asks questions orally of the participant who answers orally. There are several variants. (chap. 21)

Intraclass Correlation Coefficient (ICC)   A coefficient used to allow the researcher to calculate a reliability coefficient with two or more judges. A criterion for using the ICC is that the behavior being rated must be scaled at an interval level. (chap. 20)

Inverse Relationship   A negative relationship where persons with higher scores on one variable or test have lower scores on the second variable or test, and vice versa. (chap. 16)

Kappa Statistic   A method of calculating an intraclass correlation coefficient when the data are categorical or nominal. (chap. 20)

Kendall's Tau   A statistical test used in associational research approaches where both the independent and dependent variables are at least ordinal or one of the assumptions is markedly violated. (chap. 13)

Kruskal–Wallis (one-way ANOVA)   An alternative to a parametric one-way ANOVA, a nonparametric analysis of variance used for studies with one independent variable with two or more levels, and a dependent variable that is ordinal or ranks or when ANOVA assumptions are markedly violated. (chap. 13, 14)

Kuder–Richardson 20 (K–R 20)   A method of determining interitem reliability on tests where items are scored dichotomously. (chap. 20)

Laboratory Research   Any of several methods of isolating subjects so as to control extraneous variables. Sometimes considered to be synonymous with experimental research, but lab research can use any approach. Subjects can be isolated from contexts that might influence their behavior; hence, the research can focus on those independent variables of interest. (chap. 1)

Laws of Probability   The probability of an event, $p (X)$, is the ratio of the number of outcomes that include X to the total number of possible outcomes. (chap. 11)

Levels of a Variable   The different values, categories, or conditions of a variable, usually an independent variable (e.g., intervention versus control or married versus widowed versus divorced). Also the values of the dependent variable; usually there are many (e.g., scores on a test). The term level does not necessarily imply that values are ordered. (chap. 4)

Levels of Measurement   Similar to scales of measurement, but making distinctions that are more important for the selection of statistics. The levels are dichotomous, nominal, ordinal, and normal or normally distributed. See each term. (chap. 9)

Likert-Type Rating Scale   Individual items whose responses indicate the degree of agreement: usually strongly agree, agree, neutral, disagree, strongly disagree. (chap. 21)

Linear Regression   Based on an equation to predict the dependent variable from knowledge of the independent variable, providing that the correlation between the two variables is known. Linear regression is also used to examine the linear relationship between the independent and dependent variable. See correlation. (chap. 16)

Literature   See research literature.

Logical Positivist Paradigm   Also called the quantitative or dominant paradigm. In the extreme, asserts that reality and truth are singular and knowable. The research approach that adheres to strict scientific methodology involving deductive hypothesis testing through experimentation, quantitative data collection, and statistical analyses based on the approach of natural science research. (chap. 2)

Logistic Regression   A complex associational statistical technique used to predict a dichotomous dependent or outcome variable from a combination of several independent variables, some or all of which can be dichotomous. (chap. 19)

Longitudinal Design   One in which participants are assessed at two or more ages to determine maturation or the effect of some treatment over time. See also cross sectional designs. (chap. 12)

Main Effect   In a two or more factorial (ANOVA), it indicates the "effect" of each independent variable separately. This is the "main effect" of each independent variable by itself on the dependent variable. (chap. 14, 15, 17, 18)

Mann–Whitney U Test   A nonparametric test to determine if a significant difference exists between two groups. Commonly used instead of a t test for independent groups or samples when the dependent variable data is ordinal or the assumption of normality does not apply. (chap. 13, 14)

McNemar Test   A nonparametric test used in a design where there is one independent variable, with two levels, and the participants undergo both conditions, or pairs of participants have been matched on a relevant variable. The dependent variable is nominal or categorical data. Frequencies are the unit of measure. (chap. 13, 15)

Mean   Also called arithmetic average. Derived by summing all scores, then dividing by the number of all scores. Most common measurement of central tendency. (chap. 9)

Mean Square (MS)   An essential part of an ANOVA source table, calculated by dividing the sum of squares by the degrees of freedom. (chap. 14, 15, 17, 18)

Measurement   The assignment of numerals to objects or events according to rules. (chap. 9)

Measurement Reliability   The extent to which a measurement is consistent. There are four types of reliability indexes: test–retest, parallel forms, internal consistency, and interrater. Each provides different information about the reliability or consistency of a measure or test. (chap. 20)

Measurement Scales   According to Stevens, there are four scales or levels of measurement: nominal, ordinal, interval, and ratio. See each term, also levels of measurement. (chap. 9)

Measurement Validity   An assessment of how well an instrument measures a construct for a given purpose in a given population. Contrast with research validity. (chap. 20)

Measures of Central Tendency   Measures of the center of a frequency distribution. See mean, median, and mode. (chap. 9)

Median   The middle score. In a distribution of scores, the point below which 50% of all scores fall, derived by simply counting the number of scores above and below that point. (chap. 9)

Meta-Analysis   Quantitative procedures for summarizing or integrating the findings obtained from a number of related studies. The meta-analyst uses the results of individual research projects on the same topic (perhaps studies testing the same hypothesis) by using effect sizes to combine the results. (chap. 23)

Mixed Designs   Mixed designs have at least one between groups independent variable and at least one within subjects independent variable. They have a minimum of two independent variables. (chap. 12)

Mode   The most frequently occurring score in a distribution, derived by simply counting which score occurs most often. (chap. 9)

Multiple Regression   A complex associational statistic used to predict a normally distributed outcome or dependent variable from several normally distributed or dichotomous independent prediction variables. (chap. 19)

Multivariate Analysis of Variance (MANOVA)   A complex difference statistic used to consider several related dependent variables at a time, when there are one or more independent variables. (chap. 19)

Naturalist Paradigm   Often called qualitative. See constructivist paradigm. (chap. 1, 2)

"No Treatment" Effect   In studies in which the effects of one or more treatments are observed, a control group that does not receive a treatment is useful to determine whether or not a change may occur with "no treatment" at all. Adding a control group may increase internal validity by increasing the control of experience or environmental variables. (chap. 5)

Nominal Scale   Numerals assigned to each category stand for the name of the category, but have no implied order or value. All members of a category are considered the same but different from those in other categories. Examples: Gender, school curriculum, hair color, marital status. (chap. 9)

Non-Directional Hypothesis   A research hypothesis that does not predict the direction of the relationship between variables. Uses a two-tailed test to reject the null hypothesis. (chap. 11)

Nonparametric Statistics   Also called distribution-free statistics. Inferential statistics that do not assume the sample comes from a population that is normally distributed. The chi-square test is probably the best known example. See parametric statistics. (chap. 13, 14, 15, 16)

Nonprobability Sampling   Selecting participants from the general population such that each member of the general population has an unknown (and usually unequal) chance for inclusion in the study sample. Convenience samples are common examples of nonrandom selection. Can affect external validity of the study, but does not necessarily affect internal validity. (chap. 10)

Normal Curve   A theoretical continuous probability distribution in which the horizontal axis represents all possible values of a variable. The total area under the curve is 1.0. The scores on this variable are clustered around the mean in a symmetrical, unimodal pattern known as the bell-shaped or normal curve. In a normal distribution, the mean, median and mode are all the same. (chap. 9)

Normal Level of Measurement   A variable with ordered levels or categories on which scores are distributed approximately like the normal (bell-shaped) distribution in the population. (chap. 9)

Normality (Assumption of ...)   Assumes that the scores of the dependent variable are normally distributed in each of the populations from which samples are selected. One of the three underlying assumptions that should be met to use a *t* test or ANOVA. See also homogeneity of variance and independence. (chap. 14, 15, 17, 18)

Null Hypothesis   The hypothesis that two or more variables are not related or that two or more means are not different in the population. In accumulating evidence that the null hypothesis is false, the researcher indirectly demonstrates that the variables are related or that the means are different. The null hypothesis is central to hypothesis testing. (chap. 11)

Objective   See objectivity.

Objectivity   Treating or dealing with facts while void of personal feelings or prejudices. (chap. 1, 2, 21)

Observed Score   A score obtained from any subject on a particular instrument. According to classical test theory, the observed score is composed of the true score and error. (chap. 20)

One-Group Posttest-Only Design   In this poor quasi-experimental design, the treatment is given to one group of subjects, and then a posttest takes place. The problem with this design is that it does not satisfy even the minimum condition for a research problem, which is to investigate a relationship or comparison. There is only one level of the intervention, so it is not a variable. The value of this design is that it may serve as pilot data for a future experiment. (chap. 7)

One-Group Pretest–Posttest Design   A poor quasi-experimental design. This design provides an observation in the form of a pretest, then the intervention is given, and last, a second observation in the form of a posttest is recorded. This design is better than the one-group posttest-only design because you can compare the pre- and posttest, but without a control or comparison group, you cannot know if the dependent variable would have changed without the intervention. (chap. 7)

One-Way ANOVA   An analysis of variance to use when you have one between groups independent variable with two or more levels. (chap. 14)

Operational Definition   Describes or defines a variable in terms of the operations used to produce it or the techniques used to measure it. (chap. 4)

Operationalize   To define a concept or variable in such a way that it can be measured or identified (or "operated on"). When you operationalize a variable, you answer the questions: How will I know it when I see it? How will I record or measure it? (chap. 4)

Ordered Variable   Variable that has a set of values that vary from low to high within a certain range. (chap. 4)

Ordinal Interaction   In graphing the results of a factorial ANOVA, when an interaction F is significant and when the lines that connect the cell means for two separate groups do not intersect, the interaction is ordinal. When they intersect and are significant, the interaction is disordinal. See disordinal interaction. (chap. 17)

Ordinal Scale   Also called ordinal level of measurement. Categories are ordered from low to high in much the same way one would rank the order in which horses finish a race (first, second, third, ... last), and the intervals between the categories are not equal. Examples: 1st place, 2nd place, last; ranked preferences. (chap. 9)

Orthogonal   Statistically independent and perpendicular. The factors or components in a factor analysis. (chap. 19)

Outcome   The effect on the dependent variable of the independent variable. (chap. 4)

p   The likelihood that a statistical result would have been obtained by chance alone. This actual probability value (*p* value) is compared by a researcher with a *present* criterion, alpha, to determine whether the result has "statistical significance." If the *p* value is smaller than alpha (usually .05), the result is statistically significant. (chap. 11)

Paired Samples   Also called related samples and within subjects. Refers to a type of design in which two or more measures of the same variable are obtained on one sample of subjects, or similar measures are obtained from paired (e.g., twins, couples, sibs) or matched subjects. (chap. 15)

Paradigm   A philosophical or mental lens through which the world is viewed, based on the shared beliefs of a community. A given paradigm is a way of thinking about and conducting research. It will influence what research questions or hypotheses are generated, how they will be examined, and how gathered data will be interpreted. The two paradigms examined in the text are positivist and constructivist. (chap. 2)

Parallel Forms Reliability   Also called equivalent or alternate forms reliability. Reliability is assessed with two presumably equivalent versions of the same instrument. (chap. 20)

Parametric Statistics   Techniques designed for use when data have certain characteristics—usually when they approximate a normal distribution and are measurable with interval or ratio scales. (chap. 13, 14, 15, 16)

Participants   People of interest in a particular study; formerly called subjects.

Pearson Product–Moment Correlation (r)   Degree of linear relationship or association between two variables that are normally distributed and meet other assumptions. For example, relationship between height in inches and weight in pounds. (chap. 16)

Percentage Agreement Methods   Determines interrater reliability by having two or more raters observe behaviors and then compute a percentage. (chap. 20)

Phi Coefficient   A type of correlation coefficient that is used when both variables are dichotomous. (chap. 13, 16)

Population   The group of interest, which is usually larger than the sample. See theoretical population and accessible population. (chap. 10)

Population Parameter   A measure of a variable within a theoretical population. (chap. 11)

Positivist Paradigm   Often called the quantitative framework, the investigator establishes a detailed plan prior to the study, which includes the subjects of the investigation, how they are selected, the treatment, and how the treatment is measured. (chap. 1, 2)

Post Hoc Test   Literally, a Latin phrase meaning "after this," a post hoc test is a necessary final test in many analyses. When an overall or omnibus statistic is identified as being significant, a post hoc test helps identify where the significance occurs (e.g., a Tukey Honestly Significant Difference post hoc test makes every possible comparison of groups, two at time). (chap. 14)

Posttest-only Control Group Design   One of the randomized experimental designs. Because there is a random assignment of subjects to groups, one can assume that the two groups are equivalent prior to the intervention. Therefore, if there are differences on the dependent measure following the intervention, and all other variables are equal or controlled, it can be assumed that the differences are due to the intervention and not due to differences in subject characteristics. (chap. 7)

Power (... of a Statistic)   Power is the ability of a statistic to detect a true relationship. Parametric statistical tests are more "powerful" than nonparametric tests because there is a higher probability that parametric test results will lead the researcher to correctly reject the null hypothesis when it should be rejected (that is, when it really is false). The less likely the probability of making a type I or type II error, the more powerful the test. (chap. 23)

Predictive Evidence of Criterion Validity   The extent that one can predict how a subject will do on the criterion measure in the future based on a score on the instrument to be validated. (chap. 20)

Probability   The likelihood that a particular event or relationship will occur. The proportional expectation of a given outcome. Values for statistical probability range from 1.0 to 0. (chap. 11)

Probability Sampling   One of several methods (e.g., simple random) of obtaining a nonbiased selection of subjects where every subject or element in the population has a known, nonzero chance of being selected. (chap. 10)

Purposive Sampling   Subjects are hand picked from the accessible population and are judged to be appropriate or informative for the purpose of the study. (chap. 10)

Qualitative Data   Subjective observations that are difficult to score or classify. Such data are typically collected through open-ended interviews, observations, and documents. (chap. 1, 2)

Qualitative Research   Refers to a paradigm or approach to research that is contrasted with quantitative research. See also constructivist. (chap. 1, 2)

Quantitative Data   Observations of phenomenon, attributes or behavior, which can be numerically scored, rated, or scaled. (chap. 1, 2)

Quantitative Research   Research within the positivist framework that is usually handled numerically. (chap. 1, 2)

Quasi-experimental Approach   A type of research approach for conducting studies in field or real-life situations where there is an active independent variable that the researcher may be able to manipulate, but the researcher cannot randomly assign subjects to comparison and experimental groups. (chap. 5, 7)

Questionnaire   A general term for a data collection technique in which respondents answer a series of questions in writing. There are many variants of the types and ways that questions are asked (orally versus in writing) and the types of responses requested (open ended, multiple choice, etc.). This term includes single use surveys as well as standardized inventories. (chap. 21)

Questionnaire Item   A single question or item on the questionnaire. (chap. 21)

Quota Sampling   An attempt to make the sample representative by assigning interviewers quotas for each of several demographic variables (e.g., gender, race, census tract). A certain degree of latitude is given to interviewer about how they fill the quotas. (chap. 10)

Random Assignment of Participants to Groups   Putting subjects into experimental and control groups in such a way that each individual in each group is assigned entirely by chance. Each subject has an equal probability of being placed in each group. Using random assignment reduces the likelihood of bias. (chap. 5)

Random Assignment of Treatments to Groups   In quasi-experiments, one way to compensate for inability to randomly assign participants to groups is to randomly assign the intervention and control conditions to intact groups. (chap. 7)

Random Order of Conditions or Treatments to Each Participant   A within subjects design is considered randomized experimental if the treatment order is randomized. (chap. 12)

Random Selection or Sampling   Selecting a group of subjects (a sample) for study from a larger group (population) so that each individual (or other unit of analysis) is chosen entirely by chance. A random sample is not the same thing as a haphazard or accidental sample. (chap. 5, 10)

Randomized Experimental Research Approach   Members of a sample are randomly assigned to two or more groups in which an independent variable is manipulated and its effect on a dependent variable is observed. If well designed, it provides the best evidence about cause(s) of the differences on a dependent variable. The independent variable must be active, usually manipulated by the researcher. The greatest strength is usually high internal validity. The greatest weakness may be external validity, both population external validity, if the sample is not representative, and ecological external validity, if the setting is artificial. Includes several specific designs. (chap. 5, 7)

Rank   Put in order of first, second, third, fourth. Note the difference from rate. (chap. 9)

Rate   To indicate extent or amount (e.g., of agreement such as strongly agree, agree, neutral). (chap. 9)

Rating Scale   A measuring instrument used to obtain self-reports or observer ratings of the amount or extent of a behavior, attitude, etc. See Likert-type rating scale, summated ratings scale, semantic differential scale. (chap. 21)

Ratio Scale   Categories that have equal intervals and have a true zero. Examples: Length, weight, dollars and many other physical measures. (chap. 9)

Reality   A perception of what is not artificial or imaginary to a particular person.
   Positivist view - There is a single tangible reality fragmentable into separate variables and processes. *Constructivist view* - There are multiple constructed realities that can be studied only holistically. (chap. 2)

Related Samples   See paired samples.

Reliability   See measurement reliability. Consistency throughout a series of measurements. To the extent a test contains unsystematic variation, the lower reliability. (chap. 20)

Reliability Coefficient   According to classical test theory, the ratio of the variance of true scores to the variance of observed scores. (chap. 20)

Repeated Measures Designs   See within subjects designs.

Representative Sample   A sample that represents the population (i.e., a small replica of the population) with all the key variables in the same proportions as the whole population. (chap. 10)

Research   Systematic and disciplined method of gaining new information or answering questions. Design, methods, and conclusions must adhere to logical and verifiable standards. Duplication of the research by others should yield consistent conclusions. (chap. 1)

Research Literature   The scholarly writing (usually published) about a given researchable topic. Includes empirical research reports, theoretical articles, and reviews of research. (chap. 4)

Research Problem   The guiding interrogative statement that determines what issues will be examined in designing a research project and that helps to identify the dependent variable(s). Directs the researcher toward a critical review of concepts and theories and a clear identification of related major research issues. Helps develop clear and logical rationales for a formal hypothesis. (chap. 4)

Research Question   Stating the research problem in the form of a question. Research questions are more specific than research problems and there may be several questions to help determine an answer to a single research problem. (chap. 4, 5)

Research Validity   The quality or merit of the *whole* study. (chap. 6, 10, 23, 24)

Response Rate   The number of people interviewed or responding divided by the number of people sampled. (chap. 10)

Sample   A selected part of a larger group of participants taken with the intent of generalizing from the smaller group or sample to the theoretical population. (chap. 10)

Sample Statistics   Statistics derived from analyzing data from a sample. Inferential statistics use these numbers to make generalizations about the theoretical population. (chap. 11)

Sampling   The process of selecting part of a larger group of subjects with the intent of generalizing from the sample group, called the *sample*, to the population. (chap. 10)

Sampling Design   The process by which the selected sample is chosen. (chap. 10)

Sampling Distribution of Means   The distribution of the mean values of all the possible samples of *n* size drawn from the theoretical population. (chap. 11)

Scales of Measurement   See measurement scales. (chap. 9)

Scientific Method   From the Latin "scientia" = knowledge and Greek "methodos" = way, a view held by positivists that knowledge can be attained through a process of logical inquiry. The classic five steps are (a) observe the repeated occurrence of a phenomenon and formulate a theory that explains it, (b) from the theory, devise a general hypothesis that predicts the necessary conditions under which the specific phenomenon will occur, (c) from the hypothesis, deduce other consequences (predict other specific occurrences), (d) devise experiments to test whether or not these consequences occur. If the consequences occur, then the hypothesis is considered true and the theory is valid. Early in the twentieth century, a logical fallacy was recognized (by Popper) in the final step of this method: the theory has not been proven, rather, it has only been not disproved. In other words it has only been shown to hold true for the cases observed. Logic requires that if one counterexample can be generated, then the conclusion cannot be true. Therefore, constructivists can object that a generalization cannot be made until all possible cases, not just those examined, have been proven, which is usually impractical or impossible. This has led to a more careful approach to external validation by positivists and to a variety of alternative research approaches by constructivists. (chap. 2)

Screening   Excluding subjects that did not meet the stated purpose of the study. (chap. 10)

Selected Sample   Group of subjects who are selected by the researcher and asked to participate in the study. (chap. 10)

Self-Assignment or Selection   Once a sample is selected from the general population, subjects are allowed to assign themselves to the study or treatment group in which they choose to participate. Compromises internal validity. See random assignment. (chap. 5, 6)

Self-Report   Participants in a study report to the researcher (in writing or orally) about their attitudes, intentions, or behavior. (chap. 1, 21)

Semantic Differential Scale   Subjects rate concepts such as "my job" on sets of bipolar adjective pairs. These include Activity pairs, such as active–passive, fast–slow; Evaluative pairs, such as good–bad, valuable–worthless; Potency pairs, such as strong–weak, large–small. (chap. 21)

Significance Level (alpha level)   The probability of committing a type I error. The probability of rejecting a true null hypothesis. (chap. 11)

Simple Random Sampling   A sample in which all subjects or elements have an equal and independent chance of being included in the sample. (chap. 10)

Single Factor Design   The design of a study with one independent variable. (chap. 4, 5, 14, 15)

Snowball Sampling   Building a sample from the references of a few subjects that meet the criteria of the study. (chap. 10)

Source Table (Source of Variance Table)   In analysis of variance, a table is generated that enumerates the sums of squared deviations (SS) from the mean of each group, the degrees of freedom (df) for each group, the mean squares (MS) for each group, and finally, an F ratio is calculated. (chap. 14, 15, 17, 18)

Spearman Rank–Order Correlation   A nonparametric hypothesis testing procedure that use continuous data that has been ranked. To perform the Spearman correlation coefficient, rank the data as in other nonparametric tests and then perform a Pearson product–moment correlation on the ranks. Symbol: $r(s)$ See also correlation and Pearson product–moment correlation. (chap. 13, 16)

Split-Half Reliability   Process of determining internal consistency by correlating one half of instrument with the other half of instrument. (chap. 20)

Standard Deviation   A measure of the variance (variability) or spread of scores around the mean within a distribution. (chap. 9)

Standard Error of the Mean   The standard deviation of the distribution of the sample means. (chap. 11)

Standardization   To make uniform. Usually performed on an instrument by obtaining norms and producing a manual. (chap. 21)

Statistically Significant Difference   The probability that the difference between the population parameter and the sample statistic occurred by chance at a level less than the predetermined significance level. (chap. 11)

Statistics   A set of procedures and theory that are used to analyze data. (chap. 9)

Strata   Variables used to divide the populations into segments. (chap. 10)

Stratified Random Sampling   Grouping the sample on the basis of key variables to ensure that the sample contains the exact proportion of subjects with these key variables, as in the population. (chap. 10)

Stratified Sampling With Differential Probabilities of Selection   Oversampling underrepresented groups to have similar-sized groups to make reasonable comparisons. (chap. 10)

Strength of Association   The degree of relationship between two (or more) variables. Often the proportion of the variability in a dependent variable explained by or accounted for by the independent variable(s). Eta squared, r^2, and omega squared are common measures of strength of association. (chap. 2, 11)

Strong Positive Relationship   Those scoring high on one test or variable will also score high on the second test or variable and vice versa. (chap. 16)

Summated Rating Scale   Each subject's responses to several ratings are added together. (chap. 21)

Sums of Squares (SS).   An essential part of the ANOVA source table. The sum of squared deviations for all scores. (chap. 14)

Systematic Random Sampling   Randomly selecting the sample, but first randomly selecting the starting point and then systematically selecting each nth subject (such as every tenth one). (chap. 10)

Systematic Variation   Variation from the independent variable or intervention. (chap. 10)

t test for Correlated or Paired Samples   A common parametric statistic that compares two levels or conditions within the same group of participants. (chap. 13, 15)

t test for Independent Samples or Groups   A common parametric statistic that compares two separate groups by computing the ratio of the variance between groups to the variation within groups. (chap. 13, 14)

Theoretical or Target Population   All of the subjects of the theoretical interest to which the researcher would like to generalize. (chap. 10)

Theory   A set of interrelated constructs (concepts), definitions, and postulations that present a systematic view of phenomena by specifying relations among variables, with the purpose of explaining and predicting the phenomena. (chap. 1, 2, 4)

Time-Series Analysis   Analysis of changes in variables over time. Any of several statistical procedures used to tell whether a change in time-series data is due to some variable that occurred at the same time or is due to coincidence. (chap. 7)

Time-Series Design   A set of measures of a variable recorded periodically, before and after an event or treatment. (chap. 7)

Treatment   Also called intervention and experimental group. The study group or subjects for which an active independent variable is manipulated is said to have received a treatment, that is, the independent variable differs for that group and the effects on the dependent variable are observed. (chap. 4, 5 ff)

True Experimental Designs   See Randomized Experimental Designs.

True Score   The average of an infinite number of observed scores for one individual. (chap. 20)

Tukey HSD   A pair-wise post hoc test for a significant overall/omnibus *F* test. See post hoc test. (chap. 14)

Two-by-Two Factorial Design   (2×2 design) A study crafted to examine the effects of two independent variables on a single dependent variable. Allows three hypotheses to be tested (difference between two levels of independent variable A, differences between two levels of independent variable B, and the interaction of A and B.) (chap. 17)

Two-Factor ANOVA   Also called a two-way analysis of variance. An inferential statistic that is used to compare group means (of groups formed from two independent variables) on one dependent variable. It is similar to a one-way ANOVA, adding a second independent variable. See ANOVA. (chap. 17)

Two-Factor Designs   See Factorial Design.

Type I Error   An error made by wrongly rejecting a true null hypothesis. This might involve incorrectly concluding that the two variables are related when they are not, or wrongly deciding that a sample statistic exceeds the value that would be expected by chance. This is also called alpha error. (chap. 11)

Type II Error   An error made by wrongly retaining or failing to reject a false null hypothesis. This is also called a beta error. (chap. 11)

Unsystematic Variation   Variation that results from factors other than the intervention or independent variable. (chap. 20)

Validity   Refers to the quality of a measure or observation (i.e., measurement validity) and also to the quality of a whole study (i.e., research validity). (chap. 2, 6, 10, 20, 23, 24)

Variability   Differences between scores in a distribution. If all the scores in a distribution are the same, there is no variability. If the scores in a distribution are all different and widely spaced, the variability would be high. (chap. 9)

Variable   A characteristic of the participants or situation of a given study that has different values used in that study. (chap. 4)

Variance   A measure of variability or differences between scores in a distribution. The standard deviation squared. (chap. 9)

Within Subjects Designs   Also called repeated measure designs. Each participant is assessed on all conditions or levels of the independent variable. (chap. 12, 15)

Yates Correction   A correction used in the chi-square computation to adjust for instances in which there is only 1 degree of freedom (2×2 cross-tabulation). Effectively decreases the chi-square value. (chap. 14)

Anatomy of a Research Article

There is no unique format that is used by all journals in disseminating research information. Each discipline has some peculiarity that is common to that discipline. In addition, research formats may differ by the type of research reported. The format for qualitative research studies such as ethnographies or case studies is different from that for experimental, quasi-experimental, or survey research. The organization of this appendix is primarily styled after the *Publication Manual of the American Psychological Association* (APA, 1994) and Wilkinson and the Task Force on Statistical Inference (1999). For the most part, APA format is acceptable for research journals and required for many publications in the social sciences and education. The research format presented here has seven parts: title, abstract, introduction, method, results, discussion, and references.

Title

The title should be brief (APA, 1994, recommends a title length between 12 and 15 words), yet describe what you have studied. The title is also a selling point for the article. Few researchers have the time or energy to read every article in journals to which they subscribe. Therefore, if they are like us, on receiving the journal they skim the table of contents to see if there are any articles they wish to read. At this point, the title is the only selling feature of your article. There have been some memorable titles, like "Remember That Old Theory of Memory, Well Forget It" and "Beagles and Locks." Even statisticians have had a go at it with such titles as "On the Significance of Effects and the Effects of Significance" (Cooper, 1981); "The Religion of Statistics as Practiced in Medical Journals" (Salsburg, 1985); McNemar's famous address, "At Random: Sense and Nonsense" (1960); and Cohen's (1994) "The Earth is Round (p < .05)." The latter was influential in motivating the APA Task Force to produce their recent report, which guided much of this appendix. Our favorite is, "The Unicorn, the Normal Curve, and Other Improbable Creatures" (Micceri, 1989). For the most part, however, you cannot go wrong by being brief and to the point.

Abstract

Once the title catches the consumer's interest, the abstract is the next part of the article that usually gets read. The abstract follows the title and provides a summary of the paper. Like titles, abstracts are limited in length. APA (1994) suggests an abstract of no more than 120 words for an empirical study and no more than 100 words for a review or theoretical article. An abstract describes briefly the purpose, design, and results (in a sentence or two) of the study. Like the title, the abstract is also a selling point for the paper. We have reviewed many research studies that resulted in comments to the author(s) such as, "No one will read the paper because the abstract is not representative of what the study found," or "the wrong content has been highlighted." It is important to correctly represent the paper in the abstract.

Introduction/Literature Review

In this section we describe what should be in the introductory section of a research article. How one gets that information (e.g., from a library search) is not the purpose of this section. There are a number of good books on how to do a literature search, including Fink's (1998) *Conducting Research Literature Reviews: From Paper to the Internet.* Notice that we have put a slash between Introduction and Literature Review. In most journals, the introduction and literature review are together in one section, which is untitled in APA format. However, some of the journals you read separate the introduction and the literature review. Most master's theses and doctoral dissertations have separate chapters titled Introduction and Literature Review.

What material should go into the introduction of a journal article? The first paragraph of the introduction should be a general purpose statement of what is to be accomplished. The APA Publication Manual suggests that the first paragraph should introduce the problem. There is nothing worse than starting a journal article by reading, for instance, that Smith and Jones (1977) found one thing, and then Up and Down (1982) found something else, and then Hill and Dale (1983) supported Smith and Jones (1977), and so on. After about three or four pages, you wonder what the author(s) are doing—that is, if you are still awake. (Don't ever read a research article late at night, unless you can't afford sleeping pills.)

After the introductory paragraph, start your literature review. Although a degree of chronological order is necessary, it should only happen after the literature is *organized,* for example, into studies that support your case (hypothesis) and studies that contradict these findings. Let's say that we propose a general hypothesis that students who take a course in research design prior to a course in statistics will become better researchers than those students who take the courses in the reverse order. We would try to form two or three categories of articles. Those articles that support our hypothesis would form one category. Those articles that oppose our hypothesis would form a second category. A third category might be those articles in which the authors found no difference in their results. Within each category might be articles that are relevant to the topic and others that merely touch on the topic. The latter should only be listed as supporting or not supporting your hypothesis. Those articles that are relevant to the topic should be explored in depth, especially for why or why not they supported your hypothesis. You are leading up to why your study will make a difference in relation to the past literature. What is it about your study that is different from previous research? In summary, one good approach to a literature review, in the introduction section of a journal article, starts by categorizing studies (citing them) that support or do not support the research hypothesis, and then describes in depth a few select studies that are relevant to the present study. For studies on topics that are not well researched, another technique would be used: for example, chronological, by key variables, or by research question.

The last part of the introduction in a research article is a formal statement of the hypotheses or research questions. These statements should be presented in operational terms so that the reader knows exactly what the researcher is attempting to study.

Method

The method section for most research articles is divided into four subsections. The ultimate purpose of the method section is to instruct the reader about exactly what was done in the study and to allow the reader to replicate the study under identical conditions. According to the APA Manual, the subsections include *Participants, Apparatus* (or *Instruments/Materials*), and *Procedure.* We like to add *Design/Analyses.* The APA Task Force (Wilkinson & The Task Force, 1999) recommends a more complete description of the method than has commonly been the case in published articles. If the guidelines are adopted and implemented, it may mean that journals will publish fewer but longer, more fully documented articles.

Participants.   This subsection should contain a thorough description of the participants. Where did the participants come from? How did you contact the sample? Did the participants volunteer for the project? A sentence or two about how informed consent was obtained needs to be included.

How did you sample (select) the subjects? Were they a convenience sample, or did you use a recognized probability mode of selection (random, systematic, cluster, or stratified)? Because the interpretation of the results depends on the characteristics of the population, it is important to define the population clearly. Unfortunately, this is not always done. The description of the sampling procedures should comprise inclusion or exclusion criteria, full information about how the sample was stratified (if it was), and the sample size for each subgroup. A convenience sample should be clearly identified as such. Sometimes the case for its representativeness can be strengthened by showing how your sample compares to the population on key variables.

You should provide information about the process that led to your sample size decision. A *power analysis* (chap. 23) should be done before the data are collected. Describe the assumptions used and how the power analysis was done.

After a description of how the sample was obtained, the next part of the method section deals with characteristics of the sample. These characteristics should involve age (average and range or standard deviation) and gender. Ethnic grouping, type of disability, socioeconomic status, level of education, or a combination of characteristics should also be included.

Apparatus/Instrumentation/Materials.   This section describes in detail all of the instruments or tests that were used in the research. If an apparatus was involved, then the researcher must describe the type of equipment (including brand name), accuracy, specifications relative to the subject, and possible calibration information. If tests, questionnaires, or surveys were used in the study, information on reliability and validity *must* be included. Was the instrument standardized, or was it developed for this study? If the instrument was standardized, was it used for purposes similar to those in this study and were the standardization samples similar to those in this study? If the instrument was developed for the present study, was a pilot study performed? If the instrument has a number of items, has it been factor analyzed? Sample questions to demonstrate the content of the instrument should be included. Also, the level of measurement of the data should be given.

Each key variable should be carefully and explicitly defined. Show how such variables are related to the goals of the study and how they are measured. The measurements should fit the language used in the Introduction and Discussion. Naming an abstract variable is almost as important as how it is measured, and should be done consistently. We discussed this topic in chapter 23 as measurement validity and the generalizability of the constructs.

Procedure.   This section is a "blow-by-blow" description of how the study was conducted, and is especially important for replication to occur. Also included in this section is how the participants were assigned to the different groups under study; that is, were they randomly assigned or were they already in an intact group? It is especially important in this section to report any instructions that were given by the researcher to the participants.

Wilkinson and The Task Force (1999) and this text emphasize the distinction between the *random assignment* of participants to intervention and control (or comparison) groups, and, on the other hand, the *random selection* of participants from the population. For research intended to make causal inferences, random assignment is critical because "it allows the strongest possible causal inferences ... 'Random' does not mean 'haphazard.' Randomization is a fragile condition, easily corrupted" (Wilkinson & The Task Force, 1999, p. 595). The APA Task Force also recommends a description of how you randomized, preferably by using published tables of random numbers rather than trusting a coin, slips of paper in a hat, or physical devices.

If the participants cannot be randomly assigned to groups, you should describe how you attempted to control for initial group differences. You should try to determine the relevant covariates or confounds, and describe any methods used to adjust for them. Also describe methods to reduce bias, including minimizing dropouts, noncompliance, missing data, and experimenter bias.

Design/Analysis.   This section is usually the last subsection of the method section, but some texts place this section earlier in the method section of the article, and sometimes the design is described in the introduction. In the *design* paragraph of this subsection, the researcher first names the independent variable or variables and the number of levels within each variable. The next piece of information is the type of design (between groups, within subjects, or mixed or associational). Next, the researcher discusses whether the independent variable(s) is an active (manipulated) or attribute variable. The last part of the design section includes the specification of the dependent variable(s) and the level (scale) of measurement.

The APA Task Force report (Wilkinson & The Task Force, 1999) says:

> Make clear at the outset what type of study you are doing. Do not cloak a study in one guise to try to give it the assumed reputation of another. For studies that have multiple goals, be sure to define and prioritize those goals.

> There are many forms of empirical studies ... including case reports, controlled experiments, quasi-experiments, statistical simulations, surveys, observational studies, and studies of studies (meta-analyses). Some are hypothesis-generating .... Some are hypothesis testing .... Some are meta-analytic .... Occasionally proponents of some research methods disparage others. In fact, each form of research has its own strengths, weaknesses, and standards of practice. (p. 594)

The analysis paragraph of this subsection specifies the types of analyses that were done in the research. These analyses are determined by all of the information provided in the design paragraph. The computer program (system) that was used to carry out the analyses may be specified, for example, SPSS (Statistical Package for the Social Sciences).

Wilkinson and The Task Force (1999) recommends using relatively simple statistical analyses, such as those described in chapters 14 to 19 of this book, if they are reasonable for your research problem. The APA Task Force report goes on to state that

> The enormous variety of modern quantitative methods leaves researchers with a non-trivial task of matching analysis and design to the research question. Although complex designs and state-of-the-art methods are sometimes necessary to address research questions effectively, simpler classical approaches often can provide elegant and sufficient answers to important questions. Do not choose an analytic method to impress your readers or to deflect criticism. (p. 598)

Results

The APA Task Force report (Wilkinson & The Task Force, 1999) states:

> As soon as you have collected your data, before you compute *any* statistics, *look at your data.* Data screening is not data snooping. It is not an opportunity to discard data or change values in order to favor your hypothesis. However, if you assess hypotheses without examining your data, you risk publishing nonsense. (p. 597)

The APA Task Force also recommends that you report complications, missing data, attrition, and response rates. They also recommend that you use techniques to assure that the reported results are not due to anomalies in the data such as outliers and attrition. The Task Force also recommends graphical inspection of data by using scatterplots, boxplots, and other exploratory techniques to detect problems and errors in the data:

> the type of "atheoretical" search for patterns that we are sometimes warned against in graduate school can save us from the humiliation of having to retract conclusions we might ultimately make on contaminated data. We are warned against fishing expeditions for understandable reasons, but blind application of models without screening our data is a far graver error. (Wilkinson & The Task Force, 1999, p. 598)

These recommendations are consistent with ours earlier in the book, and it would be desirable to discuss these issues in a thesis or dissertation. However, we wonder whether many editors will allow space for presentation of these topics.

The results section is a summary of the analyses of the data collected in the study. A problem for most students is the level of description in the results. J. A. G. likes to tell a story that happened to him while in graduate school. "I submitted an article to a very prestigious journal in the field of experimental psychology. Since I had just completed two years of graduate level statistics, I made sure that I included every possible statistic, degrees of freedom, and probability level, even though most of the findings were not statistically significant. Even though the article was recommended for publication, major revisions were requested. One of the requests was to reduce the size of the results section by eliminating most of the statistical descriptions. As the section editor put it, 'Use the traumatic ocular test. If it hits you between the eyes use it. Otherwise get rid of it.'" This editor's comment is common, even today, but does not seem consistent with the recommendations of the APA Task Force.

A picture is worth a thousand words. We recommend putting a figure or a table near the beginning of the results, and then briefly describing the significant results. Wilkinson and The Task Force (1999) state that "figures attract the reader's eye and help convey global results ... it often helps to have both tables and figures" (p. 601). The APA Task Force report recommends that figures be kept small and relatively simple, and that tables have numbers rounded to a few significant digits with no decimals unless really needed. On the other hand, the Task Force report discusses in detail the failure of many published figures to include essential information, usually about the shape or distribution of the data. Again, a problem faced by persons attempting to publish articles is that editors historically have preferred to keep figures to a minimum. This potential restriction should not limit graphics in theses, however.

With regard to statistical analyses, the APA Task Force guidelines admonish researchers to assure that the underlying assumptions are reasonable, given the data. They point out that statistical programs provide tests for many assumptions, but they warn that such tests can be impractically sensitive, especially with large samples and robust tests such as ANOVA.

In accord with our recommendation in chapter 11, the APA Task Force states that effect sizes should *always* be presented for primary outcomes, and that it helps to add brief comments to put the effect sizes in context. They also say that it is almost always better to report the actual p value rather than merely to say whether the result was statistically significant or not. It is better still, they say, to report confidence intervals. Also, never use the expression "accept the null hypothesis." The Task Force recommends Cohen's (1994) article, "The Earth is Round (p<.05)" for a discussion of the issue of significance testing.

A problem in writing the results section is whether to include material that might be more appropriate for the discussion section. If the outcome you are describing pertains strictly to the analysis, then it belongs in the results section. However, if you are relating your outcome to other studies that were previously discussed in the introduction, then this material belongs in the discussion section.

Discussion

We suggest starting the discussion section with a brief review (no more than one paragraph in an article, probably a few pages in a thesis) of the hypotheses, and whether or not they were confirmed. The major purpose of the discussion section is to relate the results to the research hypotheses or questions within the context of the literature previously cited. Sometimes an outcome from the study is totally unexpected and the discussion section branches into a whole new literature review and hypothesis, indicating that the author forgot about the original intent of the study and the original hypotheses. Don't let this happen to you. Each hypothesis should be discussed with continued reference to previous findings from the literature review.

The APA Task Force report states that when you interpret your results think about whether they are credible, given the results of previous studies and theory. Do the design and analysis suggest that the results are generalizable? The report then states that:

Novice researchers err either by over-generalizing their results or, equally unfortunately, over-particularizing. Explicitly compare the effects detected in your inquiry with the effect sizes reported in related previous studies. (Wilkinson & The Task Force, 1999, p. 602)

As we have stressed throughout the book, you should be cautious about inferring causation from approaches that are not randomized experimental. Even with randomized designs, your statements should be considered carefully. Wilkinson and The Task Force (1999) support our conclusion with a strong recommendation that "inferring of causality from non-randomized designs is a risky enterprise. Researchers using non-randomized designs have an extra obligation ... to alert the reader to plausible rival hypotheses" (p. 600). Or, we would say, do not make causal statements at all.

Some discussion sections have a separate heading called Limitations. Our bias is that it is not the role of the researcher to attempt to review his or her own paper (except in a thesis or dissertation). Usually some of the limitations come out when discussing why hypotheses were confirmed or not confirmed. In short, we do not think that this additional section is necessary. However, the APA Task Force report states that:

> Speculation may be appropriate, but use it sparingly and explicitly. Note the shortcomings of your study. Remember, however, that acknowledging limitations is for the purpose of qualifying results and avoiding pitfalls in future research. Confession should not have the goal of disarming criticism. Recommendations for future research should be thoughtful and grounded in present and previous findings. (Wilkinson & The Task Force, 1999, p. 602)

Although a conclusion is not necessary, the researcher should attempt to describe, in the last paragraph or so of the discussion section, what the next step in this line of research should be. Obviously, this next step will be contingent on what was found in the present study. However, a paragraph of this nature leaves the reader with a feeling of where the researcher feels future research is headed, and also may give the reader research ideas.

References

The references should follow a particular format. For our purposes, APA format is used (see APA, 1994). Only references that were cited in the text are included in the reference section. This means that if material was read but *not* included in the text, do not cite it. Note that in this book we have used the published, or final manuscript, form of APA style in our reference list. When submitting manuscripts to an APA journal editor, double space *everything* and indent the first line of a reference, instead of using "hanging indents" as we have, and use underlines instead of italics in the references and text.

Writing Research Problems and Questions

FRAMEWORKS FOR STATING RESEARCH PROBLEMS

Although a common definition of a research problem is that it is a statement that asks what relationship exists between two or more variables, most research problems are more complex than this definition implies. The research problem should be a broad statement that covers the several more specific research questions to be investigated, perhaps by using terms that stand for several variables. One way to state the problem, which can help you determine the independent and dependent variables, is as follows (italics indicate that you fill in the appropriate name for the variable or group of variables).

Format

If your study is randomized experimental or strong quasi-experimental, you could phrase the problem as follows:

The research problem is to investigate the presumed effect of (*put independent variable 1 or group of variables here*), (*independent variable 2, if any, here*), and (*independent variable 3, if any*), on (*dependent variable 1, here*) and (*dependent variable 2, if any*) in (*population*).

Except in a totally descriptive study, there always must be at least one independent and one dependent variable. However, there can be, and often are, two or more of each variable. In the statement of the problem, in contrast to the research question or hypotheses, it is desirable to use broad descriptors for groups of similar variables. For example, demographics might cover four variables: gender, mother's education, father's education, and ethnicity. Spatial

435

performance might include a mosaic or pattern score and a visualization score. Likewise, grades and mathematics attitudes could refer to more than one variable. Concepts such as self-esteem or teaching style have several aspects that usually result in more than one variable. The first example that follows is written in a format that is most appropriate for studies that use the *randomized experimental* and *strong quasi-experimental approaches*. The second and third examples are suggested variations when the approach is moderate to weak quasi-experimental, comparative, or associational.

Examples

1. The research problem is to investigate the effect of a new curriculum on grades, math attitudes, and quantitative or spatial achievement in high school students.

If you do not have an active or manipulated independent variable and, thus, will use the *comparative* or *associational* approach, you should phrase a sample problem as follows:

2. The problem is to investigate the relationships among demographics, grades, and mathematics attitudes with quantitative and spatial achievement in high school students.

If you have more than two or three independent variables it may be best to say the following:

3. The problem is to investigate whether demographics, mathematics courses, grades, spatial scores, and mathematics attitudes are predictors of mathematics achievement. More generally, we could say the problem is to investigate the factors that predict or seem to influence mathematics achievement.

This latter format is especially useful when the approach is a complex (many independent variables) associational one.

FRAMEWORK FOR STATING RESEARCH QUESTIONS OR HYPOTHESES

Although it is fine to phrase a randomized experimental research problem (in the format of Example 1) as a "study of the effect of ... ," we think it is best to phrase your research questions or hypotheses so that they do not appear to imply cause and effect; that is, phrase them as *difference* or *associational* questions (hypotheses) or as *descriptive* questions. The former are answered with inferential statistics and the latter with descriptive statistics.

Descriptive Questions

Basic Descriptive Questions.   These questions are about an aspect of one variable. Descriptive questions ask about the central tendency, frequency distribution, percentage in each category, variability, or shape of the distribution. Some descriptive questions are intended to test assumptions. Some questions simply describe the sample demographics. Examples of descriptive questions are as follows:

1. What percentage of participants are of each gender?
2. What is the mean, mode, and median of the mathematics achievement scores?
3. Is mathematics achievement distributed approximately normally?

Complex Descriptive Questions.   These questions deal with two or more variables at a time, but do not involve inferential statistics. Cross-tabulations of two categorical variables, factor analysis, and measures of reliability (e.g., Cronbach's alpha) are examples.

An example of a complex descriptive question is as follows:

1. What is the reliability of the visualization score?

Difference Questions or Hypotheses

Basic Difference Questions.   The format for asking research questions is as follows:

Are there differences between the (*insert number*) levels (*you could name the levels here*) of (*put the independent variable name here*) in regard to the average (*put the dependent variable name here*) scores?

An example is as follows:

1. Are there differences between the three levels (high, medium, and low) of father's education in regard to the average mathematics achievement scores of the students?

Complex Difference and Interaction Questions.   When you have two categorical independent variables considered together, you will have *three* research questions or hypotheses. There are advantages of considering two or three independent variables at a time. See chapter 17 for how to interpret the *interaction* question. Sample formats for a set of three questions answered by *one* 2-way ANOVA are as follows:

1. Is there a difference between the levels of the (*insert independent variable 1*) in regard to the average (*put dependent variable 1 here*) scores?
2. Is there a difference between the levels of the (*insert independent variable 2*) in regard to the average (*dependent variable 1*) scores?
3. Is there an interaction of (*independent variable 1*) and (*independent variable 2*) in regard to the (*dependent variable 1*)?

(Repeat these three questions with the second dependent variable, if there is more than one dependent variable.)

An example is as follows:

1. Is there a difference between students having high versus low math grades in regard to their average mathematics achievement scores?
2. Is there a difference between male and female students in regard to their average math achievement scores?
3. Is there an interaction between mathematics grades and gender in regard to math achievement?

Note that the first question states the *levels* or categories of the first independent variable; that is, it states the groups that are to be compared (high vs. low math grade students). The second question does the same for the second independent variable; that is, it states the levels (male and female) to be compared. However, in the third (interaction) question, it is asked whether the first variable itself (mathematics grades) interacts with the second variable (gender). No mention is made, at this point, of the values or levels or groups.

Associational (Relationship) Questions or Hypotheses

Basic Associational Questions.   When both the independent and dependent variables are ordered and essentially continuous (i.e., have five or more ordered categories) the approach and research question are considered to be associational. The format for associational questions is as follows:

Is there an association between (*independent variable 1*) and (*dependent variable 1*)?

If there is more than one independent variable, or dependent variable, or both, which is common, and each pair of variables is associated separately, you can have a series of questions that ask whether there is an association between each independent variable and each dependent variable. If it is arbitrary which variables are independent or antecedent (predictors) and which are dependent (outcome), one might ask whether every variable is related to every other variable. This would produce a *correlation matrix.*

An example for a single association or relationship is as follows:
1. Is there an association between grades in high school and mathematics achievement?

An example that would produce a correlation matrix is as follows:
2. Are there associations among the three mathematics attitude scale scores?

Note that what is said to be associated in these questions is the variable itself; no mention is made of the levels or values.

Complex Associational Questions.   In the associational approach, when two or more *independent* variables are considered together, rather than separately as in the basic format, you get a new kind of question. The format can be phrased something like the following:

Is there a combination of factors (*list the several specific independent variables here*) that predict (*put dependent variable here*) better than any one alone?

An example of a complex associational question is as follows:

1. Is there a combination of the number of mathematics courses, gender, father's education, mathematics grades, and motivation for mathematics that predicts mathematics achievement better than any one predictor variable alone?

References

Altman, E., & Hernon, P. (1997). *Research misconduct: Issues, implications, and strategies.* Greenwich, CT: Ablex.

American Psychological Association. (1992). Ethical principles of psychologists and code of conduct. *American Psychologist, 47*, 1597–1611.

American Psychological Association. (1994). *Publication manual of the American Psychological Association* (4th ed.). Washington, DC: Author.

Anastasi, A. (1988). *Psychological testing* (6th ed.). New York: Macmillan.

Ary, D., Jacobs, L. C., & Razavieh, A. (1996). *Introduction to research in education* (5th ed). Fort Worth, TX: Harcourt Brace College Publishers.

Atler, K. E., & Gliner, J. A. (1989). Post stroke activity and psychosocial factors. *Physical and Occupational Therapy in Geriatrics, 7*, 28–33.

Bakan, D. (1966). The test of significance in psychological research. *Psychological Bulletin, 66*, 1–29.

Bakshi, R., Bhambhani, Y., & Madill, H. (1991). The effects of task preference on performance during purposeful and nonpurposeful activities. *American Journal of Occupational Therapy, 45*, 912–916.

Bambara, L., & Ager, C. (1992). Using self-scheduling to promote self-directed leisure activity in home and community settings. *The Journal of the Association for Persons with Severe Handicaps, 17*, 67–76.

Bartko, J. J., & Carpenter, W. T. (1976). On the methods and theory of reliability. *The Journal of Nervous and Mental Disease, 163*, 307–317.

Beatty, W. W., & Gange, J. J. (1977). Neuropsychological aspects of multiple sclerosis. *The Journal of Nervous and Mental Disease, 164*, 42–50.

Bergin, D. A. (1995). Effects of a mastery versus competitive motivation situation on learning. *Journal of Experimental Education, 63*, 303–314.

Berkowitz, L., & Lutterman, K. (1968). The traditionally socially responsible personality. *Public Opinion Quarterly, 32*, 169–185.

Bernspang, B., & Fisher, A. G. (1995). Differences between persons with right or left CVA on the Assessment of Motor and Process Skills. *Archives of Physical Medicine and Rehabilitation, 76*, 1144–1151.

Bradley, D. R., Bradley, T. D., McGrath, S. G., & Cutcomb, S. D. (1979). Type 1 error rate of the chi-square test of independent in R X C tables that have small expected frequencies. *Psychological Bulletin, 86*, 1290–1297.

Bryze, K. A. (1991). *Functional assessment of adults with developmental disabilities.* Unpublished master's thesis, University of Illinois at Chicago, Chicago.

Burleigh, S.A., Farber, R.S., & Gillard, M. (1998). Community integration and life satisfaction after traumatic brain injury: Long-term findings. *American Journal of Occupational Therapy, 52,* 45–52.

Camilli, G., & Hopkins, K. D. (1978). Applicability of chi-square to 2 × 2 contingency tables with small expected cell frequencies. *Psychological Bulletin, 85,* 163–167.

Campbell, D. T., & Stanley, J. C. (1966). *Experimental and quasi-experimental designs for research.* Chicago: Rand McNally.

Caracelli, V. J., & Greene, J. C. (1993). Data analysis strategies for mixed-method evaluation designs. *Educational Evaluation and Policy Analysis, 15,* 195–207.

Chambers, T. (1994). Criteria to evaluate student leadership programs: What leadership educators consider important. *NASPA Journal, 31,* 225–234.

Chiara, T., Carlos, J., Martin, D., Miller, R., & Nadeau, S. (1998). Cold effect on oxygen uptake, perceived exertion, and spasticity in patients with multiple sclerosis. *Archives of Physical Medicine and Rehabilitation, 79,* 523–528.

Cohen, J. (1988). *Statistical power analysis for the behavioral sciences* (2nd ed.). Hillsdale, NJ: Lawrence Erlbaum Associates.

Cohen, J. (1990). The things I have learned (so far). *American Psychologist, 45,* 1304–1312.

Cohen, J. (1994). The earth is round ($p < .05$). *American Psychologist, 49,* 997–1003.

Cook, T. D., & Campbell, D. T. (1979). *Quasi-experimentation: Design and analysis issues for field settings.* Boston: Houghton Mifflin.

Cook, T. D., Cooper, H., Cordray, D. S., Hartmann, H., Hedges, L.V., Light, R. J., Louis, T. A., & Mosteller, F. (1992). *Meta-analysis for explanation.* New York: Russell Sage Foundation.

Cooper, H. M. (1981). On the significance of effects and the effects of significance. *Journal of Personality and Social Psychology, 41,* 1013–1018.

Cooper, H., & Hedges, L. (1994). *The handbook of research synthesis.* New York: Russell Sage Foundation.

Cortina, J., & Dunlap, W. P. (1997). On the logic and purpose of significance testing. *Psychological Methods, 2,* 161–172.

Cosby, P. C. (1989). *Methods in behavioral research* (4th ed.). Mountain View, CA: Mayfield.

Creagh, U., Reilly, T., & Lees, A. (1998). Kinematics of running on 'off-road' terrain. *Ergonomics, 41,* 1029–1033.

Creswell, J. W. (1994). *Research design: Qualitative and quantitative approaches.* Thousand Oaks, CA: Sage.

Cromack, T.R. (1989). Measurement considerations in clinical research. In C. B. Royeen (Ed.), *Clinical research handbook.* Thorofare, NJ: Slack Inc.

Cronbach, L. J. (1960). *Essentials of psychological testing* (2nd ed.). New York: Harper & Row.

Cronbach, L. J. (1970). *Essentials of psychological testing* (3rd ed.). New York: Harper & Row.

Czerniecki, J .G., Deitz, J. C., Crowe, T. W., & Booth, C. L. (1993). Attending behavior: A descriptive study of children aged 18 through 23 months. *American Journal of Occupational Therapy, 47,* 708–716.

Daniel, L. G., & Witta, E. L. (1997, March). *Implications for teaching graduate students correct terminology for discussing validity and reliability on a content analysis of three social science measurement journals.* Paper presented at American Education Research Association, Chicago, Il.

Davis, J. A. (1985). *The logic of causal order.* Newbury Park, CA: Sage.

Dickerson, A. E., & Fisher, A. G. (1993). Age differences in functional performance. *American Journal of Occupational Therapy, 47,* 686–692.

Dillman, D. A. (1978). *Mail and telephone surveys: The total design method.* New York: Wiley.

DiPasquale–Lehnerz, P. (1994). Orthotic intervention for development of hand function with C-6 quadriplegia. *American Journal of Occupational Therapy, 48,* 138–144.

Dittmar, C. M., & Gliner, J. A. (1987). Bilateral hand performance with divided attention following cerebral vascular accident. *American Journal of Occupational Therapy, 41,* 96–101.

Drew, C. (1980). *Introduction to designing and conducting research.* (2nd ed.). St. Louis, MO: C.V. Mosby Company.

Dunlap, G., Foster–Johnson, L, Clarke, S., Kern, L., & Childs, K. (1995). Modifying activities to produce functional outcomes: Effects on the problem behaviors of students with disabilities. *The Journal of the Association for Persons with Severe Handicaps, 20*, 248–258.

Dunn, O. J. (1961). Multiple comparisons among means. *Journal of the American Statistical Association, 56*, 52–64.

Durr, R., Guglielmino, L., & Guglielmino, P. (1995). Self directed readiness and occupational categories. *Human Resource Development Quarterly, 7*, 351–357.

Dunnett, C. W. (1955). A multiple comparison procedure for comparing several treatments with a control. *Journal of the American Statistical Association, 50*, 1096–1121.

Edgington, E. (1992). Nonparametric tests for single-case experiments. In T. Kratochwill & J. Levin (Eds.), *Single-case research design and analysis* (pp. 15–40). Hillsdale, NJ: Lawrence Erlbaum Associates.

Fine, M. A., & Kurdek, L. A. (1993). Reflections on determining authorship credit and authorship order on faculty-student collaborations. *American Psychologist, 48*, 1141–1147.

Fink, A. (1998). *Conducting research literature reviews: From paper to the Internet.* Thousand Oaks, CA: Sage.

Fisher, A. G. (1993). The assessment of IADL motor skills: An application of many-faceted Rasch analysis. *American Journal of Occupational Therapy, 47*, 319–338.

Fisher, A. G. (1995). *Assessment of motor and process skills.* Fort Collins, CO: Three Star Press.

Fisher, A. G., Liu, Y., Velozo, C. A., & Pan, A. W. (1992). Cross-cultural assessment of process skills. *American Journal of Occupational Therapy, 46*, 876–885.

Fisher, R. A. (1935). *The design of experiments.* Edinburgh, Scotland: Oliver & Boyd.

Fowler, F. J., Jr. (1993). *Survey research methods* (2nd ed.). Newbury Park, CA: Sage.

Frone, M.R. (1998). Predictors of work injuries among employed adolescents. *Journal of Applied Psychology, 83*, 565–576.

Gerst, J. (1994). *An ethnography of the medically indigent within the context of prenatal care.* Unpublished doctoral dissertation, Colorado State University, Fort Collins.

Ghiselli, E. E., Campbell, J. P., & Zedeck, S. (1981). *Measurement theory for the behavioral sciences.* San Francisco: W.H. Freeman.

Gilfoyle, E. M., & Gliner, J. A. (1985). Attitudes toward handicapped children: Impact of an educational program. *Physical and Occupational Therapy in Pediatrics, 5*, 27–41.

Glass, G. V., McGaw, B., & Smith, M. L. (1981). *Meta-analysis in social research.* Beverly Hills, CA: Sage.

Gliner, J. A. (1994). Reviewing qualitative research: Proposed criteria for fairness and rigor. *The Occupational Therapy Journal of Research, 14*, 78–92.

Gliner, J. A., Bedi, J. F., & Horvath, S. M. (1979). Somatic and nonsomatic influences on the heart: Hemodynamic changes. *Psychophysiology, 16*(4), 358–362.

Gliner, J. A., Bunnell, D. E., & Horvath, S. M. (1982). Hemodynamic and metabolic changes prior to speech performance. *Physiological Psychology, 10*, 108–113.

Gliner, J. A., Haber, E., & Weise, J. (1999). Use of controlled vignettes in evaluation: Does type of response method make a difference? *Evaluation and Program Planning, 22*, 313–322.

Gliner, J. A., & Sample, P. (1993). *Participatory action research: An approach to evaluate community integration for persons with developmental disabilities.* Paper presented at the American Evaluation Association, Dallas, TX.

Gliner, J. A., & Sample, P. (1996). A multimethod approach to evaluate transition into community life. *Evaluation and Program Planning, 19*, 225–233.

Griffin, M. M. (1992). Do student-generated rational sets of examples facilitate concept acquisition? *Journal of Experimental Education, 61*(2), 104–115.

Grimm, L. G., & Yarnold, P. R. (1997). *Reading and understanding multivariate statistics.* Washington, DC: American Psychological Association.

Hanpachern, C., Morgan, G. A., & Griego, O. V. (1998). Extension of the theory of margin: A framework for assessing readiness for change. *Human Resource Development Quarterly, 9*, 339–350.

Harter, S. (1985). *Manual for the self-perception profile for children.* Unpublished manuscript, University of Denver, CO.

Harvey, R. F., Silverstein, B., Venzon, M. A., Kilgore, K. M., Fisher, W. P., Steiner, M., & Harley, J. P. (1992). Applying psychometric criteria to functional assessment in medical rehabilitation: III. Construct validity and predicting level of care. *Archives of Physical Medicine and Rehabilitation, 73*, 887–892.

Heinsman, D. T., & Shadish, W. R. (1996). Assignment methods in experimentation: When do nonrandomized experiments approximate answers from randomized experiments? *Psychological Methods, 1*, 154–169.

Heller, J. (1972, July 26). Syphilis victims in U.S. study without therapy for 40 years. *The New York Times*, pp. 1, 8.

Hendricks, B., Marvel, M. K., & Barrington, B. L. (1990). The dimensions of psychological research. *Teaching of Psychology, 17*, 76–82.

Howe, K. R. (1985). Two dogmas of educational research. *Educational Researcher, 44*, 10–18.

Hsieh, C., Nelson, D. L., Smith, D. A., & Peterson, C. Q. (1996). A comparison of performance in added-purpose occupations and rote exercise for dynamic standing balance in persons with hemiplegia. *American Journal of Occupational Therapy, 50*, 10–16.

Huck, S. W., Cormier, W. H., & Bounds, W. G., Jr. (1974). *Reading statistics and research*. New York: Harper & Row.

Huck, S. W., & McLean, R. A. (1975). Using a repeated measures ANOVA to analyze the data from a pretest-posttest design: A potentially confusing task. *Psychological Bulletin, 32*, 511–518.

Humphreys, L. (1970). *Tearoom trade: Impersonal sex in public places*. Chicago: Aldine.

Hunter, J. E., & Schmidt, F. L. (1990). Methods of meta-analysis: Cumulating research findings across studies. Beverly Hills, CA: Sage.

Iverson, A. M., Iverson, G. L., & Lukin, L. E. (1993). Frequent, ungraded testing as an instructional strategy. *Journal of Experimental Education, 62*(2), 93–101.

Janelle, S. (1992). Locus of control in nondisabled versus congenitally physically disabled adolescents. *American Journal of Occupational Therapy, 46*, 334–342.

Jones, J. H. (1982). *Bad blood*. New York: Free Press.

Jongbloed, L., Stacey, S., & Brighton, C. (1989). Stroke rehabilitation: Sensorimotor integrative treatment versus functional treatment. *American Journal of Occupational Therapy, 43*, 391–397.

Kazdin, A. (1982). *Single-case research designs*. New York: Oxford University Press.

Keppel, G. (1991). *Design and analysis: A researcher's handbook* (3rd ed.). New York: Prentice Hall.

Keppel, G., & Zedeck, S. (1989). *Data analysis for research designs*. New York: W. H. Freeman.

Kerlinger, F. (1986). *Foundations of behavioral research* (3rd ed.). New York: Holt, Rinehart & Winston.

King, G. A., Specht, J. A., Schultz, I., Warr–Leeper, G., Redekop, W., & Risebrough, N. (1997). Social skills training for withdrawn unpopular children with physical disabilities: A preliminary evaluation. *Rehabilitation Psychology, 42*, 47–60.

Kircher, M. A. (1984). Motivation as a factor of perceived exertion in purposeful versus nonpurposeful activity. *American Journal of Occupational Therapy, 38*, 165–170.

Kirchner, G. L., & Holm, M. B. (1997). Prediction of academic and clinical performance of occupational therapy students in an entry-level master's program. *American Journal of Occupational Therapy, 51*, 775–779.

Kirk, R. E. (1982). *Experimental design: Procedures for the behavioral sciences* (2nd ed.). Belmont, CA: Wadsworth, Inc.

Komesaroff, P. A. (1986). *Objectivity, science and society*. London: Routledge & Kegan Paul.

Kraemer, H. C., & Thiemann, S. (1987). *How many subjects: Statistical power analysis in research*. Newbury Park, CA: Sage.

Krathwohl, D. R. (1993). *Methods of educational and social science research*. New York: Longman.

Kratochwill, T., & Levin, J. (Eds.) (1992). *Single-case research design and analysis*. Hillsdale, NJ: Lawrence Erlbaum Associates.

Kuhn, T. S. (1970). *The structure of scientific revolutions* (2nd ed.). Chicago: University of Chicago Press.

Laconte, M. A., Shaw, D., & Dunn, I. (1993). The effects of a rational-emotive affective education program for high-risk middle school students. *Psychology in the Schools, 30*, 274–281.

Lafferty, A., & Gliner, J. A. (1991). *Execution of rapid bimanual tasks in patients with unilateral cerebral hemisphere damage.* Unpublished master's thesis, Colorado State University, Fort Collins.

Lan, W. Y., & Repman, J. (1995). The effects of social learning context and modeling on persistence and dynamism in academic activities. *Journal of Experimental Education, 64,* 53–67.

Lancy, D. F. (1993). *Qualitative research in education.* New York: Longman.

Levin, J., Marascuilo, L., & Hubert, L. (1978). *N* = 1 nonparametric randomization tests. In T. Kratochwill (Ed.), *Single subject research: Strategies for evaluating change* (pp. 167–196). New York: Academic Press.

Likert, R. (1932). A technique for the measurement of attitudes. *Archives of Psychology.* No. 140.

Lincoln, Y. S., & Guba, E. G. (1985). *Naturalistic inquiry.* Newbury Park, CA: Sage.

Lipsey, M. W. (1990). *Design sensitivity: Statistical power for experimental research.* Newbury Park, CA: Sage.

Lipsey, M. W. (1992). Juvenile delinquency treatment: A meta-analytic inquiry into the variability of effects. In T. D. Cook, H. Cooper, D. S. Cordray, H. Hartmann, L. V. Hedges, R. J. Light, T. A. Louis, & F. Mosteller, (Eds.), *Meta-analysis for explanation: A casebook.* New York: Russell Sage Foundation.

Lipsey, M. W., & Wilson, D. B. (1993). The efficacy of psychological, educational, and behavioral treatment: Confirmation from meta-analysis. *American Psychologist, 48,* 1181–1209.

Locke, L. F., Silverman, S. J., & Spirduso, W. W. (1998). *Reading and understanding research.* Thousand Oaks, CA: Sage.

Loftus, G. R., & Loftus, E. F. (1982). *Essence of statistics.* Monterey, CA: Brooks/Cole.

Lord, F.M., & Novick, M.R. (1968). *Statistical theories of mental test scores.* Reading, MA: Addison-Wesley Publishing Co.

Louth, R., McAllister, C., & McAllister, H. A. (1992). The effects of collaborative writing techniques on freshman writing and attitudes. *Journal of Experimental Education, 61,* 215–224.

Luft, J. A., & Pizzini, E. L. (1998). The demonstration classroom in-service: Changes in the classroom. *Science Education, 82,* 147–163.

MacPhee, D., Kreutzer, J. C., & Fritz, J. J. (1994). Infusing a diversity perspective into human development courses. *Child Development, 65,* 699–715.

McCleary, R., & Welsh, W. (1992). Philosophical and statistical foundations of time-series experiments. In T. Kratochwill & J. Levin (Eds.), *Single-case research design and analysis* (pp. 41–92). Hillsdale, NJ: Lawrence Erlbaum Associates.

McDougall, D., & Granby, C. (1996). How expectation of questioning method affects undergraduates' preparation for class. *The Journal of Experimental Education, 65,* 43–54.

McNemar, Q. (1960). At random: Sense and nonsense. *American Psychologist, 15,* 295–300.

Mental Measurements Yearbooks. Lincoln, NE: Buros Institute of Mental Measurements, University of Nebraska.

Meltzoff, J. (1997). *Critical thinking about research: Psychology and related fields.* Washington, DC: American Psychological Association.

Micceri, T. (1989). The unicorn, the normal curve, and other improbable creatures. *Psychological Bulletin, 105*(1), 156–166.

Milgram, S. (1974). *Obedience to authority: An experimental view.* New York: Harper & Row.

Moisan, M. O. (1990). *Effects of an adaptive ski program on the self-perception and performance of children with physical disabilities.* Unpublished master's thesis, Colorado State University, Fort Collins.

Morgan, G. A., & Griego, O. V. (1998). *Easy use and interpretation of SPSS for Windows: Answering research questions with statistics.* Mahwah, NJ: Lawrence Erlbaum Associates.

Morgan, G. A., Harmon, R. J., & Maslin–Cole, C. A. (1990). Mastery motivation: Definition and measurement. *Early Education and Development, 1,* 318–339.

Morgan, G. A., Maslin–Cole, C. A., Harmon, R. J., Busch–Rossnagel, N. A., Jennings, K. D., Hauser–Cram, P., & Brockman, L. (1993). Parent and teacher perceptions of young children's mastery motivation: Assessment and review of research. In D. Messer (Ed.), *Mastery motivation in early childhood: Development, measurement and social processes* (pp. 109–131). London: Routledge.

Morgan, G. A., & Ricciuti, H. N. (1969). Infants' responses to strangers during the first year. In B. M. Foss (Ed.), *Determinants of infant behavior* (pp. 272–353). London: Methuen.

Murphy, J. B., & Gliner, J. A. (1988). Visual and motor sequencing in normal and dyspraxic children. *Occupational Therapy Journal of Research, 8*, 89–103.

National Commission for the Protection of Human Subjects of Biomedical and Behavioral Research. (1978). *The Belmont Report: Ethical principles and guidelines for the protection of human subjects of research* (DHEW Publication No. (OS) 78-0012). Washington, DC: Government Printing Office.

Nelson, D. L., & Peterson, C. Q. (1989). Enhancing therapeutic exercise through purposeful activity: A theoretical analysis. *Topics in Geriatric Rehabilitation, 4*, 12–22.

Nunnally, J. C. (1978). *Psychometric theory.* New York: McGraw-Hill.

Osgood, C. E., Suci, G. J., & Tannenbaum, P. H. (1957). *The measurement of meaning.* Urbana, IL: University of Illinois Press.

Ottenbacher, K. (1986). *Evaluating clinical change.* Baltimore, MD: Williams & Wilkins.

Parsonson, B., & Baer, D. (1992). The visual analysis of data, and current research into the stimuli controlling it. In T. Kratochwill & J. Levin (Eds.), *Single-case research design and analysis* (pp. 15–40). Hillsdale, NJ: Lawrence Erlbaum Associates.

Patton, M. Q. (1990). *Qualitative evaluation and research methods* (2nd ed.). Newberry Park, CA: Sage.

Pedhazur, E. J., & Schmelkin, L. P. (1991). *Measurement, design, and analysis: An integrated approach.* Hillsdale, NJ: Lawrence Erlbaum Associates.

Phillips, D. C. (1992). *The social scientist's bestiary.* Oxford, UK: Pergamon Press.

Porter, A. C. (1997). Comparative experiments in educational research. In Jaeger, R.M. (Ed), *Complementary methods for research in education* (2nd ed., pp.524–544). Washington, DC: American Educational Research Association.

Pross, C. (1992). Nazi doctors, German medicine, and historical truth. In G. J. Annas & M. A. Grodin (Eds.), *The Nazi doctors and the Nuremburg Code* (pp. 32–52). New York: Oxford University Press.

Puderbaugh, J. K. & Fisher, A. G. (1992). Assessment of motor and process skills in normal young children and children with dyspraxia. *Occupational Therapy Journal of Research, 12*, 195–216.

Redding, R., Morgan, G. A., & Harmon, R. J. (1988). Mastery motivation in infants and toddlers: Is it greatest when tasks are moderately challenging? *Infant Behavior and Development, 11*, 423–434.

Reichardt, C. S. (1979). The statistical analysis of data from nonequivalent group designs. In T. D. Cook & D. T. Campbell (Eds.), *Quasi-experimentation: Design and analysis issues for field settings* (pp. 147–205). Boston: Houghton Mifflin.

Rennie, D., Yank, V., & Emanuel, L. (1997). When authorship fails: A proposal to make contributors accountable. *Journal of the American Medical Association, 278*, 579–585.

Rheingold, H. L., & Eckerman, C. O. (1973). Fear of the stranger. In H.W. Reese (Ed.), *Advances in child development and behavior* (pp. 185–222). New York: Academic Press.

Richardson, A .G., & Fergus, E. E. (1993). Learning style and ability grouping in the high school system: Some Caribbean findings. *Educational Research, 35*, 69–74.

Robinson, D. H., Katayama, A. D., Dubois, N. F., & Devaney, T. (1998). Interactive effects of graphic organizers and delayed review on concept application. *Journal of Experimental Education, 67*, 17–31.

Robinson, D. H., & Levin J. R. (1997). Reflections on statistical and substantive significance, with a slice of replication. *Educational Researcher, 26*, 21–26.

Robnett, R., & Gliner, J. A. (1995). Qual-OT: A quality of life assessment tool. *Occupational Therapy Journal of Research, 15*, 198–214.

Roethlisberger, F. S., & Dickson, W. J. (1939). *Management and the worker.* Cambridge, MA: Harvard University Press.

Rosenthal, R. (1979). The "file drawer problem" and tolerance for null results. *Psychological Bulletin, 86*, 638–641.

Rosenthal, R. (1985). Writing meta-analytic reviews. *Psychological Bulletin, 118*, 169–312.

Rosenthal, R. (1994). Parametric measures of effect size. In H. Cooper & L. Hedges (Eds.), *The handbook of research synthesis* (pp. 231–244). New York: Russell Sage Foundation.

Rozeboom, W.W. (1960). The fallacy of the null hypothesis significance test. *Psychological Bulletin, 57,* 416–428.

Rumrill, P. D., & Garnette, M. R. (1997). Career adjustment via reasonable accommodations: The effects of an employee-empowerment intervention for people with disabilities. *Work, 9,* 57–64.

Salant, P., & Dillman, D. A. (1994). *How to conduct your own survey.* New York: Wiley.

Salsburg, D. S. (1985). The religion of statistics as practiced in medical journals. *The American Statistician, 39,* 220–223.

Schalock, R., Keith, K., Hoffman, K., & Karan, O. (1989). Quality of life: Its measurement and use. *Mental Retardation, 27,* 25–31.

Scheffe, H. (1953). A method for judging all contrasts in the analysis of variance. *Biometrika, 40,* 87–104.

Schmitt, N. (1996a). Statistical significance testing and cumulative knowledge in psychology: Implications for training of researchers. *Psychological Methods, 1,* 115–129.

Schmitt, N. (1996b). Uses and abuses of coefficient alpha. *Psychological Assessment, 8,* 350–353.

Shavelson, R. J. (1981). *Statistical reasoning for the behavioral sciences.* Boston: Allyn & Bacon.

Shavelson, R. J. (1988). *Statistical reasoning for the behavioral sciences* (2nd ed.). Boston: Allyn and Bacon.

Shuster, E. (1997). Fifty years later: The significance of the Nuremberg code. *The New England Journal of Medicine, 337,* 1436–1440.

Sieber, J. E. (1992). *Planning ethically responsible research: A guide for students and internal review boards.* Newbury Park, CA: Sage.

Siegel, S., & Castellan, N. J. (1988). *Nonparametric statistics for the behavioral sciences* (2nd ed.). New York: McGraw-Hill.

Silverstein, B., Kilgore, K. M., Fisher, W. P., Harley, J. P., & Harvey, R. F. (1991). Applying psychometric criteria to functional assessment in medical rehabilitation: I. Exploring unidimensionality. *Archives of Physical Medicine and Rehabilitation, 73,* 507–518.

Smith, M. L. (1981). Naturalistic research. *Personnel and Guidance Journal, 59,* 585–589.

Smith, M. L., Gabriel, R., Schott, J., & Padia, W. L. (1976). Evaluation effects of Outward Bound. In G.V. Glass (Ed.), *Evaluation studies review annual* (Vol. 1, pp. 400–421). Beverly Hills, CA: Sage.

Spector, P. E. (1992). *Summated rating scale construction: An introduction.* Newbury Park, CA: Sage.

Spitz, R. A. (1965). *The first year of life.* New York: International Universities Press.

Stevens, J. (1986). *Applied multivariate statistics for the social sciences.* Hillsdale, NJ: Lawrence Erlbaum Associates.

Stevens, S. S. (1951). Mathematics, measurement, and psychophysics. In S. S. Stevens (Ed.) *Handbook of experimental psychology.* New York: Wiley.

Stone, W. L., Lemanek, K. L., Fishel, P. T., Fernandez, M. C., & Altemeier, W .A. (1990). Play and imitation skills in the diagnosis of autism in young children. *Pediatrics, 86,* 267–272.

Stuart, A. (1984). *The idea of sampling* (3rd ed.). New York: Macmillan.

Sudman, S., & Bradburn, N. (1989). *Asking questions: A practical guide to questionnaire design.* San Francisco: Jossey-Bass.

Suen, H. K. (1990). *Principles of test theories.* Hillsdale, NJ: Lawrence Erlbaum Associates.

Tabachnick, B. G., & Fidell, L. S. (1989). *Using multivariate statistics* (2nd ed.). New York: Harper Colling.

Tarr, S.J., & Bishop, P. (1992). Effects of instructional approaches on motor performance of boys with developmental disabilities. *Clinical Kinesiology, 45,* 18–22.

Tate, S. (1997). Peppermint oil: A treatment for postoperative nausea. *Journal of Advanced Nursing, 26,* 543-549.

Test critiques (annually). Austin, TX: Pro-Ed.

Tests (3rd ed.). (1991). Austin, TX: Pro-Ed.

Tests in print (4th ed.). (1994). Lincoln, NE: Buros Institute for Mental Measurements.

Thompson, B. (1995). Stepwise regression and stepwise discriminant analysis need not apply here: A guidelines editorial. *Educational and Psychological Measurement, 55,* 525–534.

Thompson, B. (1996). AERA editorial policies regarding statistical significance testing: Three suggested reforms. *Educational Researcher, 25,* 26–30.

Thorndike, R. L., & Hagen, E. (1992). *Measurement and evaluation in psychology and education* (5th ed.). New York: John Wiley and Sons.

Tuckman, B. W. (1992). The effect of student planning and self-competence on self-motivated performance. *Journal of Experimental Education, 60,* 119–127.

Tuckman, B. W. (1996). The relative effectiveness of incentive motivation and prescribed learning strategy in improving college students' course performance. *Journal of Experimental Education, 64,* 197–210.

Tukey, J. W. (1953). The problem of multiple comparisons. Unpublished manuscript, Princeton University, Princeton, NJ.

Tukey, J. W. (1977). *Exploratory data analysis.* Reading, MA: Addison-Wesley.

Tun, C. G., Tun, P. A., & Wingfield, A. (1997). Cognitive function following long-term spinal cord injury. *Rehabilitation Psychology, 42,* 163–182.

Webster, P.E., Plante, A. S., & Couvillion, L.M. (1997). Phonologic impairment and prereading: Update on a longitudinal study. *Journal of Learning Disabilities, 30,* 365–375.

Webster's seventh new collegiate dictionary (1972). Springfield, MA: C & G Merriam.

Weinfurt, K. P. (1997). Multivariate analysis of variance. In L. G. Grimm & P. R. Yarnold (Eds.), *Reading and understanding multivariate statistics.* Washington, D.C.: American Psychological Association.

White, O. (1974). *The "split middle": A "quickie" method of trend estimation* (3rd revision). Unpublished manuscript, University of Washington, Experimental Education Unit, Child Development and Mental Retardation Center, Seattle, WA.

Wilkinson, L., & The Task Force on Statistical Inference. (1999). Statistical methods in psychology journals: Guidelines and explanations. *American Psychologist. 54,* 594–604

Winer, B. J. (1962). *Statistical principles in experimental design.* New York: McGraw-Hill.

Woodward, J., & Goodstein, D. (1996). Conduct, misconduct and structure of science. *American Scientist, 84,* 479–490.

Young, E. D. (1999). *Research involving human subjects: Historical review, ethical theory, and Stanford guidelines.* Unpublished manuscript, Stanford University School of Medicine, Stanford, CA.

Author Index

Subject Index